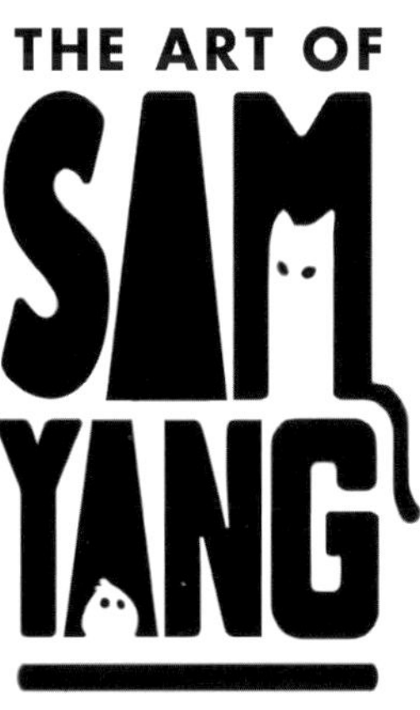

3dtotalPublishing

3dtotal Publishing

Correspondence: **publishing@3dtotal.com**
Website: **store.3dtotal.com**

First published in the United Kingdom, 2024, by 3dtotal Publishing.

Address: 3dtotal.com Ltd, 29 Foregate Street, Worcester WR1 1DS, United Kingdom.

Hard cover ISBN: 978-1-912843-68-8

Printed and bound in China by C&C Offset Printing Co., Ltd

Visit **store.3dtotal.com** for a complete list of available book titles.

Editorial Project Manager: Rhiannon Joseph
Lead Editor: Samantha Rigby
Lead Designer: Joseph Cartwright
Studio Manager: Simon Morse
Managing Director: Tom Greenway

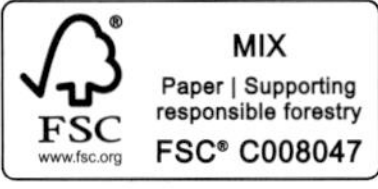

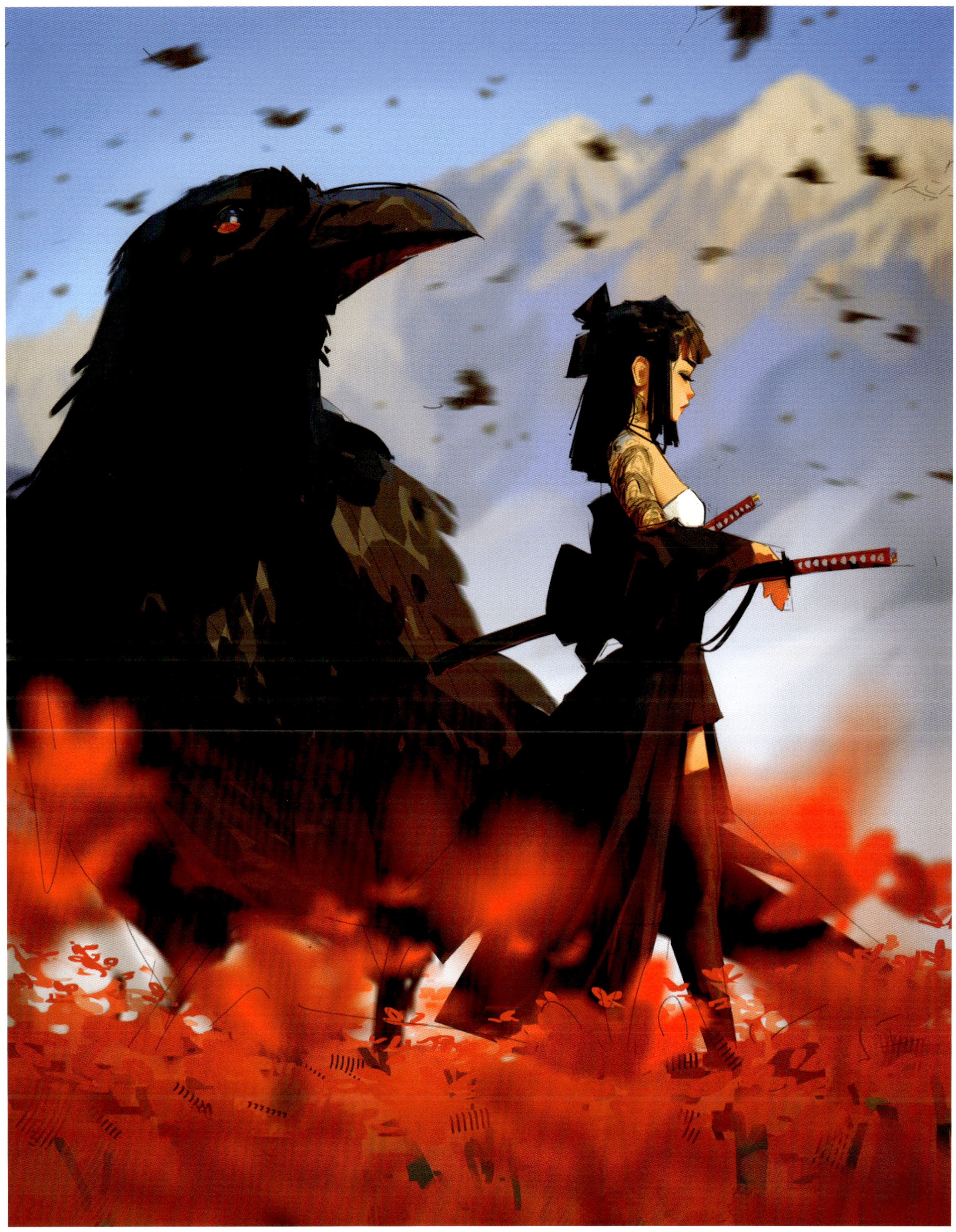

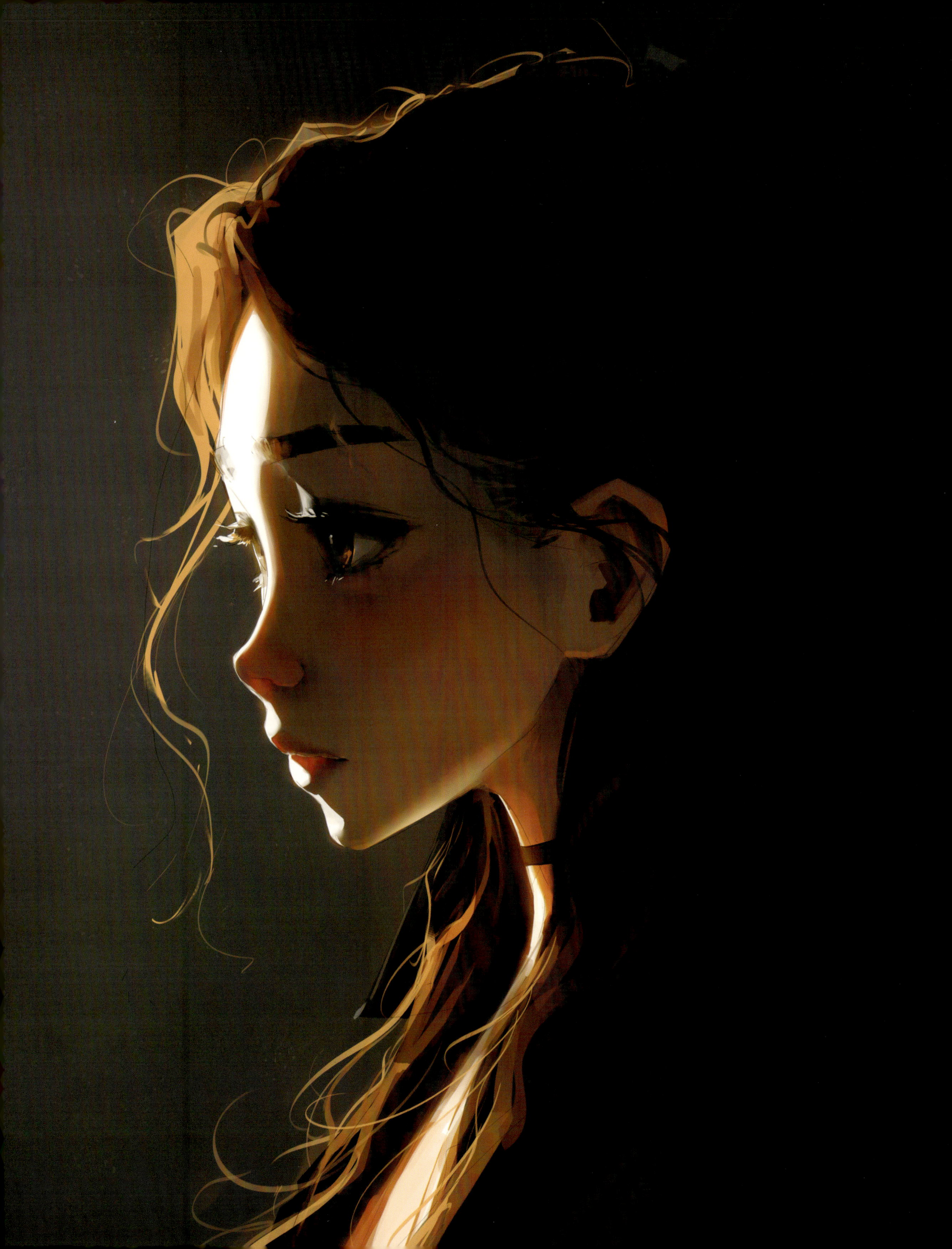

contents.

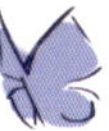

Dedicated to my mom and dad

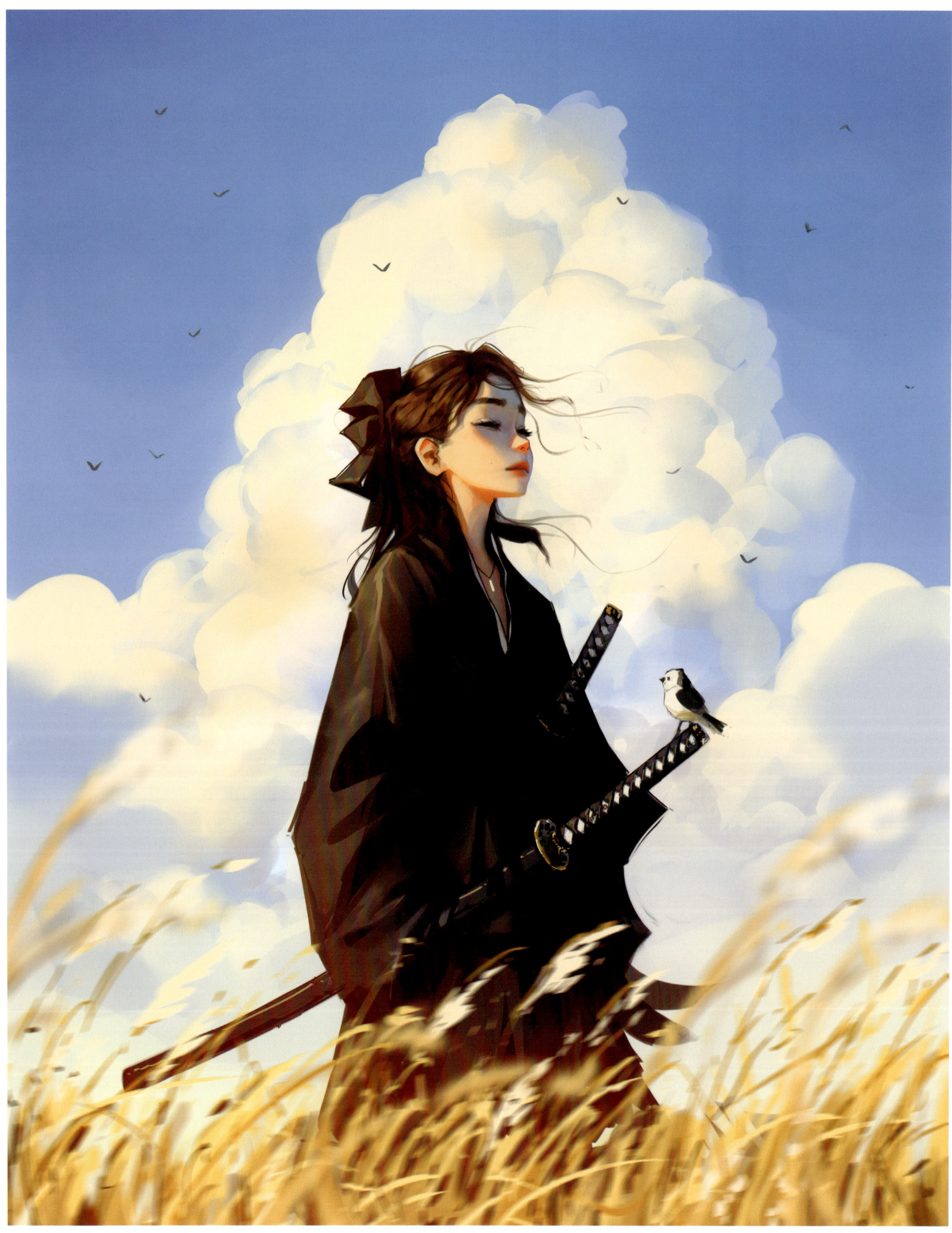

introduction

Ever since I was young, I've loved flipping through art books. It's fascinating to look behind the scenes and read about the processes used to create the artworks, characters, and worlds I adore. Each page is a new realm and every paragraph a new journey.

I made this book to give you a place of escape where I hope you'll find inspiration for your own journey. It's a collection of work, some previously published and others kept private, where a snapshot of my artistic journey can be found. My work is always changing as I learn and grow. In a few years, maybe I'll look back and think, 'What was I thinking, putting that image in there ...'

But that's the beauty of art – we're never really finished.

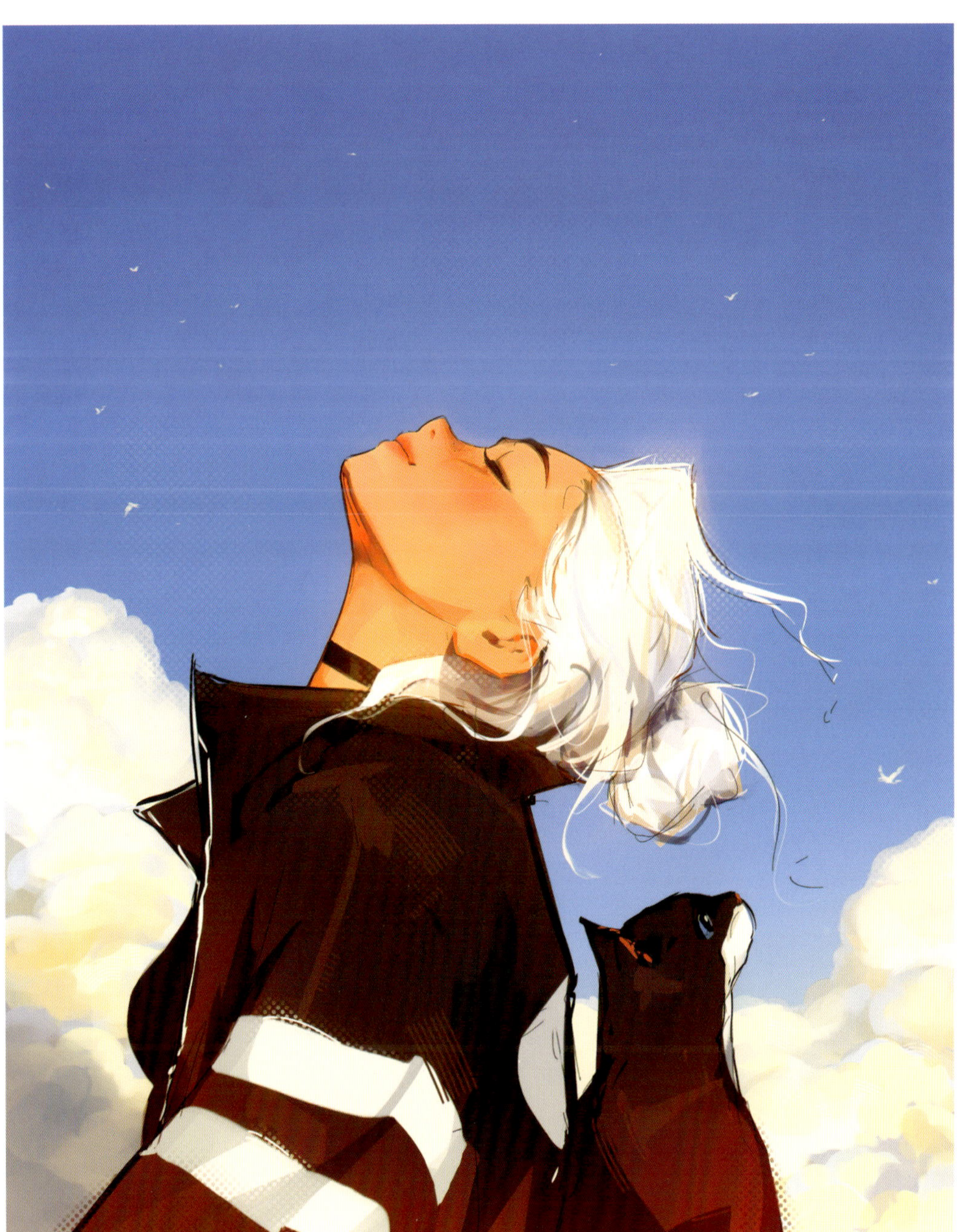

This book is me giving it my best shot. I hope it can act as a window into my own process of artistic creation and show you what my behind the scenes looks like. With luck, it will also give you some helpful tips and ideas that you can take with you on your own journey. I wish I'd had something like this when I was younger so, really, this is for you!

Our artistic selves are always growing, learning, and reflecting the changes of the world around us. We seek to push ourselves further and escape comfort zones, and we all have our bad pieces and terrible days that we'd love to wipe from our memories. But, behind all the struggles, we push through and pick up our pens time and time again because of a profound love for art.

I'd like nothing more than to share this love with you.

Sam Yang

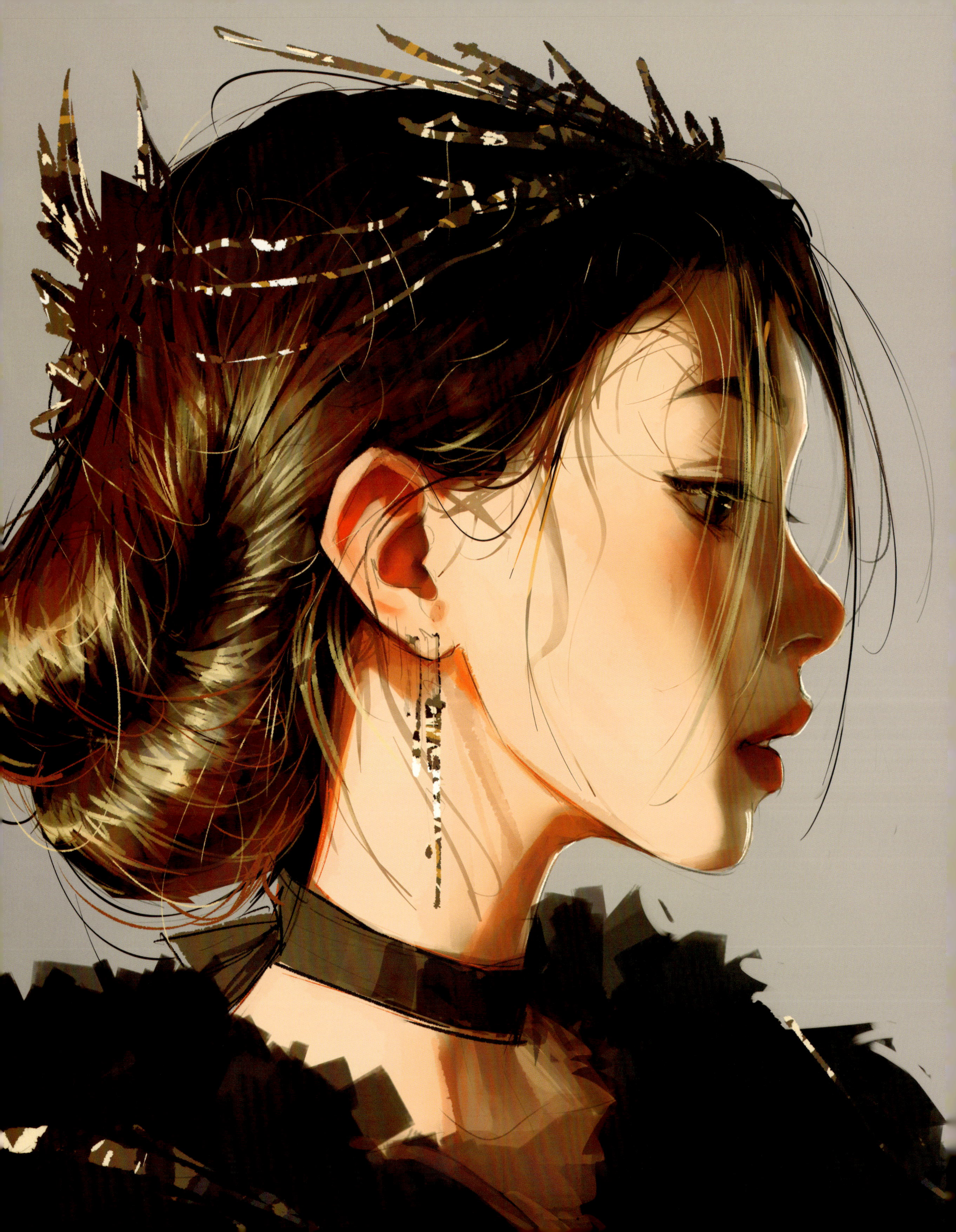

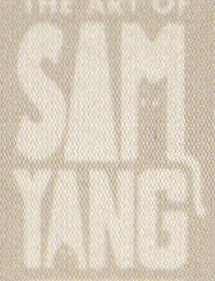

intro gallery

A collection of introductory works

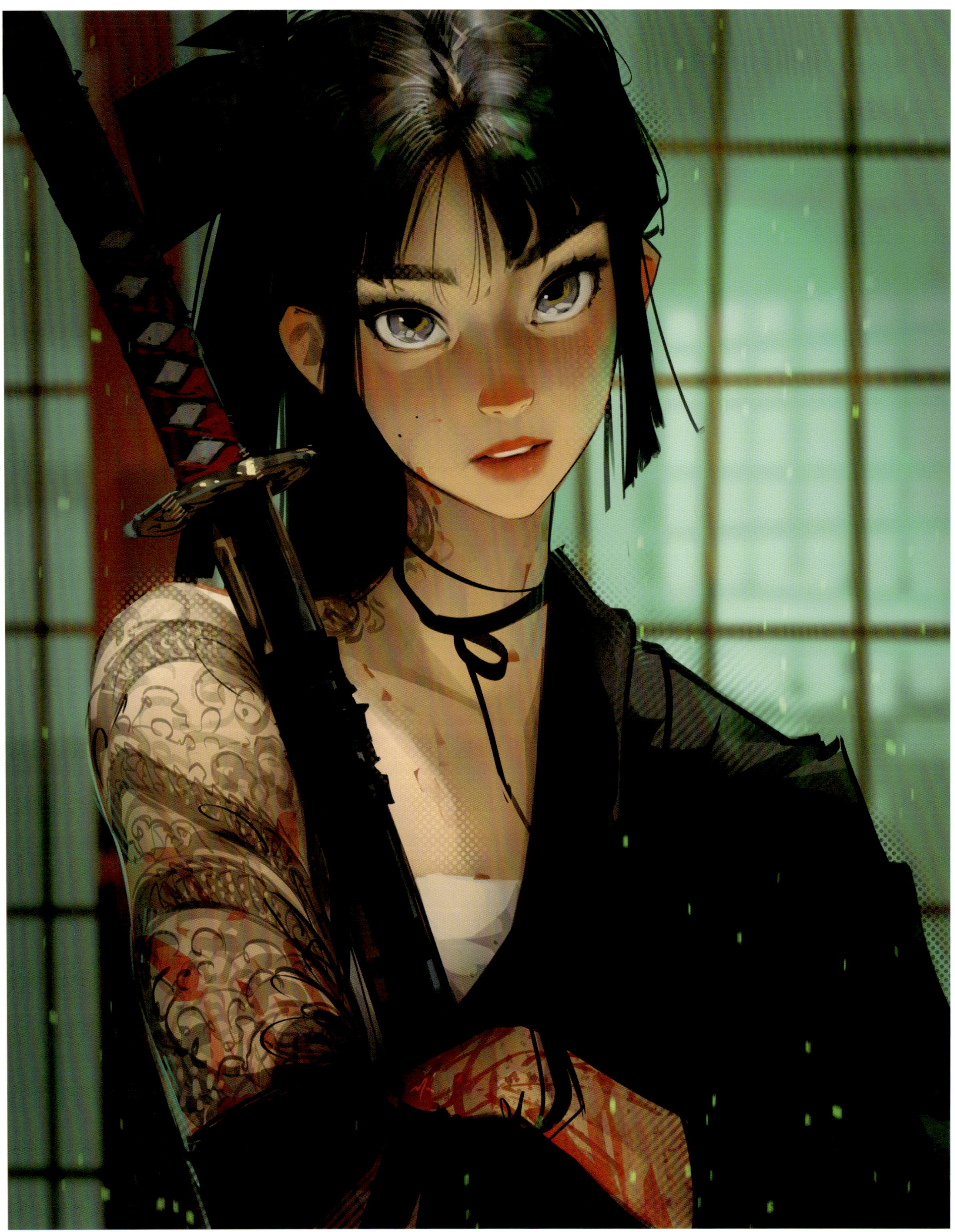

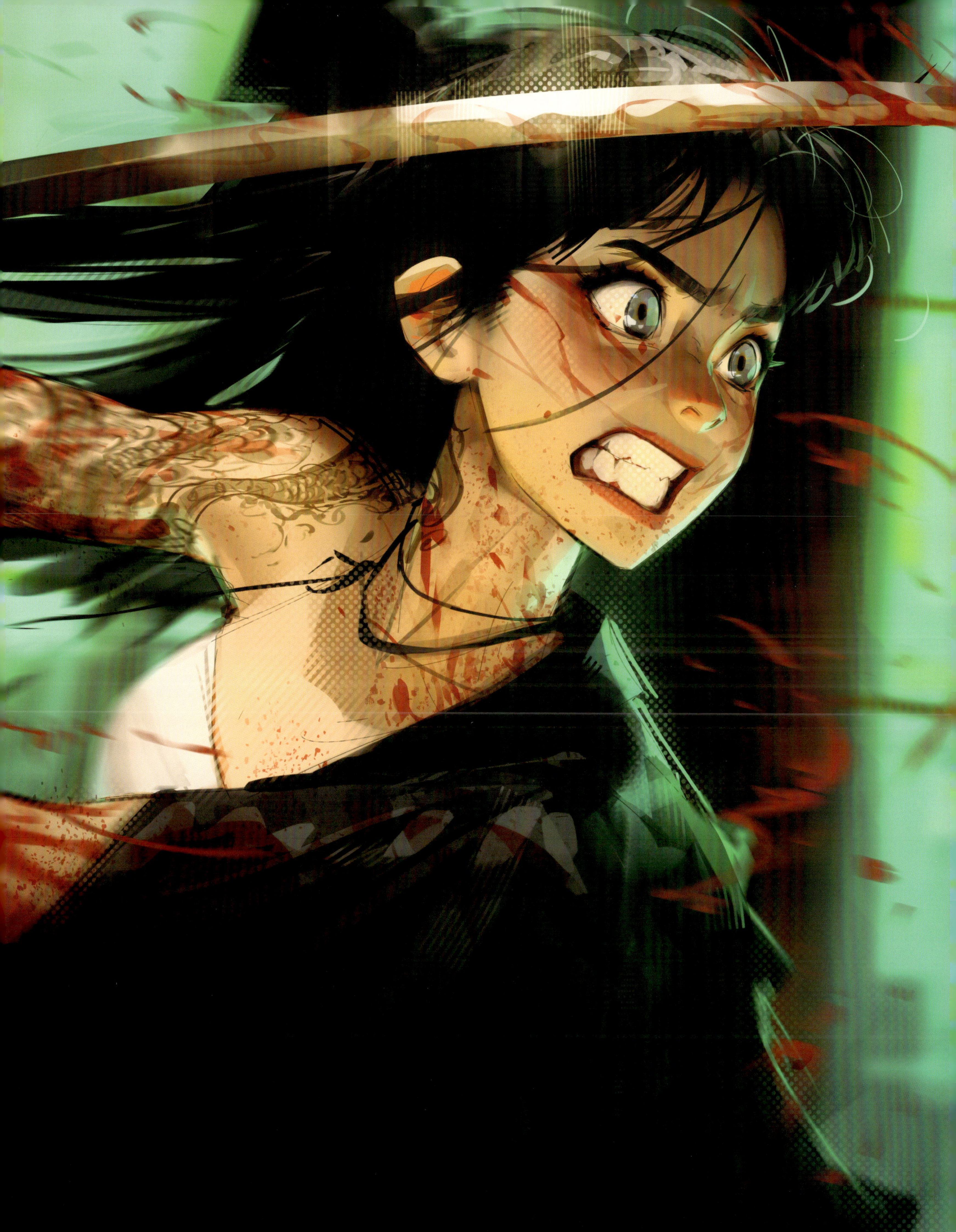

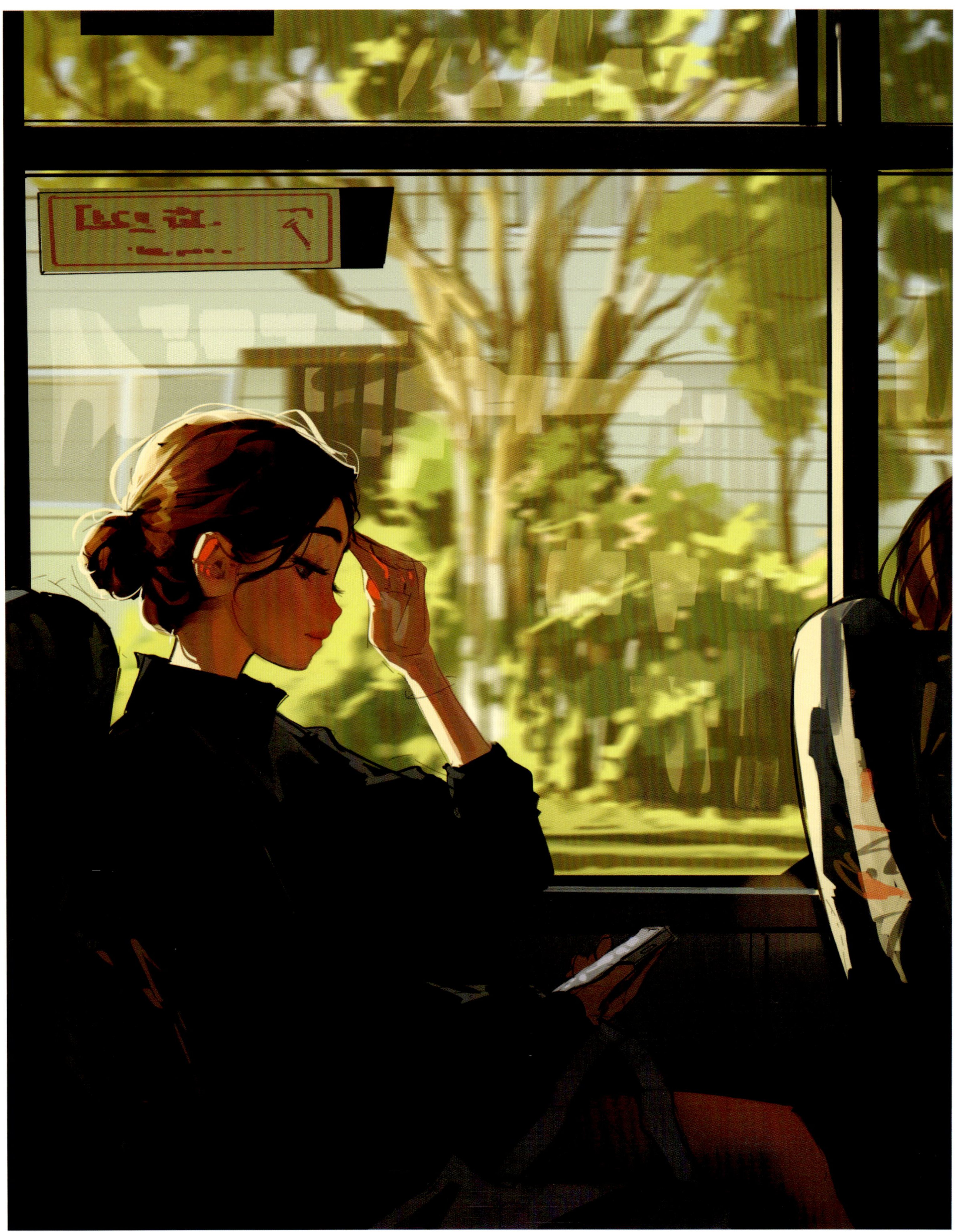

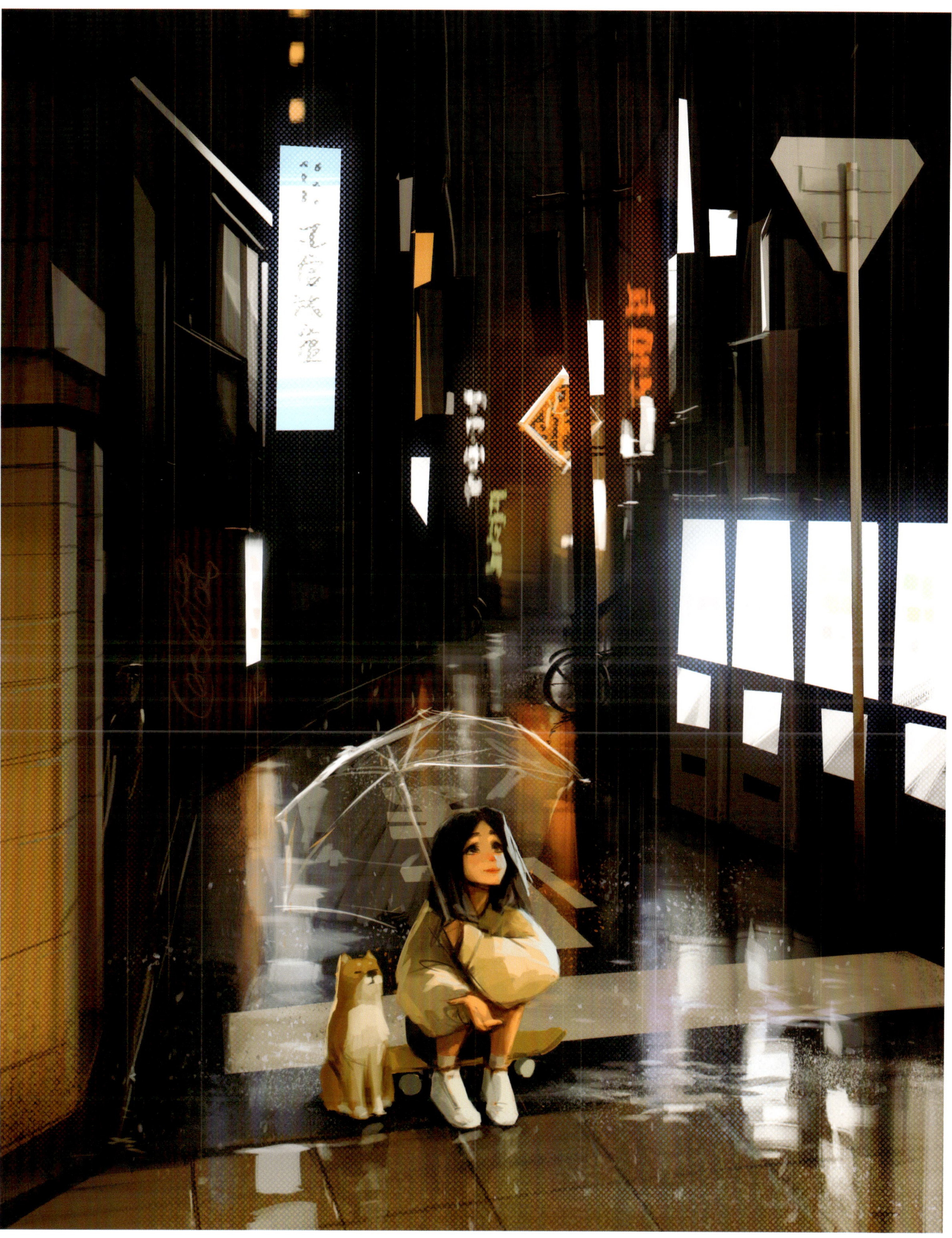

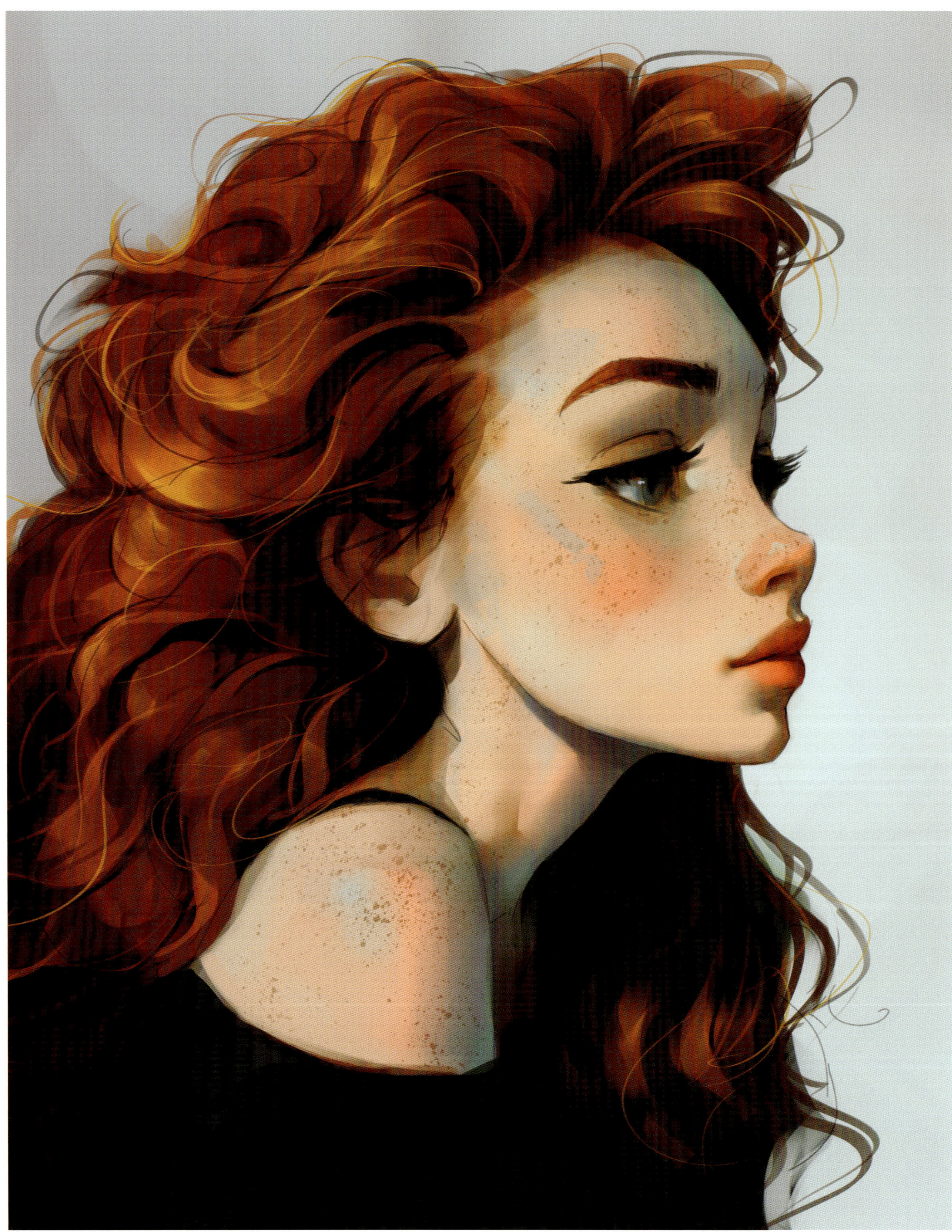

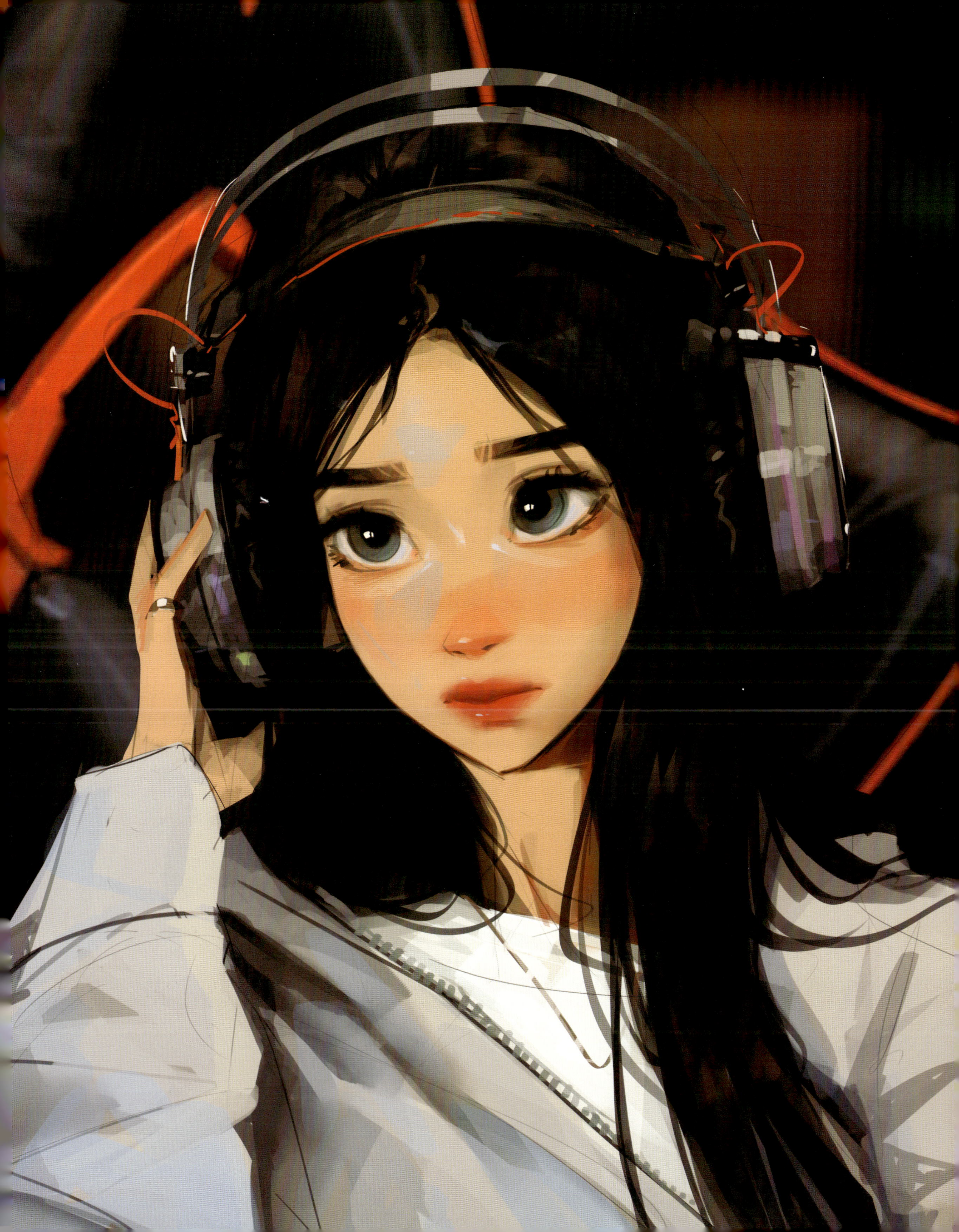

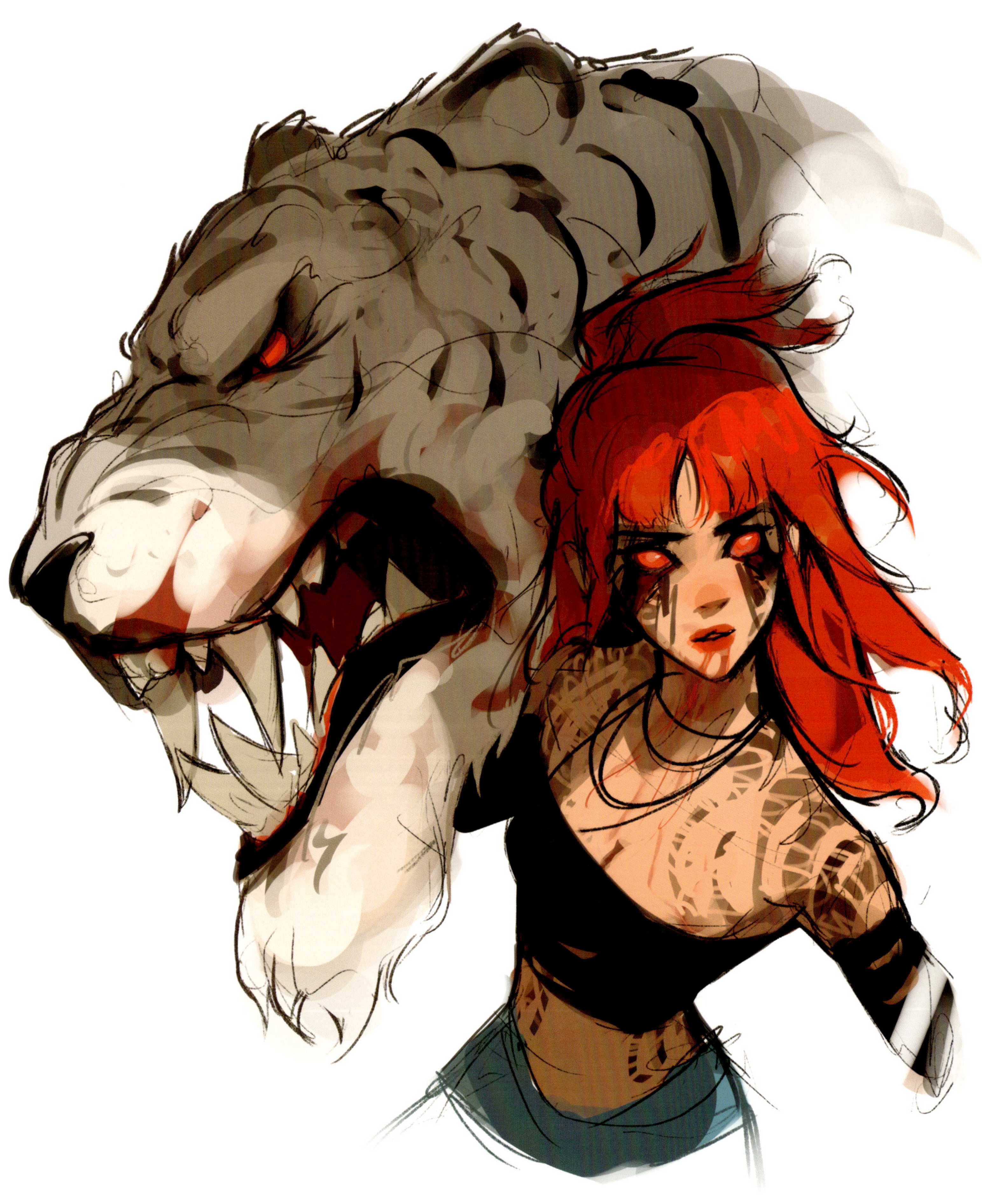

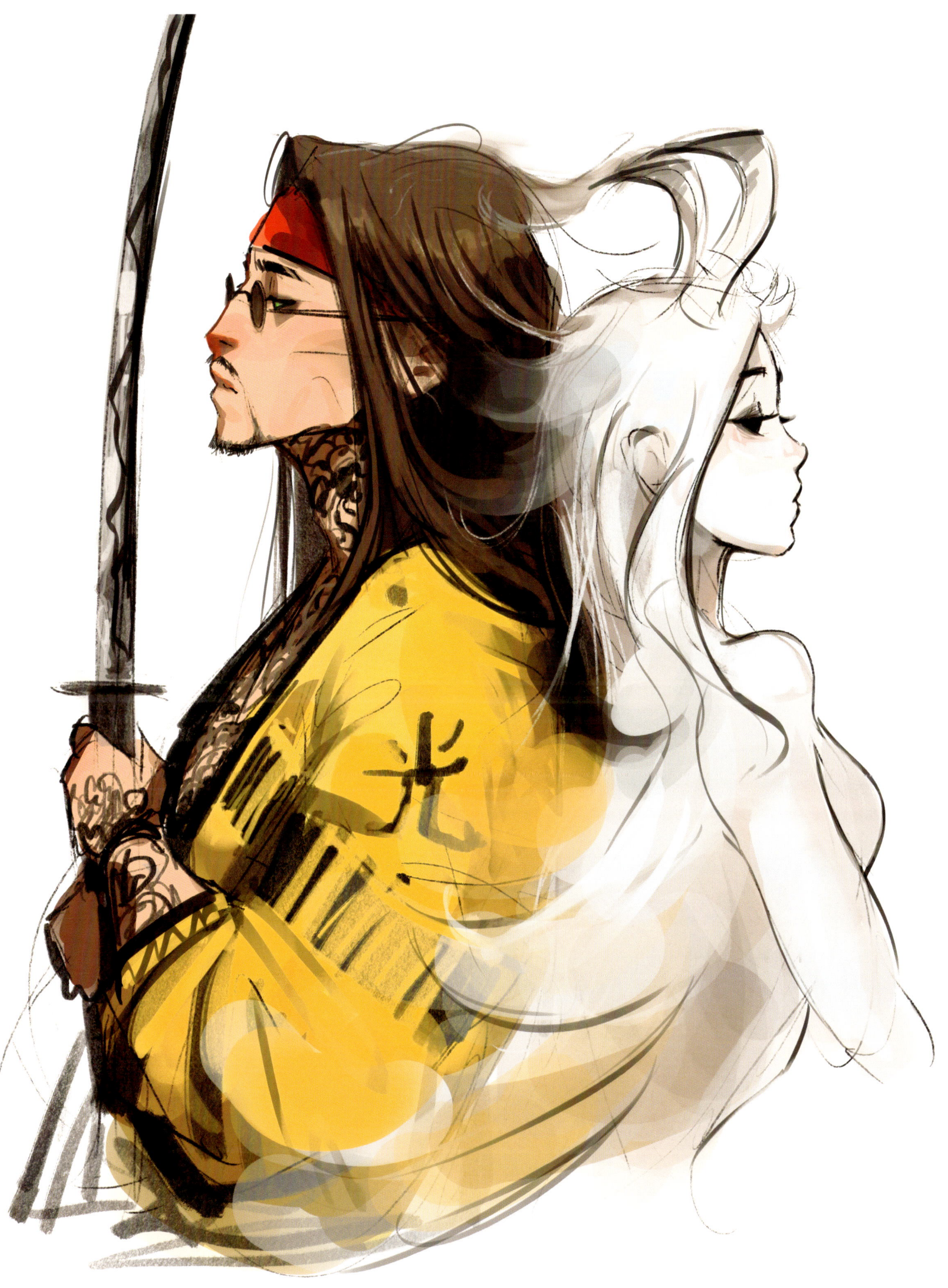
光

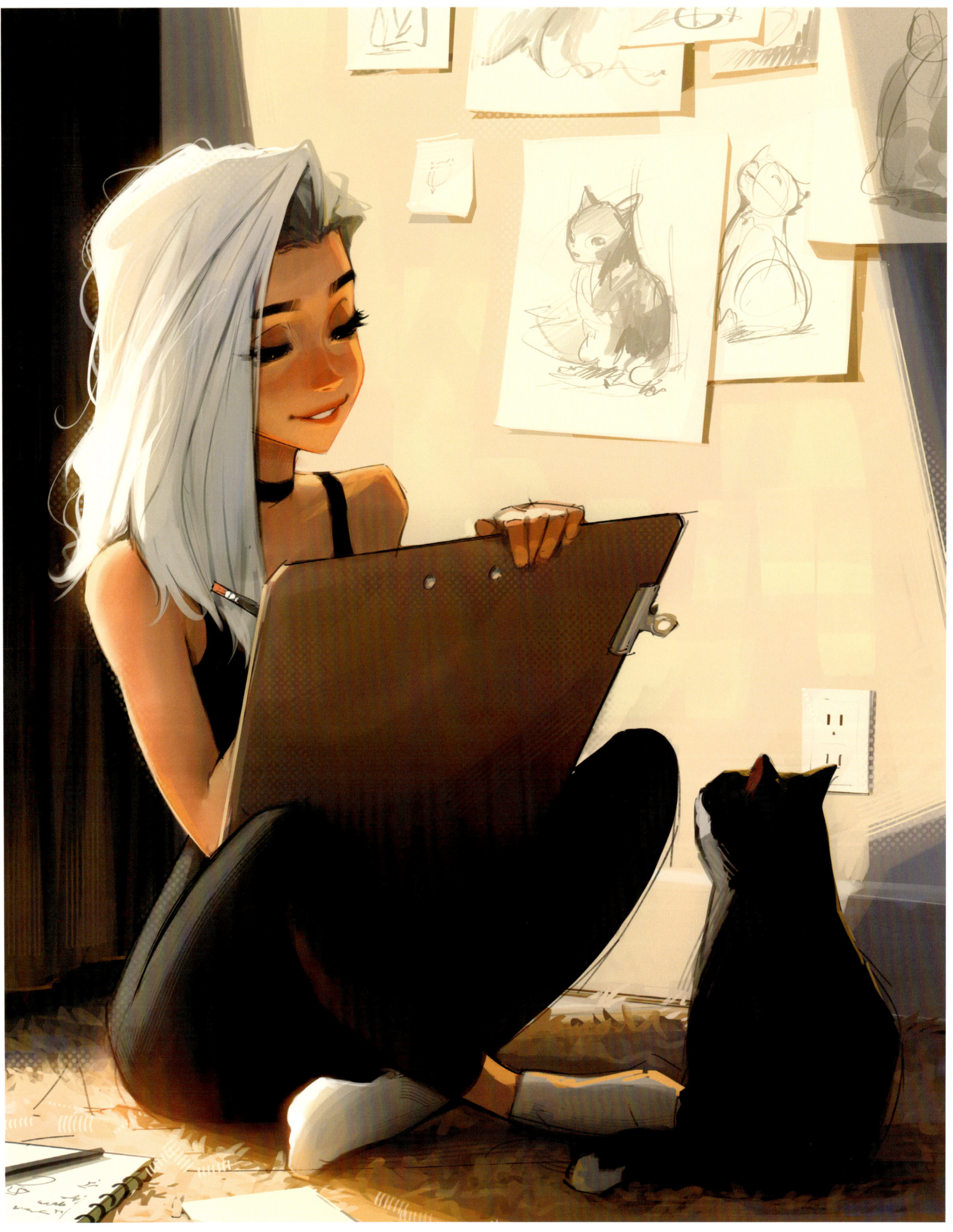

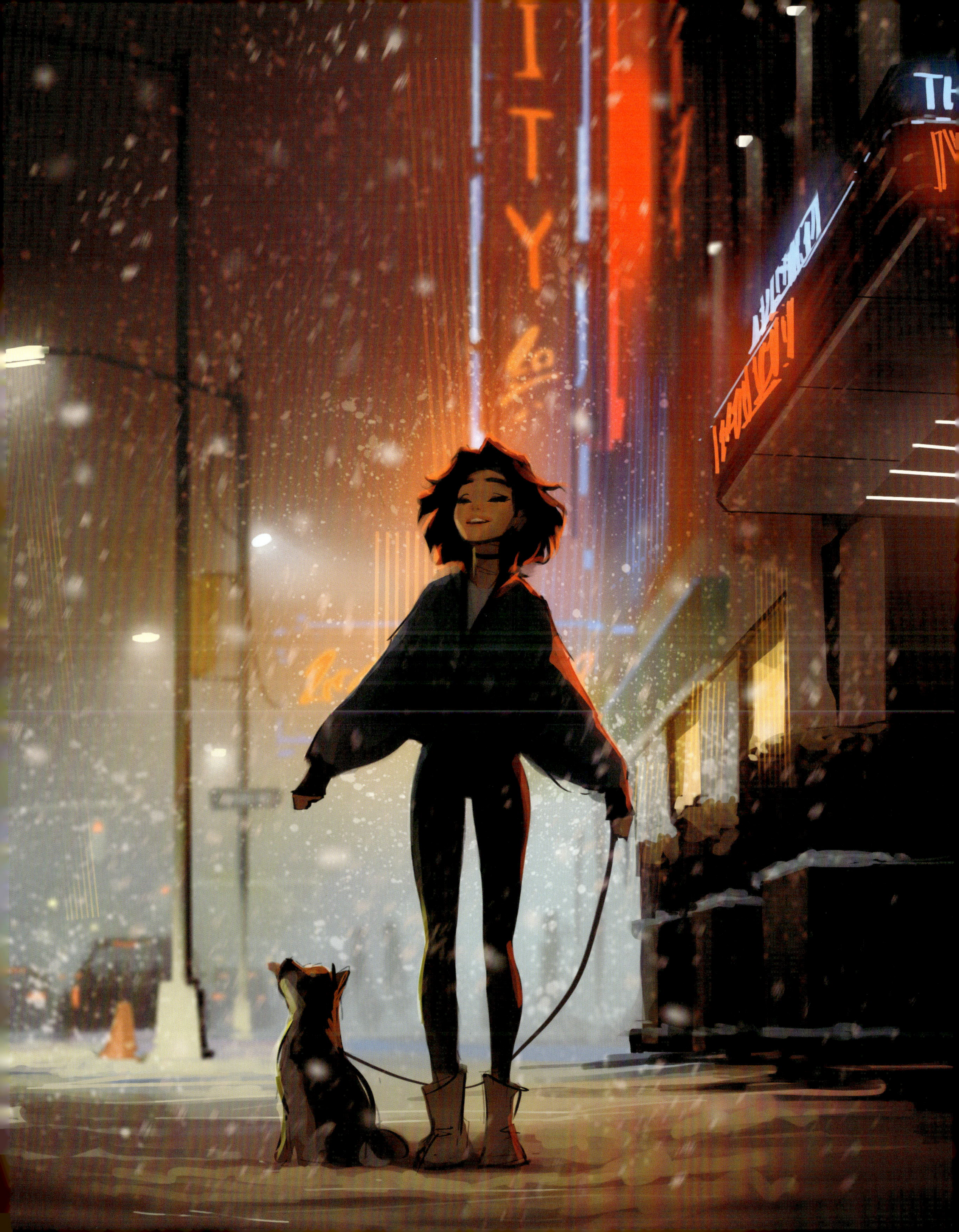

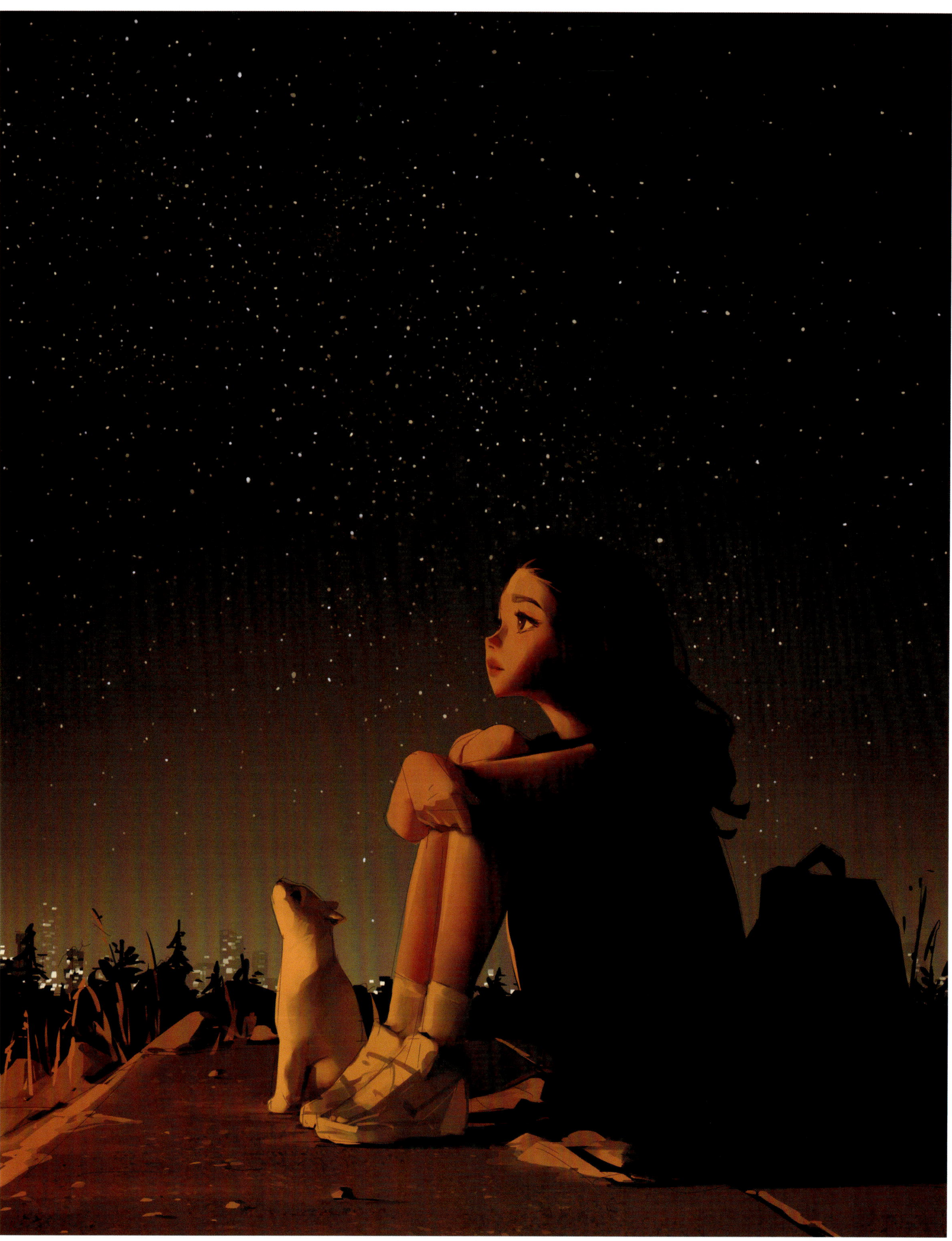

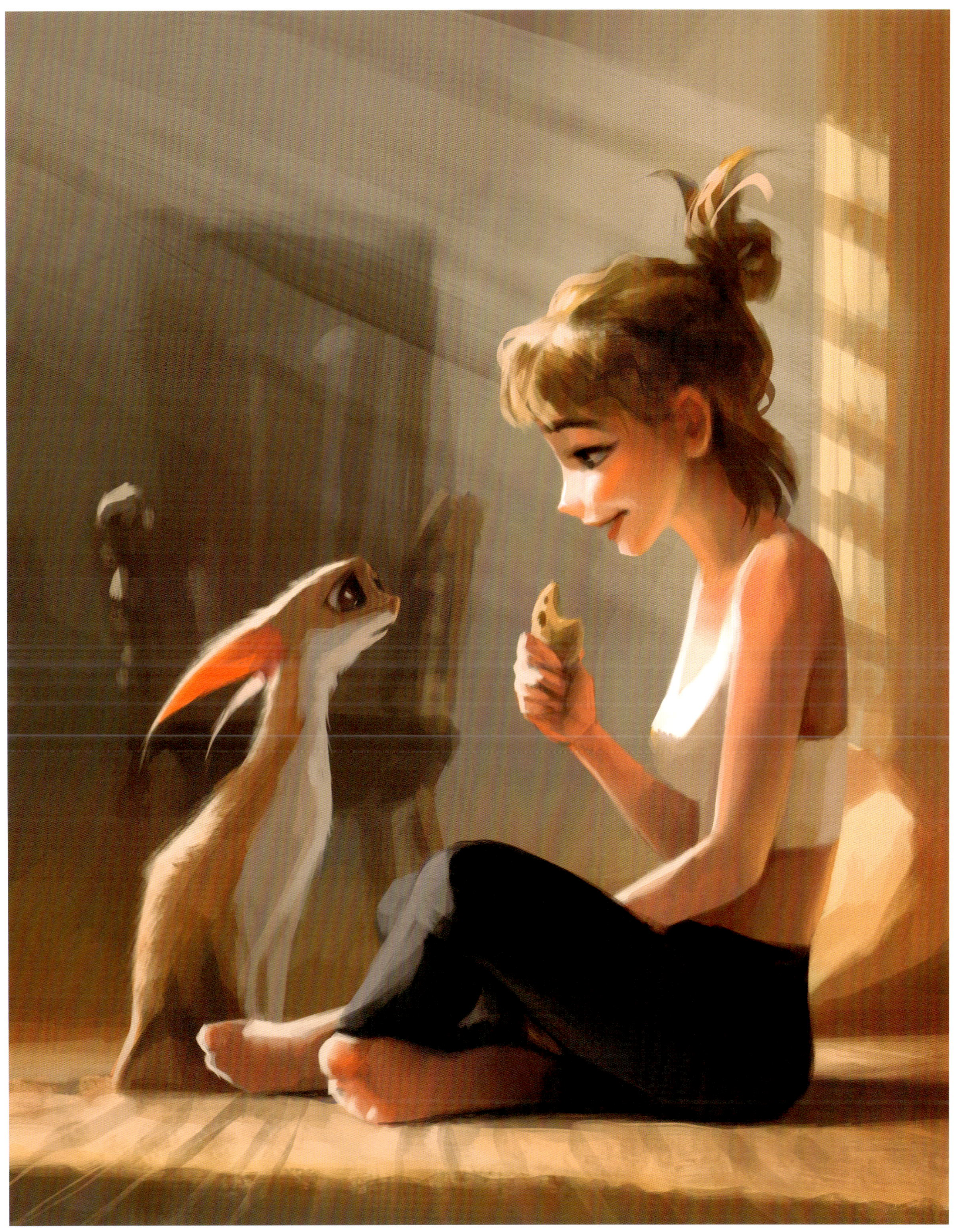

my artistic journey

Early works, learning & pursuing art

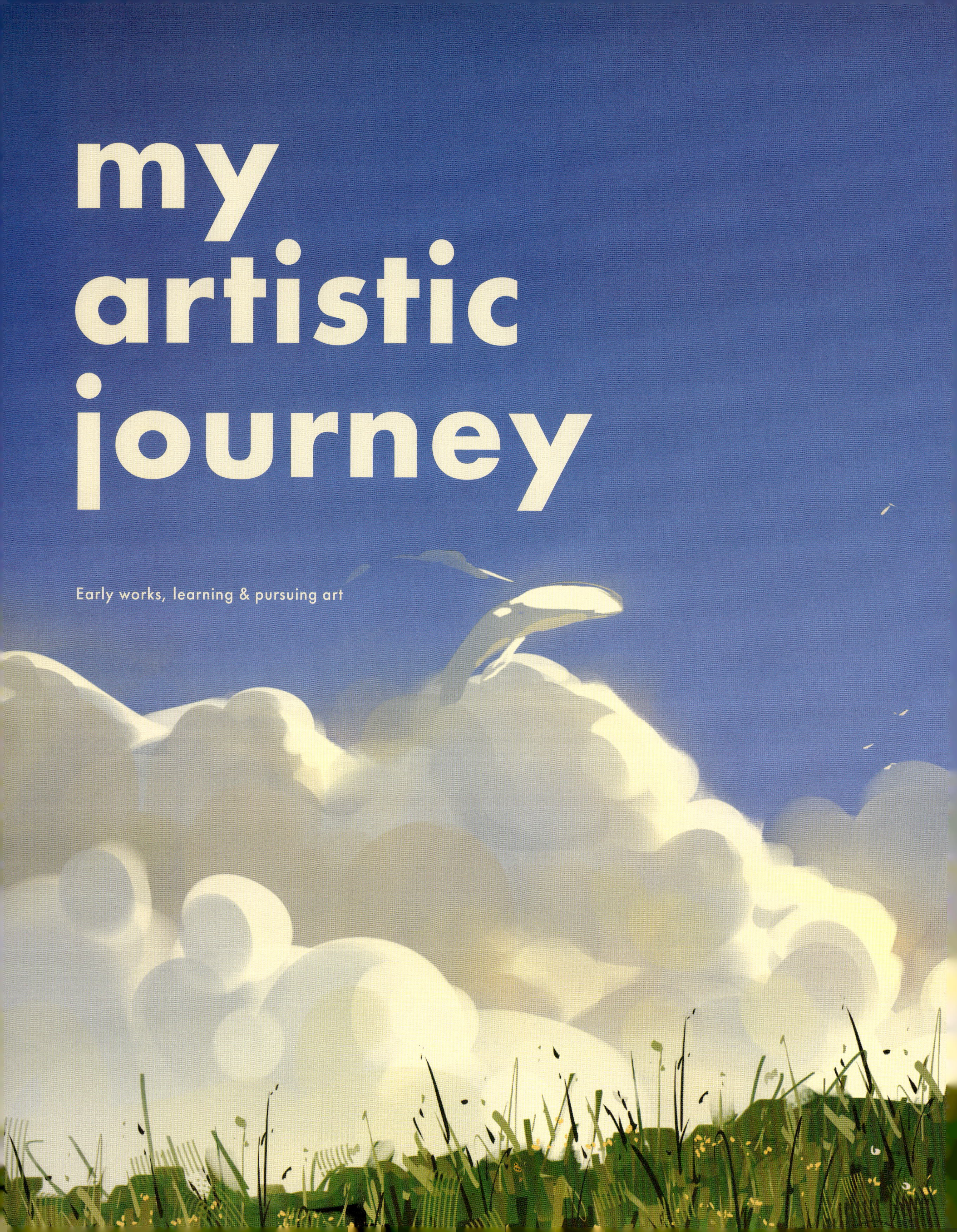

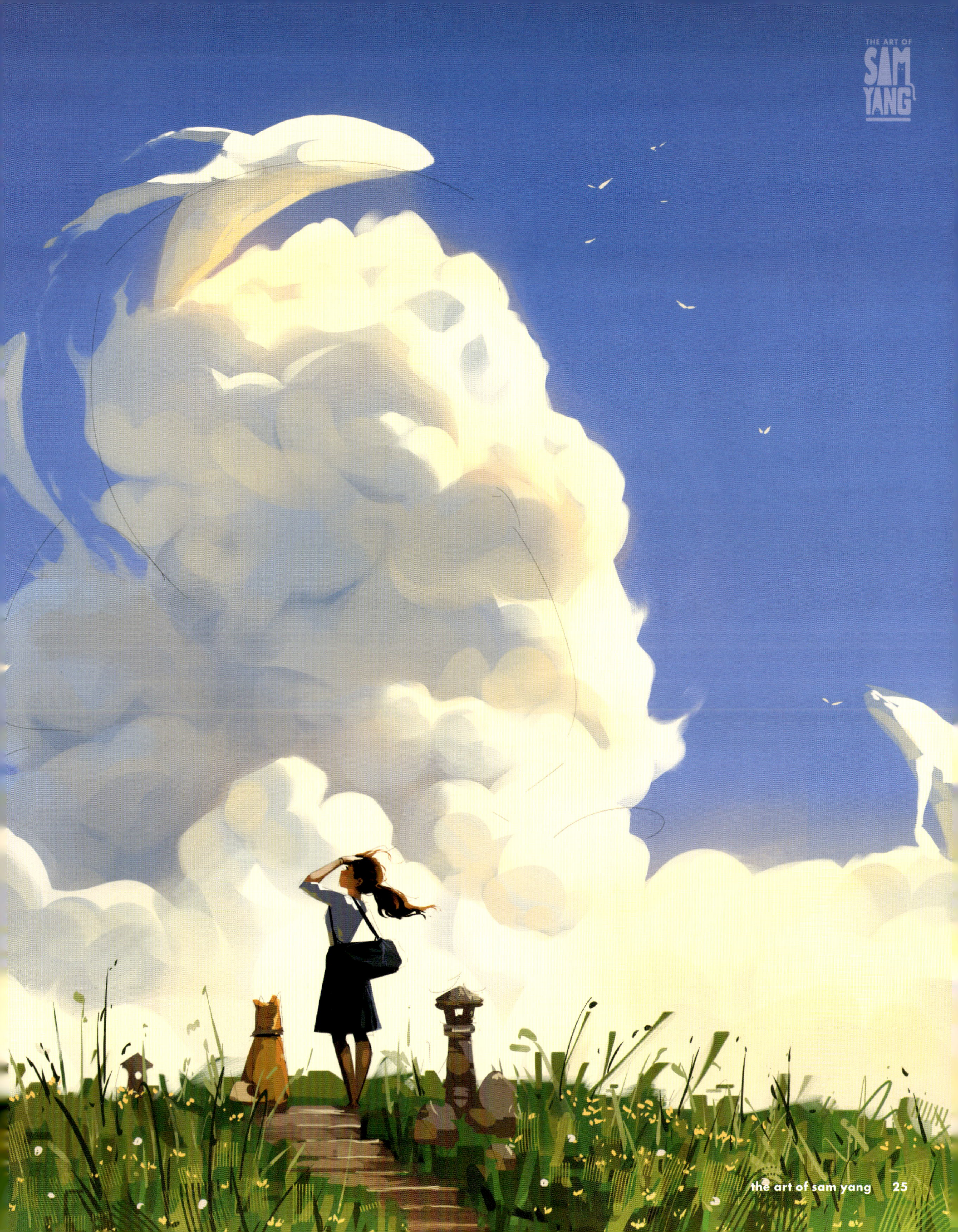
THE ART OF
SAM
YANG

FIRST MEMORIES OF DRAWING

Like many other kids, the first thing I ever drew was a dinosaur. My earliest memory of this is from around three or four years old, sitting on the floor of my bedroom with a coloured pencil, scribbling away on a thin sheet of A4 printing paper. I recall my pencil passing over the bumpy, uneven surface of the wood beneath it, and my mom and dad watching me. At the time, my dinos only consisted of a few straight lines and two dots for eyes. But one day, my mom picked up a pencil and showed me how to make a shape with those lines. You could say she was my first teacher; and as you can see, my dino drawings definitely took off after that.

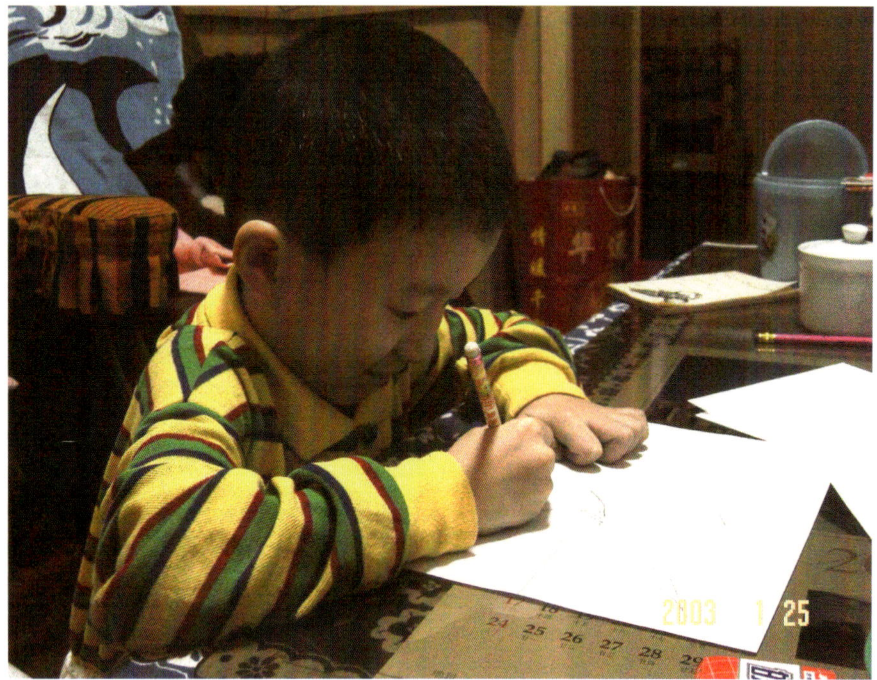

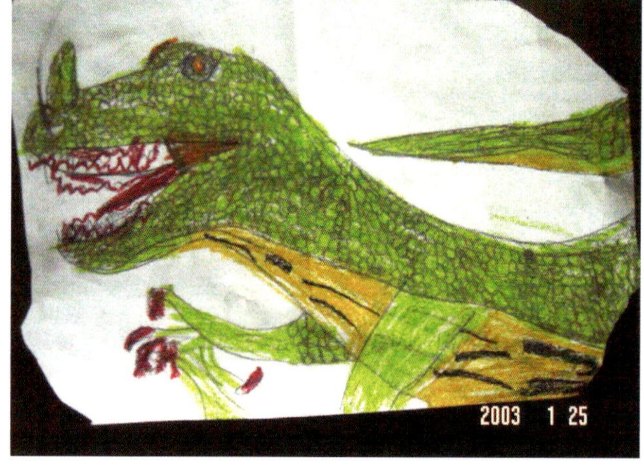

Above | *Young Sam Doing Art*, 2003, aged four

Right | *Dinosaur Drawing*, 2003, aged four. This was drawn with graphite and crayon. Most of my early passion for dinosaurs actually came from my interest in prehistoric-nature documentaries. *Walking with Dinosaurs* was one of my favourites. Looking back at this, I'm very impressed with the attention to the scale texture, as well as the two-tone colour scheme reminiscent of a lizard. Pretty good stuff

My parents clearly saw my love for drawing. Though our family didn't have much back in China before we moved, they always supported me by providing an endless supply of paper and coloured pencils. Sometimes, they'd entertain me by drawing with me. When I turned six, they even signed me up for art classes. I didn't really enjoy the classes at the time, but looking back, I'm so grateful I did them. I owe everything to my parents for their unwavering support and the courage to leave their home behind for the chance of a better future for us.

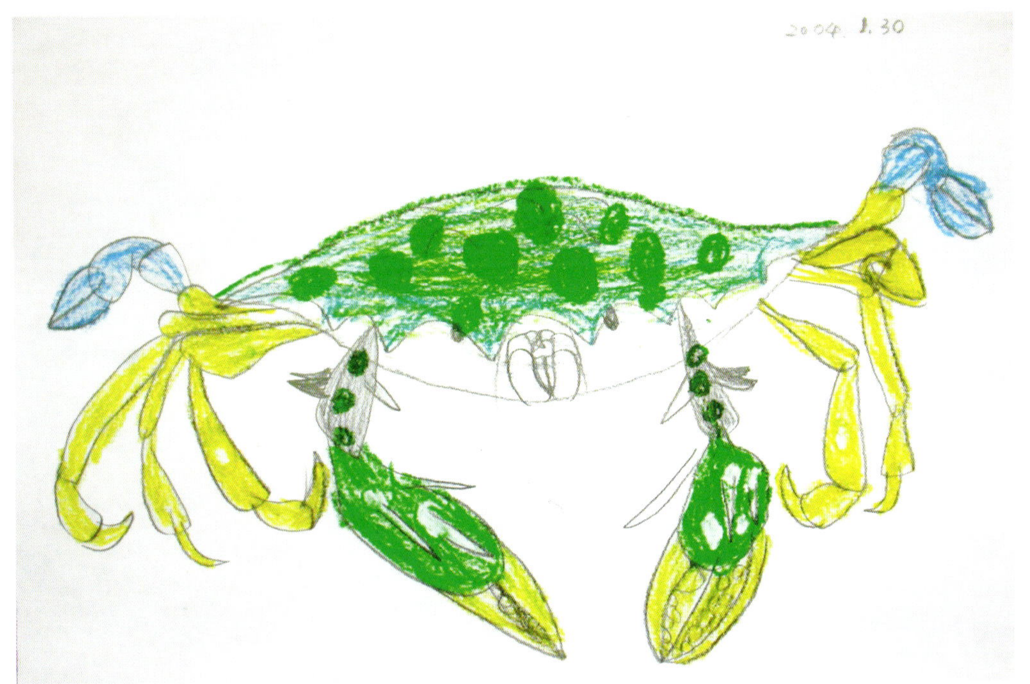

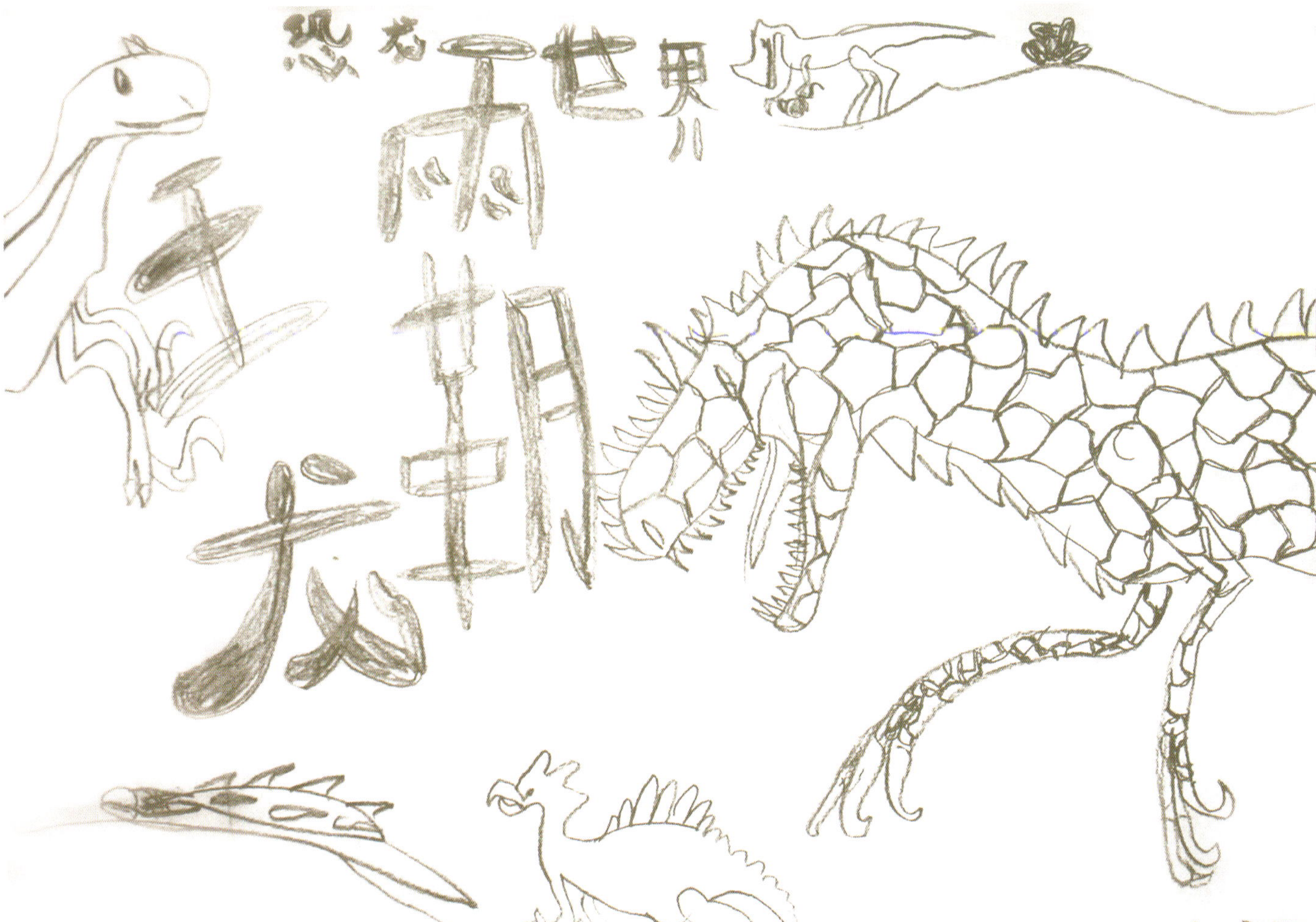

Left | *Mister Krabs*, 2004, aged five

Below | *Dinosaur*, 2003, aged five

Below | *Painting from my art tutor class*, 2009, aged eleven

Opposite page (above) | *Budgies on a Branch*, 2010, aged twelve

Opposite page (below) | *Gift Shop*, 2010, aged twelve. I took a picture of this gift shop in southern Ontario while I was on an autumn hike with my parents. It served as a great reference for this watercolour piece. In fact, all of the paintings on pages 28–31 are done using watercolour. It was my favourite coloured medium to work with; it's unforgiving, impressionistic, and has a very distinct aesthetic. It was also the easiest one to clean up

While I'm most known for my digital artworks today, I actually grew up doing mainly traditional art. I attended art schools and classes in China until the age of ten, when my family immigrated to Canada. Most of my earliest learning consisted of boring, dry, and repetitive fundamentals.

I remember drawing white plaster shapes and meticulously shading them with a 2B pencil over the course of a three-hour art class every weekend. We'd later move on to watercolours, painting still-life scenes, and sometimes imitating the works of the old masters. Up until high school, I attended this type of art class every week.

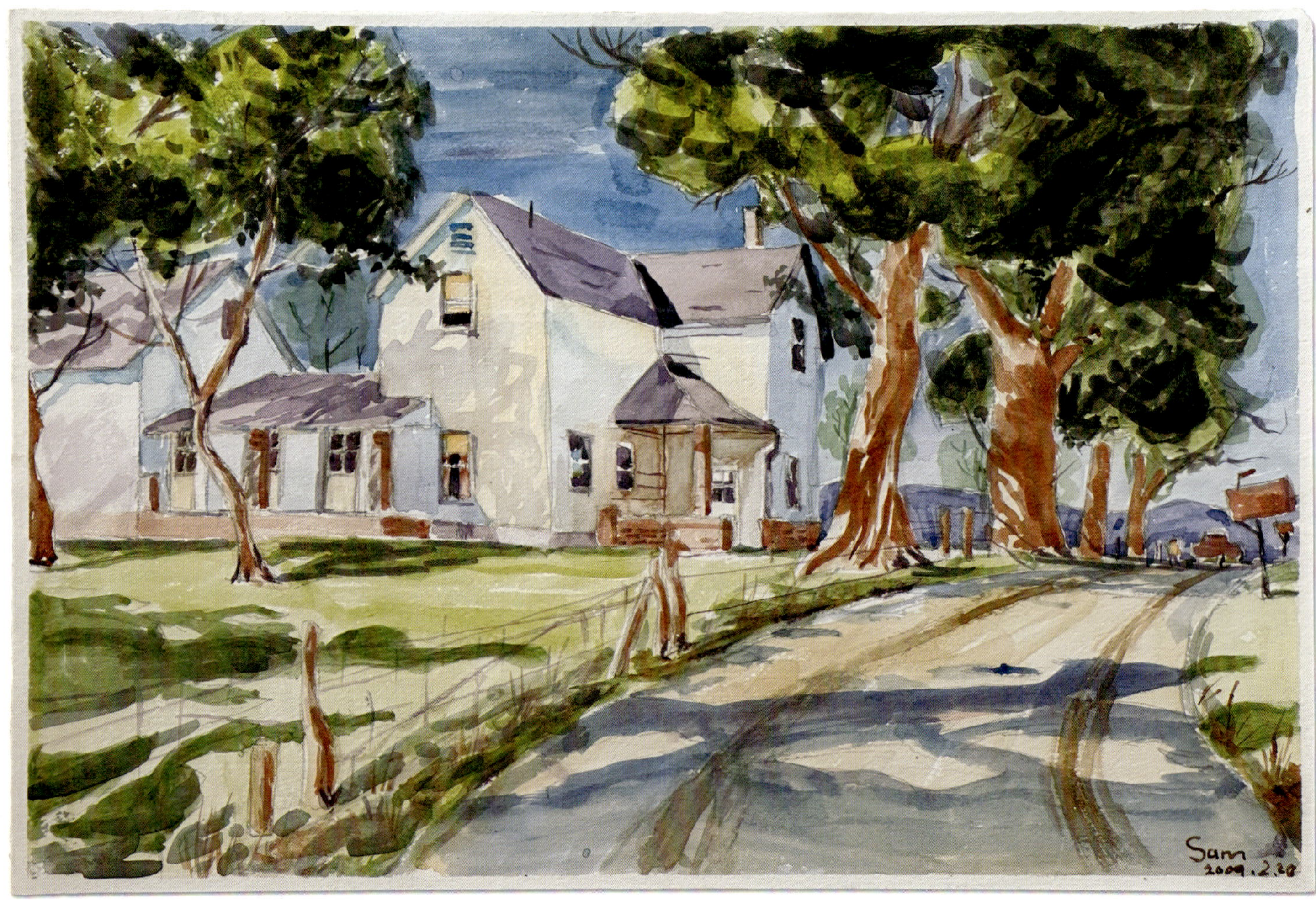

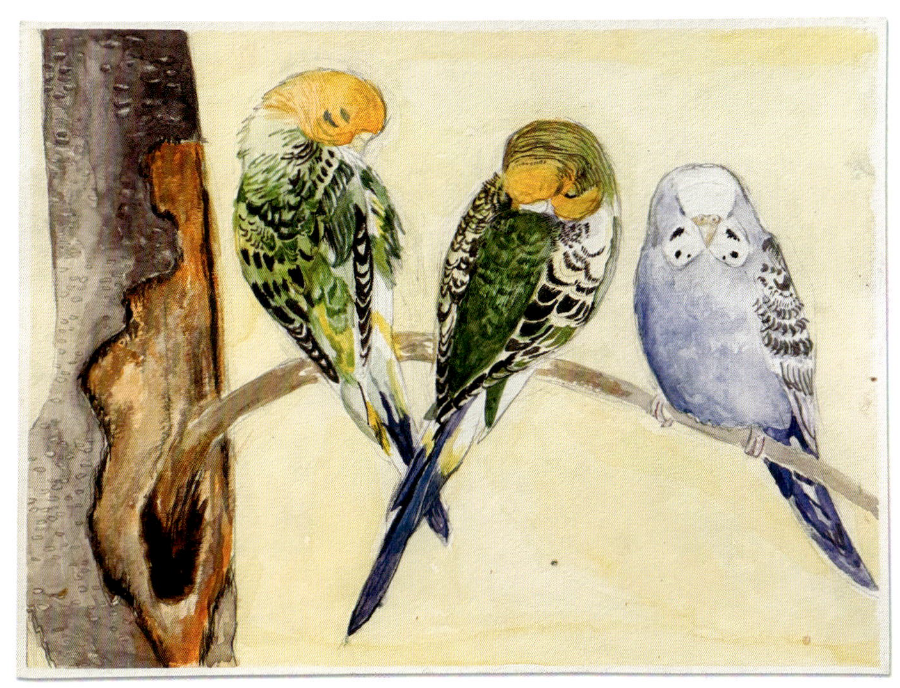

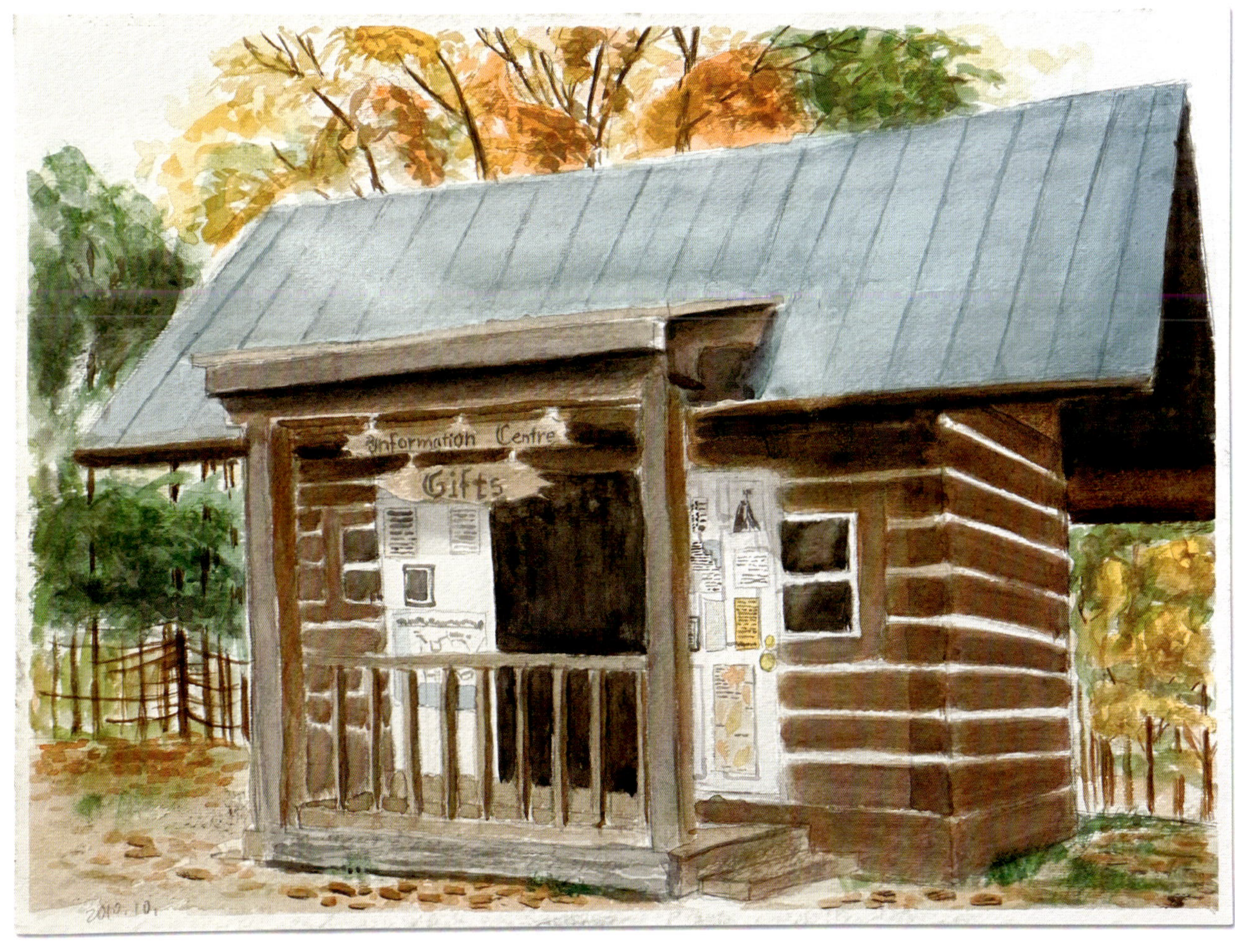
Information Centre
Gifts

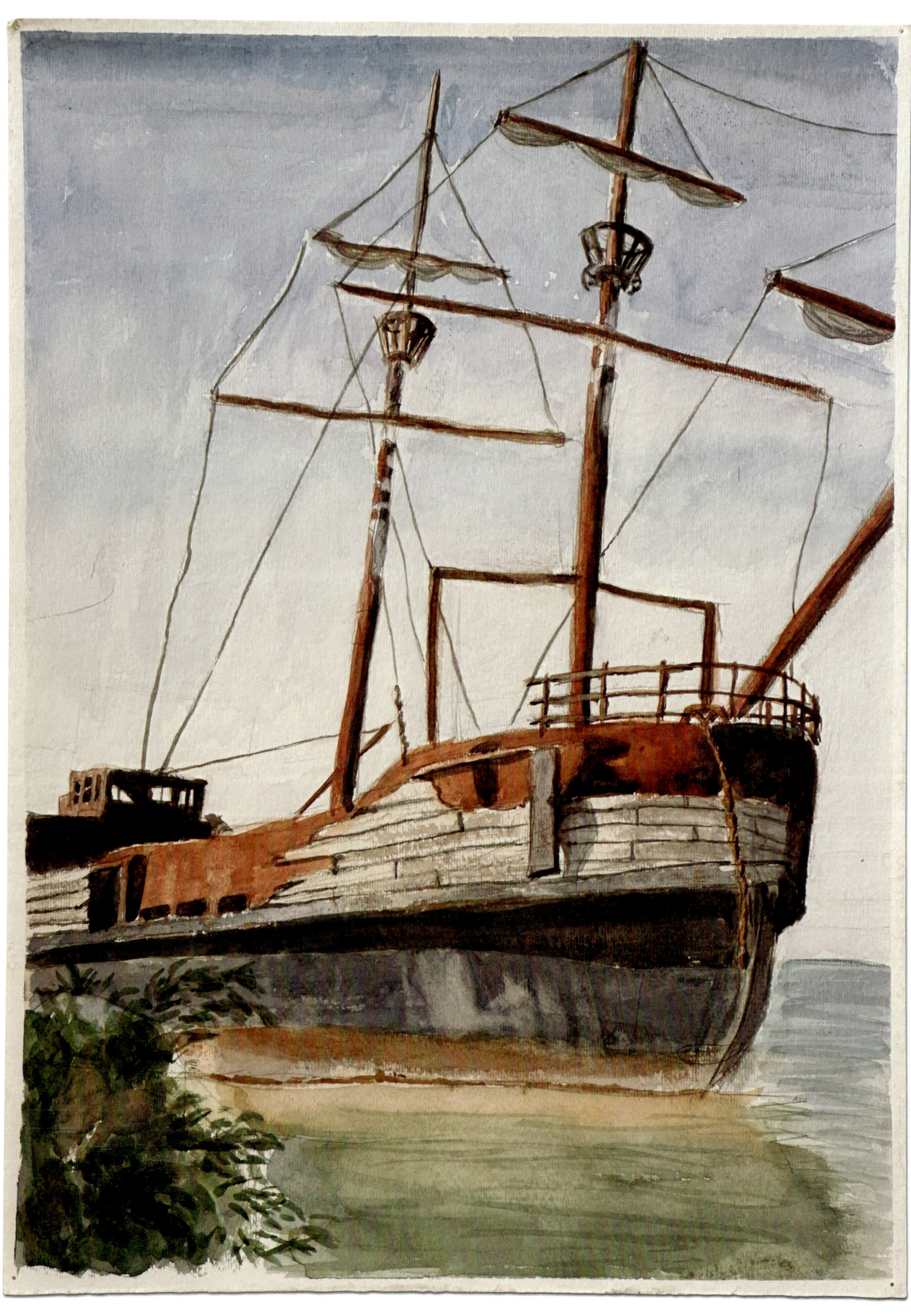

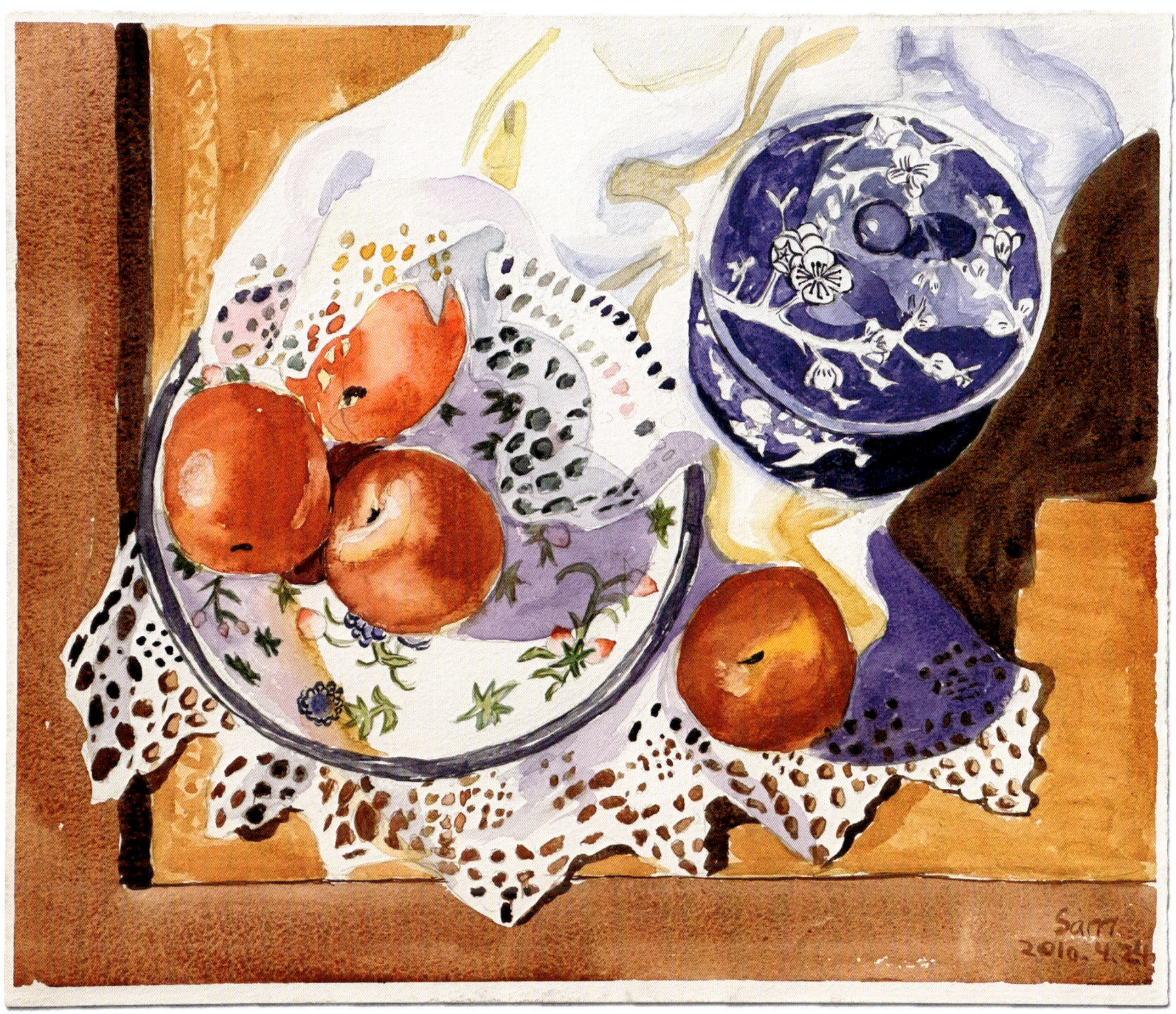

Left | *Abandoned Boat*, 2010, aged twelve

Above | *Study of a Still-Life Painting*, 2010, aged thirteen

Looking back now, I'm glad I went through all of those gruelling drawing sessions. If it wasn't for the repeated practice of these fundamental skills in traditional art, the learning curve for digital art would have been immense. I liken fundamentals to the forging of a sword; the repeated hammering and layering of steel is what gives it shape and rigidity while removing impurities. Without it, the blade would bend and break the moment it meets any resistance. Having a solid foundation makes a world of difference as you try to build on your skill set and venture out of your comfort zone. Don't skip out on perspective in your portraits just because you feel like you can get away without understanding it. Don't neglect colour theory just because your rendering doesn't look bad. There's always more to learn. Just like building a skyscraper, the stronger your foundation, the higher you can go.

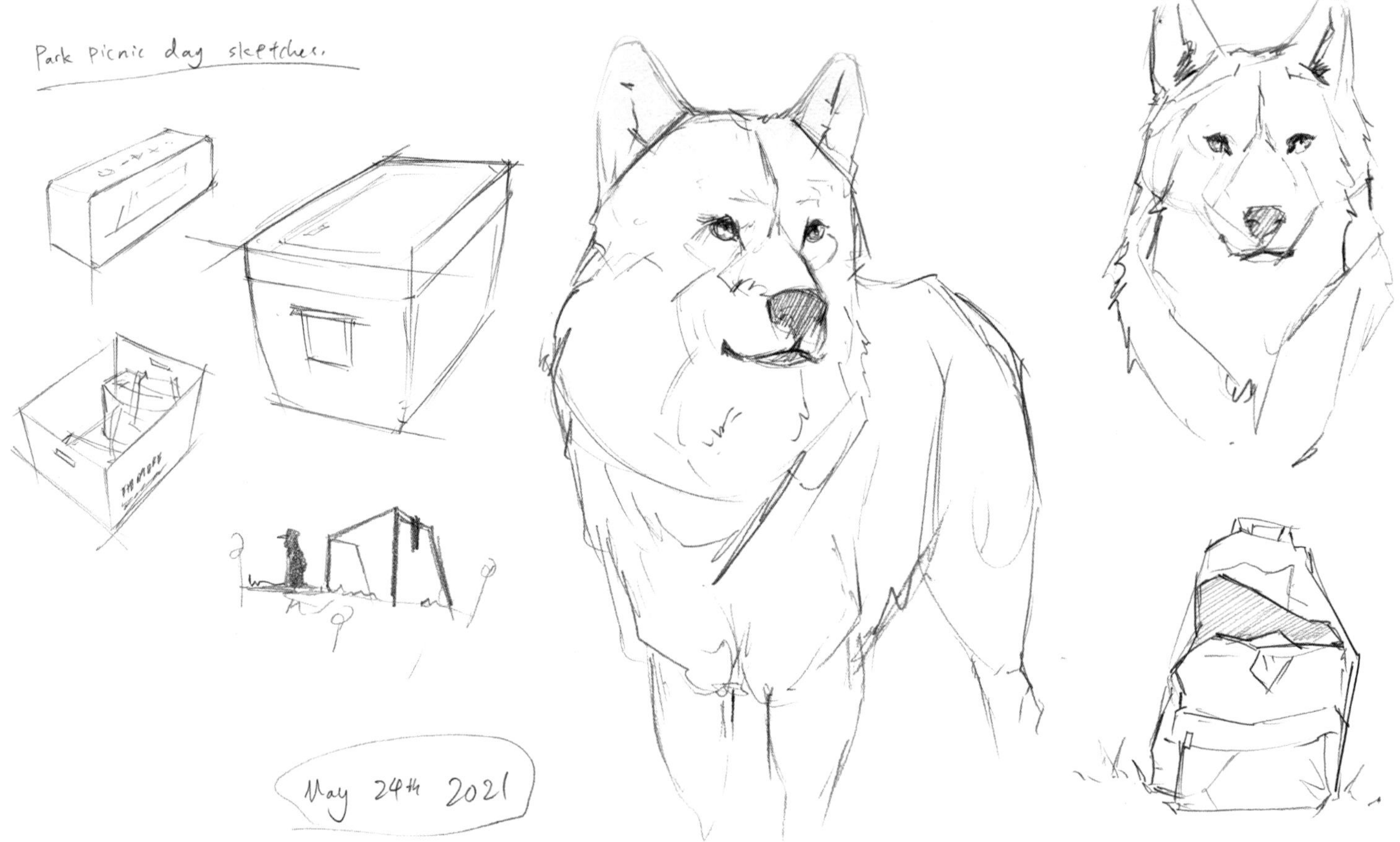

GROWING UP WITH ART

Art is, and will always be, a universal language that everyone can understand.

This was especially true when my family moved to Canada. Sitting in that grade-four classroom on my first day, I did not understand a single word from anyone. But I did have a piece of paper and a pencil on my desk, so I started drawing. I drew a car, and during my very first recess, the kids from my class crowded around my desk to look at it. Though I couldn't make out anything they were saying to me, I understood their expressions – they loved it! I still cherish that memory because that drawing made me feel less like an outsider in that new world.

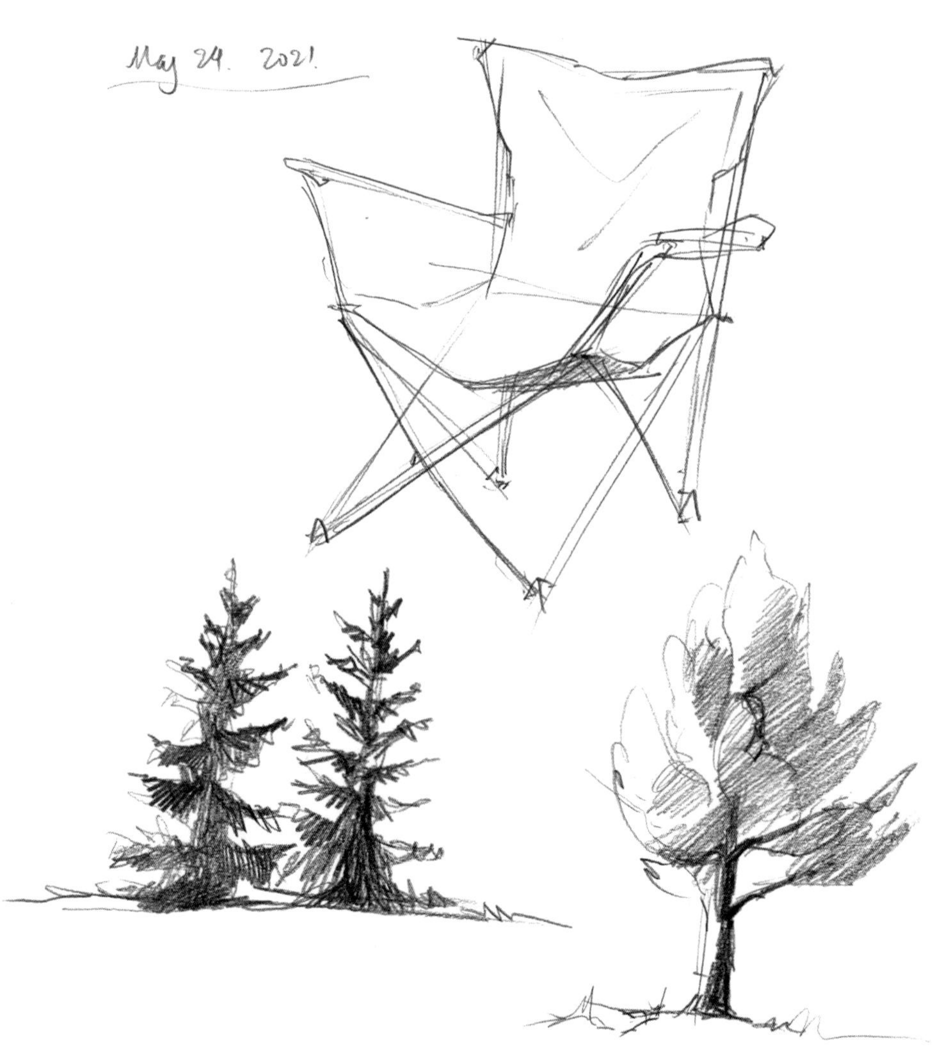

Sketchbook Studies, 2021.
These sketches are usually very fast and loose, no more than five minutes. When I have a subject I want to study, I'll make a few of these kinds of sketches to help build up a mental library of visual information. They're also just a lot of fun to do. Nothing beats the tactile feeling of pencil on paper. Not having an undo button can actually result in much more expressive lines and energetic pieces

Car studies

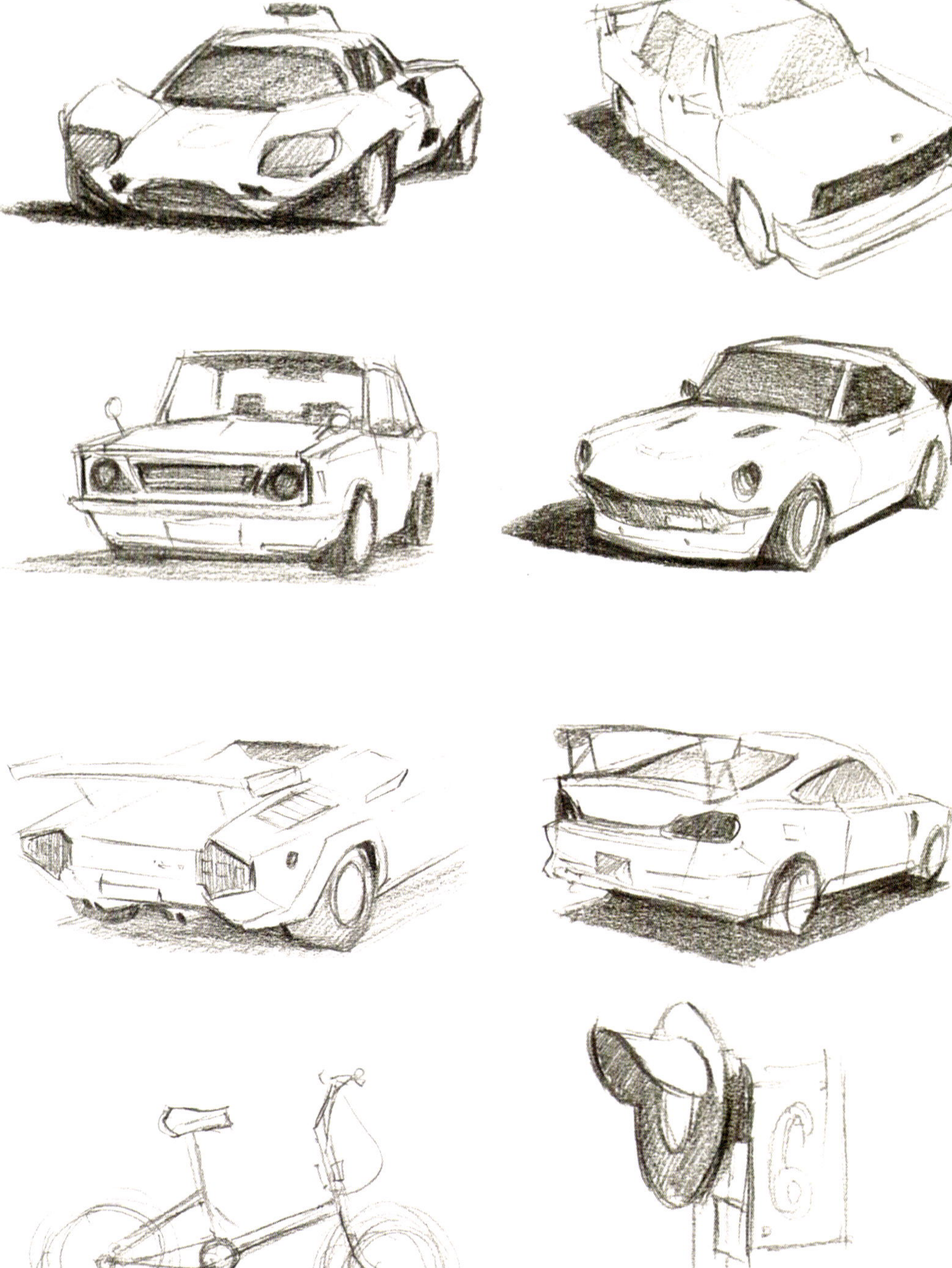

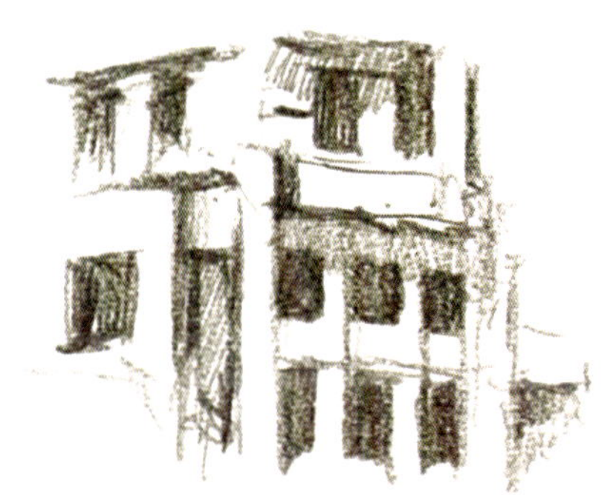

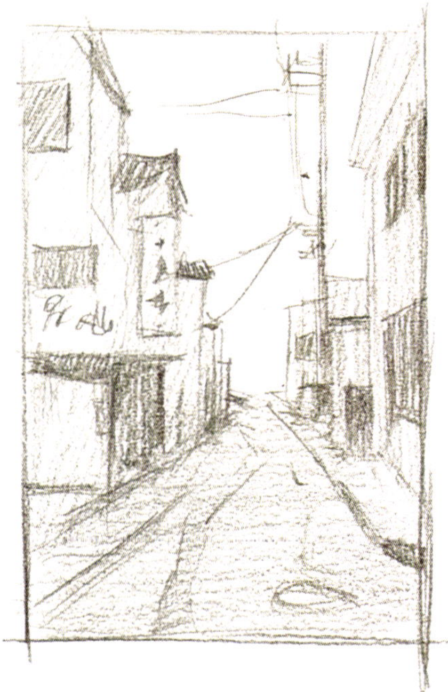

My family played a big role in nurturing my love for drawing. I was very lucky to have parents and grandparents who actually supported my passion and didn't try to mould me into something else. I was given the necessary environment for continuing my pursuit of drawing, and that played a very big part in how I managed to get to where I am today.

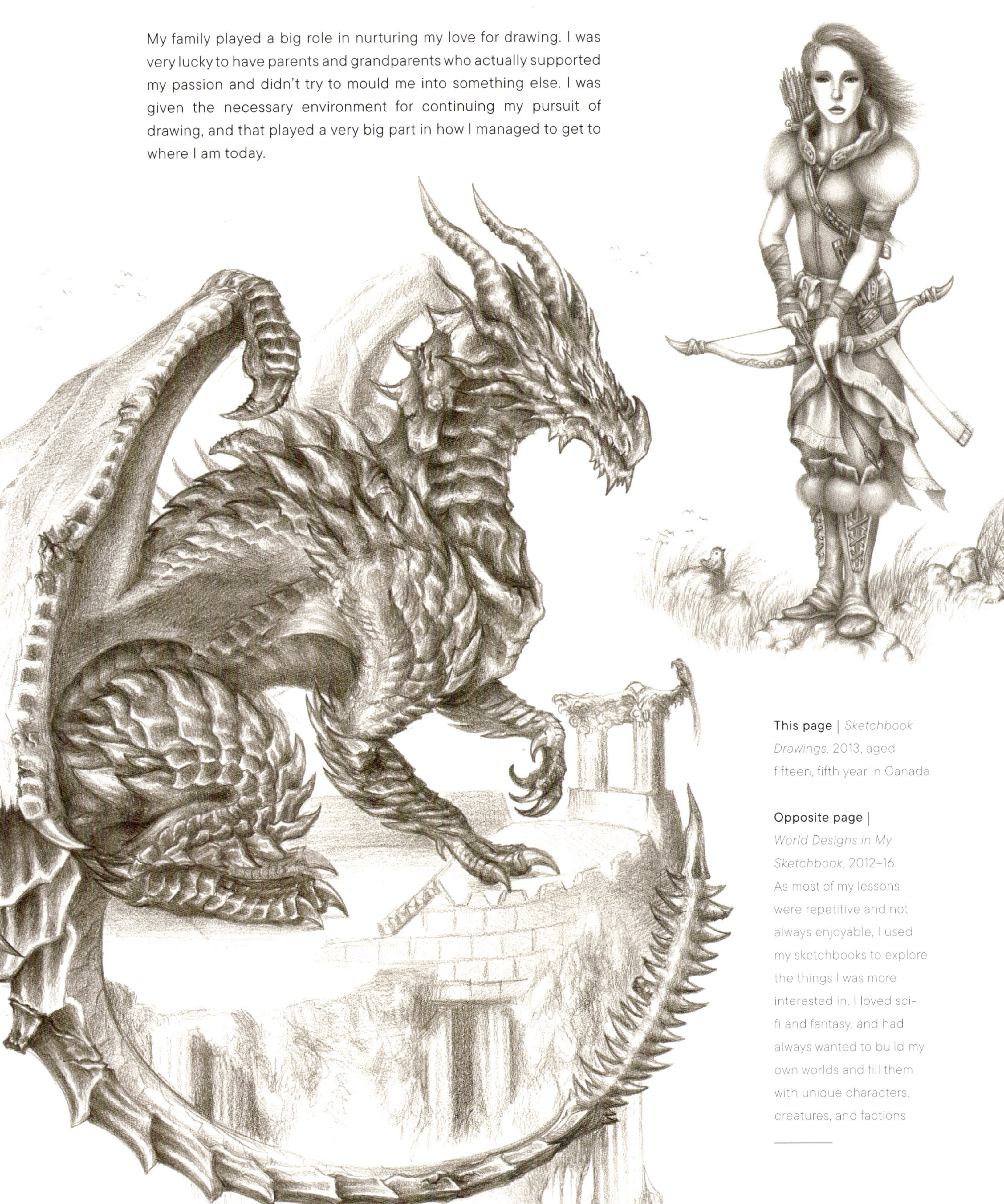

This page | *Sketchbook Drawings*, 2013, aged fifteen, fifth year in Canada

Opposite page | *World Designs in My Sketchbook*, 2012–16. As most of my lessons were repetitive and not always enjoyable, I used my sketchbooks to explore the things I was more interested in. I loved sci-fi and fantasy, and had always wanted to build my own worlds and fill them with unique characters, creatures, and factions

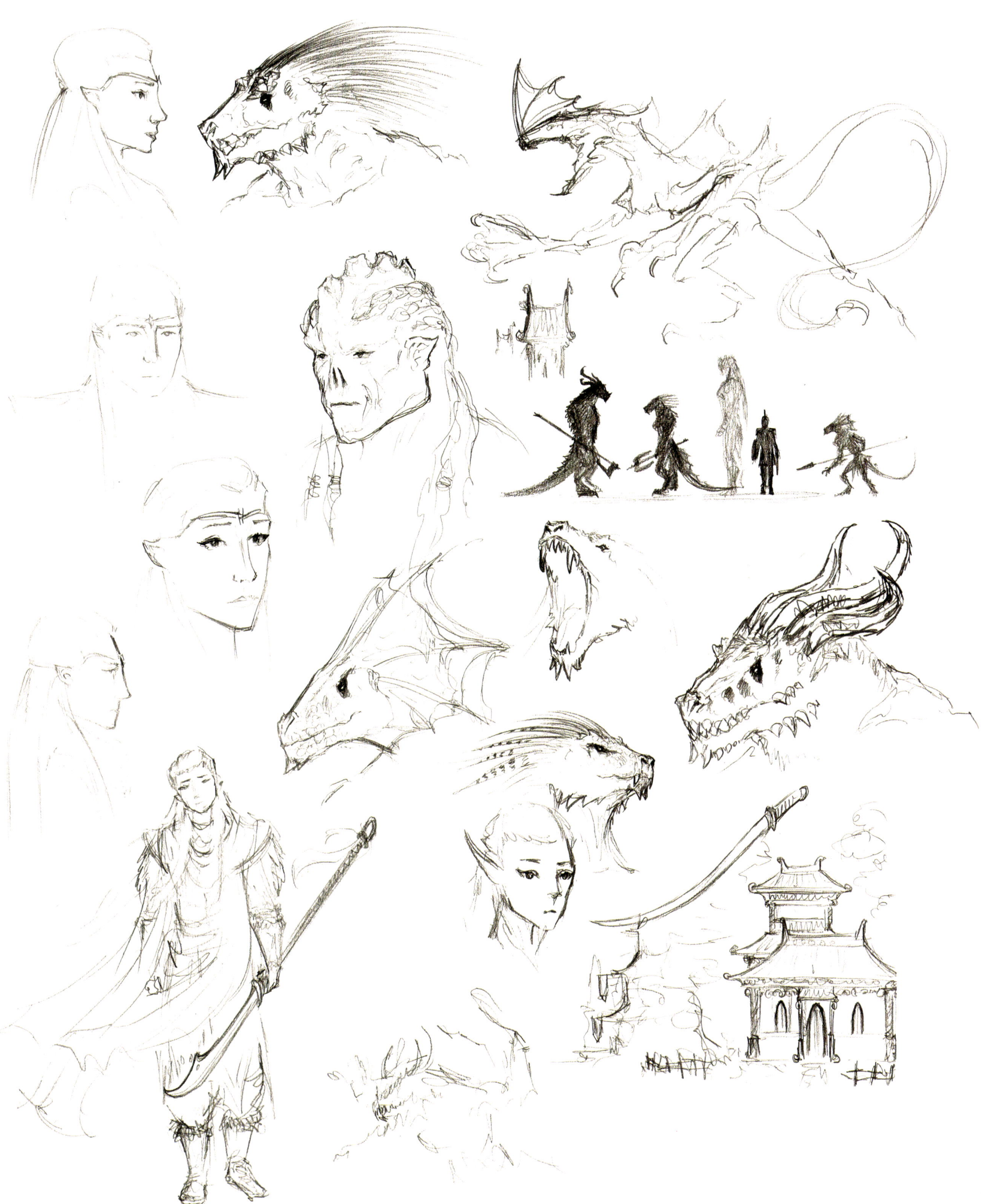

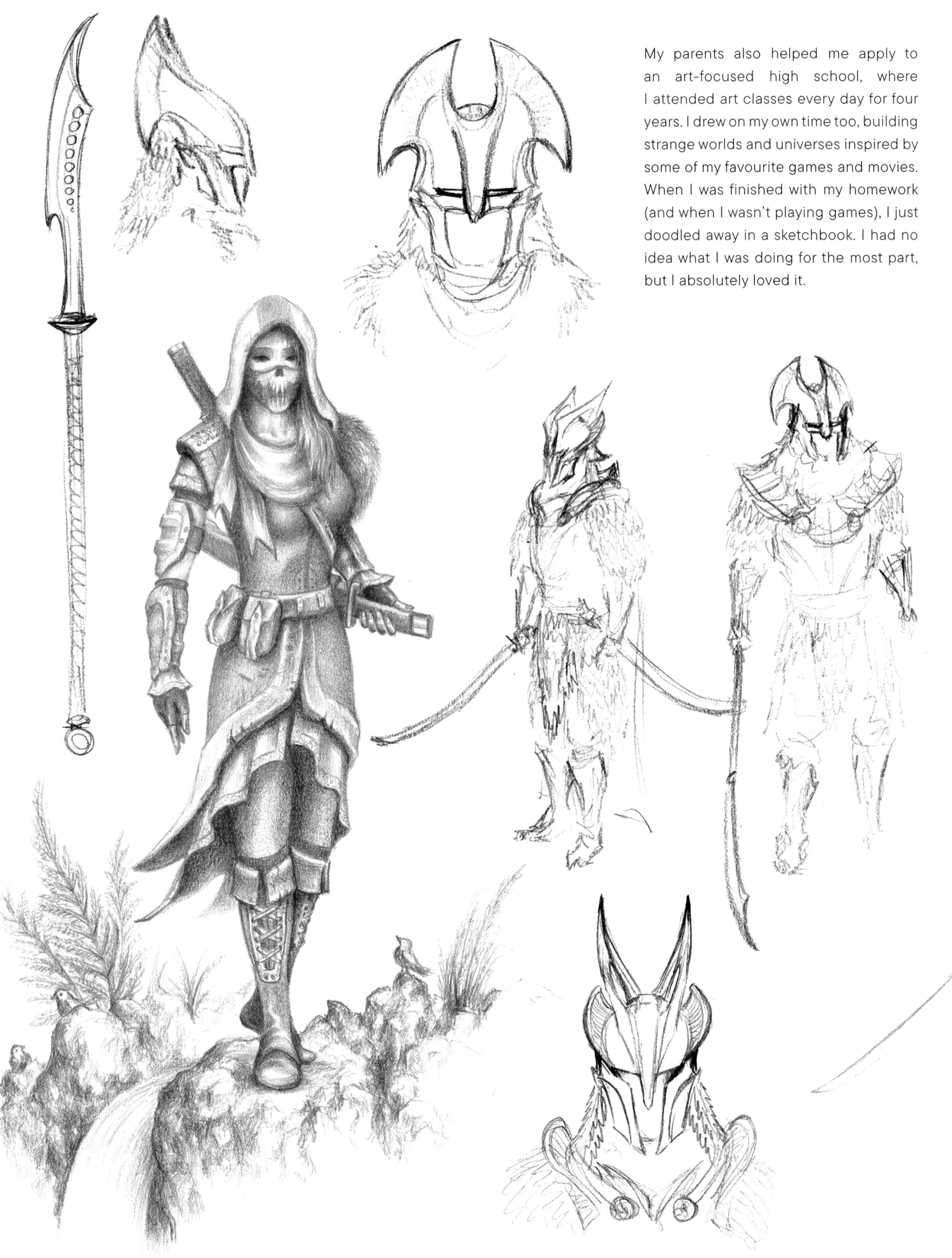

My parents also helped me apply to an art-focused high school, where I attended art classes every day for four years. I drew on my own time too, building strange worlds and universes inspired by some of my favourite games and movies. When I was finished with my homework (and when I wasn't playing games), I just doodled away in a sketchbook. I had no idea what I was doing for the most part, but I absolutely loved it.

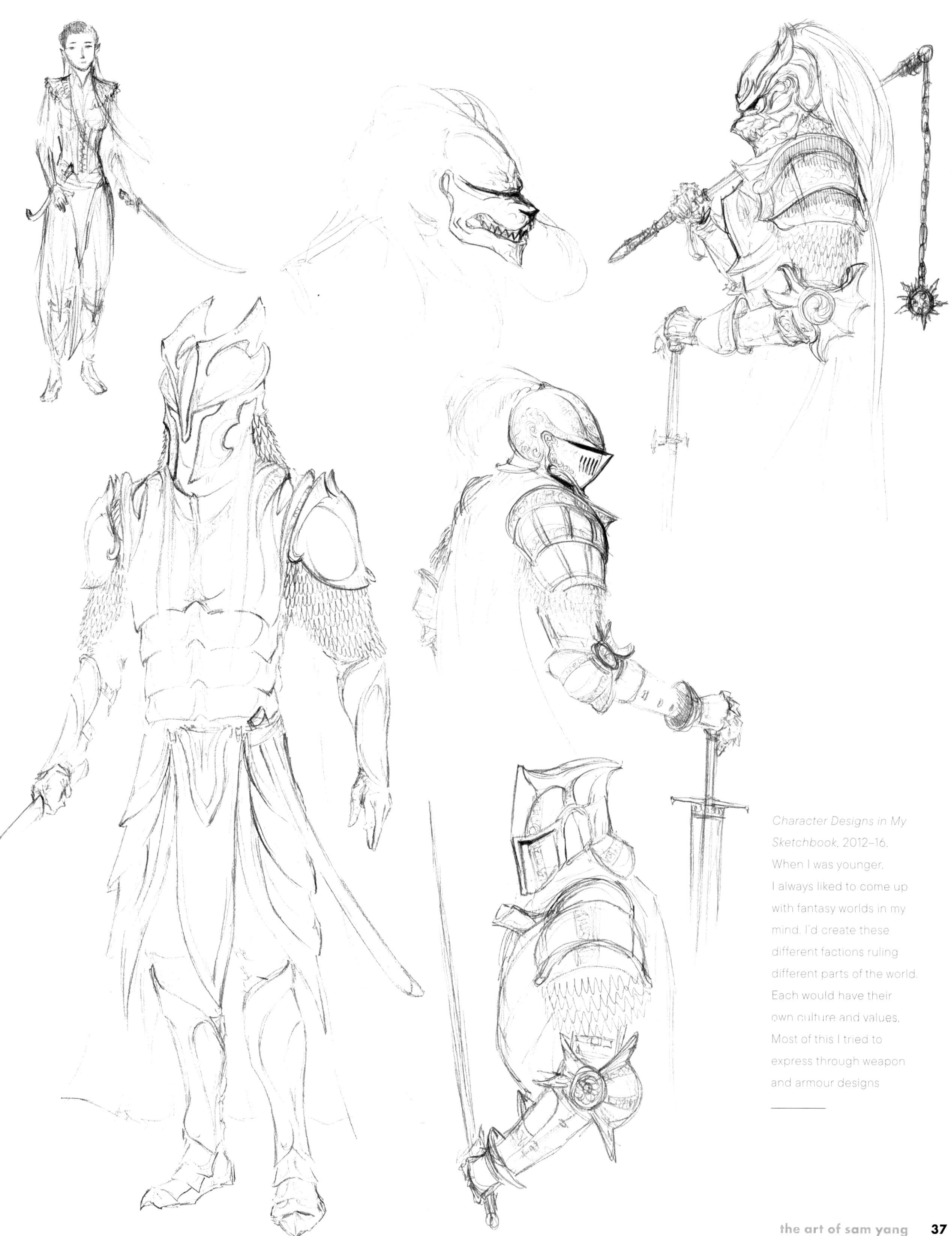

Character Designs in My Sketchbook, 2012–16.
When I was younger, I always liked to come up with fantasy worlds in my mind. I'd create these different factions ruling different parts of the world. Each would have their own culture and values. Most of this I tried to express through weapon and armour designs

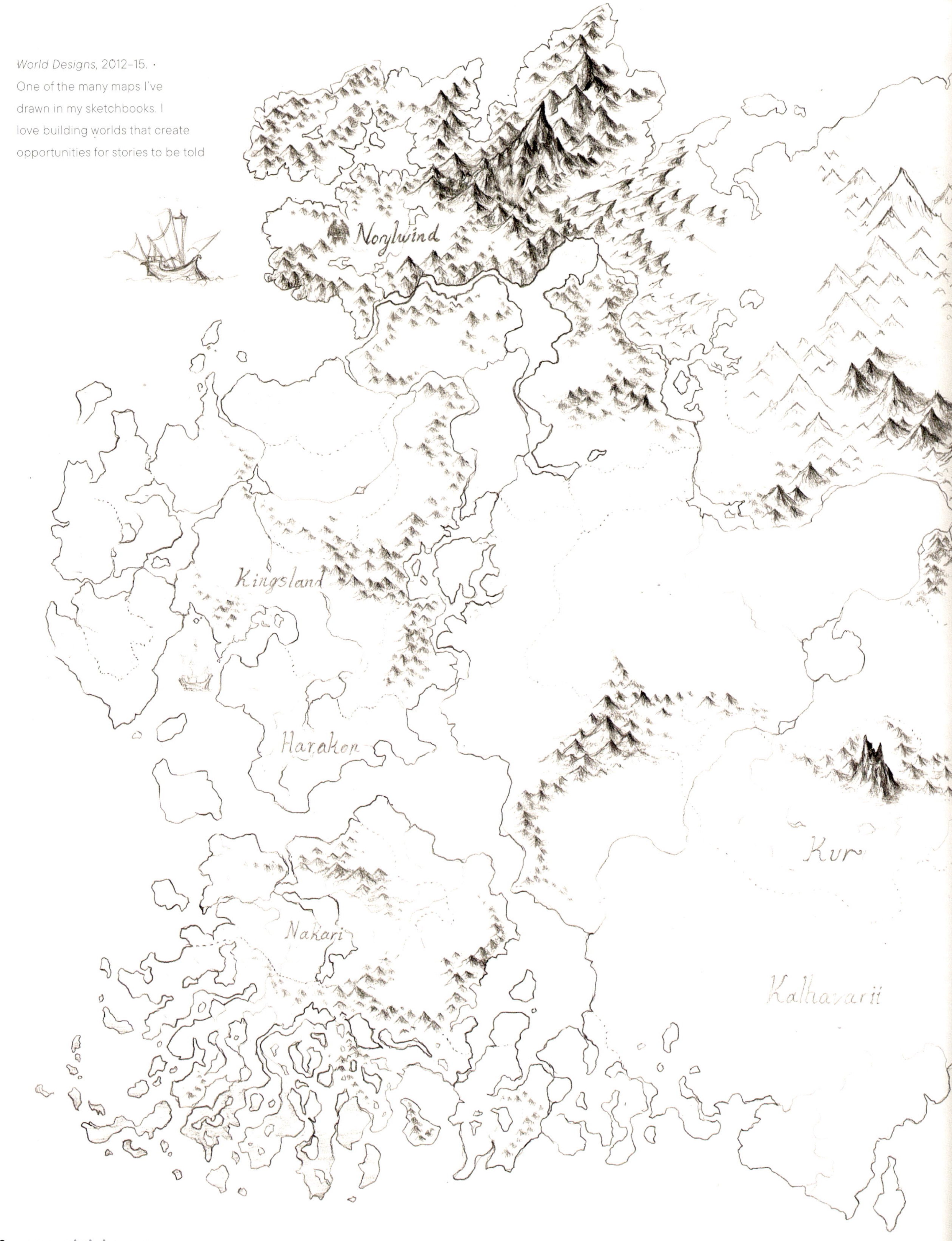

World Designs, 2012–15. · One of the many maps I've drawn in my sketchbooks. I love building worlds that create opportunities for stories to be told

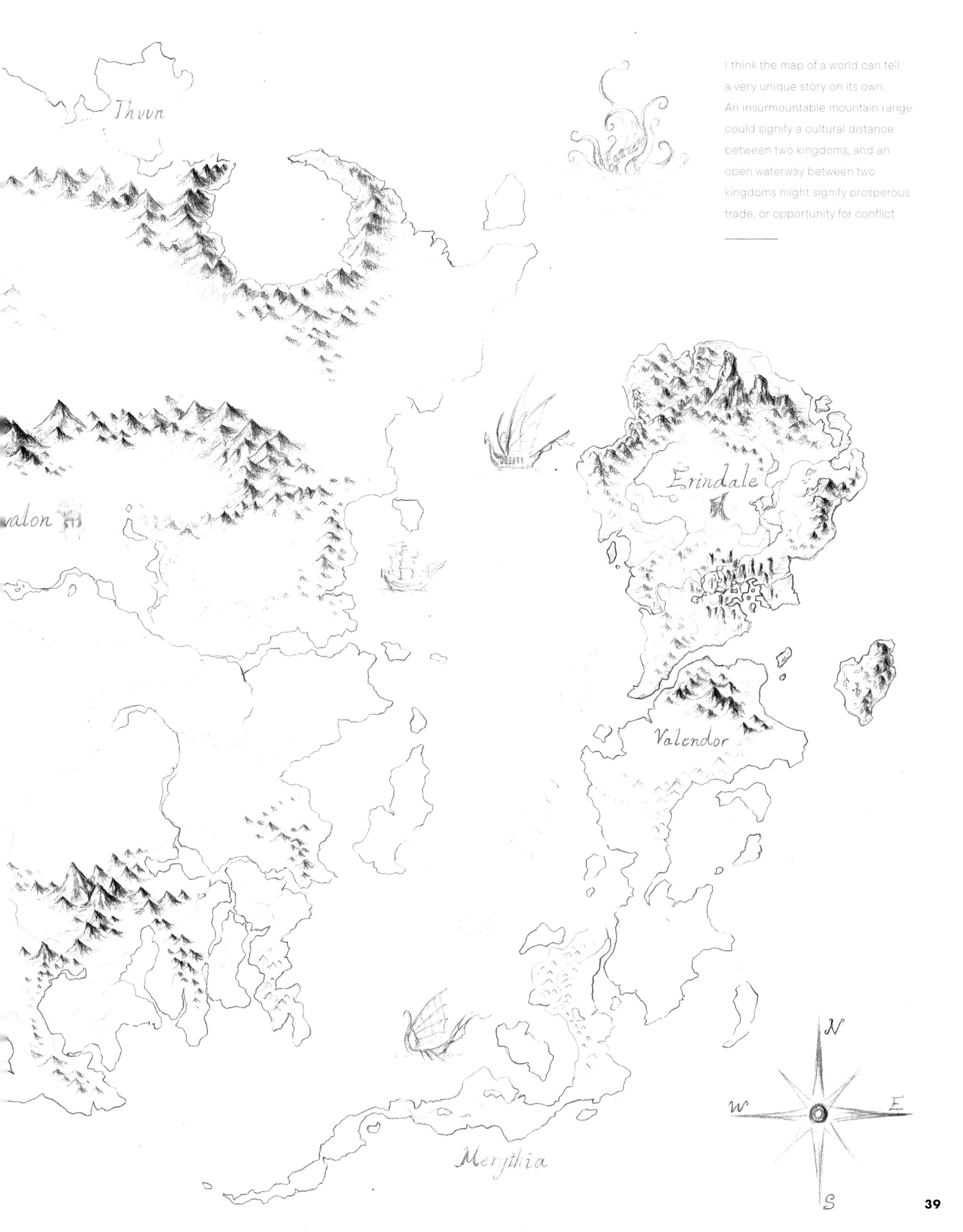

I think the map of a world can tell a very unique story on its own. An insurmountable mountain range could signify a cultural distance between two kingdoms, and an open waterway between two kingdoms might signify prosperous trade, or opportunity for conflict

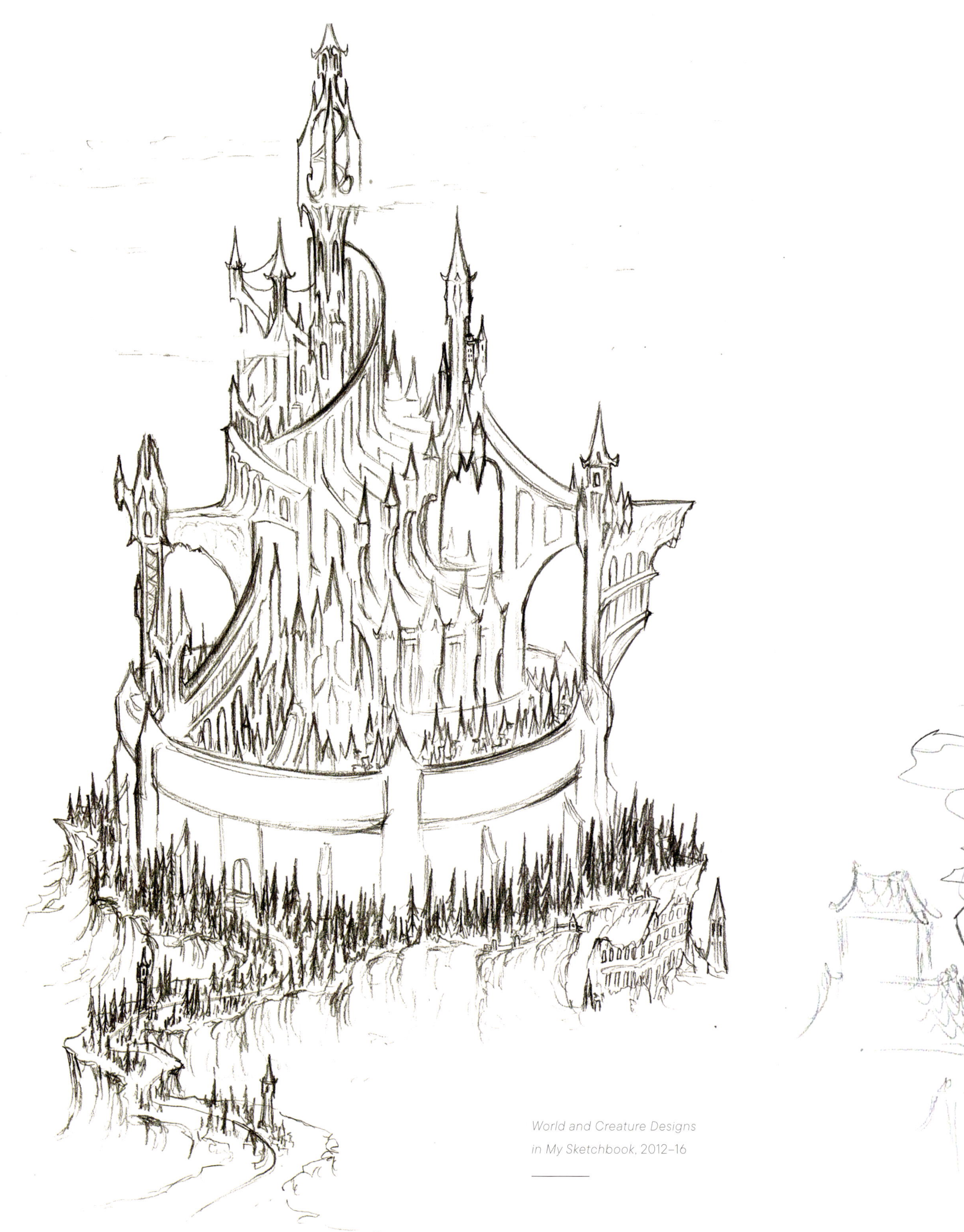

World and Creature Designs in My Sketchbook, 2012–16

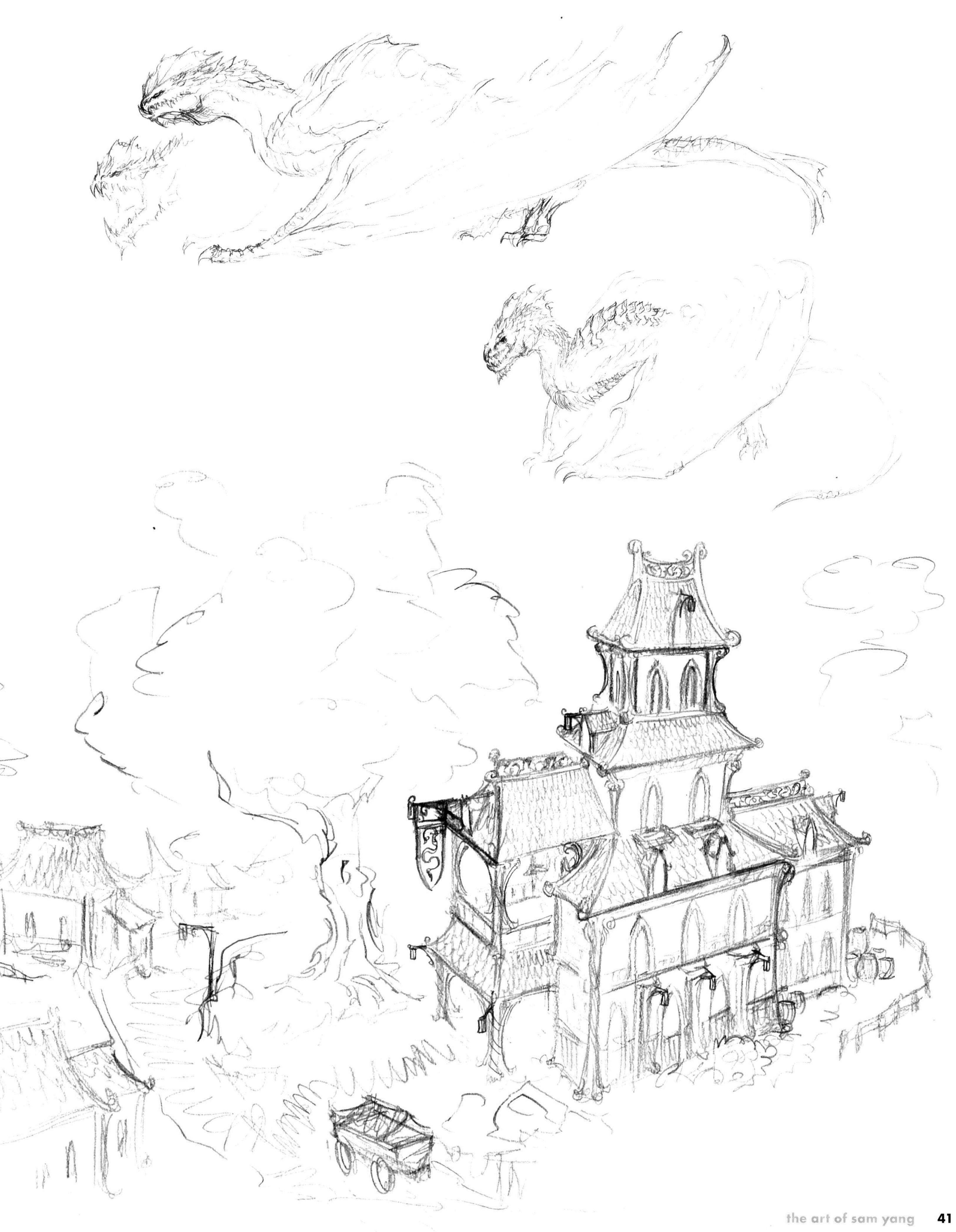

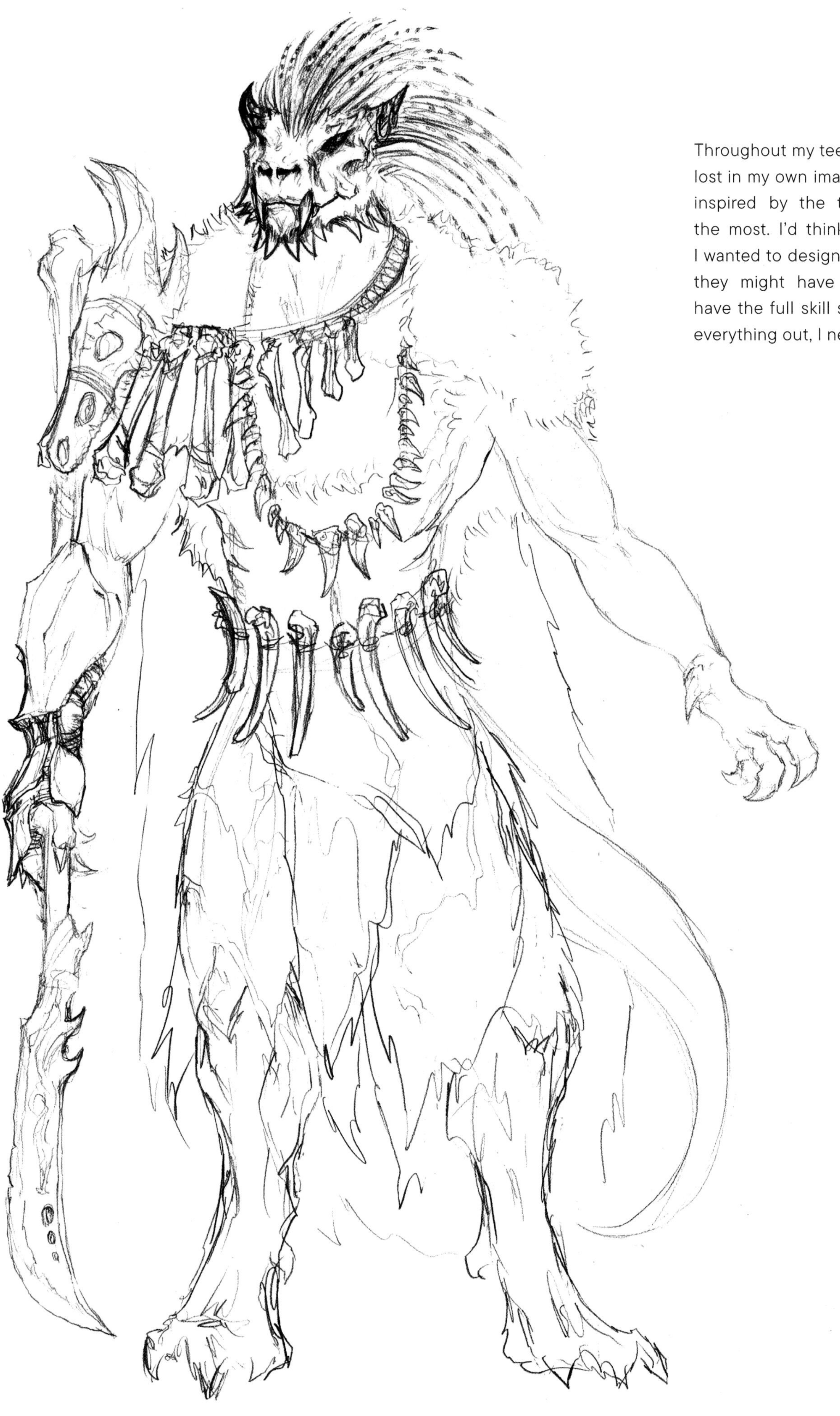

Throughout my teenage years, I was always lost in my own imagination, creating worlds inspired by the things that interest me the most. I'd think about what characters I wanted to design and the worlds in which they might have lived. Though I didn't have the full skill set needed to truly flesh everything out, I never let that stop me.

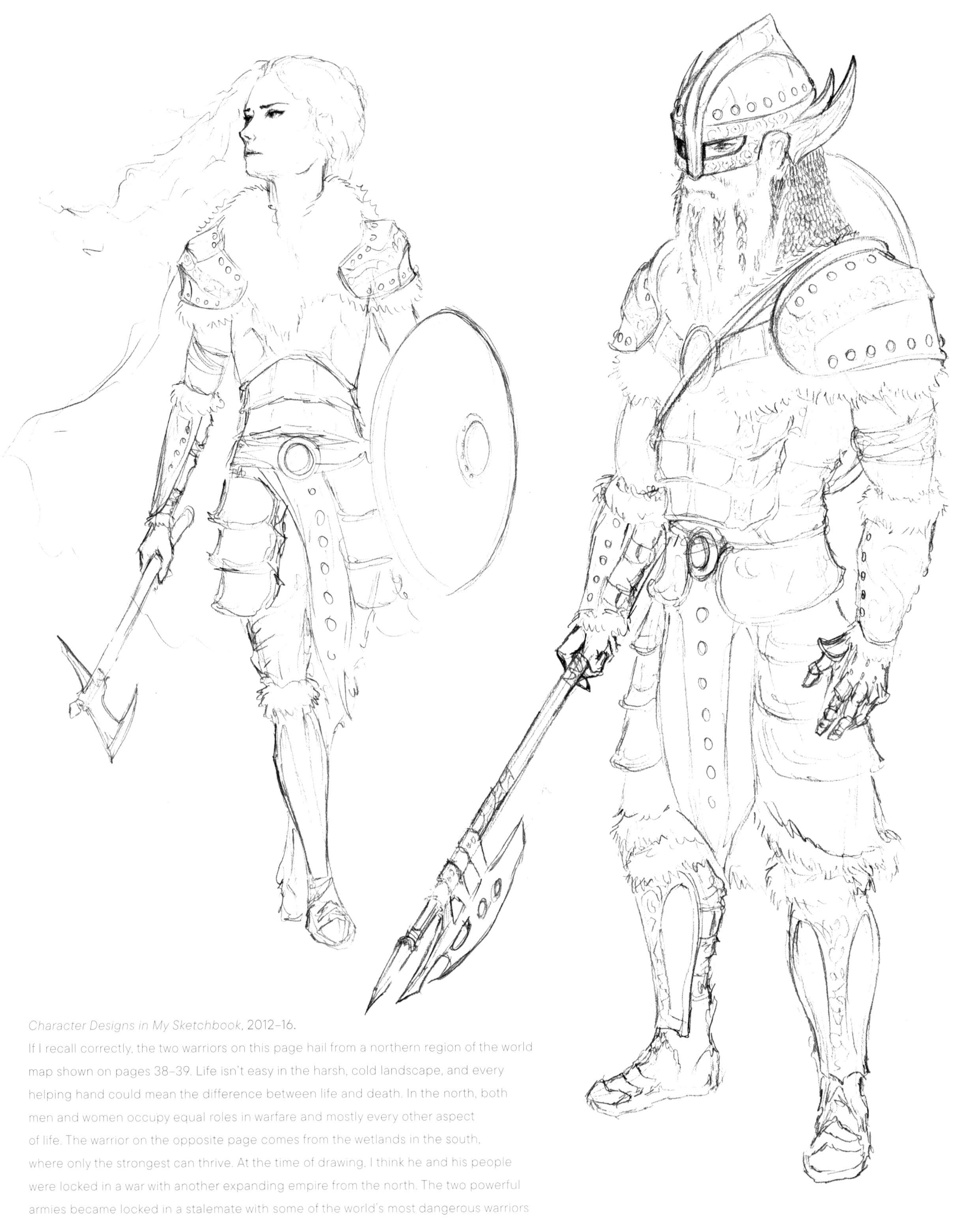

Character Designs in My Sketchbook, 2012–16.

If I recall correctly, the two warriors on this page hail from a northern region of the world map shown on pages 38–39. Life isn't easy in the harsh, cold landscape, and every helping hand could mean the difference between life and death. In the north, both men and women occupy equal roles in warfare and mostly every other aspect of life. The warrior on the opposite page comes from the wetlands in the south, where only the strongest can thrive. At the time of drawing, I think he and his people were locked in a war with another expanding empire from the north. The two powerful armies became locked in a stalemate with some of the world's most dangerous warriors

PURSUING ART AFTER HIGH SCHOOL

When university rolled around, I was accepted into an animation programme, but didn't really fit in and felt like it wasn't my vibe. So, I decided to pursue graphic design instead. My life had taken a different trajectory, moving ever so slightly further from art with each passing year. I could almost feel it slipping away from me. At times, it made me feel sad that so many years of drawing and attending art classes were being tossed away for the sake of a more stable future. Luckily, the story didn't end there.

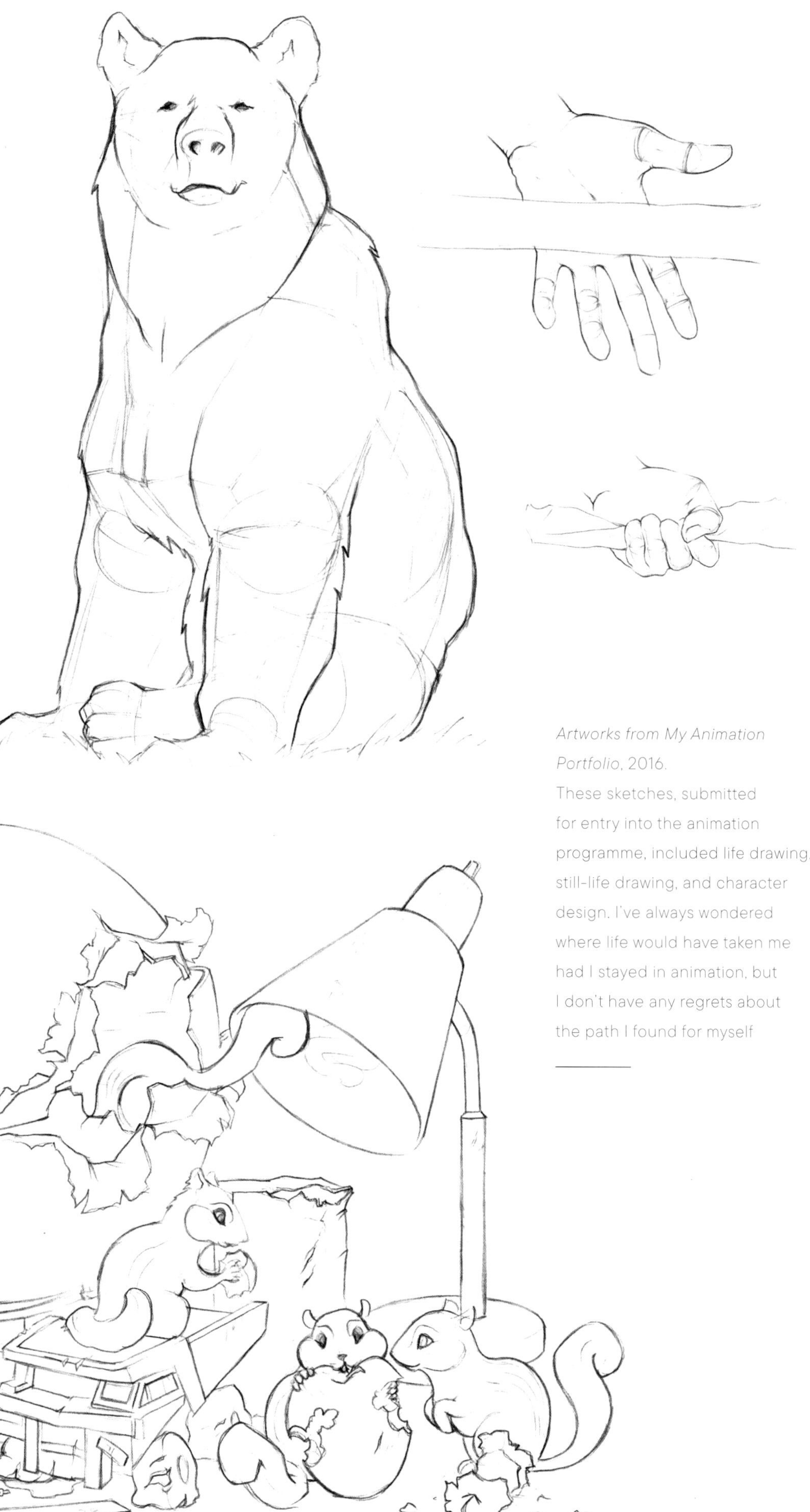

Artworks from My Animation Portfolio, 2016.
These sketches, submitted for entry into the animation programme, included life drawing, still-life drawing, and character design. I've always wondered where life would have taken me had I stayed in animation, but I don't have any regrets about the path I found for myself

MY INSPIRATIONS

During the pandemic in spring 2020, three years into my university graphic-design programme, we were all ordered to stay home here in Toronto. I no longer had to commute hours to class, and I wasn't able to go out to socialize, so I occupied my time by drawing again. It was during this period of rediscovery that I found some of my biggest and earliest artistic influences, such as Ross Tran, Atey Ghailan, Glen Keane, WLOP, Aaron Blaise, and so many more.

Viv & Luna Environment, July 2020. This was one of my earliest environment-learning attempts in digital art. There are undoubtedly many aspects I would approach differently now.

I think I came up with a perspective grid first, just to afford myself more certainty and clarity. While I do find the lack of details very charming, I think a bit more visual interest in the foreground could take this to the next level.

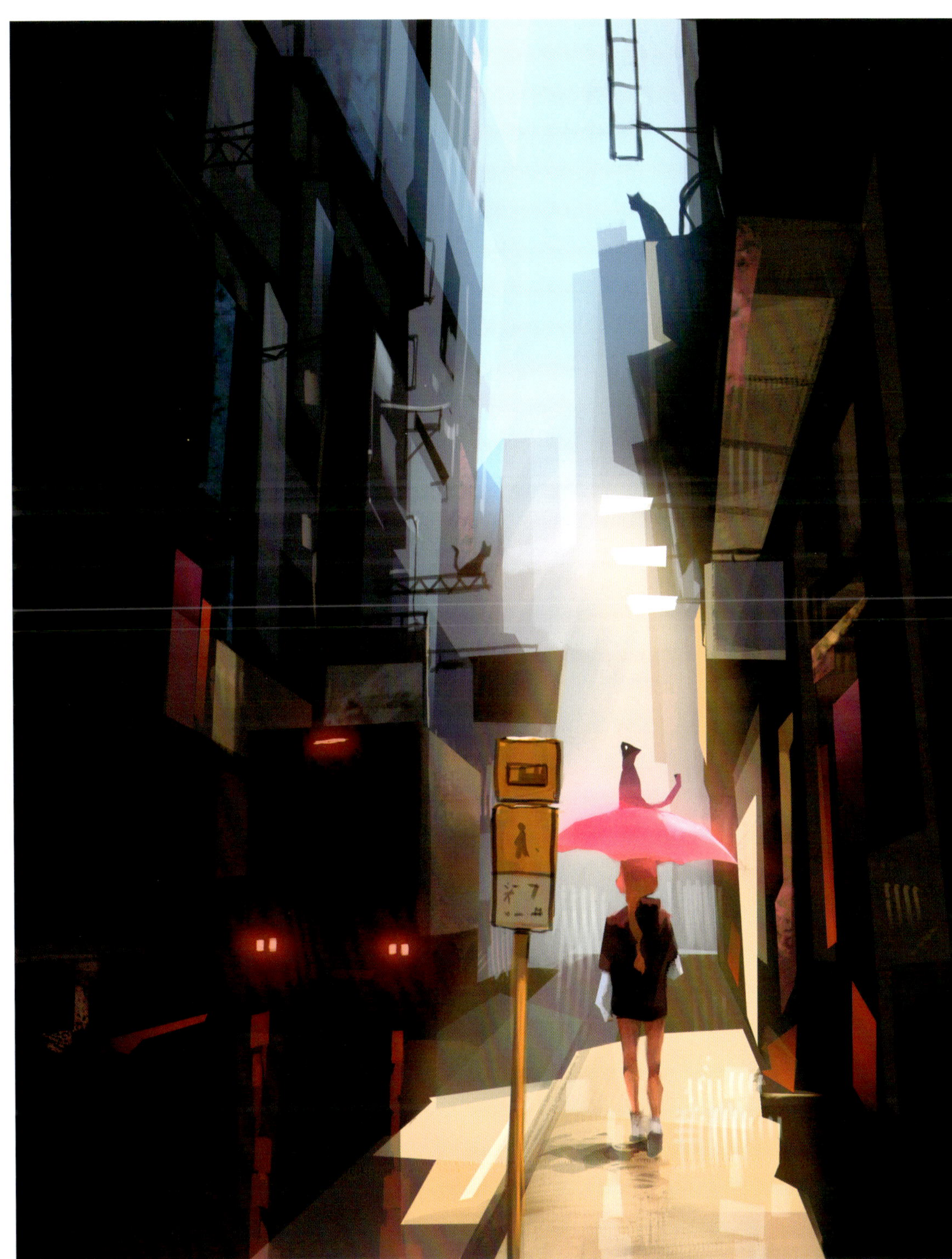

I loved Ross's beautiful, vibrant colour palettes and Atey's environments, which were imbued with a sense of wonder and nostalgia. Seeing one of Atey's process videos on YouTube made me wonder what could be possible for me if I put in the hard work and genuinely tried to be better. These artists were my heroes and I wanted to be like them. So, I started learning again. I owe so much of what I've learned to these incredibly skilled artists who shared their work with the world.

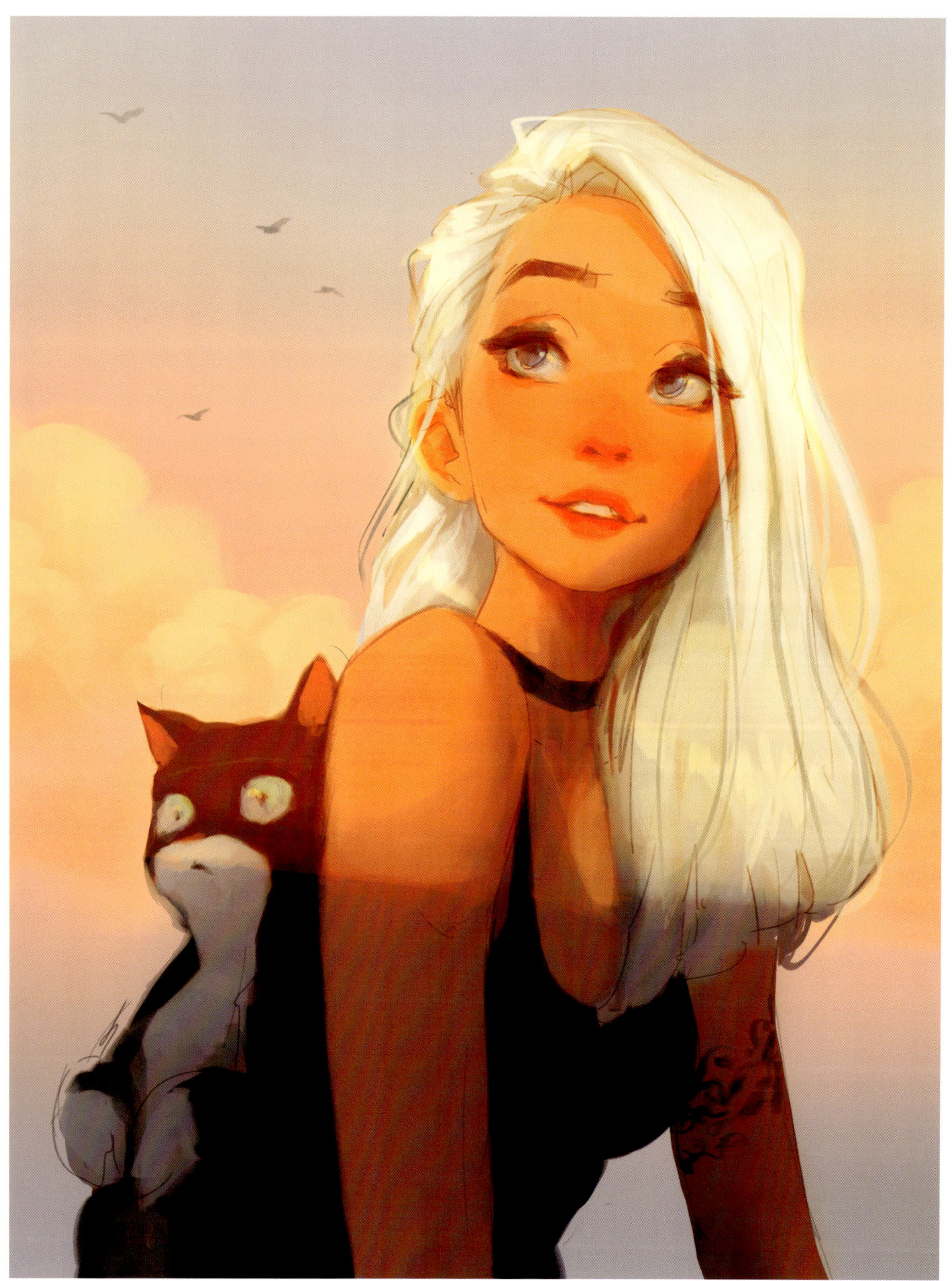

Left | *Kara*, October 2020.
I've always loved the look of warm sunlight on a character. Good lighting can breathe life into a scene and generate a feeling that nothing else can achieve. Throughout 2020 and onwards, I dedicated a lot of my time to studying, understanding, and interpreting light in my own way

Right | *Portrait*, August 2020

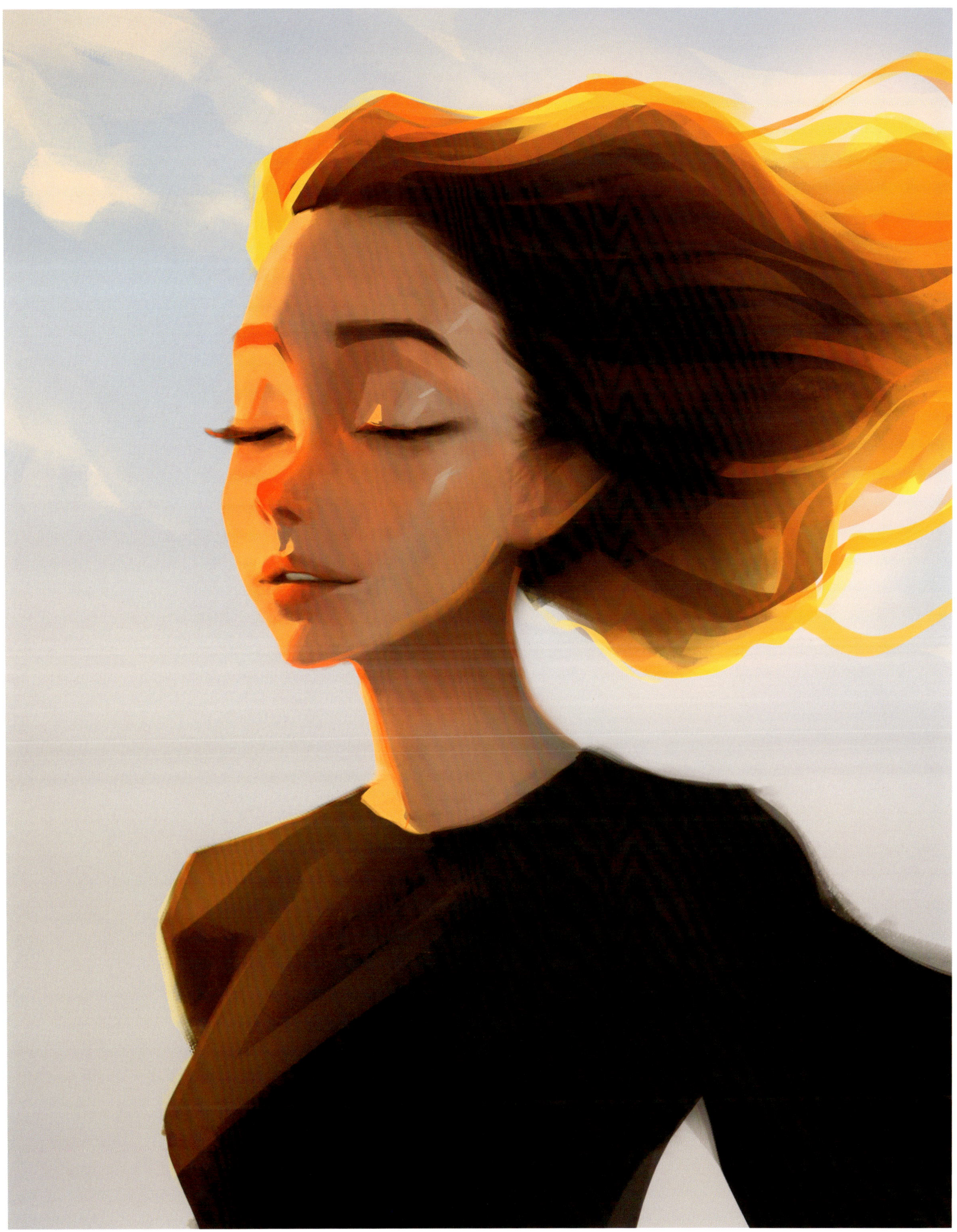

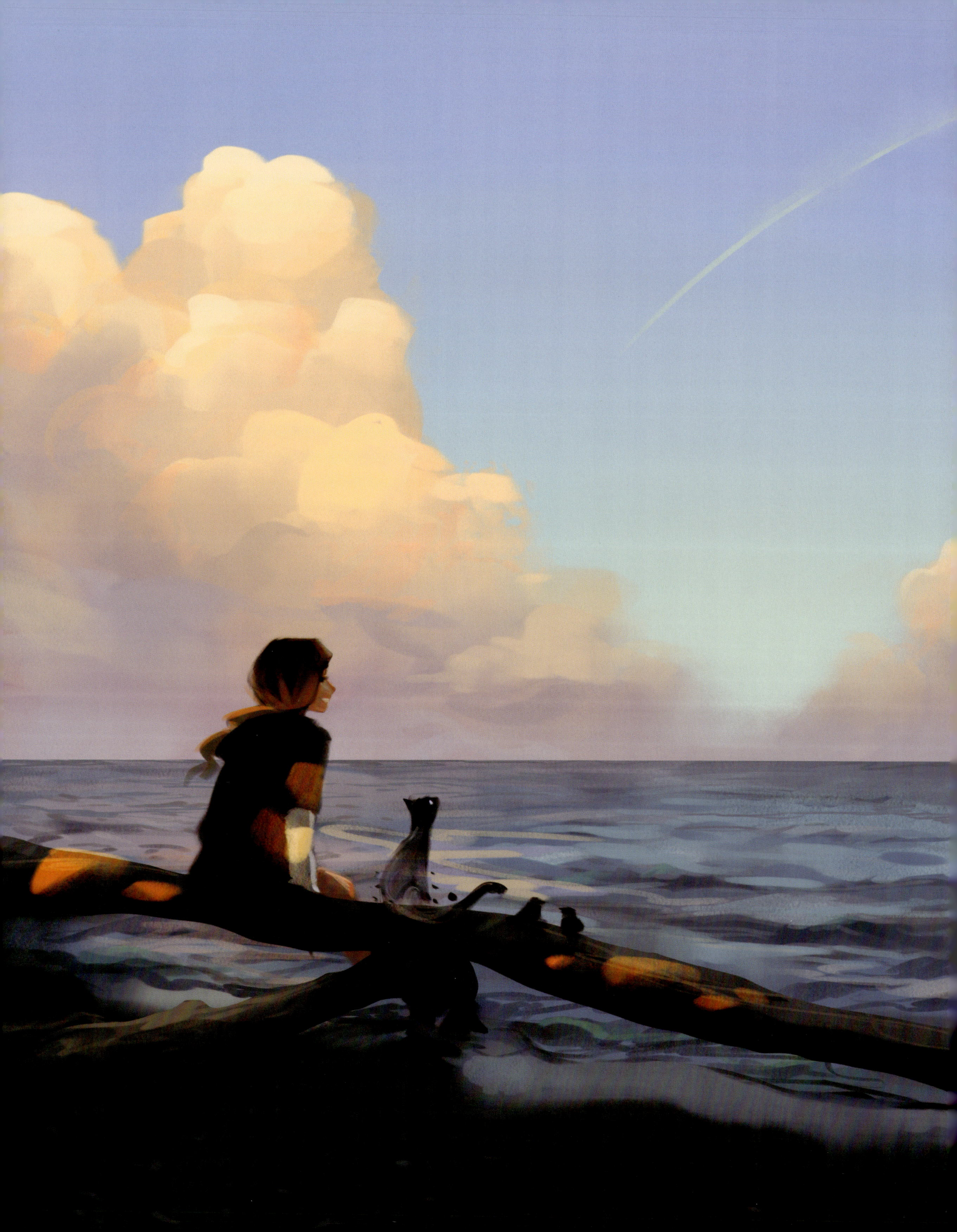

One of the biggest hurdles for me to cross was my previous notion that I was 'good'. Growing up, I'd always been good at art among my peers. I'd always received validation for the work I produced and it put me in the mindset of: 'I'm good enough, I don't need to go out of my way to learn.' In my high-school years, I nurtured this mindset until it had become fully ingrained. I'd stopped actively looking to others for inspiration; I was content. Sure, my art was good at the time, but there was so much room for improvement. I truly had no idea of how little I actually knew.

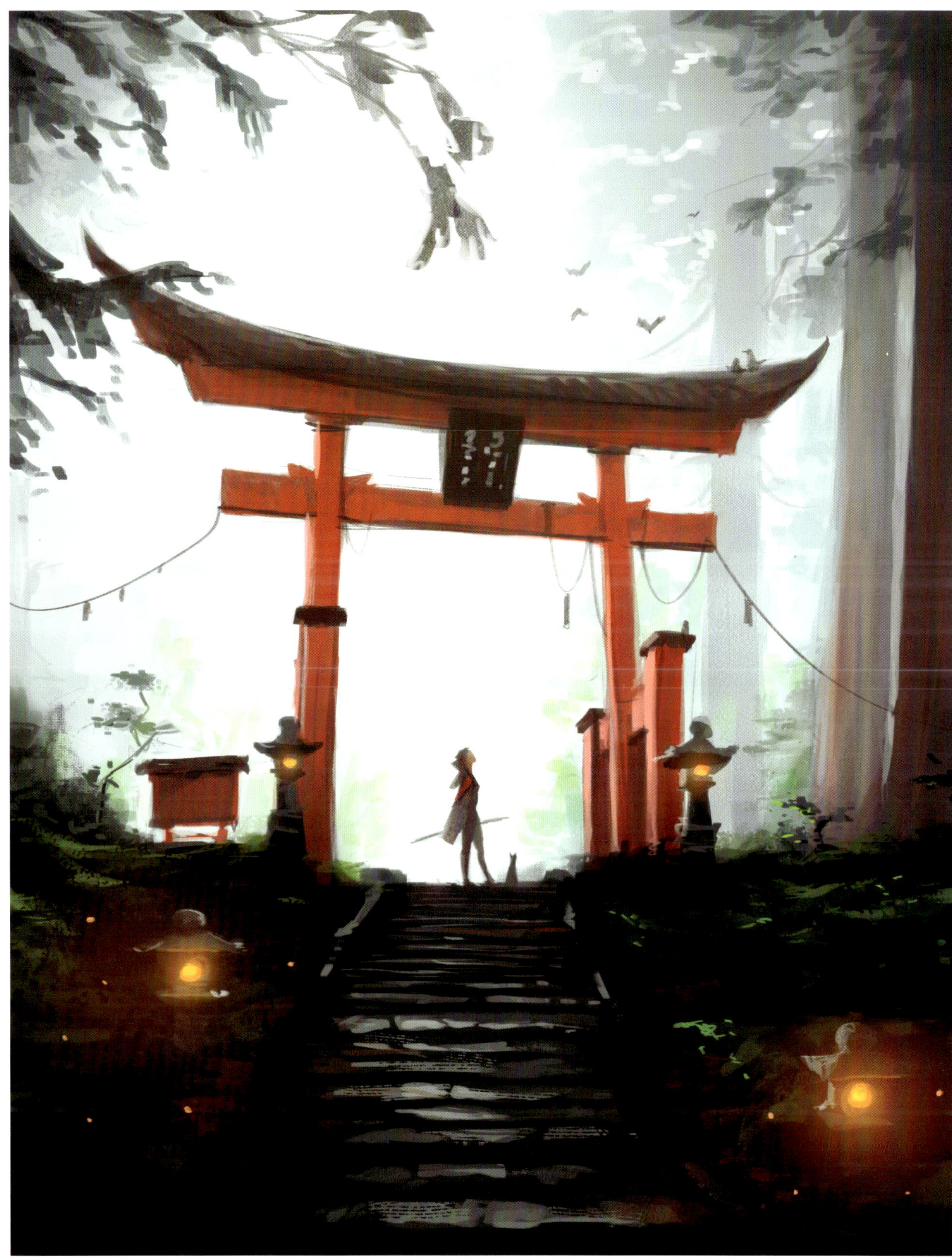

Left | *Luna by the Lake*, August 2020

Right | *The Torii Gate*, December 2020

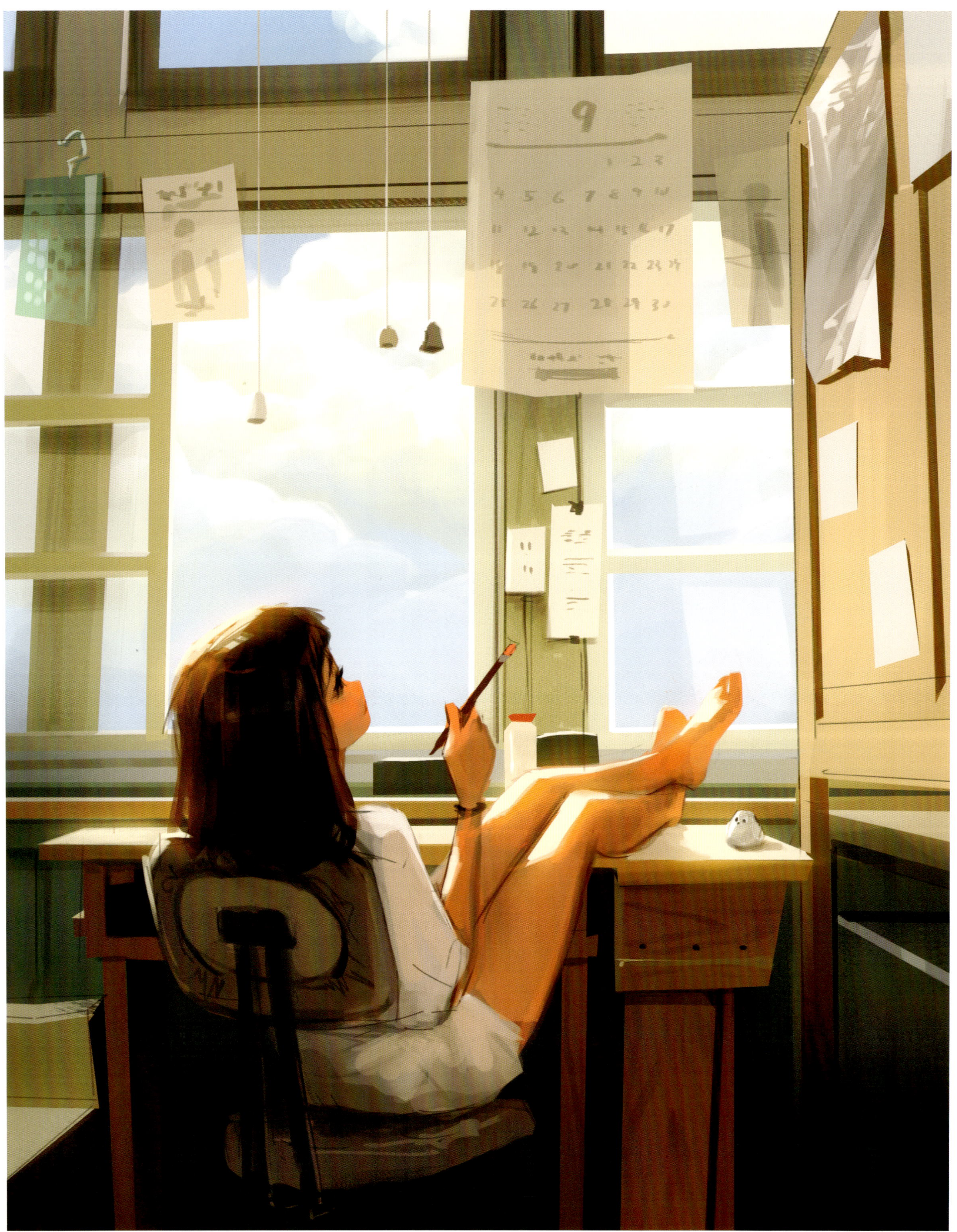

Left | *Dreaming*, January 2021.

Environments have always fascinated me. They tell stories of their own. I love using a painted world to convey a fleeting feeling of nostalgia. Sometimes these worlds give us a chance to escape to somewhere simpler than the one we live in.

Below | *Dumplings*, January 2021

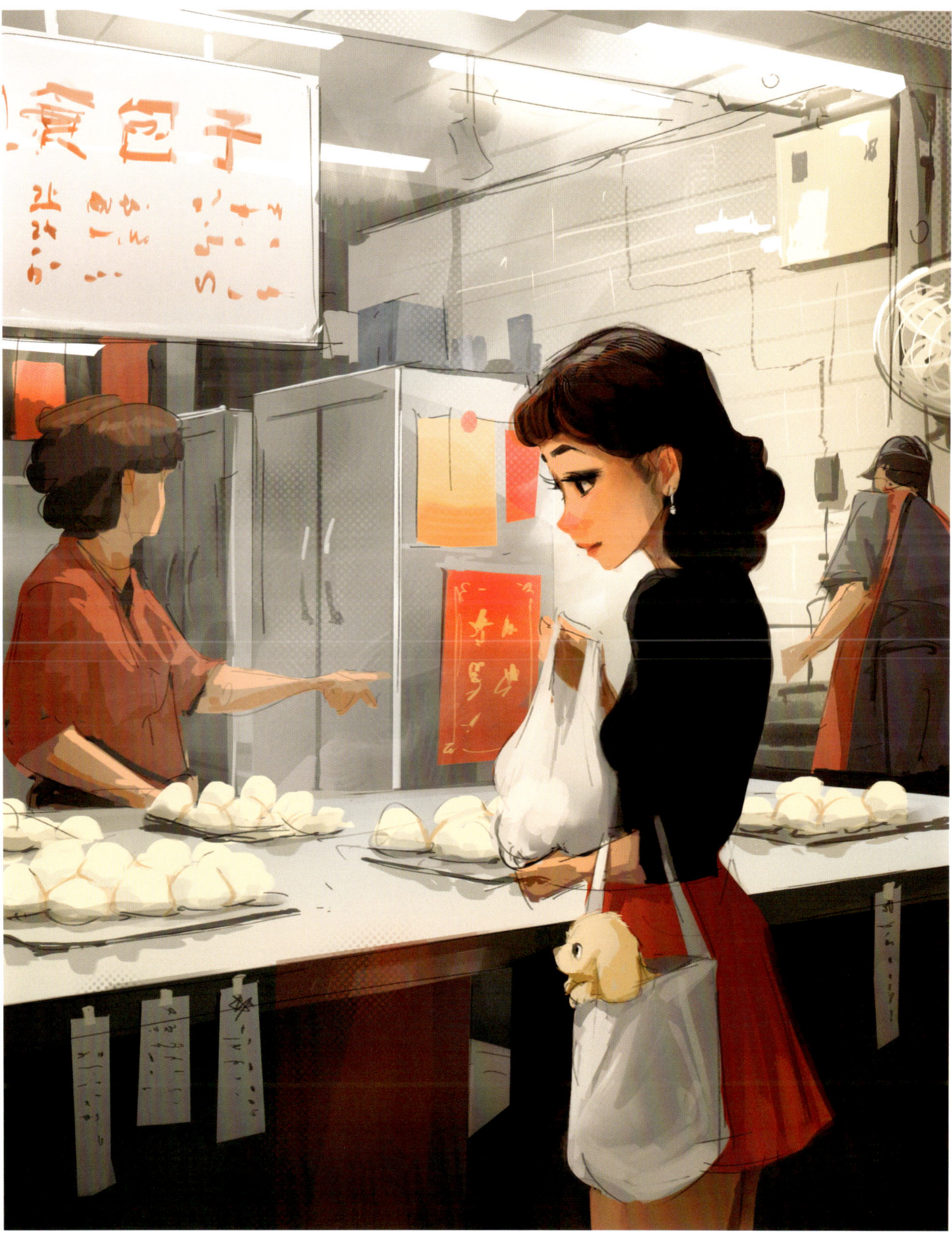

Breaking down this mentality meant shifting my mindset. I started to look for things I really loved in other people's work, and for the first time, I tried to seriously figure out how they did it. I would study references with an image belonging to one of my favourite artist's work pulled up next to it, just so I could try to understand how they interpreted things like colour or stylization. I even tried to implement some of their visual elements into my work. As I drew, I'd frequently compare my art to theirs, see where my style differed, and try to learn from that.

I stepped so far out of my comfort zone to learn things like lighting and simplification. Even now, I am still always learning new things about how light works in different settings and how I can express the beautiful colours of light in my own way. At the start, this involved abandoning my previous way of drawing and shading that revolved around ambiguous light sources and overly soft shadows and blending.

I expanded the saturation of my palette too. By studying the works of those who inspired me, I saw the possibilities one could achieve with a rich saturation in colour. I learned more about colour theory and how each colour interacts with those around it. These areas of study have had such a lasting impact on my work, and are now some of the hallmarks of my personal style.

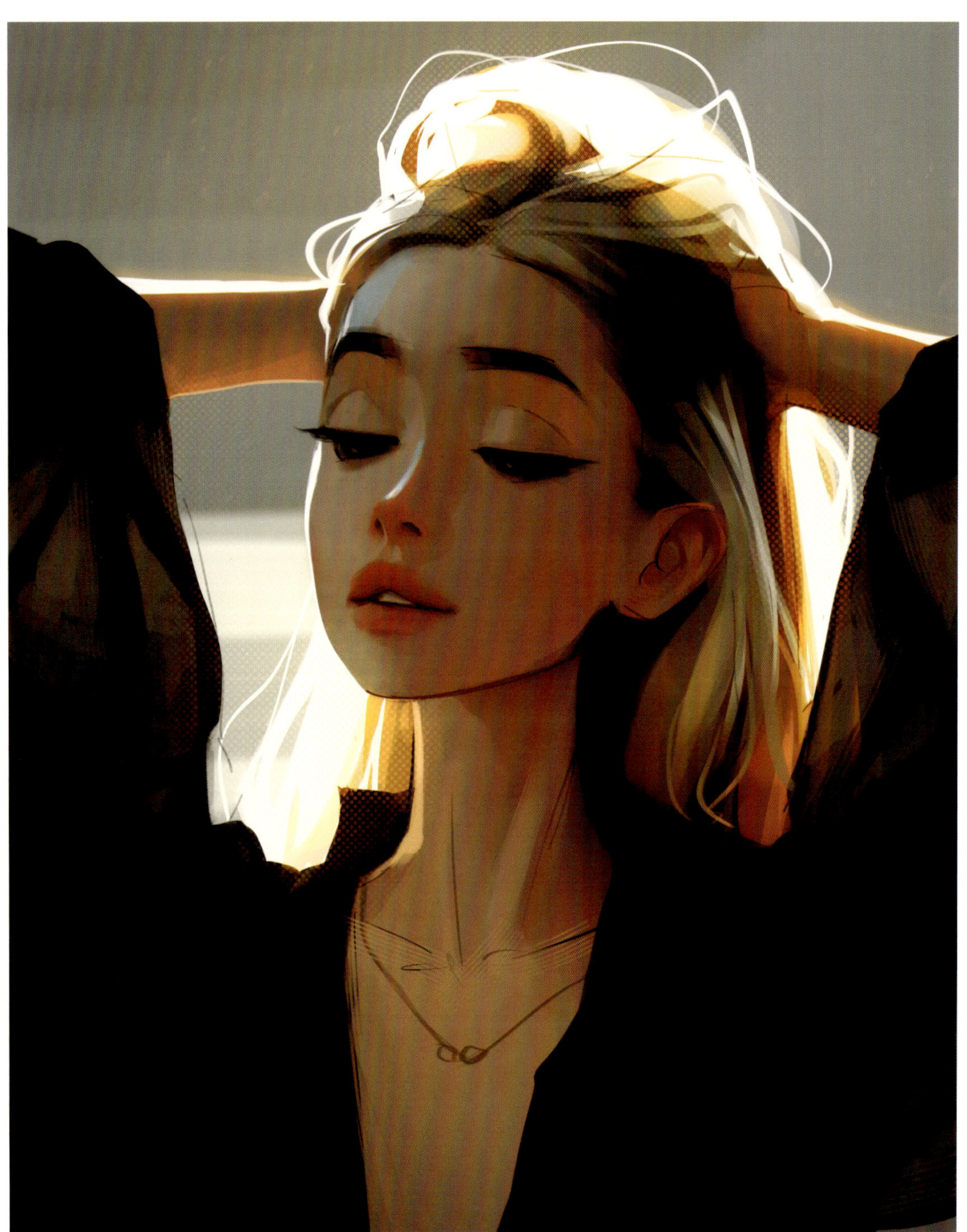

Left | *Light Study*, April 2021

Right | *Character Pose*, July 2021. This character was drawn from a style study of the great Glen Keane's work, as well as a pose study. I paid the most attention to the proportions and fluidity of lines. It's similar but also quite different from how I normally draw, as I tend to use more geometric lines and shapes

I also had the absolute hardest time trying to stylize my work and break free from realism. While growing up in China, I was taught that realism is the ultimate form of art. Many traditional art schools and everyday people tend to see realism as the true essence of what it means to be a good artist. I was taught that anime wasn't art and that cartoonish illustrations were childish and not to be taken seriously. This was ingrained in me when I was young and severely limited my mindset as an artist.

My sketchbooks back then were almost all composed of drawings done in the pursuit of realism. No matter how outlandish the idea seemed, I always tried to make the drawings realistic because that's the only thing I thought was good. It also limited the number of artists I could look up to, as prior to stepping out of my own bubble, I had no desire to learn from ones who drew in more stylized ways. But now, having tried it myself, I can fully understand the sheer skill and intuition required to stylize effectively.

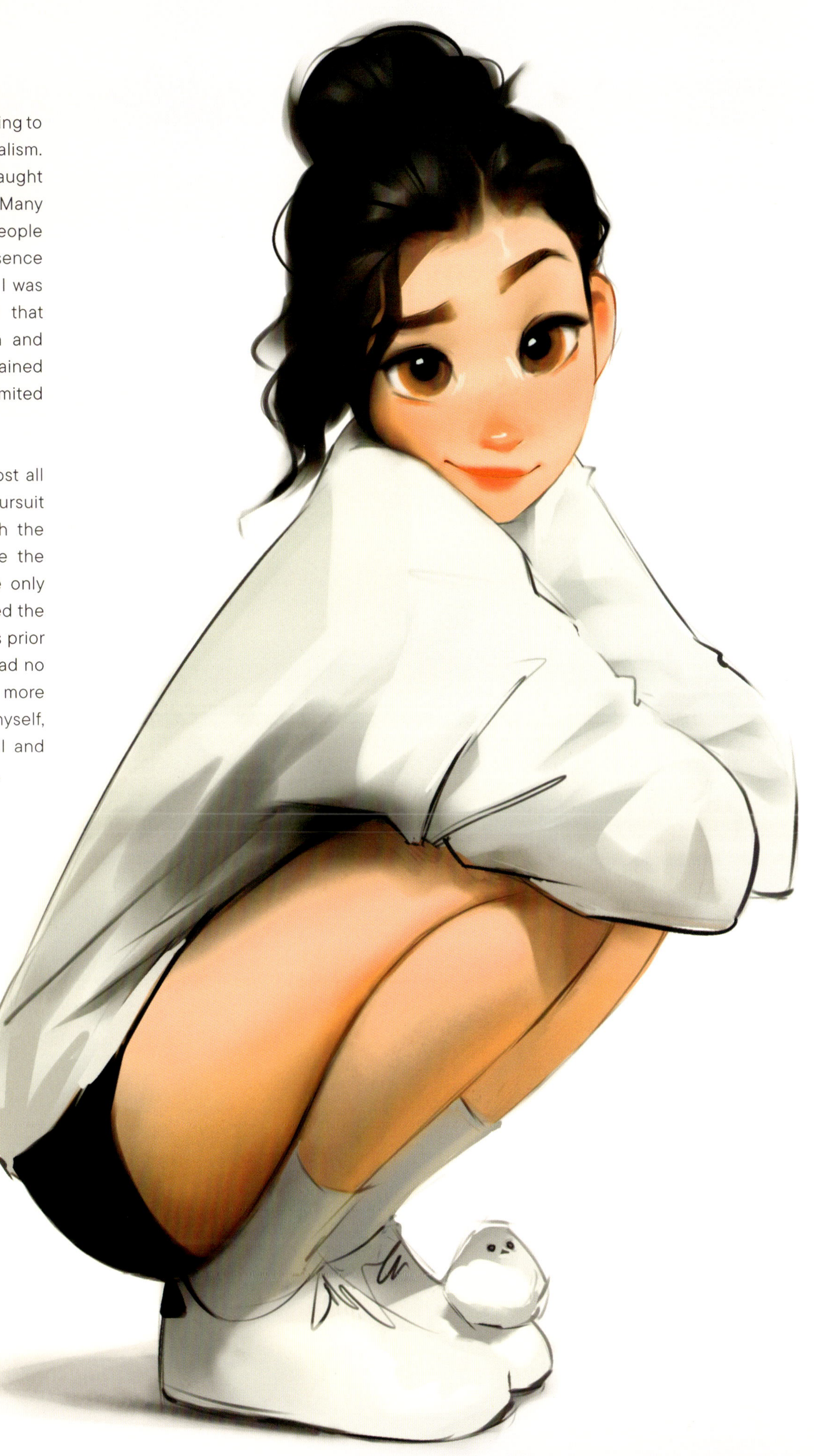

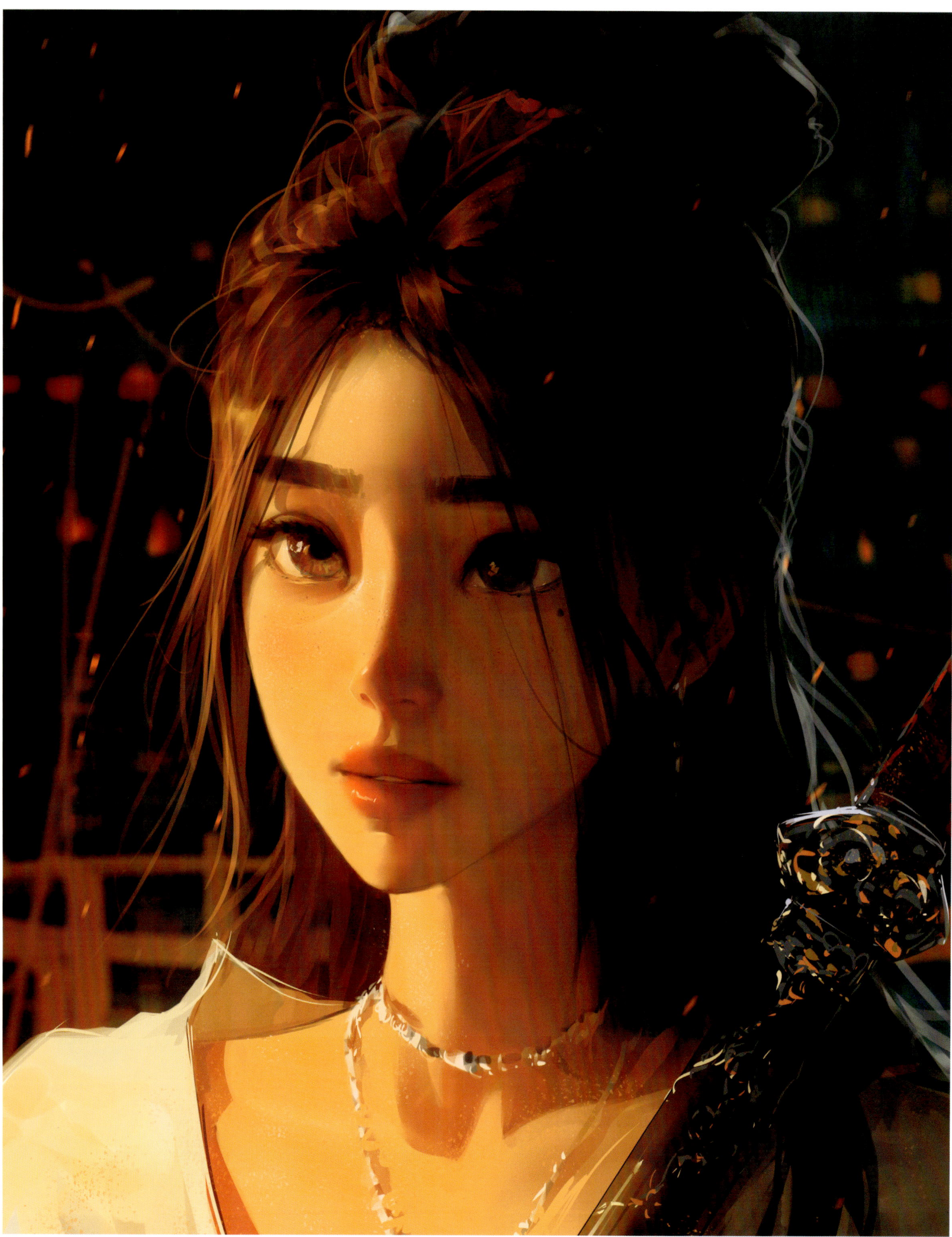

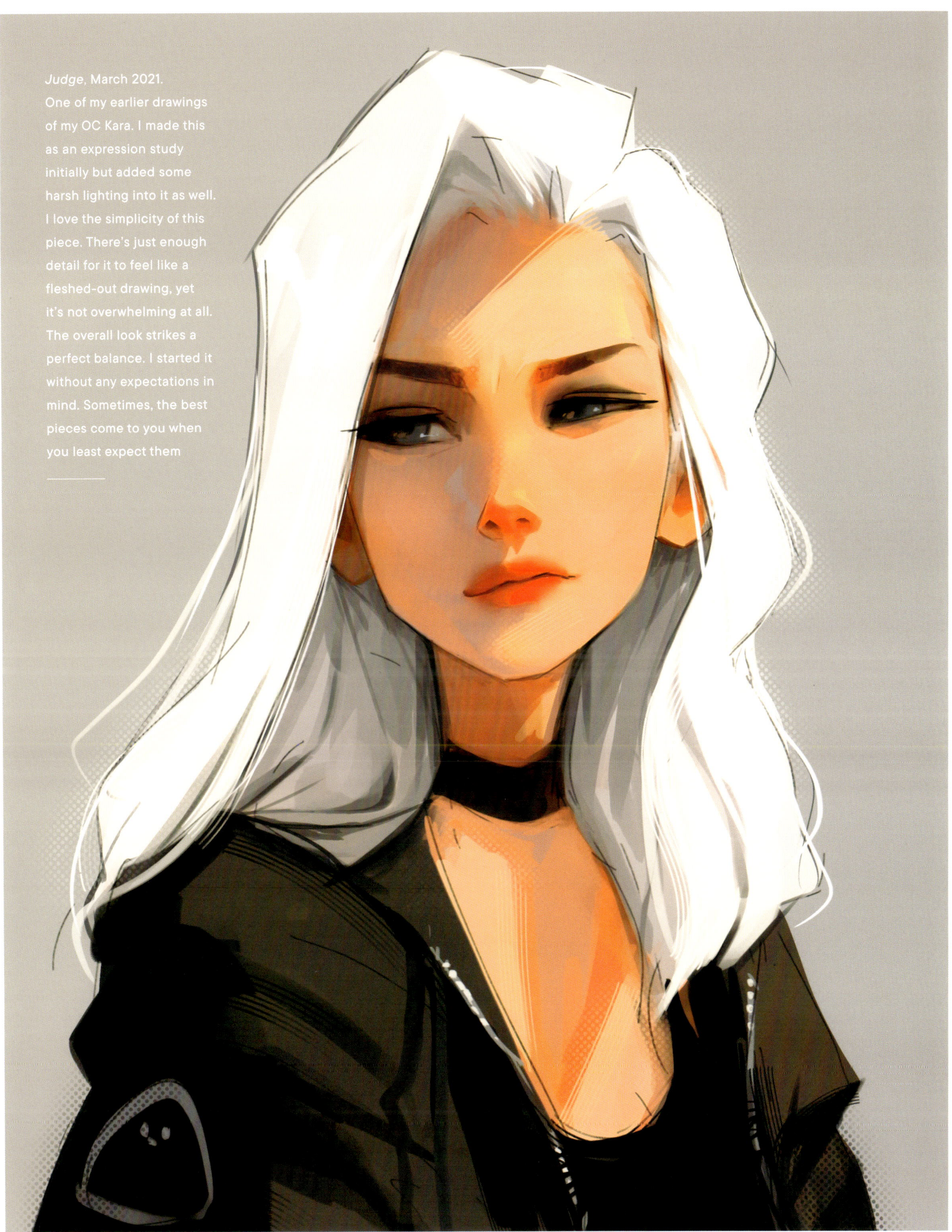

Judge, March 2021.
One of my earlier drawings of my OC Kara. I made this as an expression study initially but added some harsh lighting into it as well. I love the simplicity of this piece. There's just enough detail for it to feel like a fleshed-out drawing, yet it's not overwhelming at all. The overall look strikes a perfect balance. I started it without any expectations in mind. Sometimes, the best pieces come to you when you least expect them

Grayscale, March 2021.

Today, many of us have access to painting with colours through drawing tablets and digital media. Technology has made colours much more accessible overall; not having to constantly buy paint and materials removes a big barrier for many. But I feel this also made many younger artists skip the very crucial step of learning values through drawing in greyscale. Knowing your values is an irreplaceable building block in being an effective artist

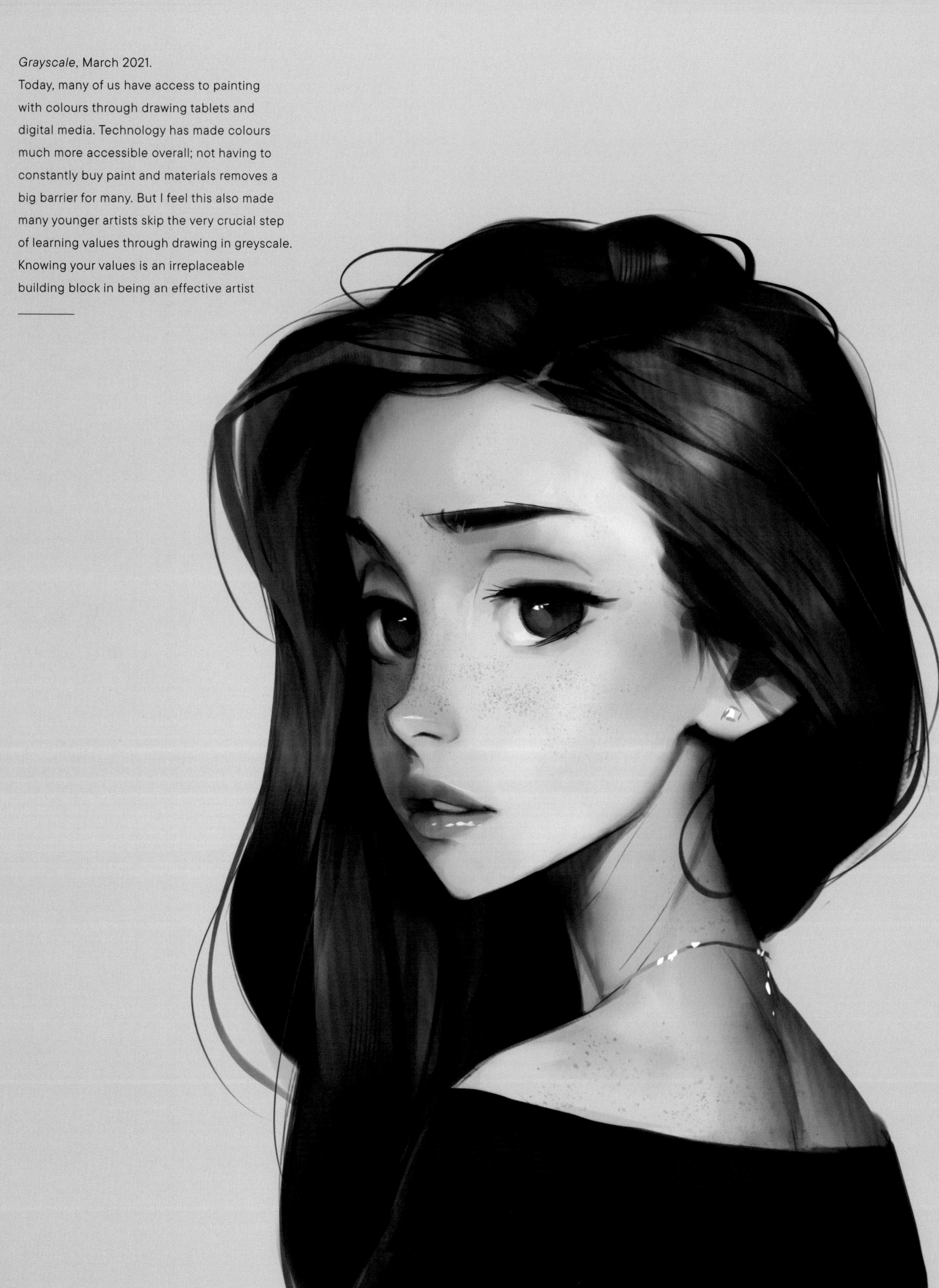

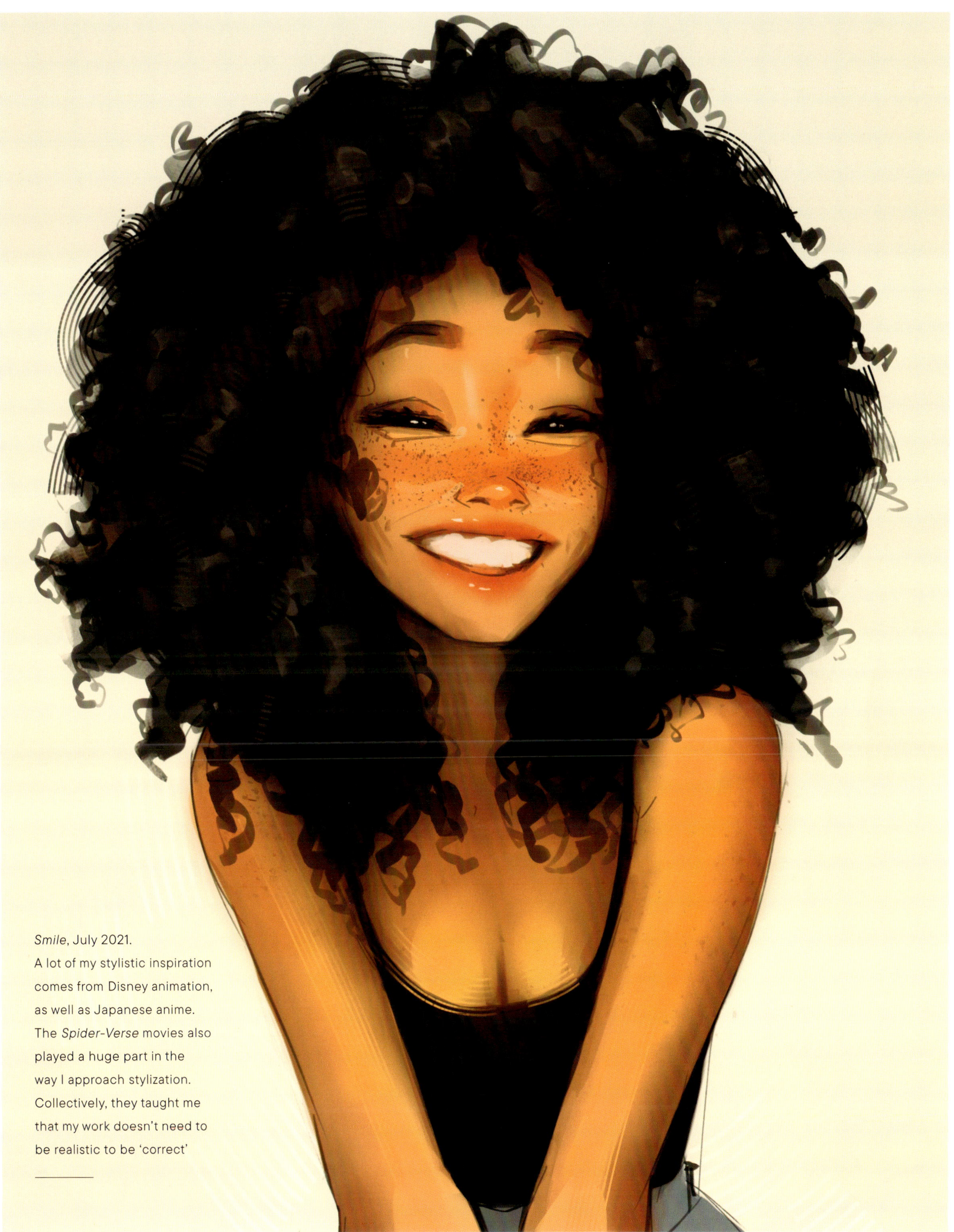

Smile, July 2021.
A lot of my stylistic inspiration comes from Disney animation, as well as Japanese anime. The *Spider-Verse* movies also played a huge part in the way I approach stylization. Collectively, they taught me that my work doesn't need to be realistic to be 'correct'

As I discovered more artists, I slowly began to gain more and more appreciation for stylization, and what really made everything click for me was trying to do it myself. My repeated inability to stylize my references made me realize just how much skill and knowledge is needed to stylize effectively. Now, I look at artists who are able to stylize well with great admiration.

This period of learning and stepping out of my bubble slowly shaped my work into what it is today. For that, I'm very grateful to my former self.

At the time of writing this book, I'm still trying to figure out stylization. It's the thing I have the most trouble with. I'm not sure if it's something I'm not naturally gifted at, or if I've just been raised with the mindset of realism for so long that it'll take longer than a few years to truly break free. Regardless, it's something I'm working on.

Light, December 2022

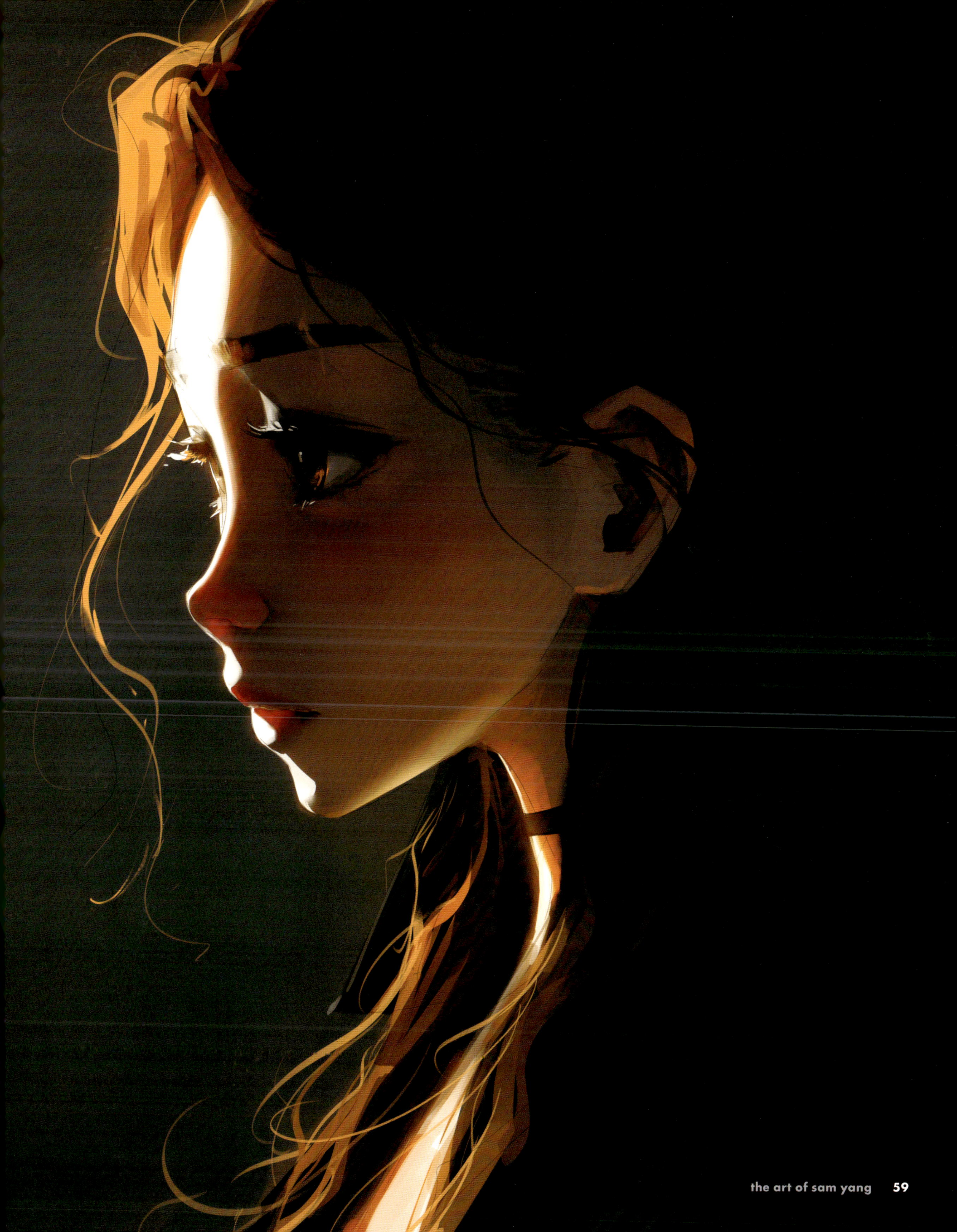

Below | *Cry*, April 2021 | Right | *Winter*, November 2023

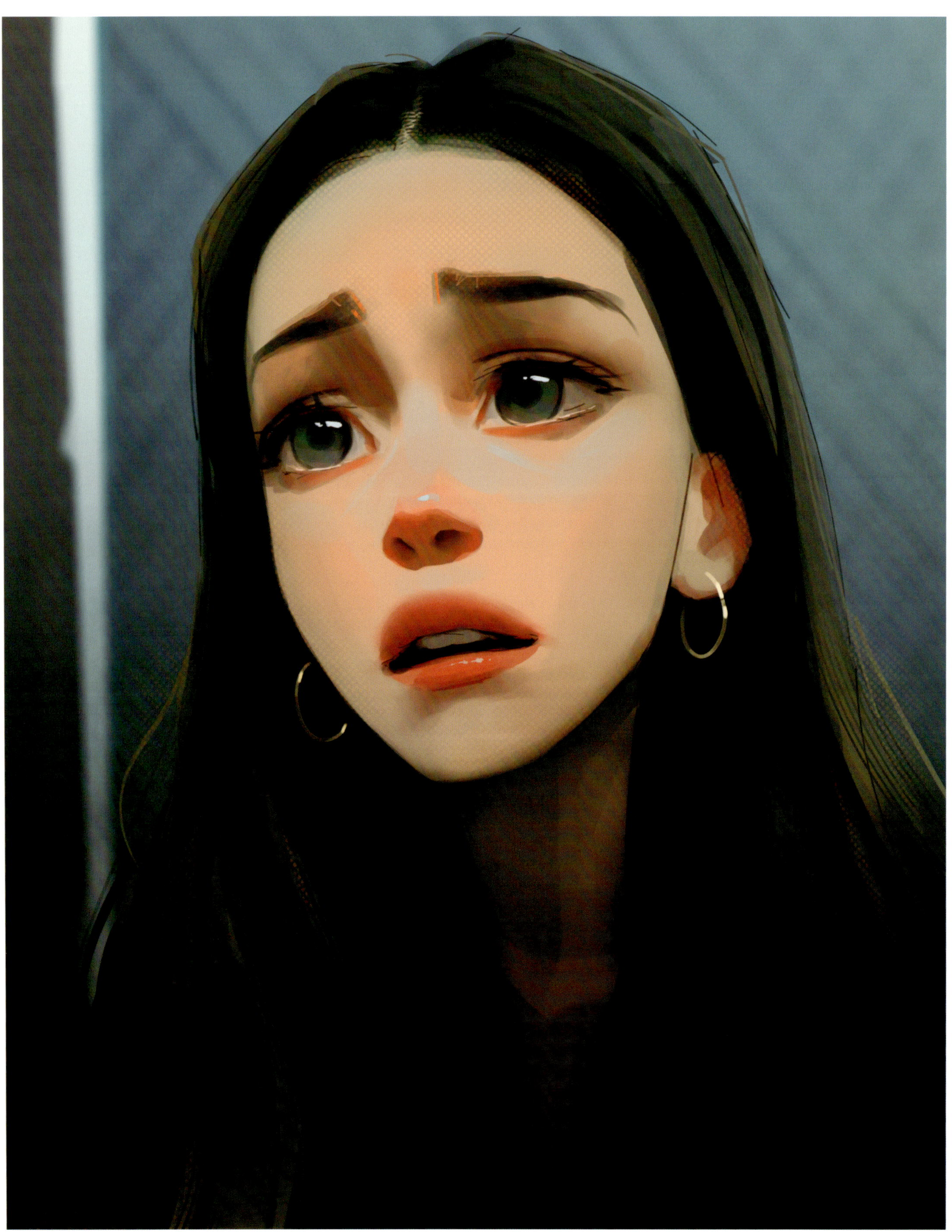

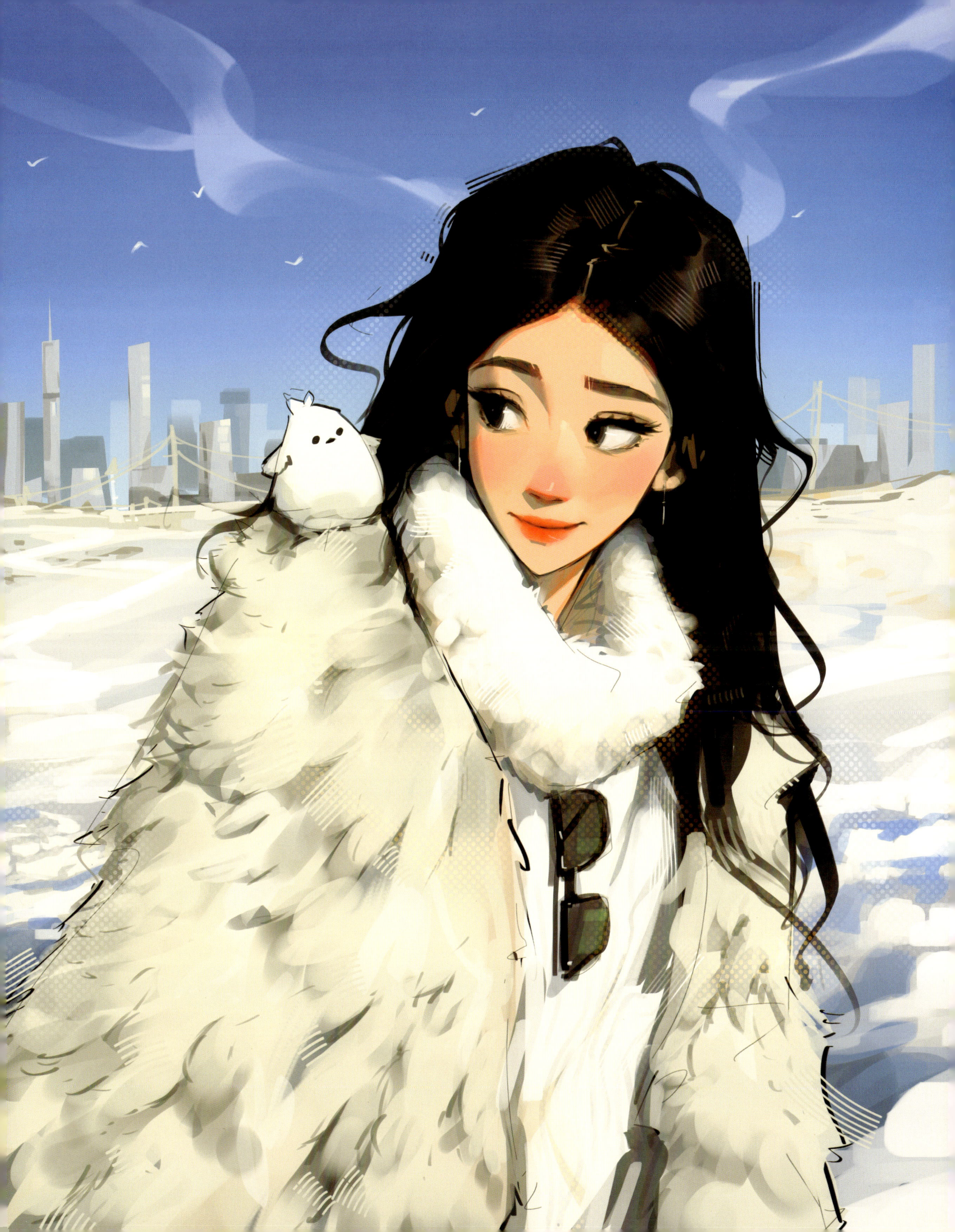

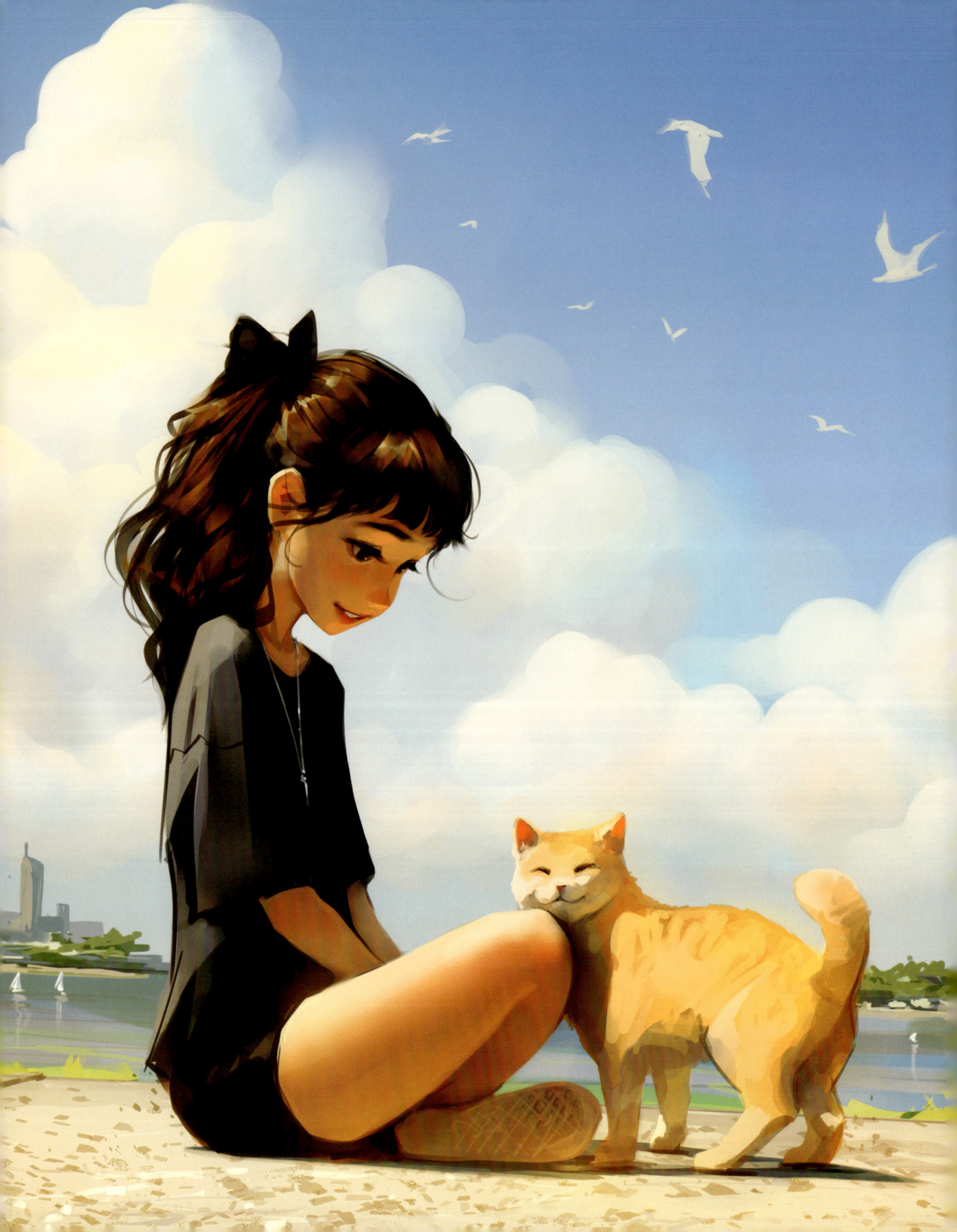

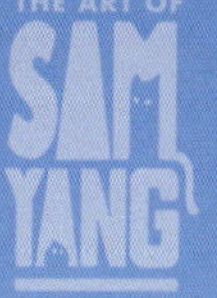

life as an artist

Work habits, inspirations, motivation & learning

WORK HABITS

As a digital artist, I primarily work on a drawing tablet in Adobe Photoshop. At the time of writing, my main workstation is the Wacom Cintiq Pro 24 because the larger surface area allows me to freely move my drawing arm, incorporating my shoulder, elbow, and wrist for bigger brushstrokes. I'm very cautious not to put too much strain on any part of my body during the drawing process. Drawing takes hours at a time, and bad habits can often lead to chronic pain or injuries.

While the vast majority of my work is done on my Wacom tablet or iPad, I do occasionally switch over to my sketchbook. I sometimes miss the tactile feeling of pencil on paper and the inability to remove your mistakes without consequences.

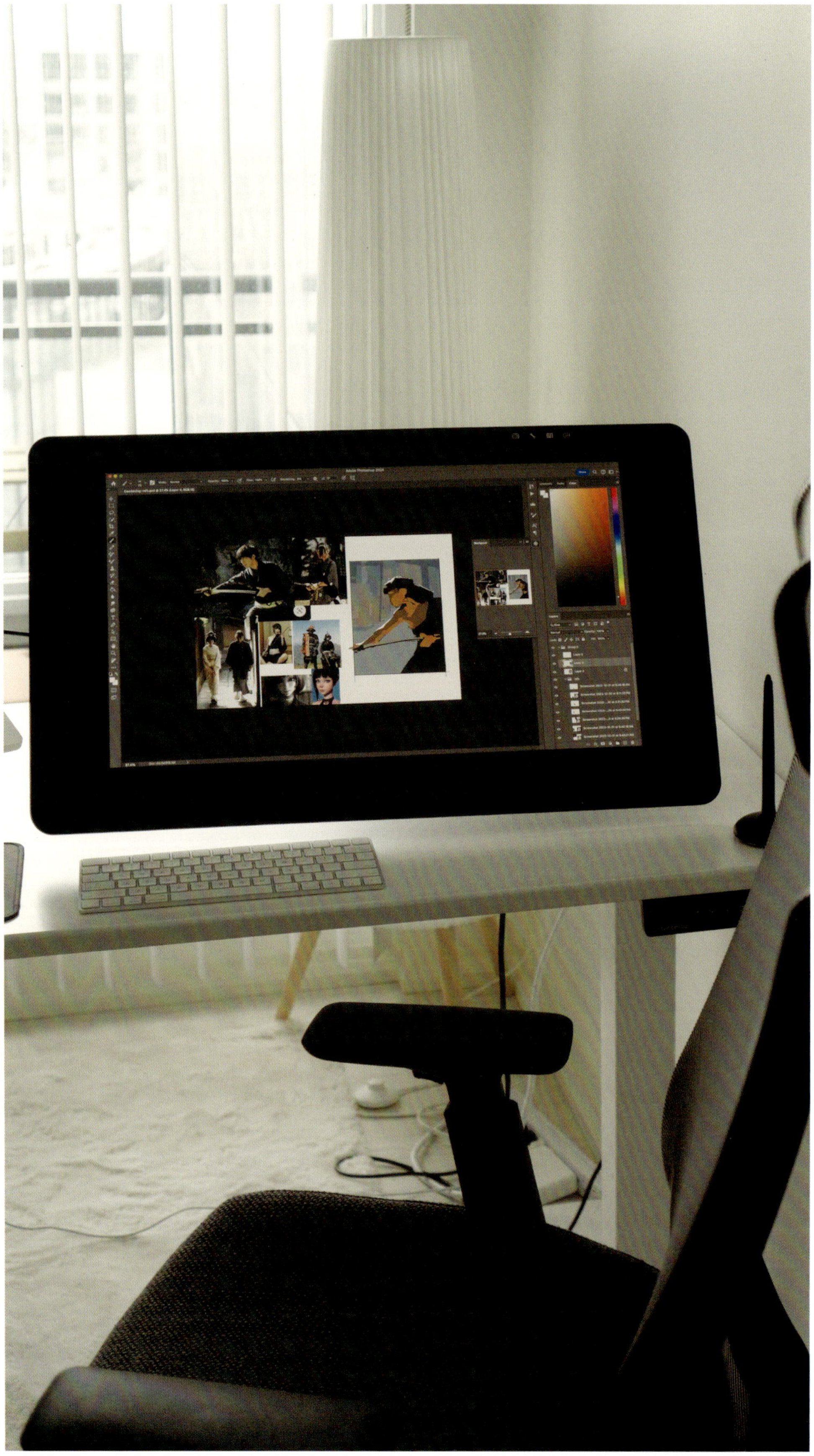

This page | My Wacom tablet

Opposite page | *Sketchbook Style Studies, Practice Work and Personal Work*, 2021–22. I often use sketchbooks as a place to do quick and simple practice work. In the lower-page examples, I'm breaking down some of the shape language and stylization of Glen Keane's artwork

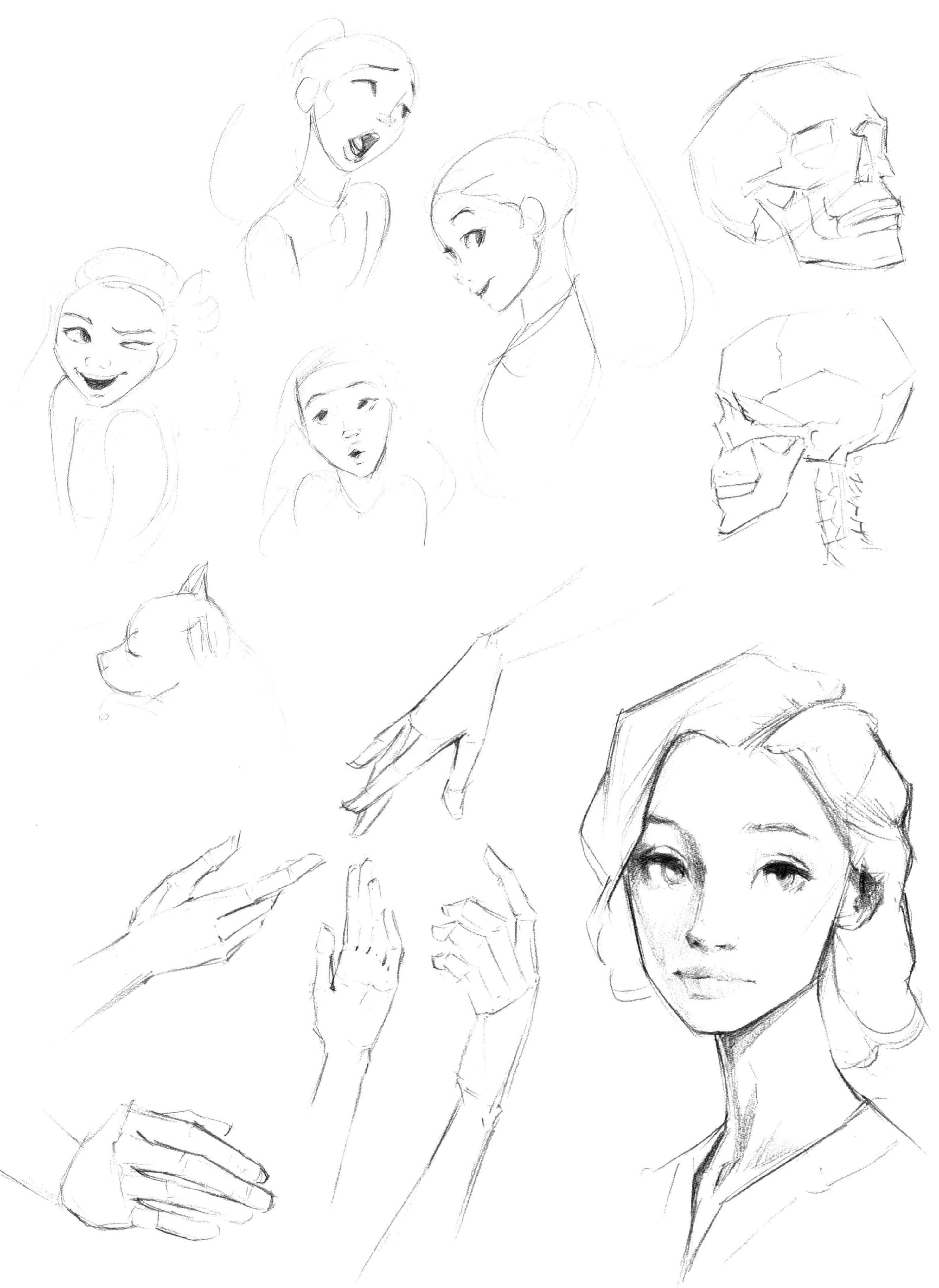

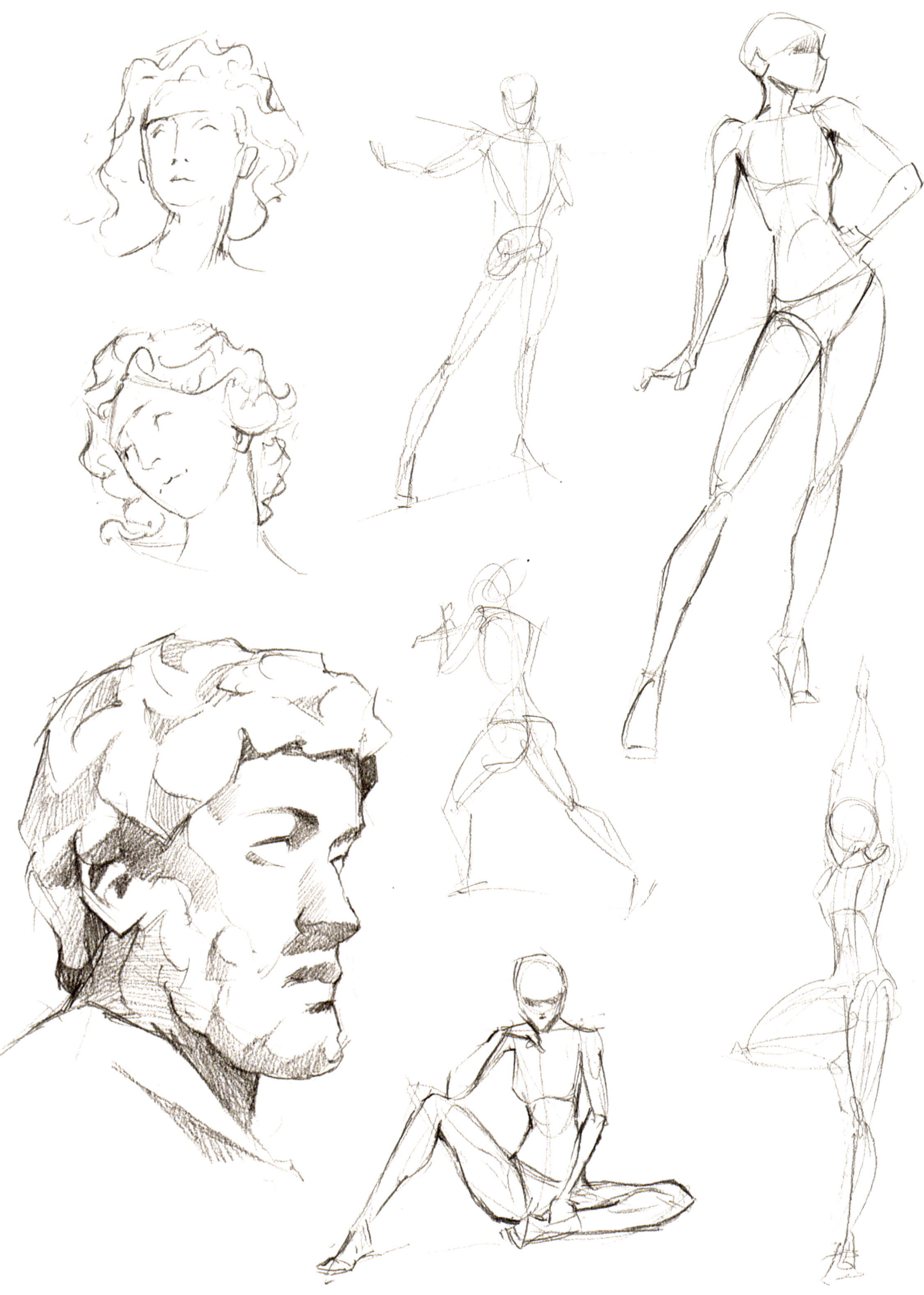

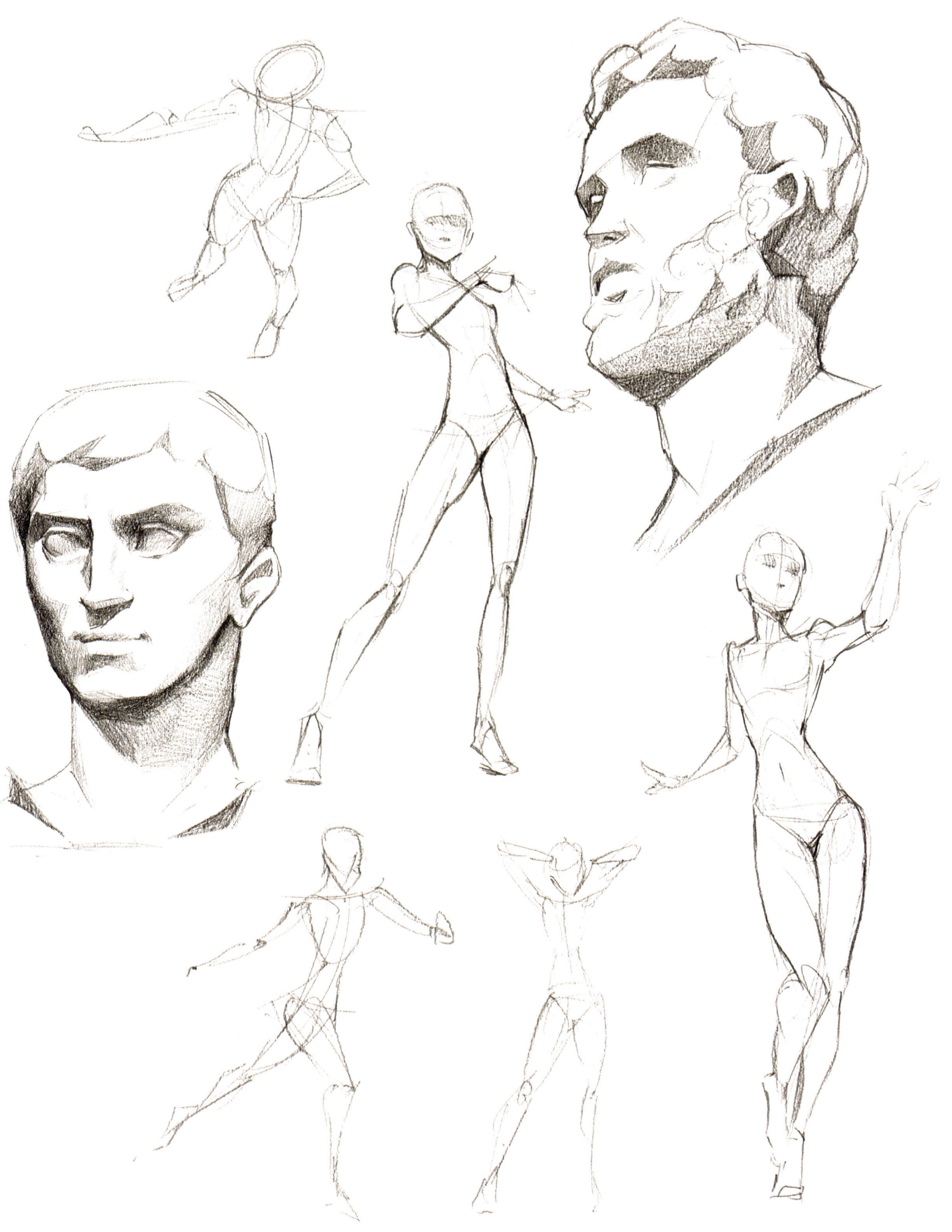

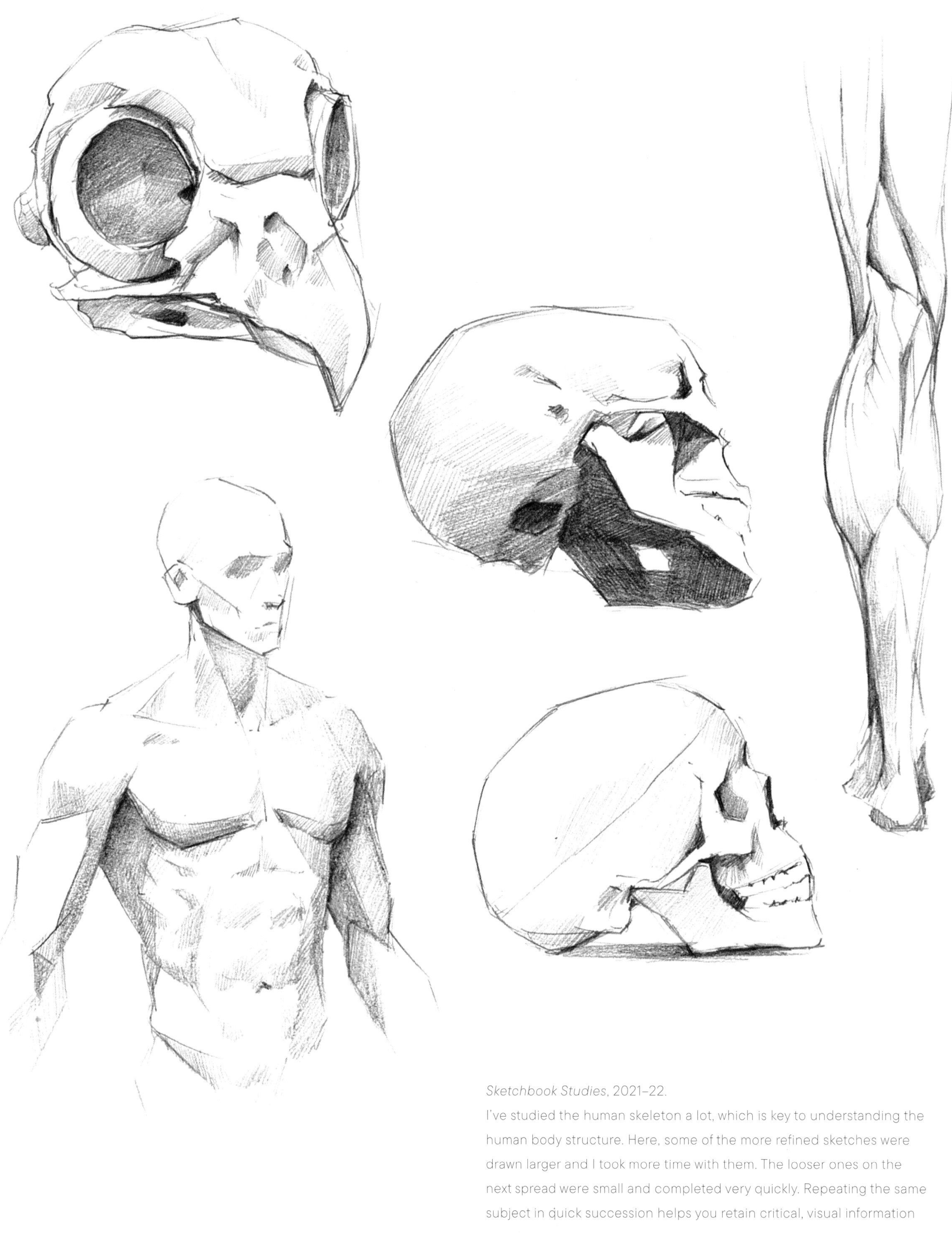

Sketchbook Studies, 2021–22.
I've studied the human skeleton a lot, which is key to understanding the human body structure. Here, some of the more refined sketches were drawn larger and I took more time with them. The looser ones on the next spread were small and completed very quickly. Repeating the same subject in quick succession helps you retain critical, visual information

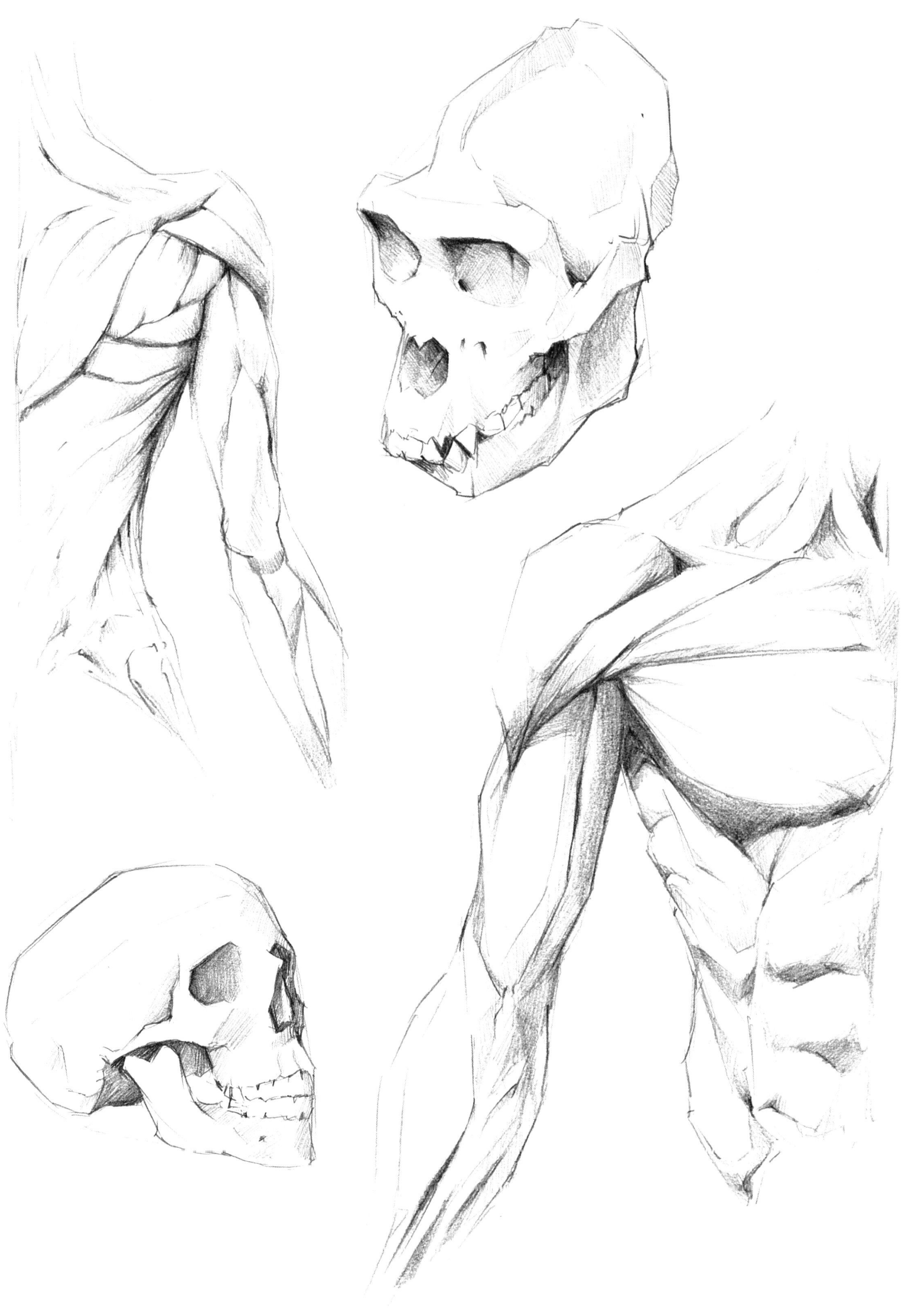

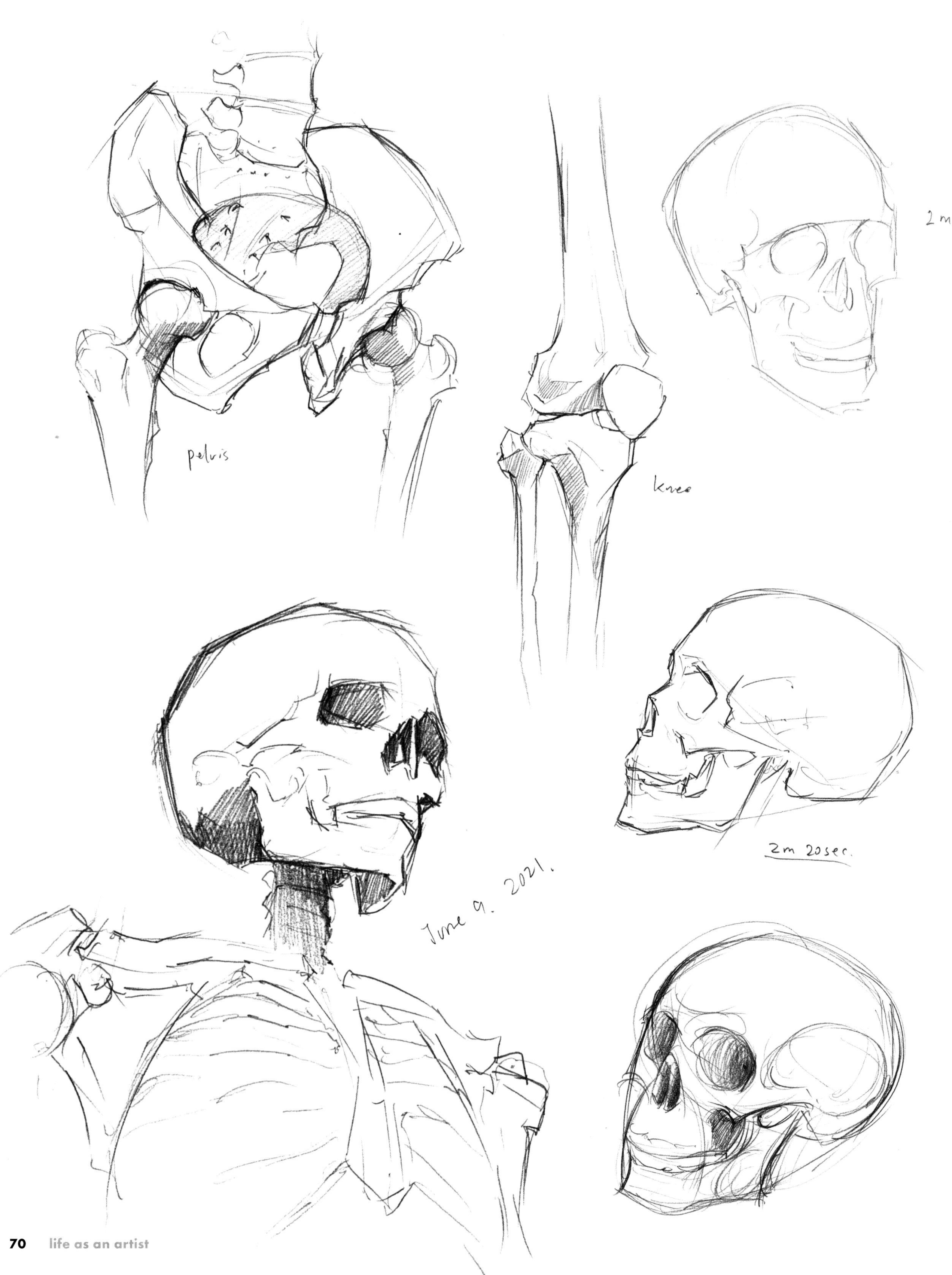
pelvis
knee
2m
2m 20sec.
June 9. 2021.

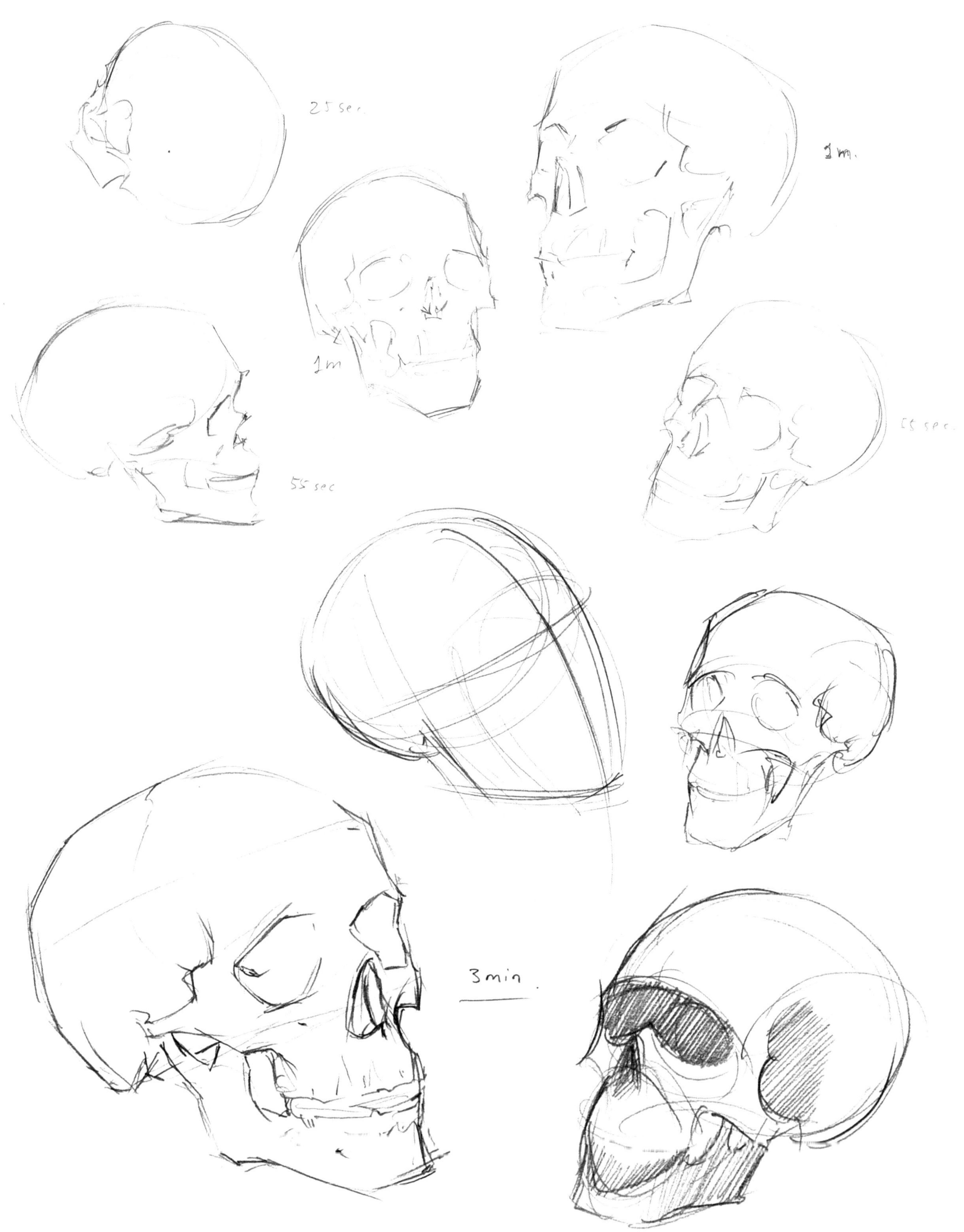
25 sec.
1m
55 sec
3min.

Repaint | *Golden Hour*, October 2020.
I like to revisit my older works and paint over them to see the things I'd do differently. This process reminds me of the progress I've made. Seeing the contrast between past and present is very encouraging for me. It's easy to get lost in the day to day, which is why taking a step back is so important. Compared to the old piece (this page), the new one demonstrates much more clarity and confidence. This confidence comes from repeated practice, which gives me a level of certainty regarding the lines, shapes, and colours I lay down. You'll also see more contrast between the lights and shadows, which happens to be another sign of confidence and familiarity

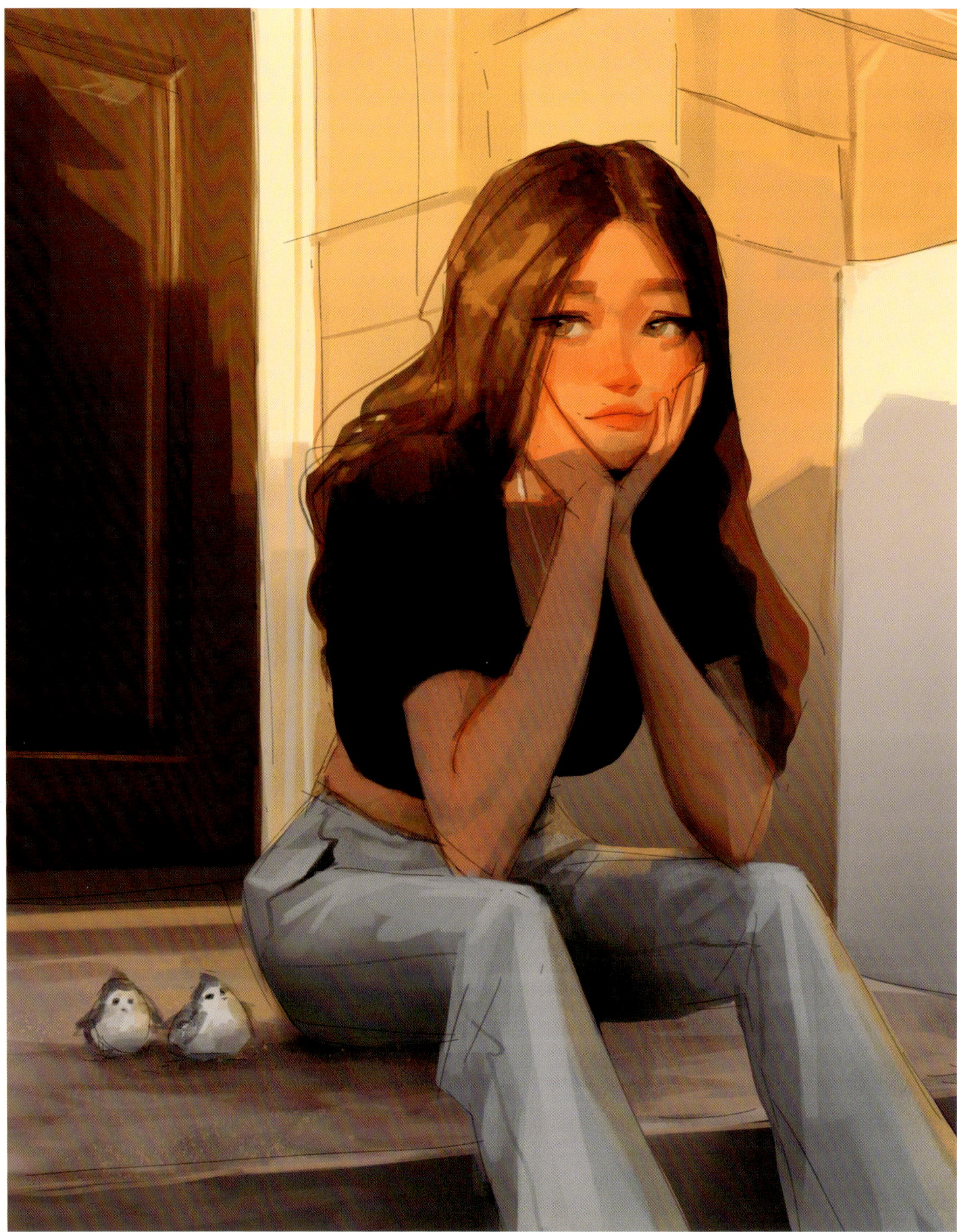

To me, the most rewarding aspect of drawing is learning and improving. There's a new challenge to face in every piece, and embracing that challenge is what makes us better artists. However, admittedly, I don't do this all the time. I try not to make every single painting a struggle, as too much of that would take away some of the joy of creating art. A balance should be achieved. At a very fundamental level, I make art because I love making art, and getting better at it helps me love it even more.

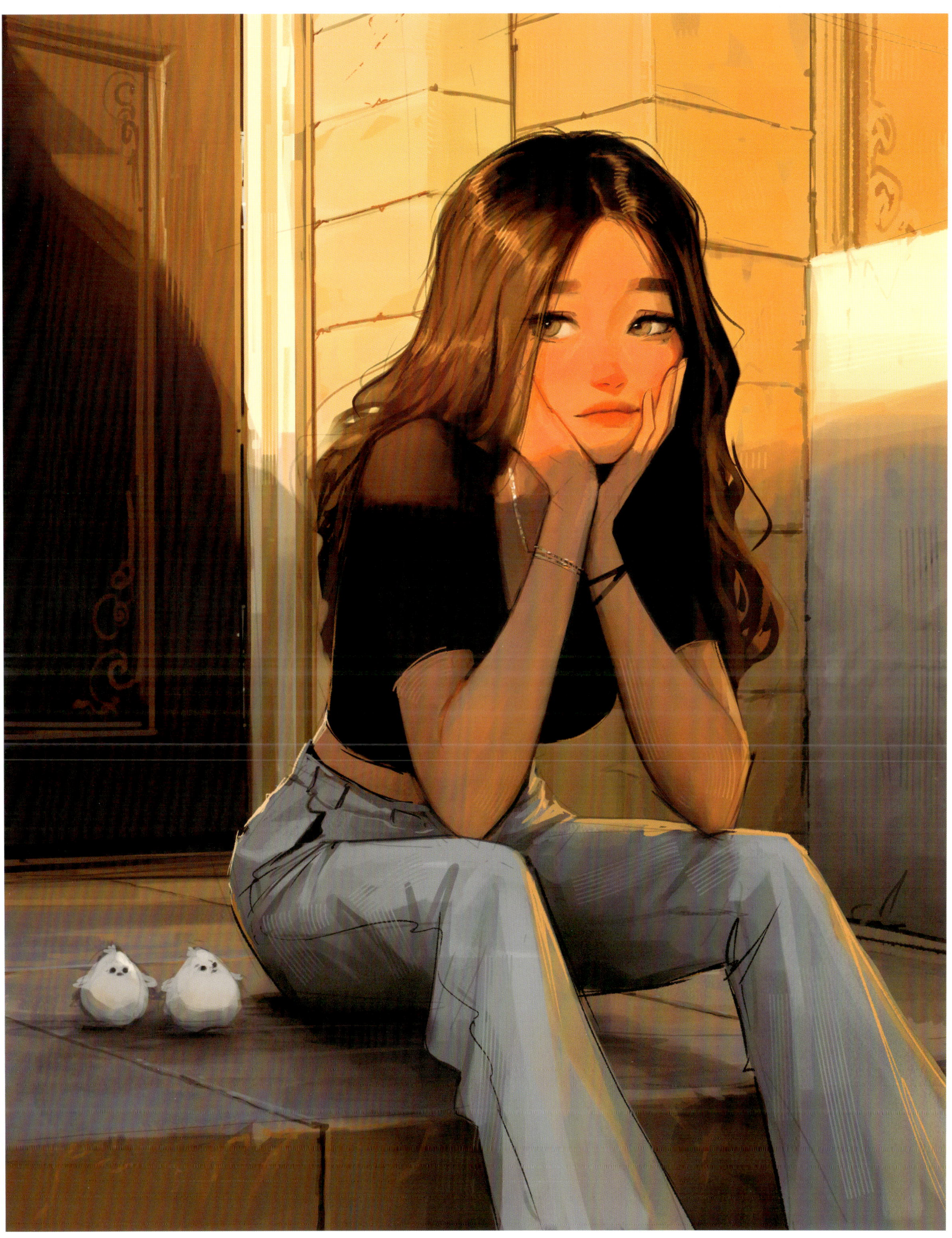

I try to draw almost every day, sometimes every few days. It's important for me to be consistent. I feel that hard work almost always contributes to success more than natural talent does. If someone is naturally gifted at drawing, they may pick up concepts quicker; if they don't stay consistent and determined in their practice, however, they will be surpassed in skill by those who work harder, smarter, and more determinedly than them. This is not to say that talent doesn't matter at all – if you're both talented and hard working, you're far more likely to succeed than someone who only possesses one of the two.

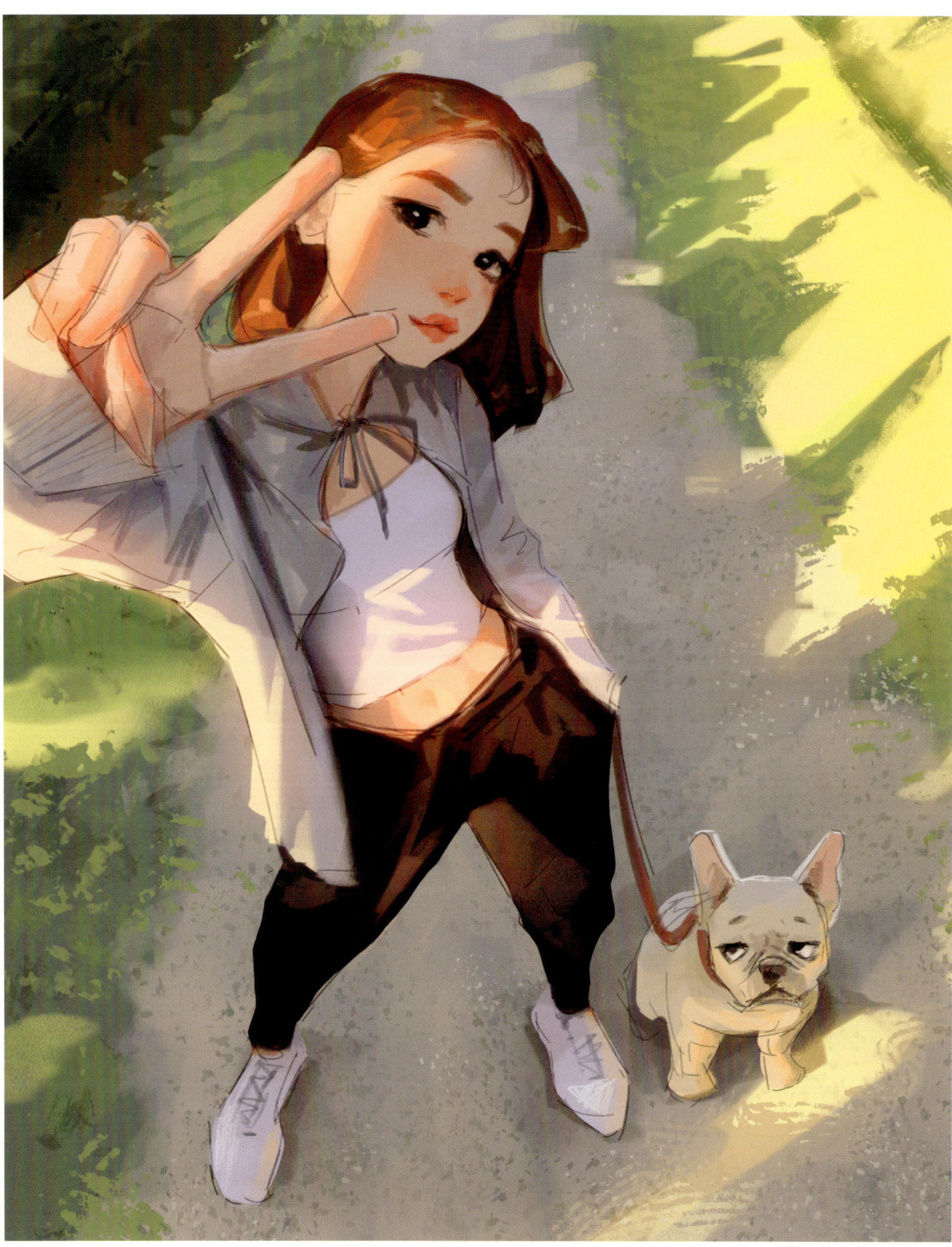

Opposite page | *Girl with Frenchie*, October 2020

This page | *Character Design*, September 2022.
In this character study, I focused on simplicity. I wanted the lines and shapes to flow into each other in an energetic way. There's not much rendering of light versus shadow here, and this was done deliberately to force myself to embrace the simplicity and not overthink things

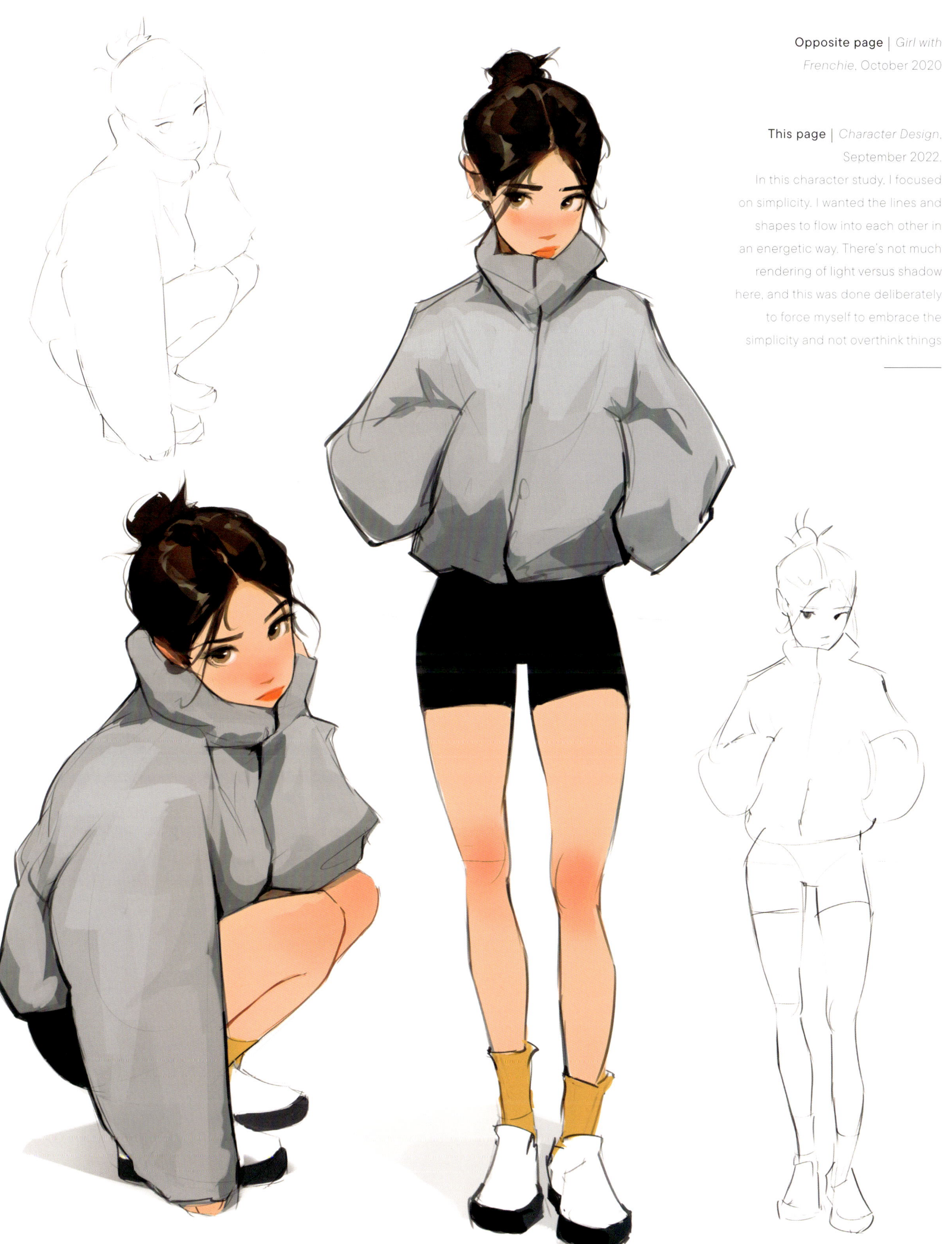

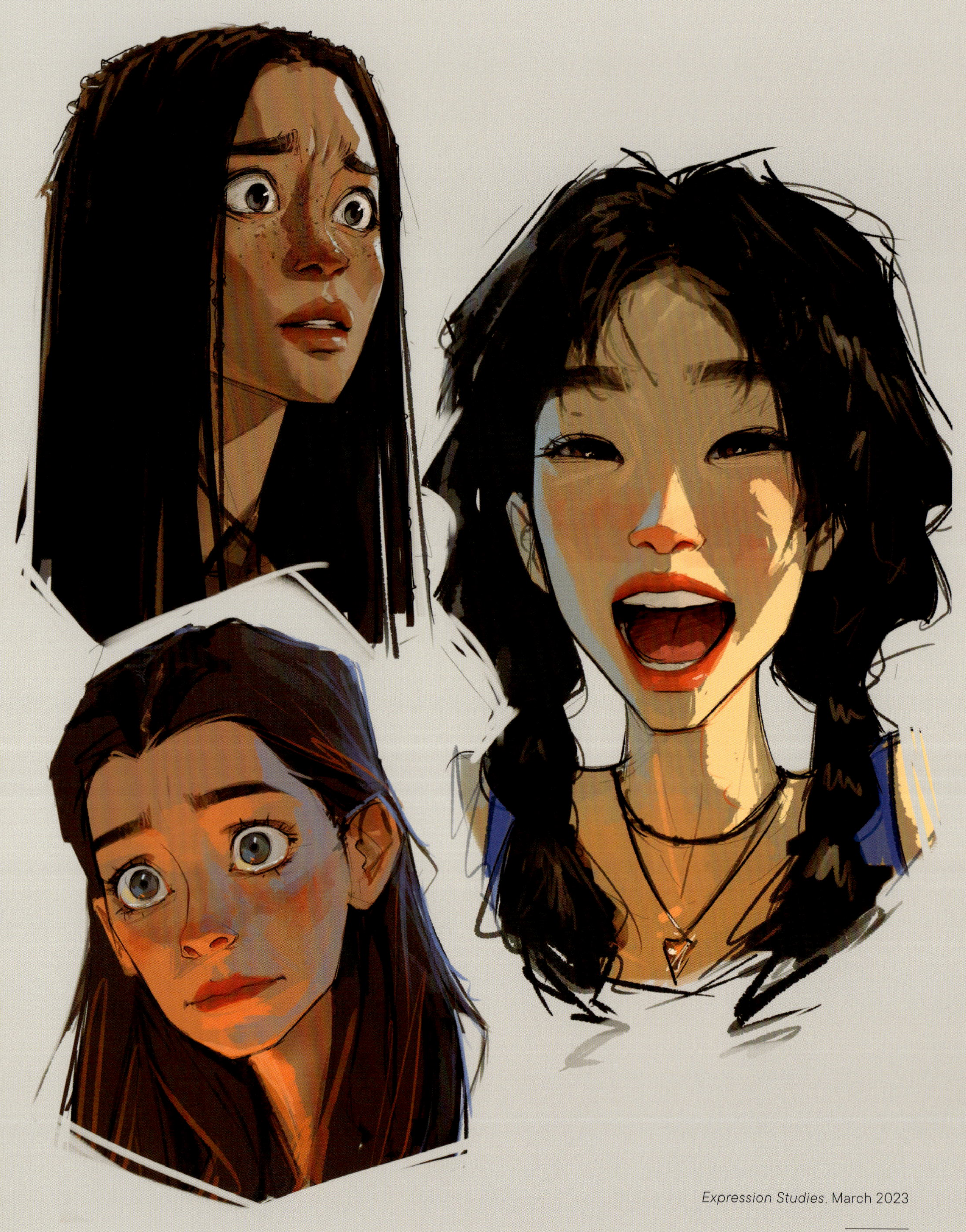

Expression Studies, March 2023

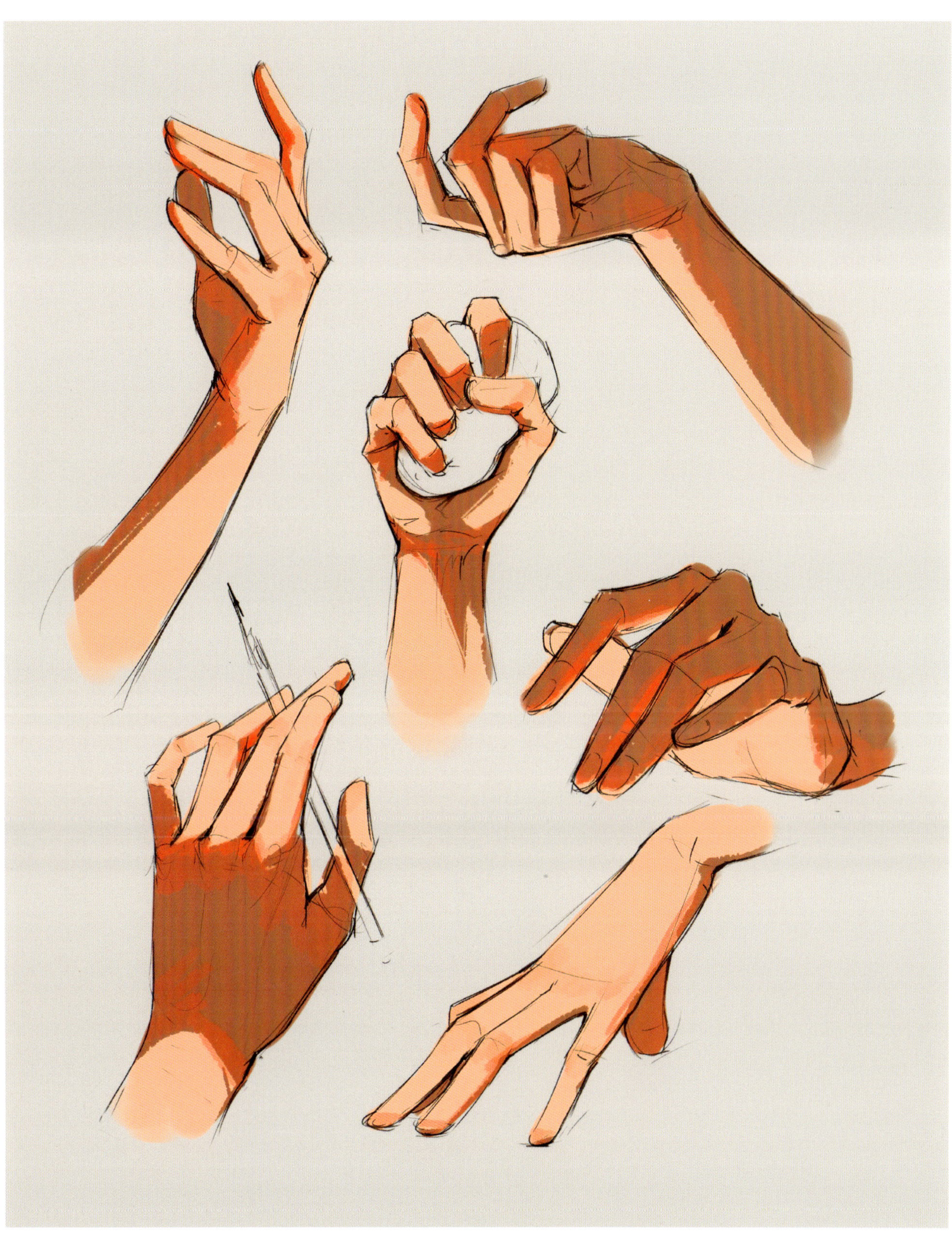

Hand Studies, March 2020

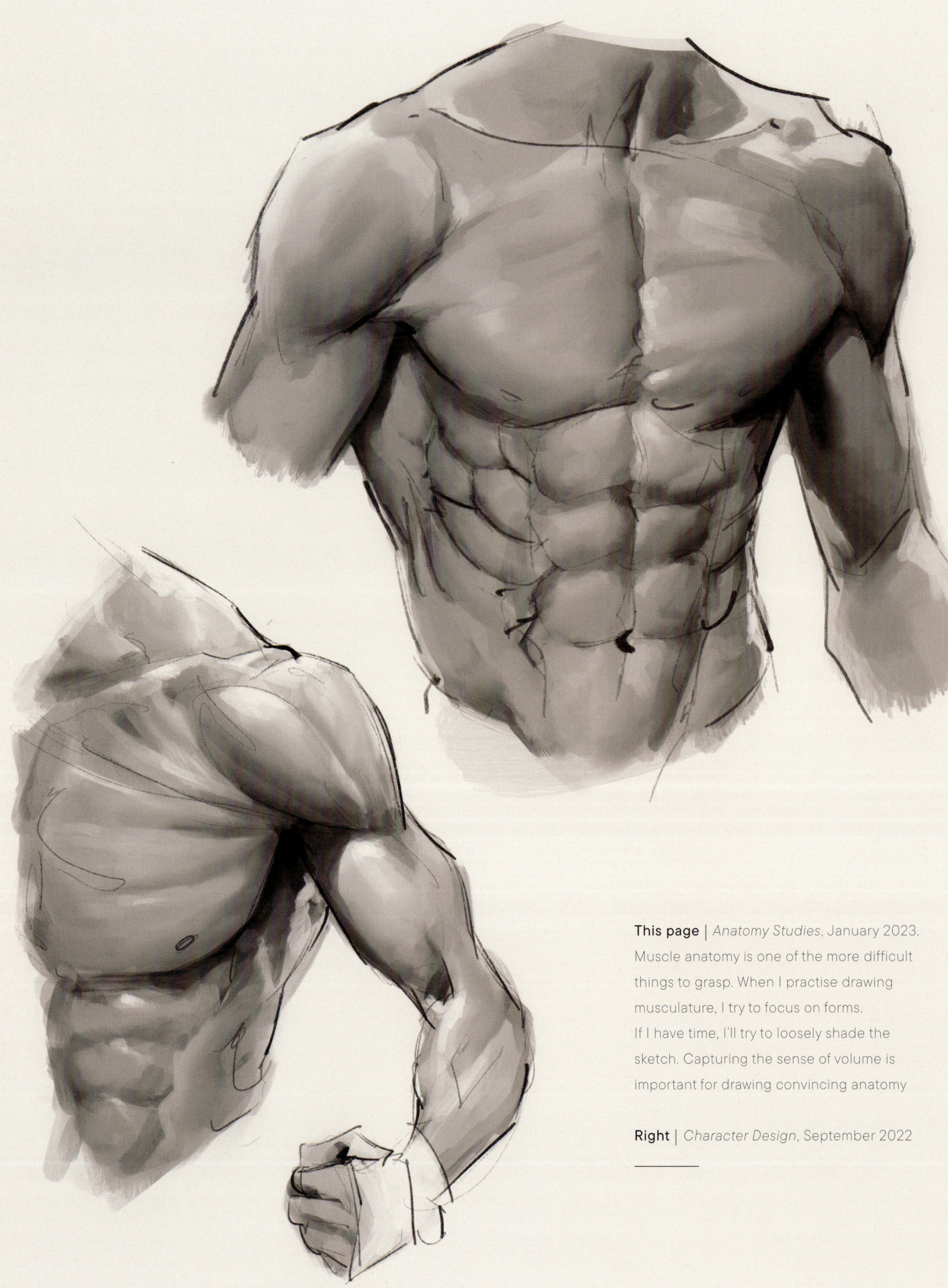

This page | *Anatomy Studies*, January 2023. Muscle anatomy is one of the more difficult things to grasp. When I practise drawing musculature, I try to focus on forms. If I have time, I'll try to loosely shade the sketch. Capturing the sense of volume is important for drawing convincing anatomy

Right | *Character Design*, September 2022

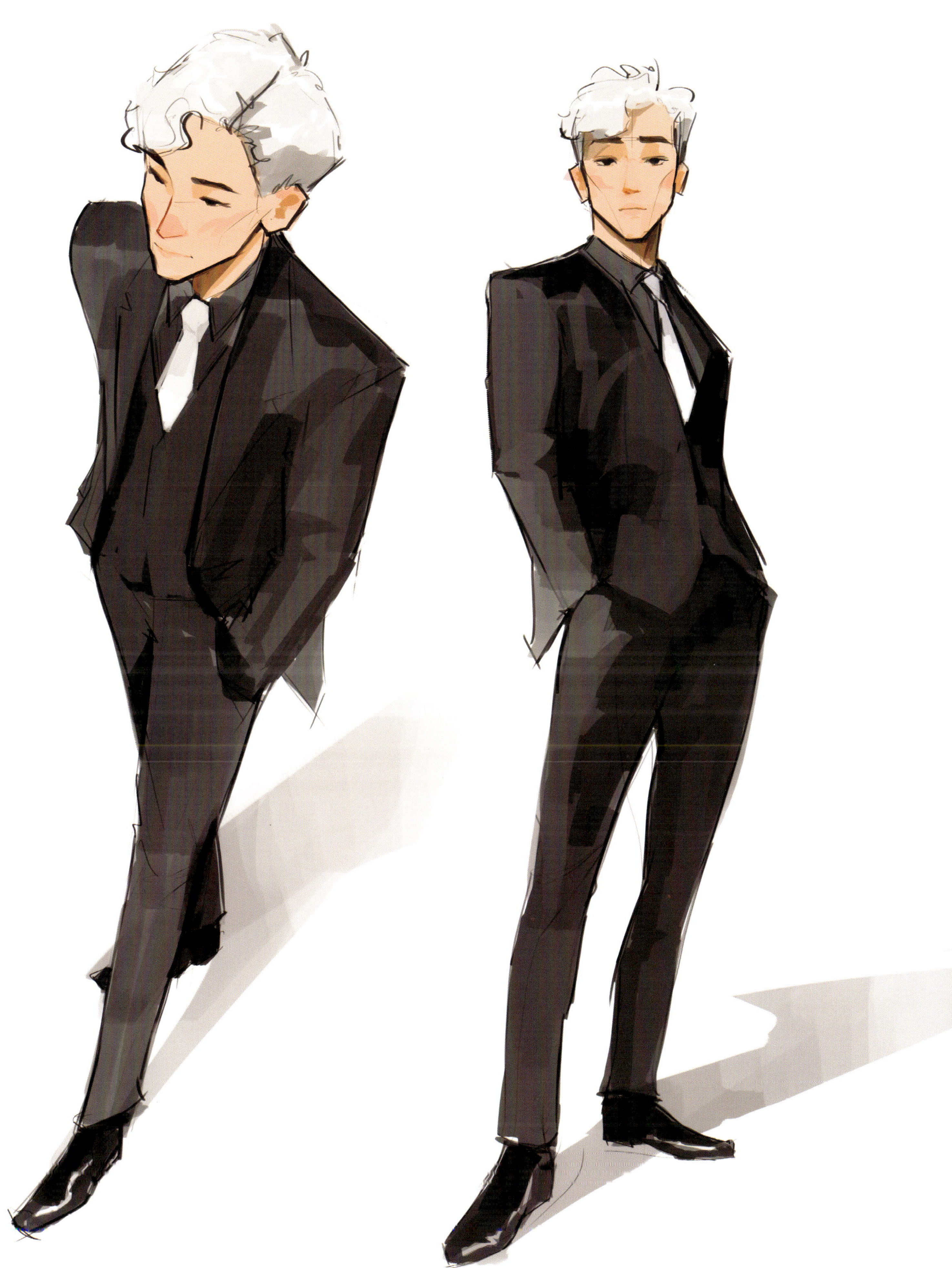

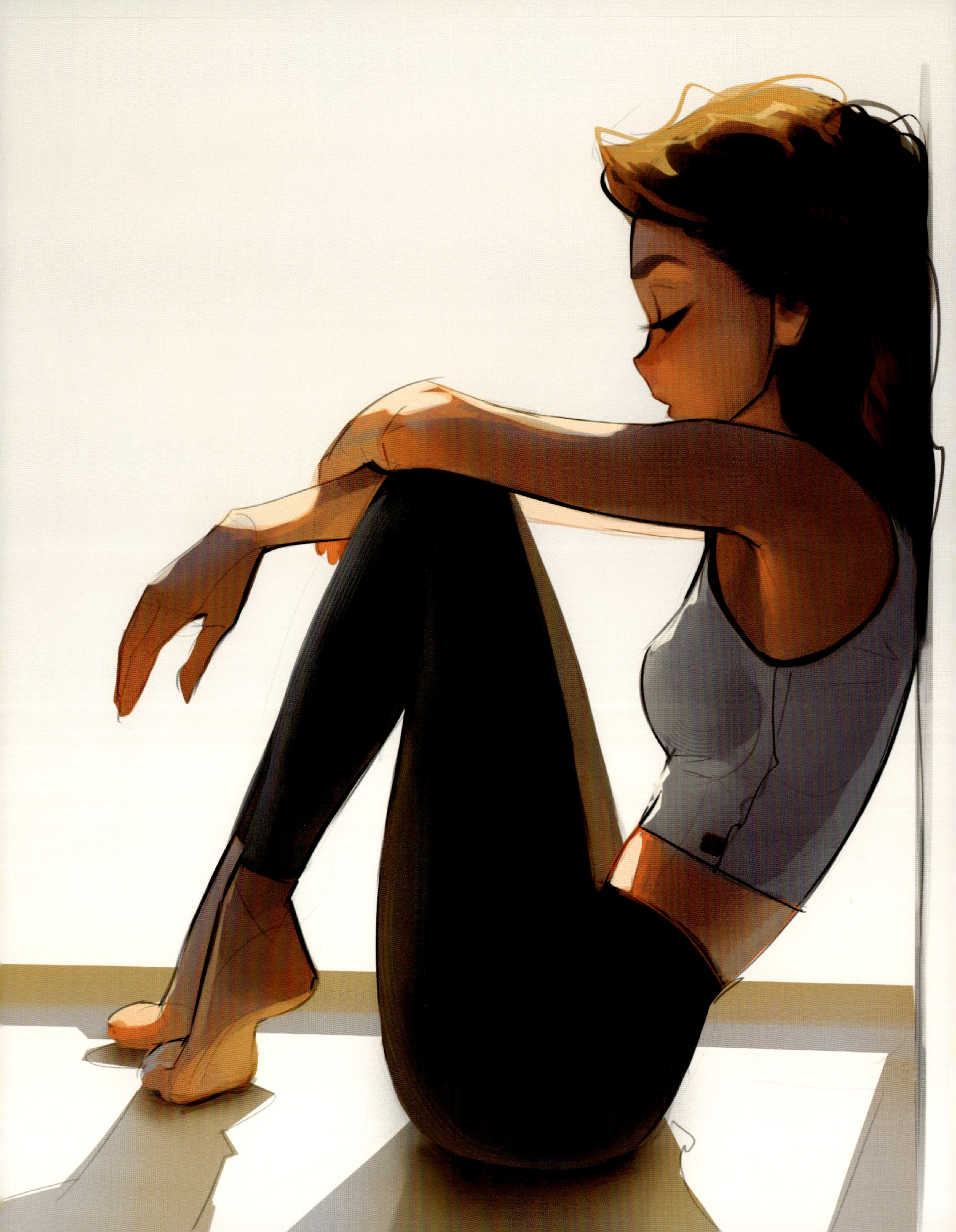

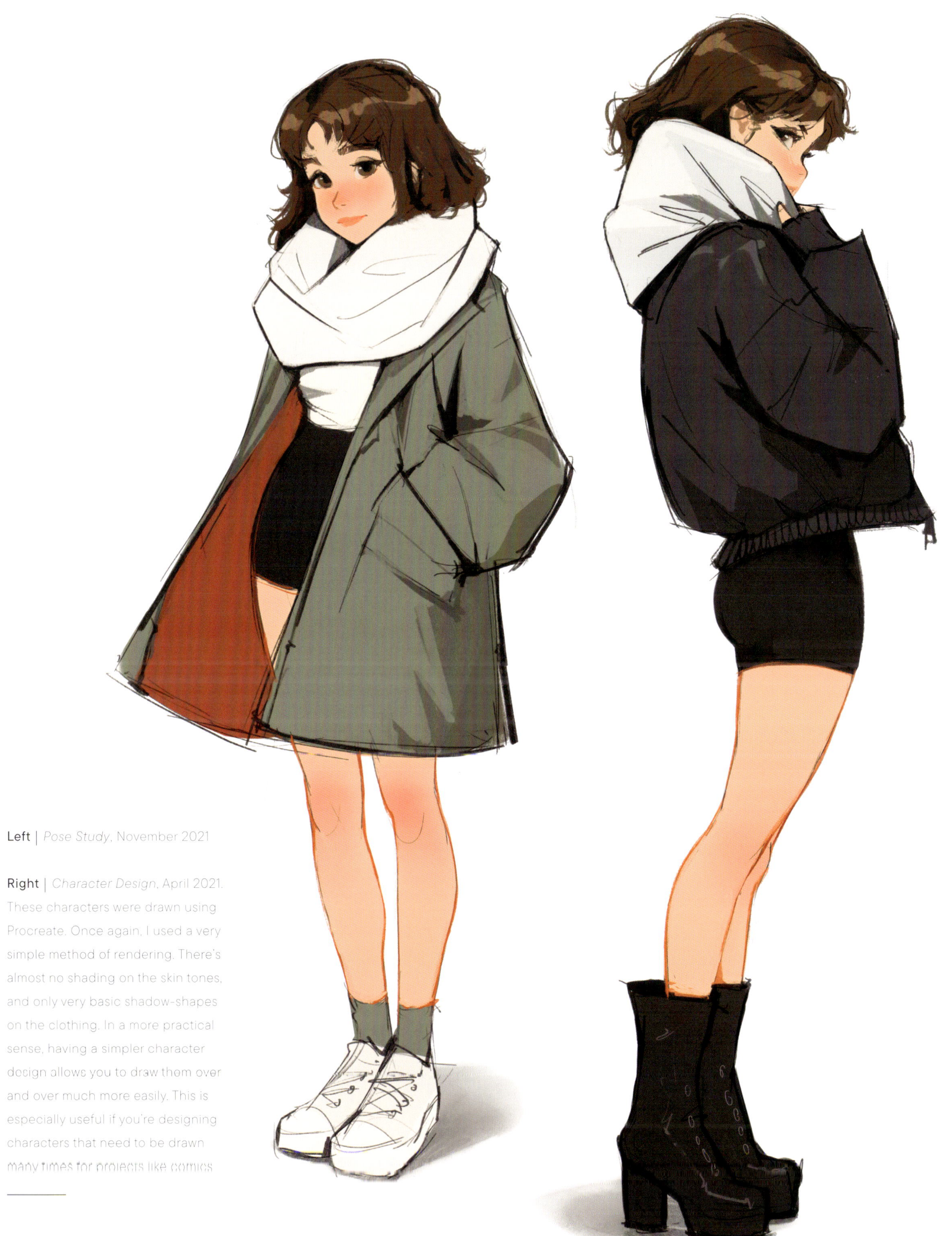

Left | *Pose Study*, November 2021

Right | *Character Design*, April 2021. These characters were drawn using Procreate. Once again, I used a very simple method of rendering. There's almost no shading on the skin tones, and only very basic shadow-shapes on the clothing. In a more practical sense, having a simpler character design allows you to draw them over and over much more easily. This is especially useful if you're designing characters that need to be drawn many times for projects like comics

FINDING INSPIRATION

I'm much more driven when I feel strongly about something, so having inspiring references, ideas, or goals usually helps produce great results.

I love Pinterest for finding references; a lot of ideas that inspired me were found on that website. The ability to save different visual concepts and images to their own category boards is extremely valuable to an artist. I have quite a few private boards where I keep my references – they could contain images that inspire me or perhaps just plain learning material for something like perspective or anatomy. I tend to divide my boards into categories such as faces, environments, lighting, and so on. I also like to keep a more general board of references for each year – it allows me to step back and glimpse the things that have interested me year after year. It's quite interesting to see your own progression.

Though I post my art frequently, many of my artworks don't actually end up online. There is a decent number of unfinished or unpublished pieces that I'm just not happy with.

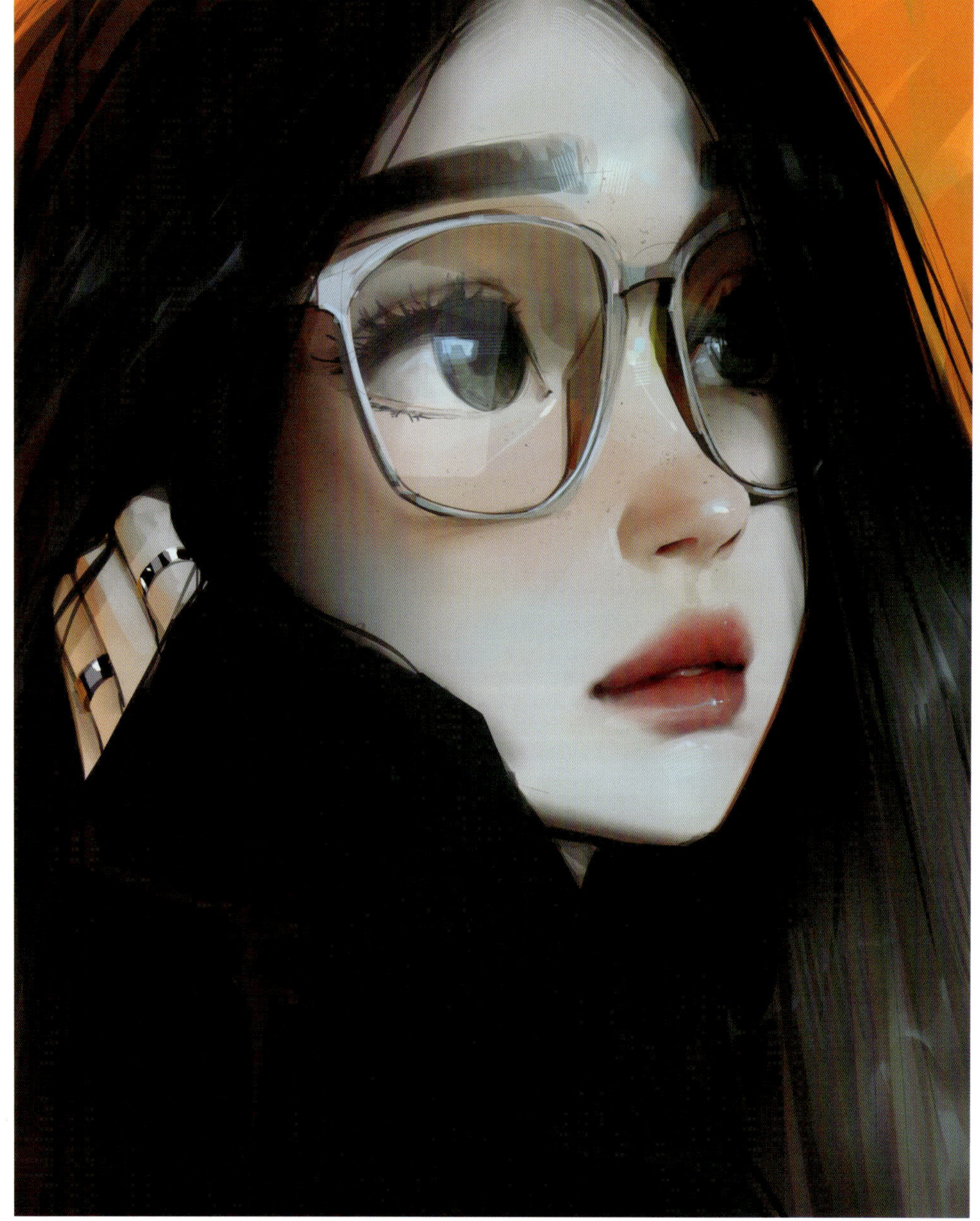

This page | *Glasses*, January 2023

Opposite page | *Fish*, April 2023

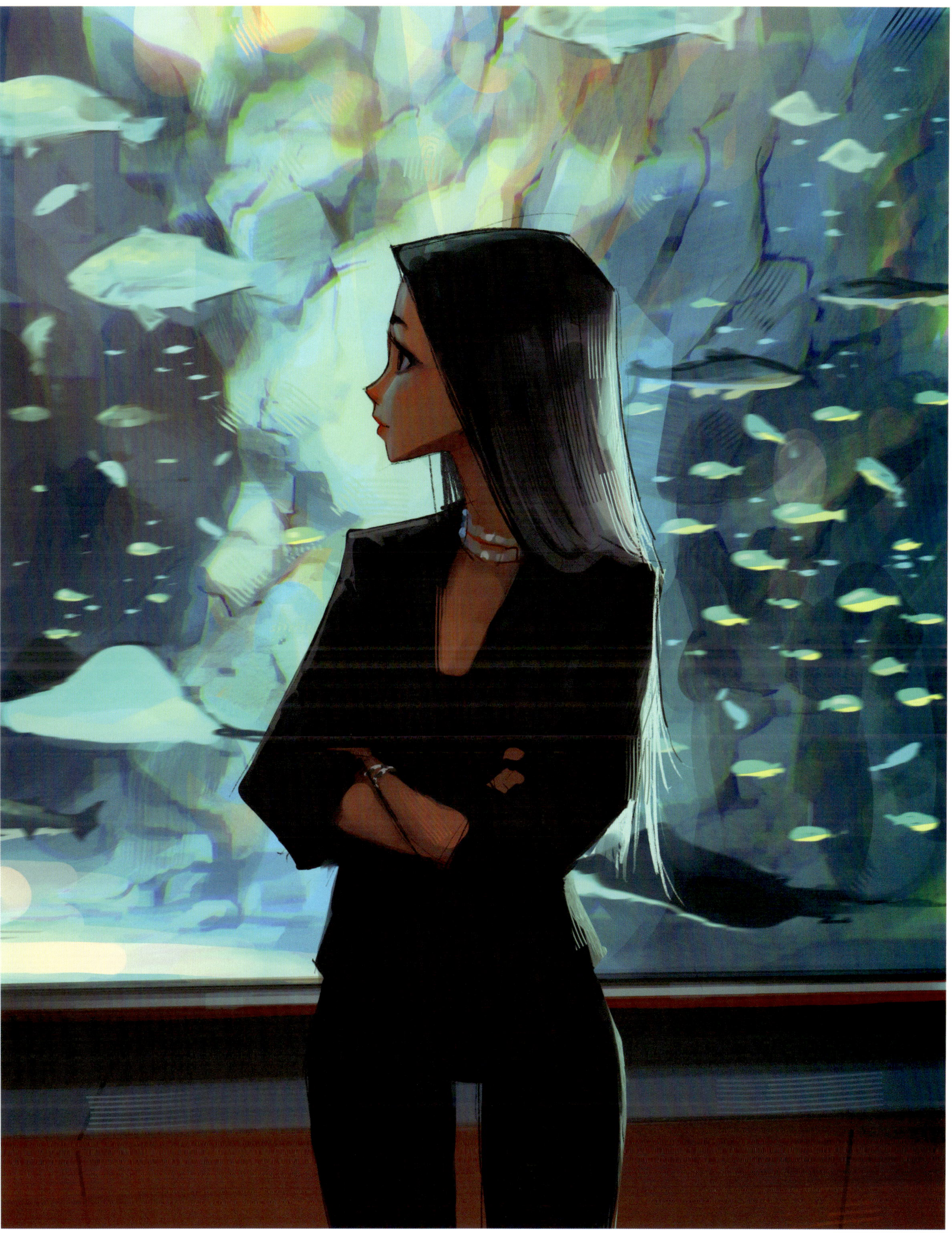

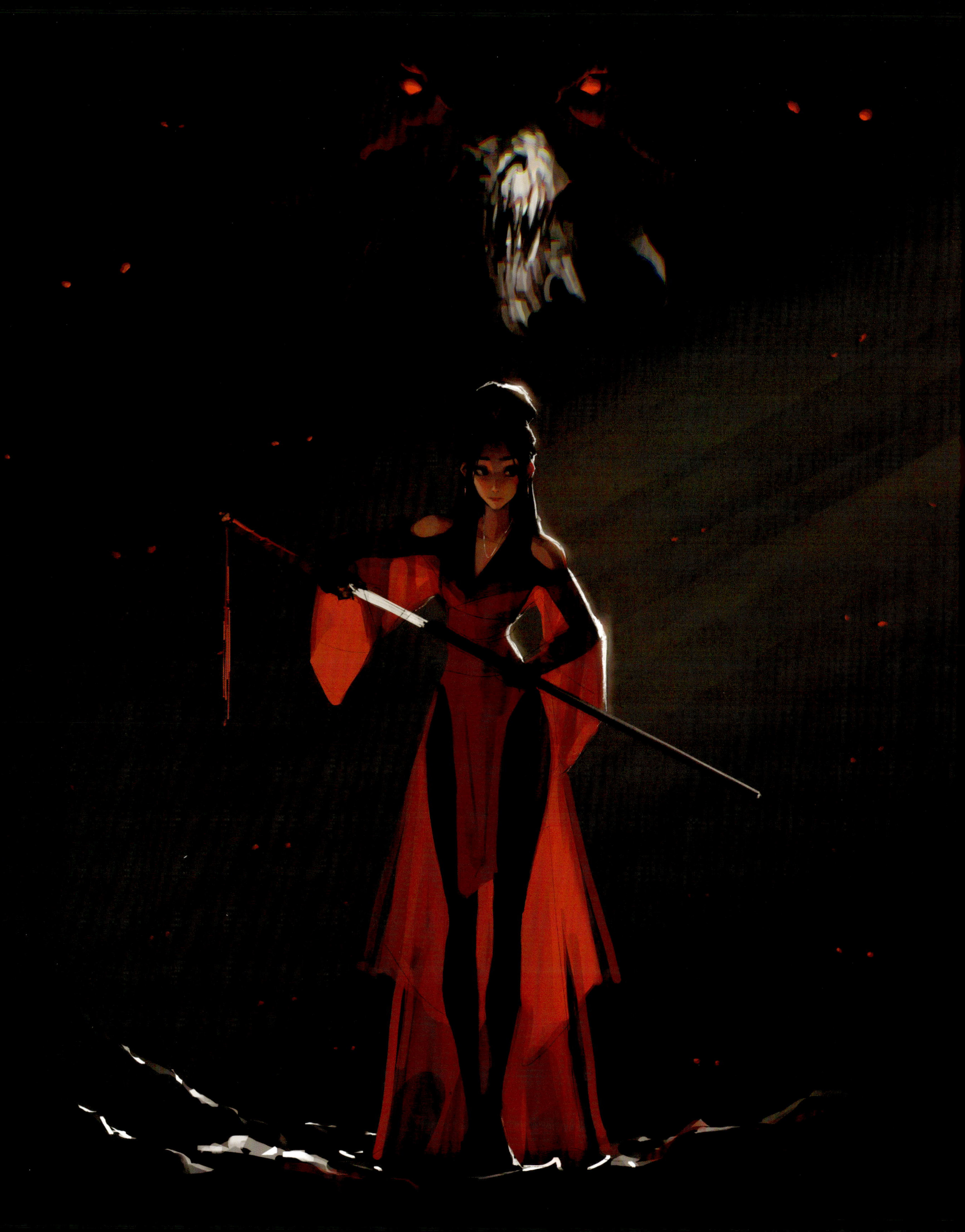

When it comes to more well-known artists, you're usually only seeing the best they have to offer. Not many of us will regularly share failed pieces or work that we're unsatisfied with. I think it's so important to keep this in mind as a fellow artist, or someone who simply appreciates art. We are all human and we all stumble and mess up. I think this is part of the beauty of our handmade artworks. The pieces that we do end up cherishing and sharing with the world are that much more special because of this.

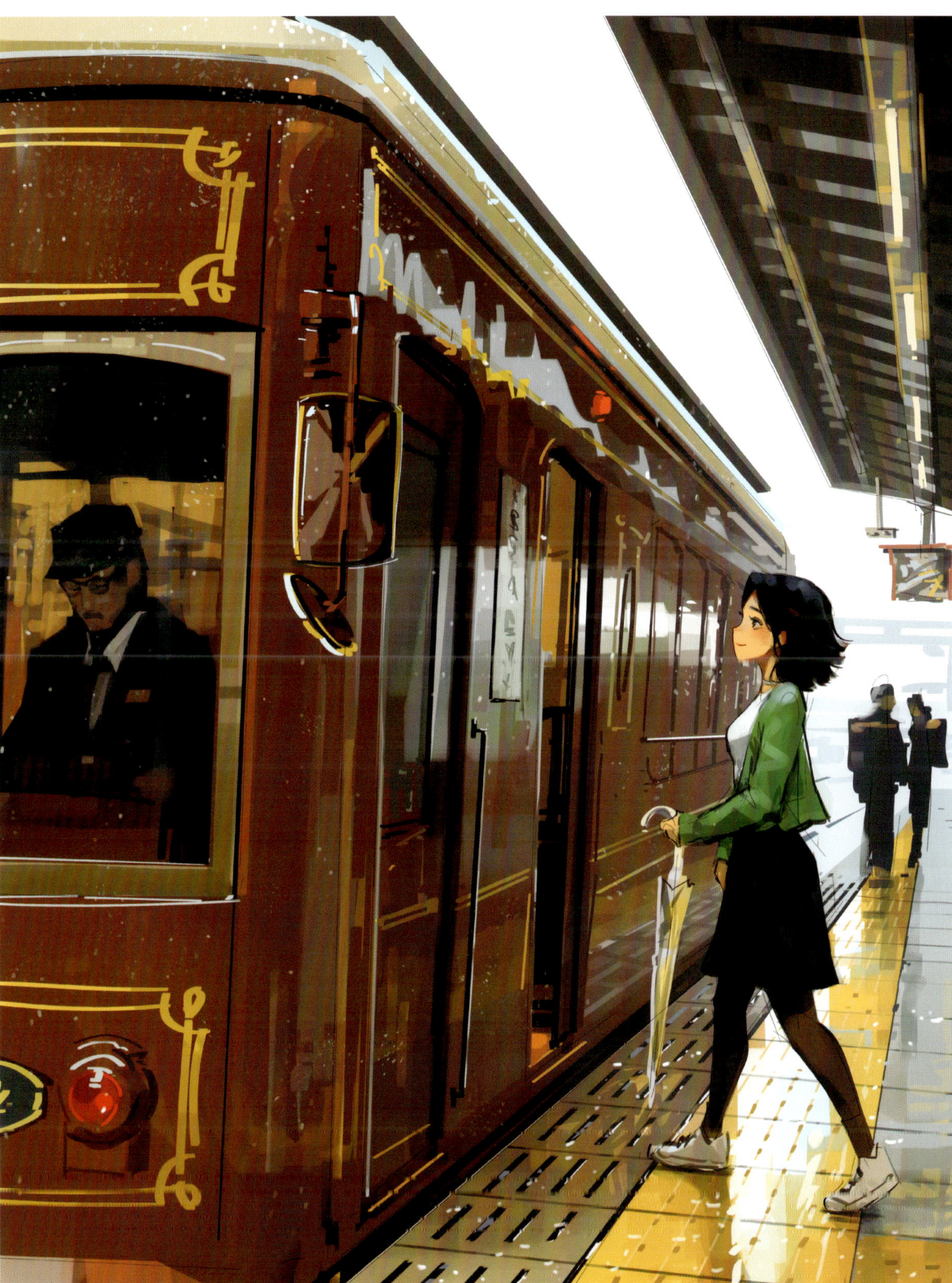

Left | *Demons*, January 2023. This is an example of a piece that didn't end up online. Most of the time there's nothing critically wrong with the work. I just usually have a rough idea of how I'd like it to look, and when it fails to live up to those expectations, I don't feel confident in sharing it with the world. Not every piece makes it to the final state, and that's okay, because they're all learning experiences

Right | *Train*, May 2023

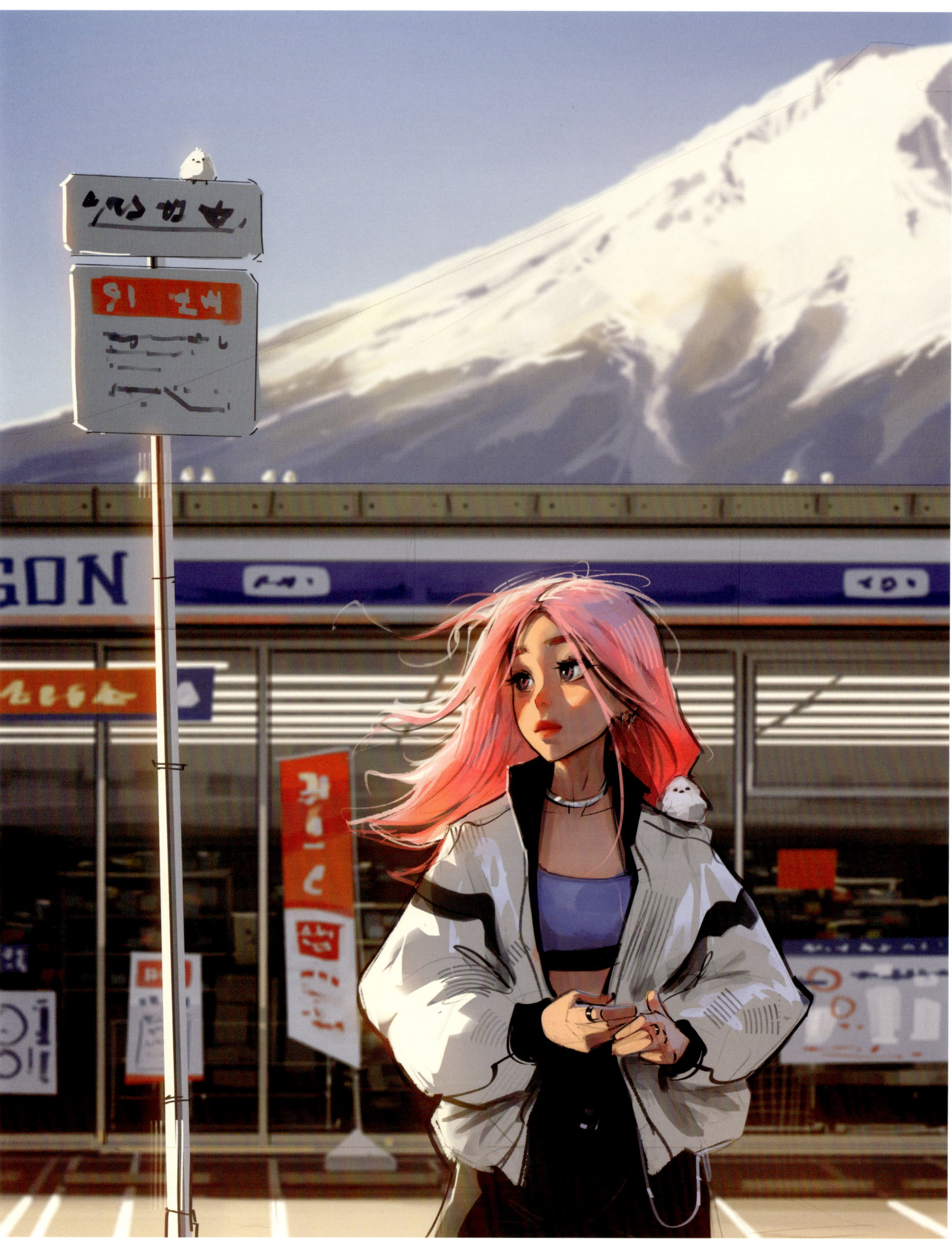
GON

Left | *Fuji*, May 2023 | Below | *Borb*, November 2022

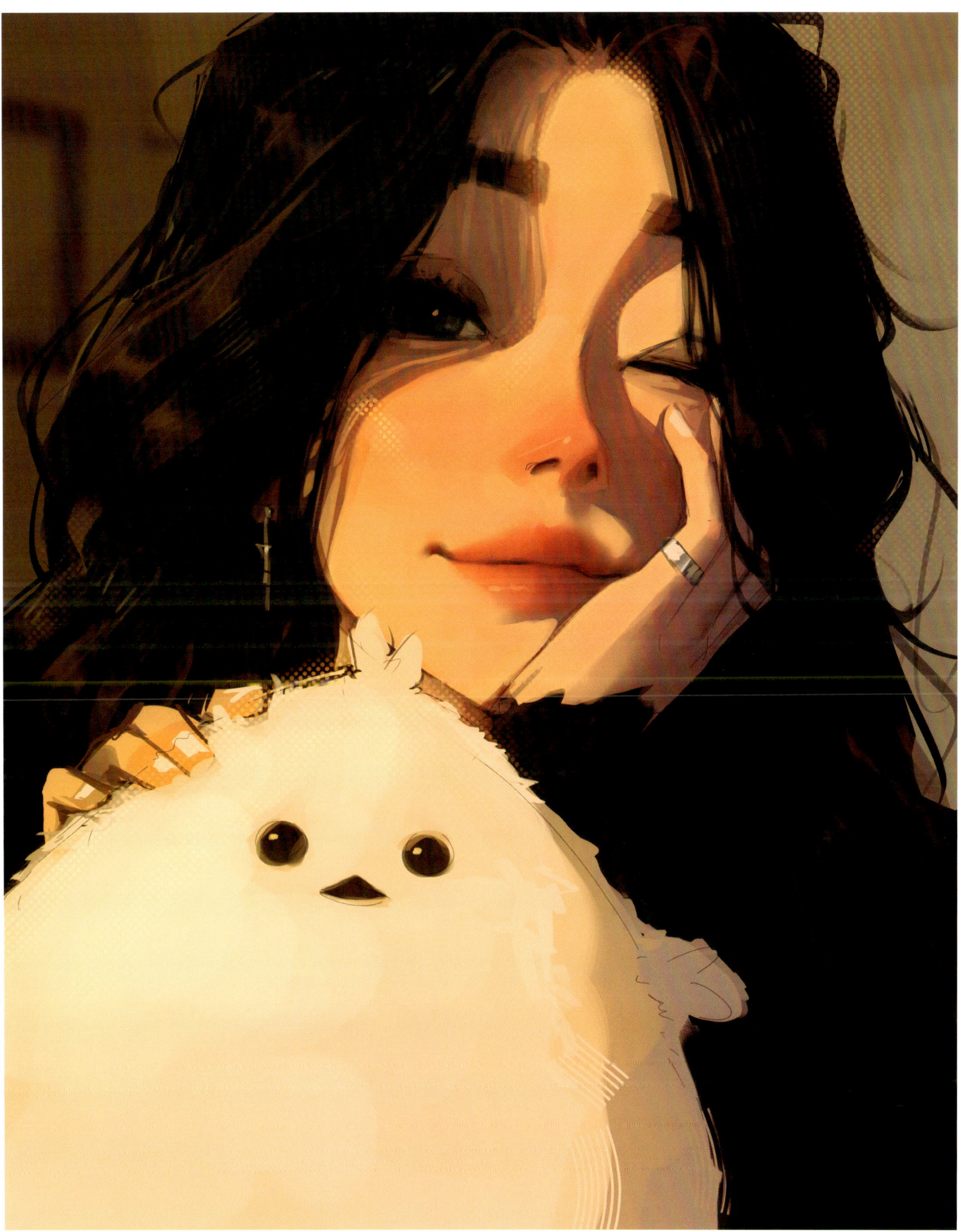

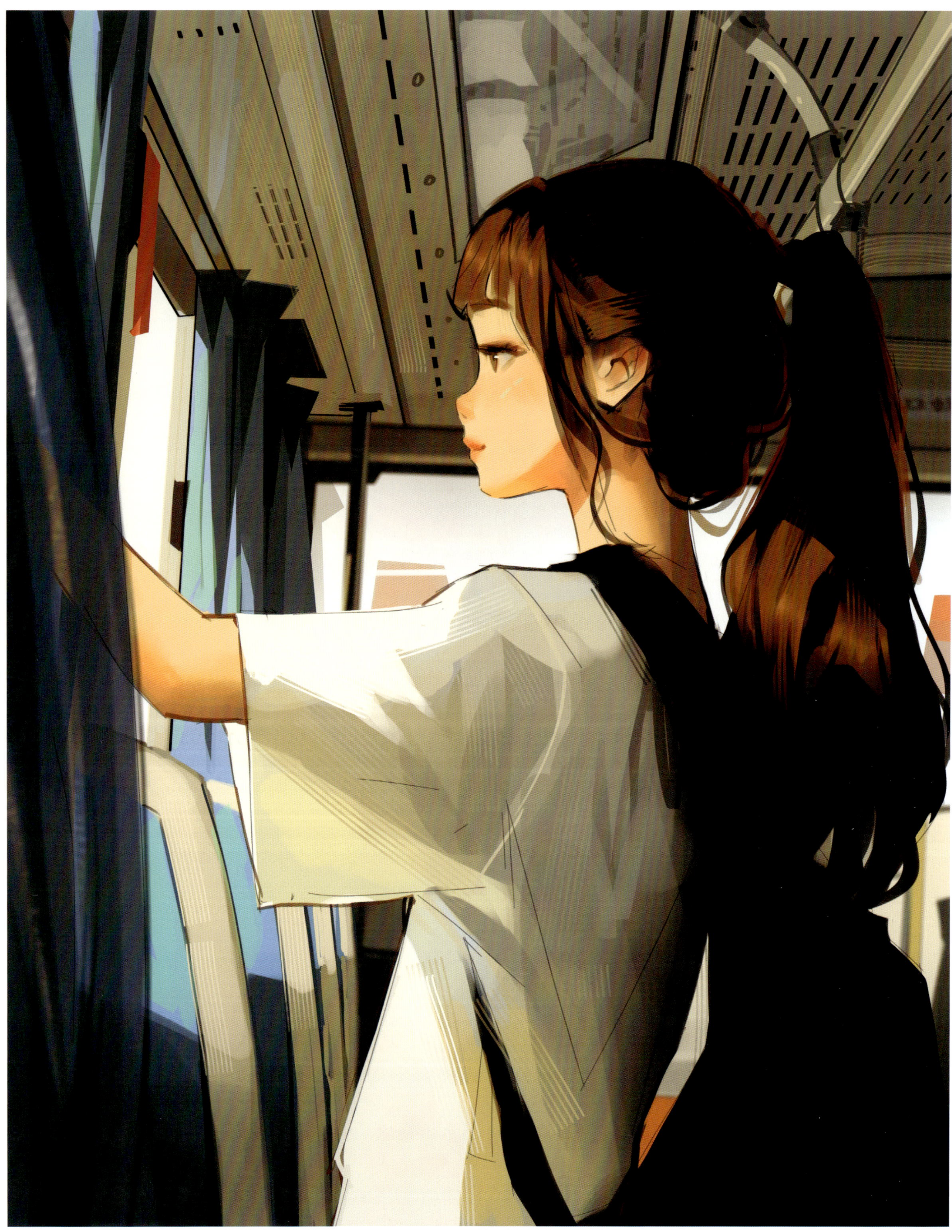

Only ever seeing someone else's best work can be mentally taxing on artists as they struggle along their journeys. Personally, it helps to remember that everyone started off as an amateur. No one was born with a brush in their hand and the ability to draw masterpieces without training. If I'm stuck on a piece, and it's just not working out, I don't force it. Sometimes, you need to take a step back and ask yourself what went right, what went wrong, and what lessons can be learned – then move on to the next piece. That unfinished, unpublished artwork that you're ashamed of is not actually a failure on your part; that piece is an irreplaceable stepping stone for your journey to finding your artistic voice.

It's important to be patient with yourself and understand that no one becomes a master like Hayao Miyazaki or Glen Keane overnight. Look up to those you admire and hold yourself to a high standard, but also remember to be kind to yourself. A failed piece is always an opportunity to learn.

Left | *Commute*, February 2022

MOTIVATION

One of the most common questions I get asked is: 'How do you stay motivated?' My answer is always 'define your goals'. Don't just have random goals, either – be precise about them and actually change your routine to act on them.

I usually feel the most motivated to draw when I know I'm working towards something. Ask yourself what you ultimately want to achieve with your artwork. Perhaps you'd like to be an animator at a prestigious studio, or to create a popular web comic to tell your own stories. If you're younger, maybe your goal is to attend a specific art school. A long-term goal gives you something to work towards.

When I find a long-term goal, I like to break it down and start backwards by asking a couple of questions: *How do I go from where I am right now to where I want to be?* and *What are the things I need to overcome to reach that stretch goal?* For example, if you'd like to work in animation, you'll need to learn how to make your characters move by practising anatomy, shape language, and character drawing. It's also important to be specific and set smaller goals, which will help chip away at your larger, long-term goals. This could be something like practising facial expressions in your sketchbook for thirty minutes a day for thirty days, if expressions are a weak spot for you. Identify your long-term goal, compartmentalize it, and form smaller, short-term goals. Always try to work towards something.

Also make sure to continuously challenge yourself by stepping out of your comfort zone. Growth is what brings me the most joy when it comes to the pursuit of art, so this is the angle I approach it from. However, it's important to note that everyone functions differently; something that works for me may not work for you, and that's perfectly okay! Experiment and find your own path. There's no 'one size fits all'.

LEARNING FROM OTHER ARTISTS

I often catch myself looking at the works of other artists, wondering, 'Why can't I draw like *that*?' It's a routine piece of inner dialogue that emerges when I see works that truly inspire me. If you're an artist, I'm sure you've asked yourself the same thing. When I find myself doing this, I always try to figure out what '*that*' is. What is it about this piece that inspires me? Could it be the colours? The simplification? When you can home in and identify one or more aspects of that artwork that really speaks to you, you'll have something tangible to work with. Be specific about it and avoid saying things like, 'I just like the way it looks.' Ask yourself why! Do you like it because of the line quality? The stylization? Find the specific things that inspire you and see if you can learn how that artist did it. Again, I like to work backwards here, which means examining the artist's work and absorbing it in any way I find helpful. I can trace over it (but not publish it and claim it as my own, obviously), or I can try to draw exactly what they've drawn, mimicking the style, colours, and so on. This helps me see things from another artist's perspective. It can be very difficult to break free from your own drawing-style bubble without some external motivation.

At the end of the day, we all take inspiration from others. For many people, the most beneficial aspect of art school is not the classes themselves; it's actually the other students who present challenges and inspiration. Don't get caught up in your own bubble. Instead, observe how others do things. There's something you can learn from everyone.

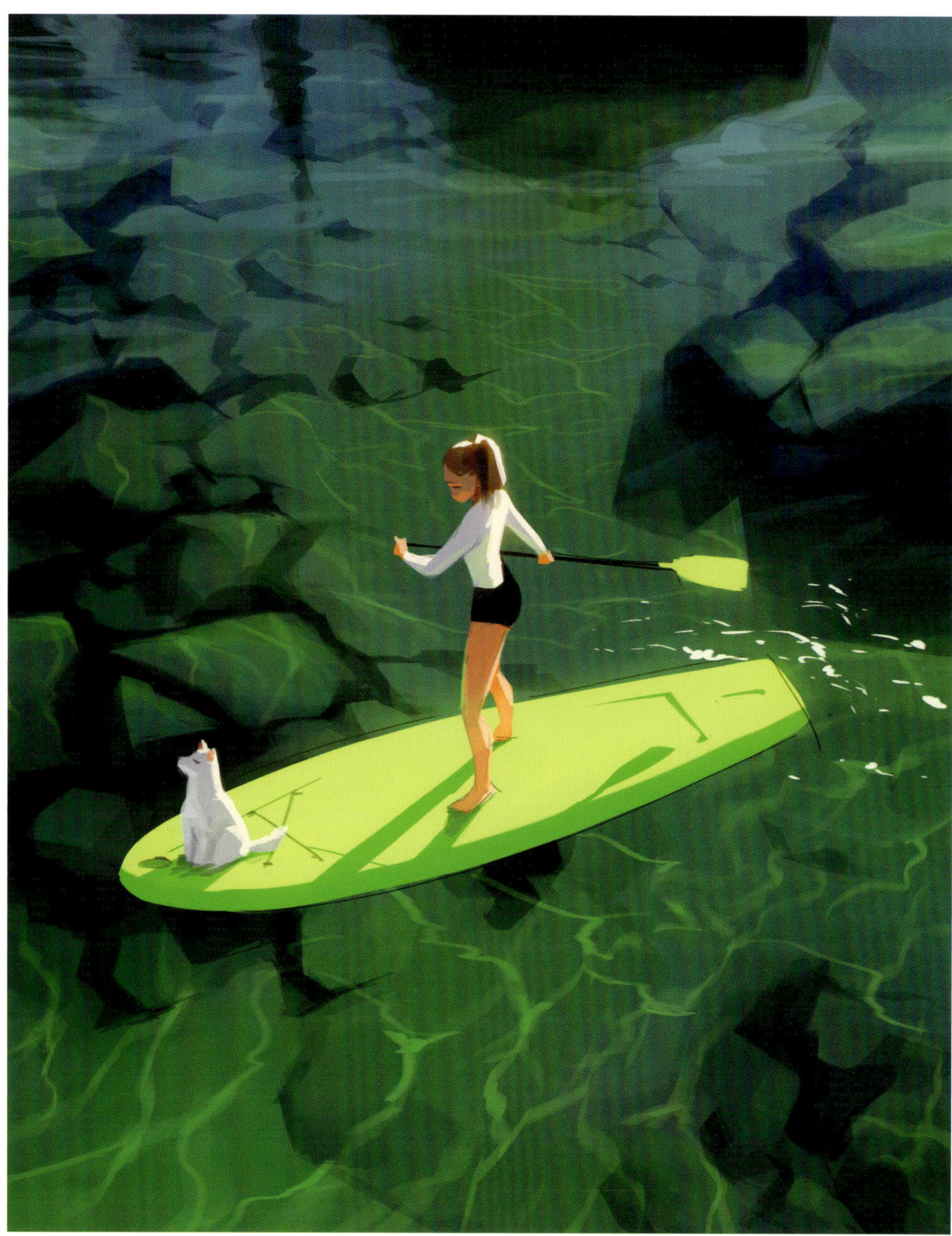

Above | *Board Doggo*, April 2021.
The style that inspired this study is the work of Atey Ghailan. The environment here is constructed using highly simplified geometric shapes. In this case, less is more. Today, I've found myself rendering in a more complex style. I think this level of simplicity is something I'd like to return to

Right | *Driving*, September 2020.
This piece was heavily inspired by the work of Ramón Nuñez. His influence is most notable in the more exaggerated character stylization and very rough overall render style. And of course, the crazy big eyes

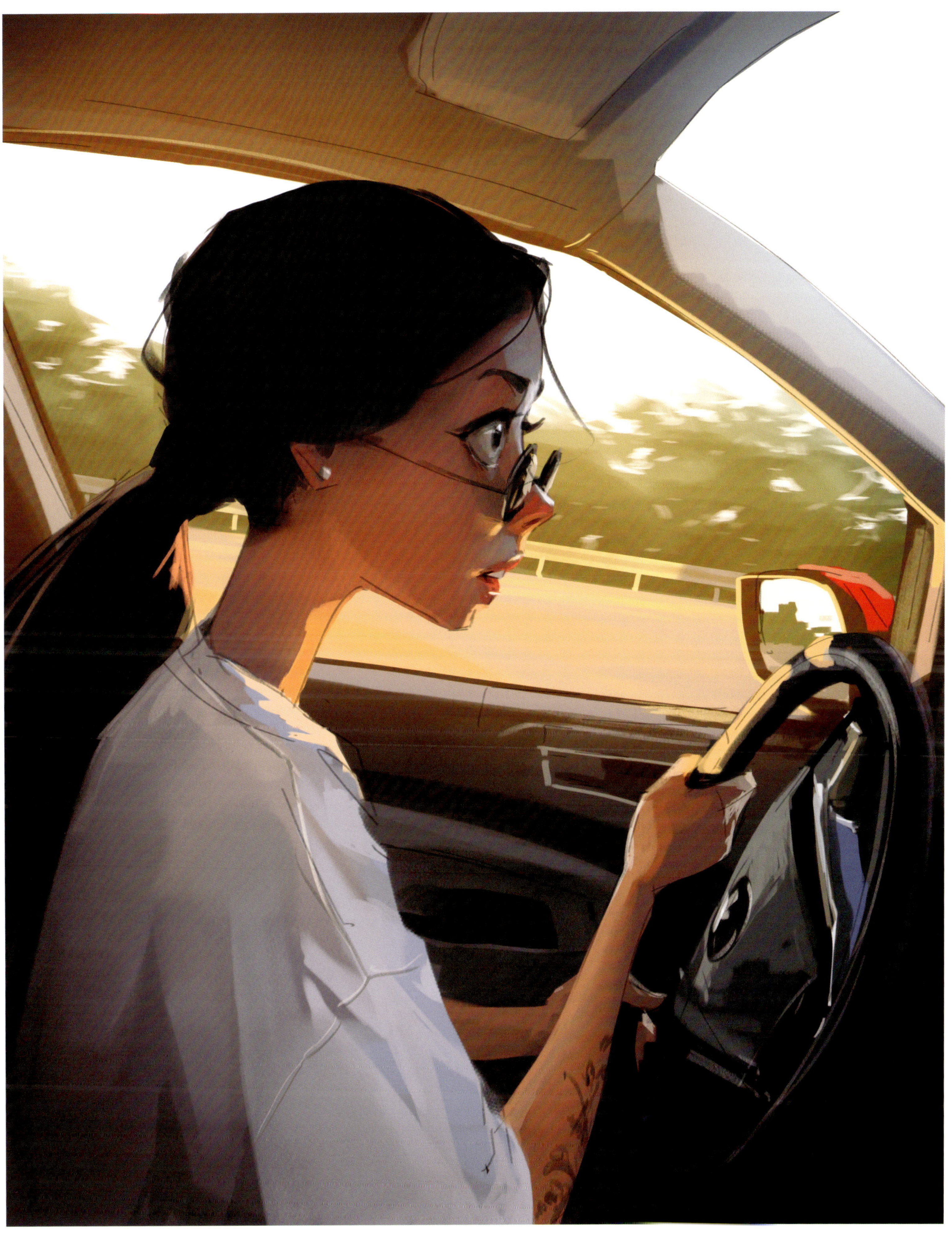

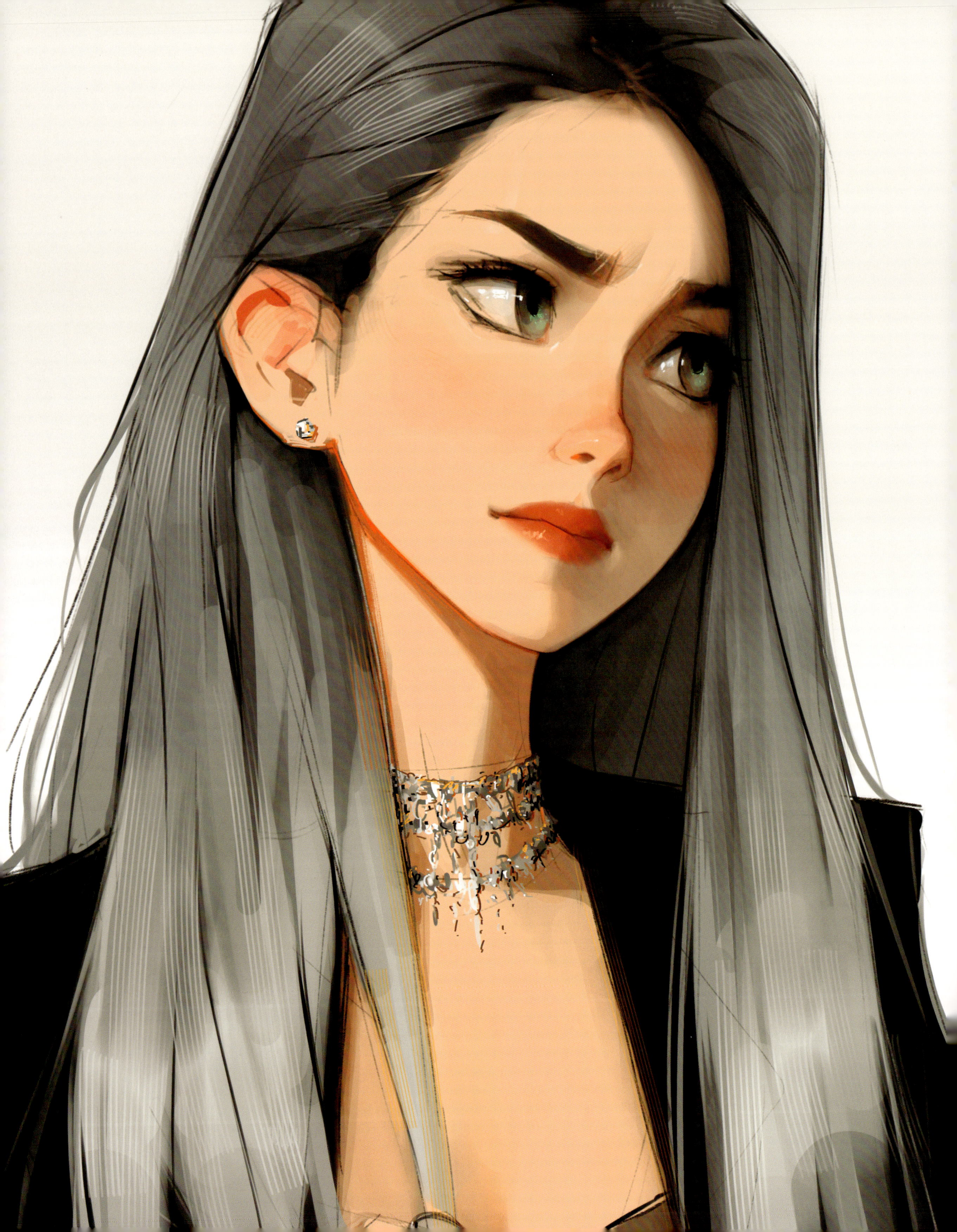

gallery 1

Selection of works from my portfolio

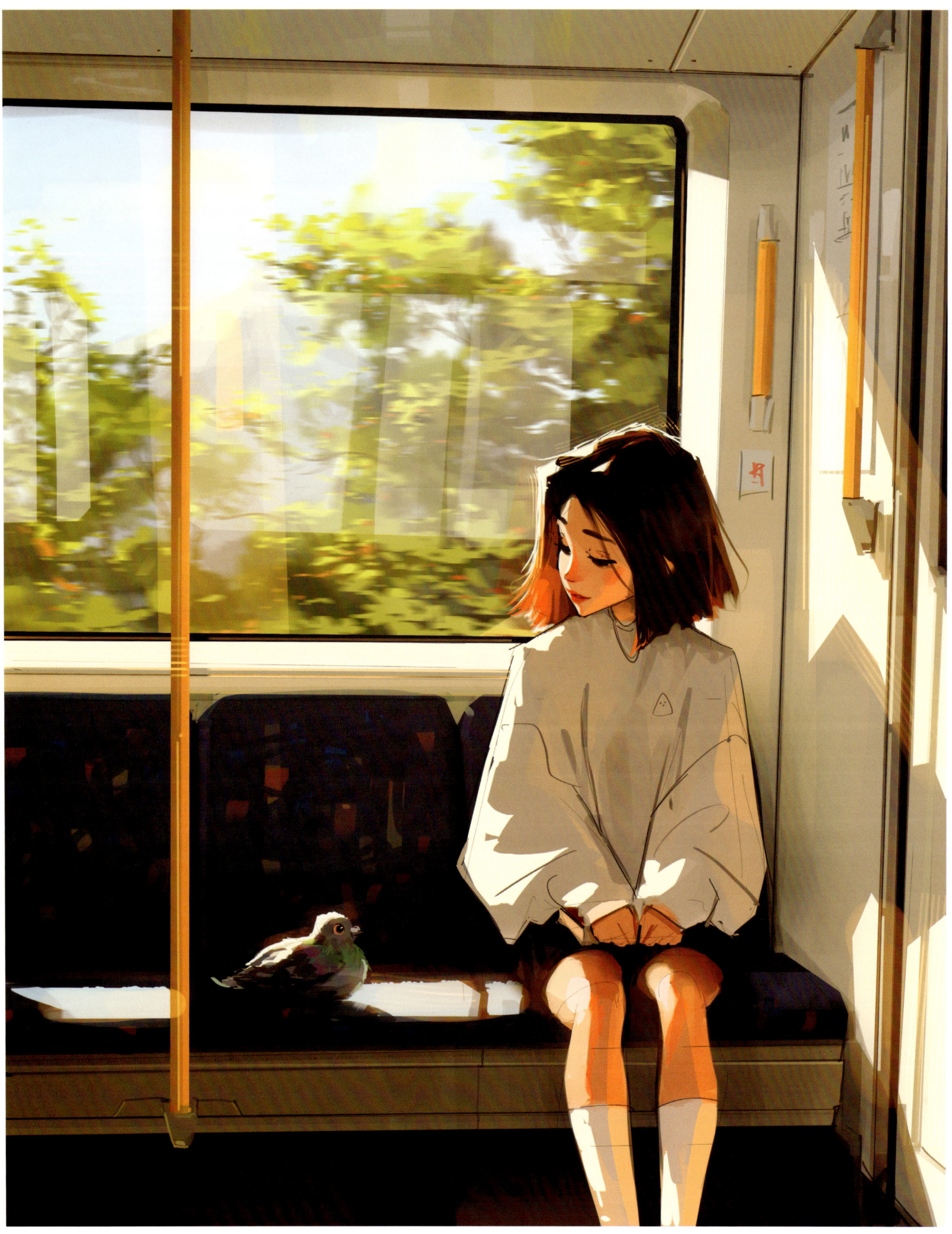

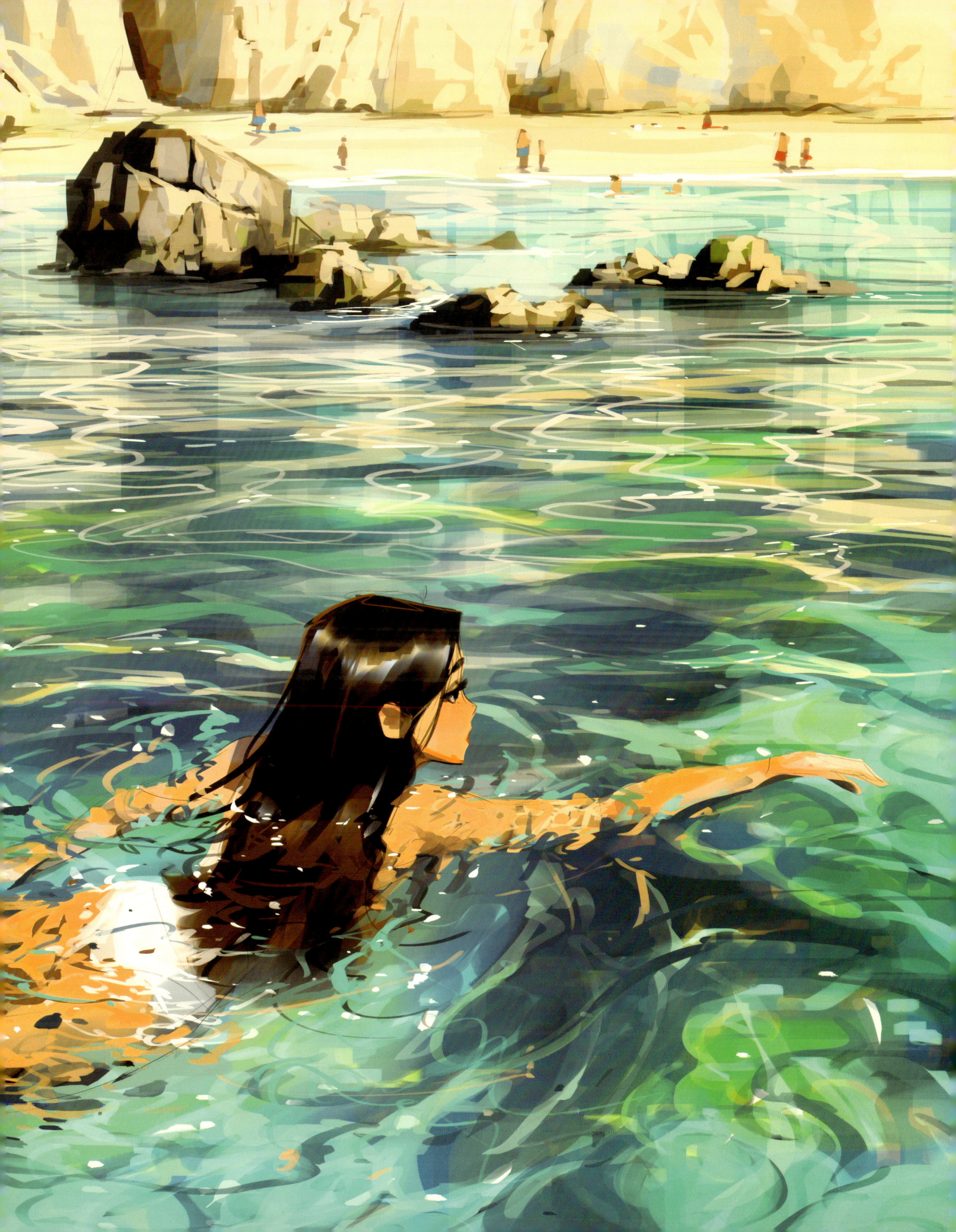

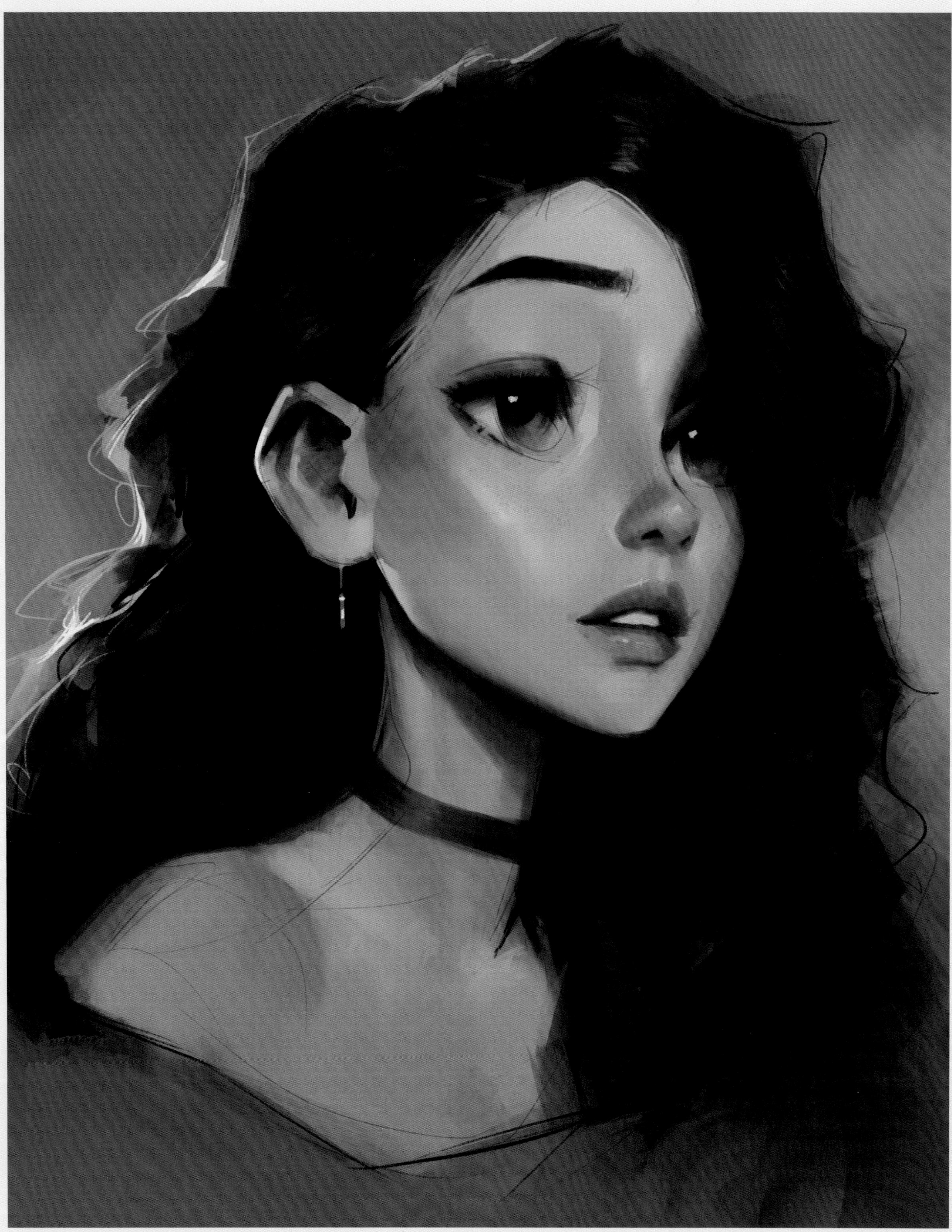

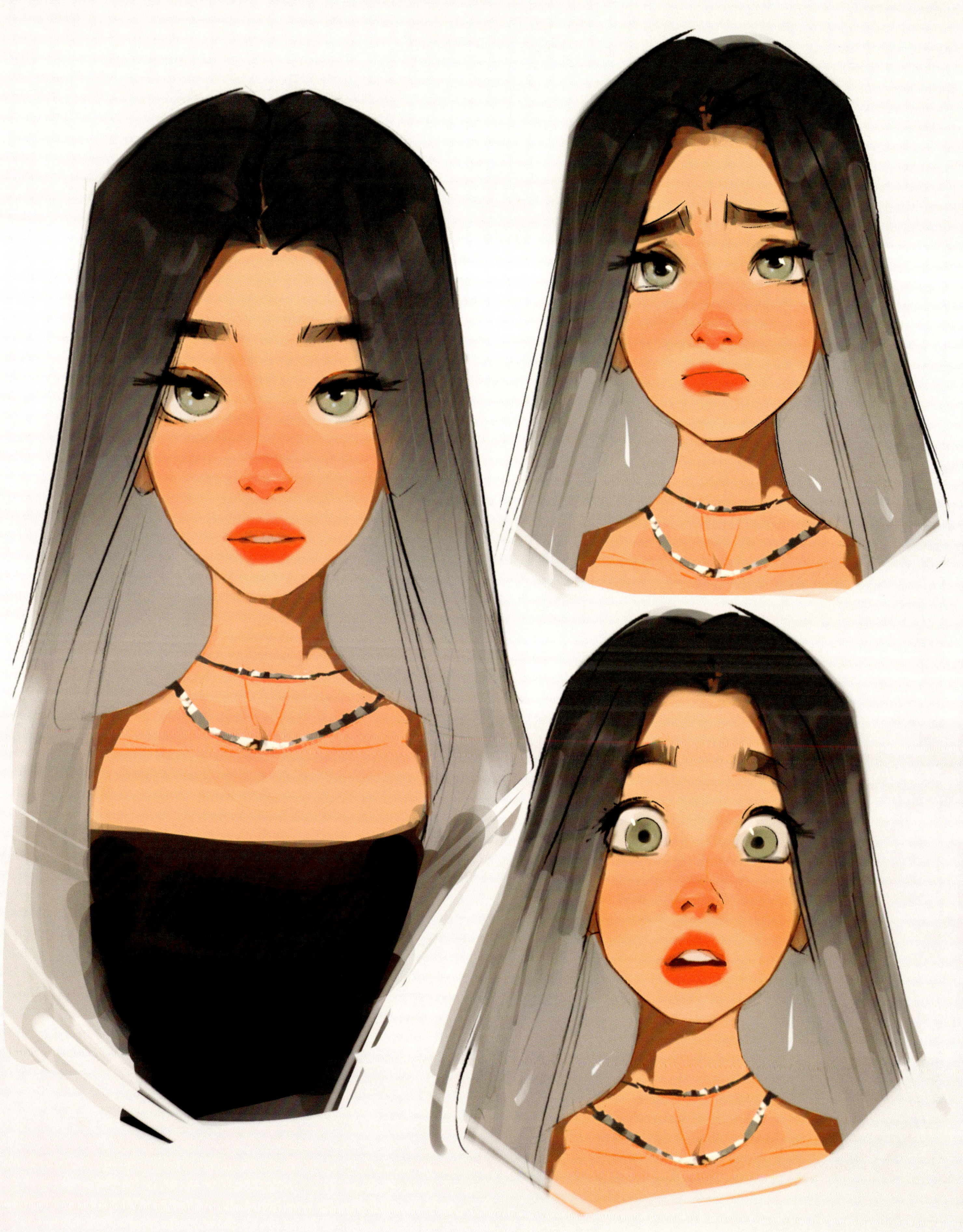

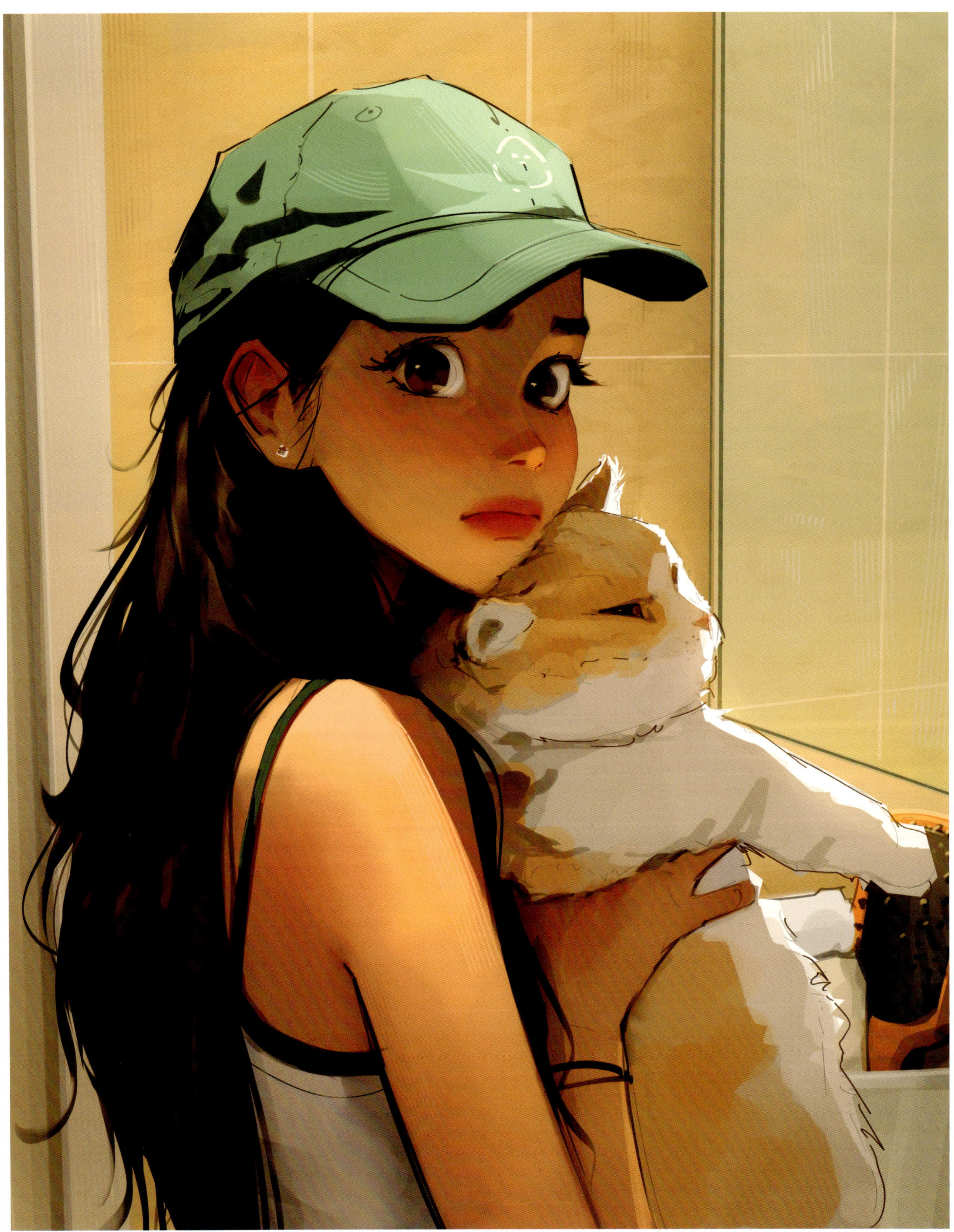

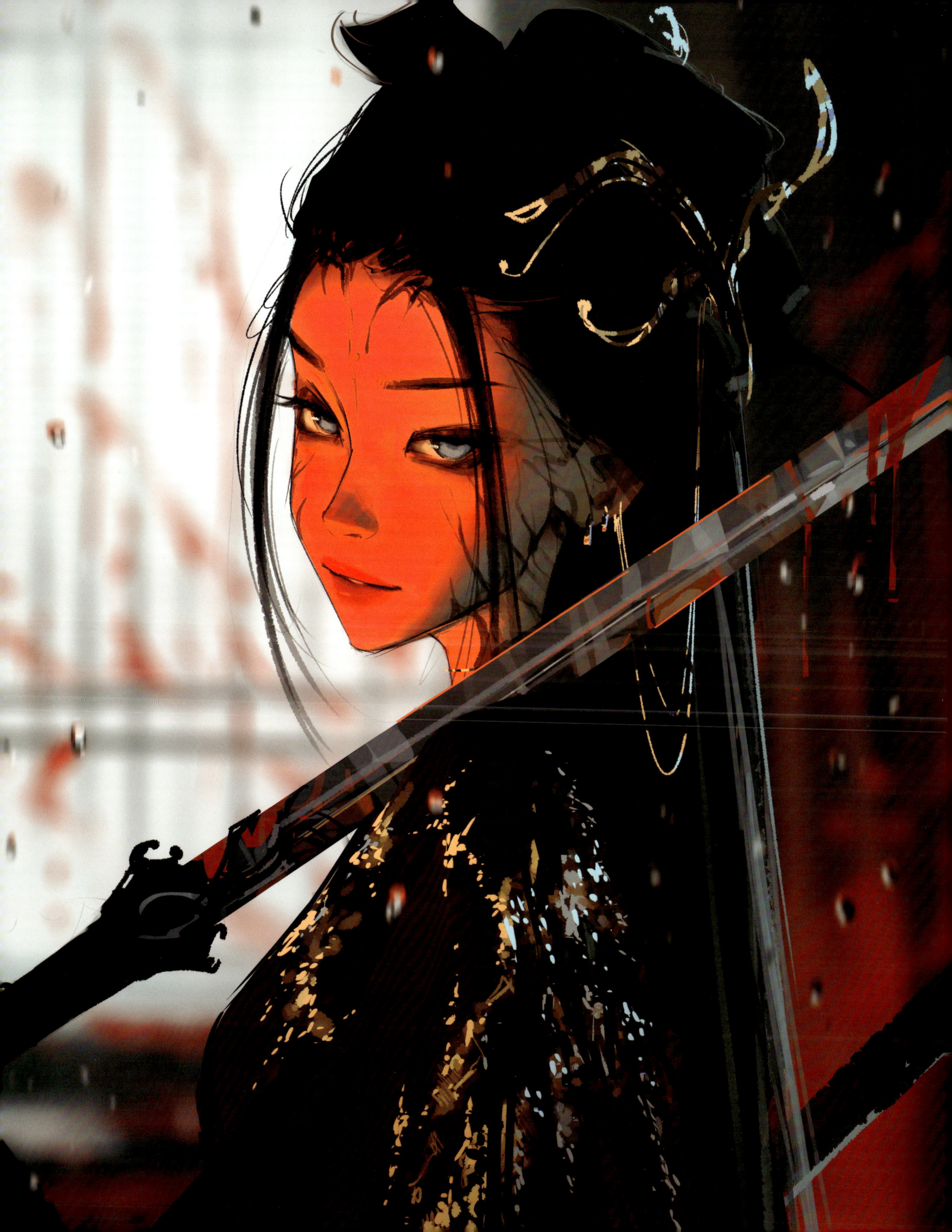

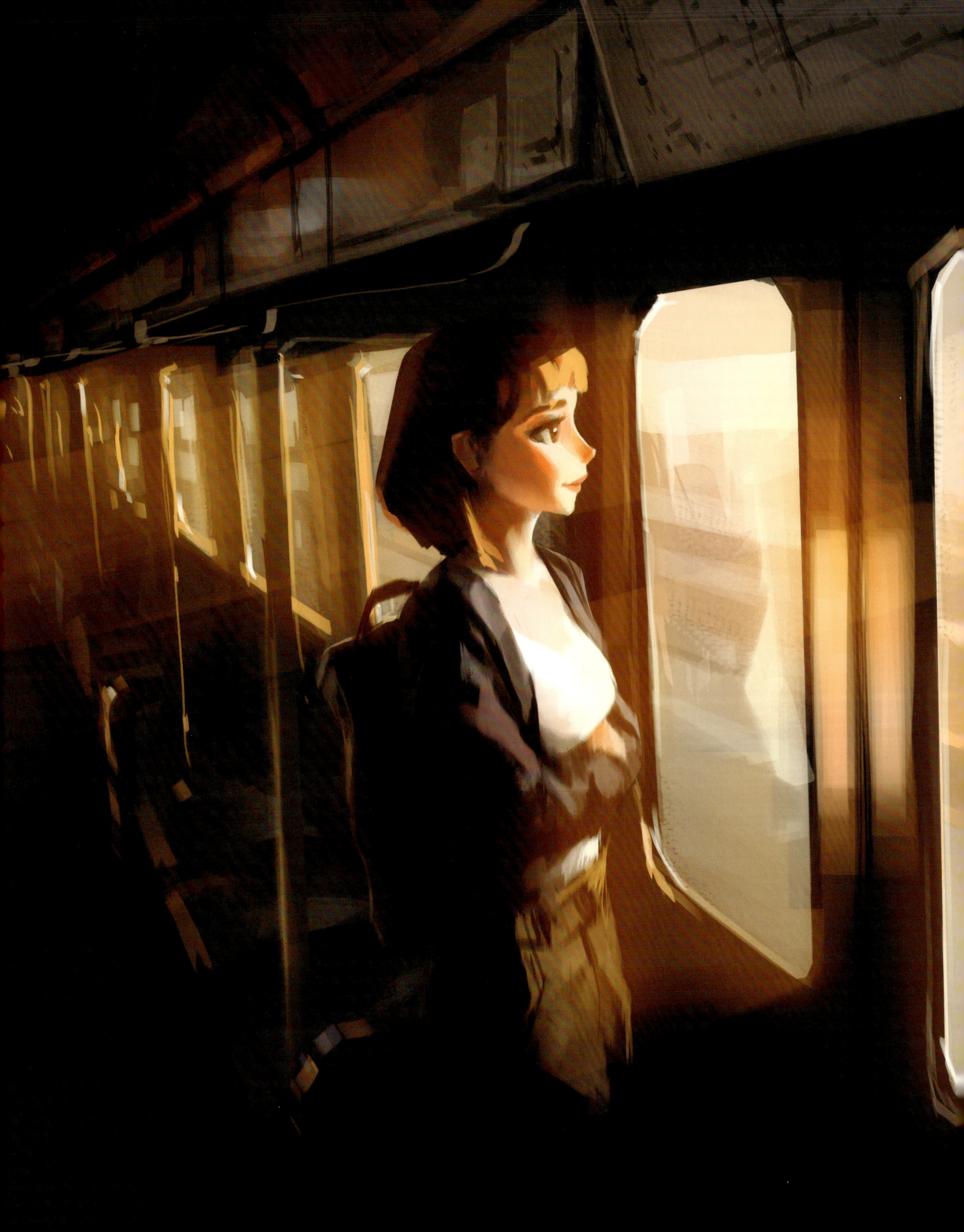

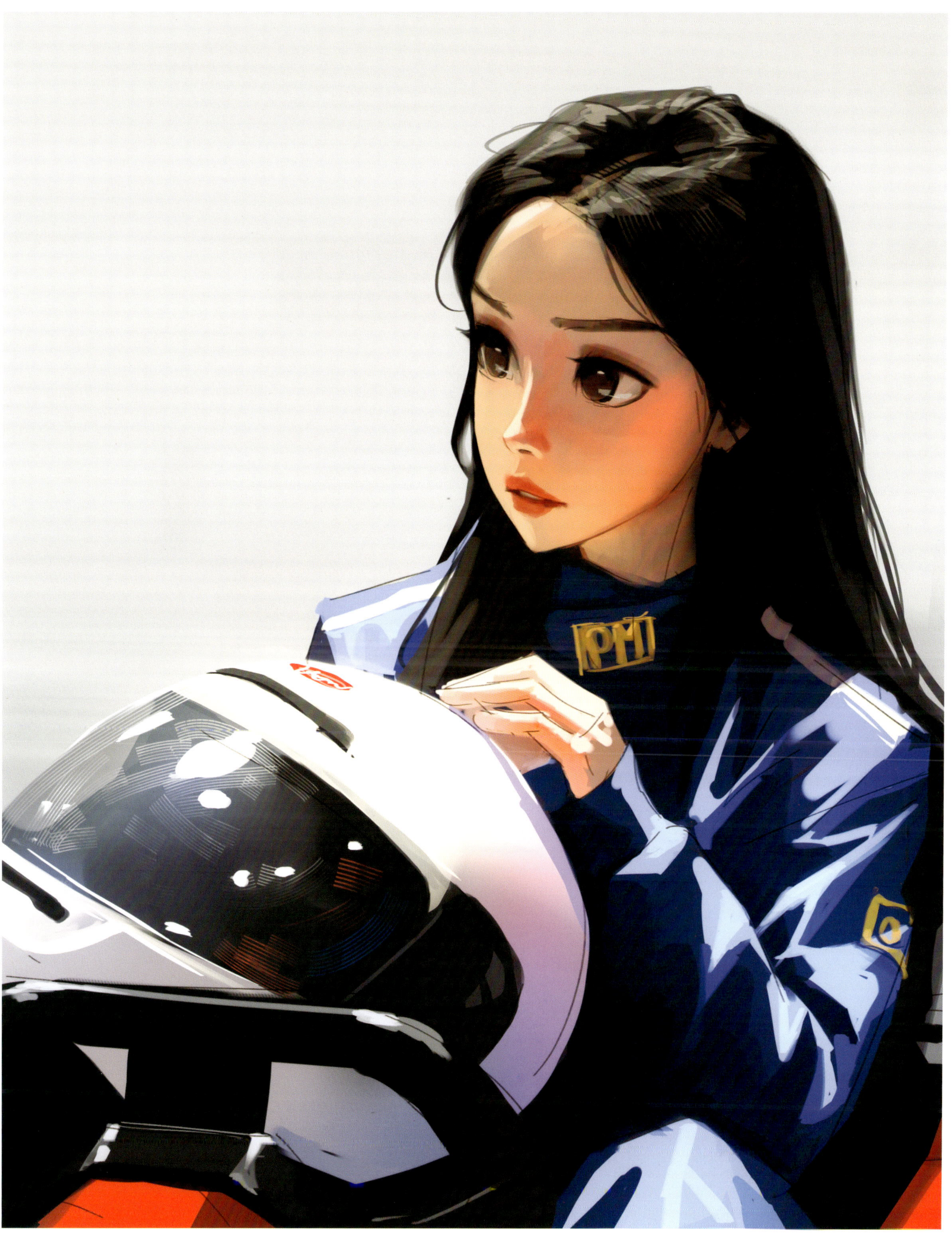

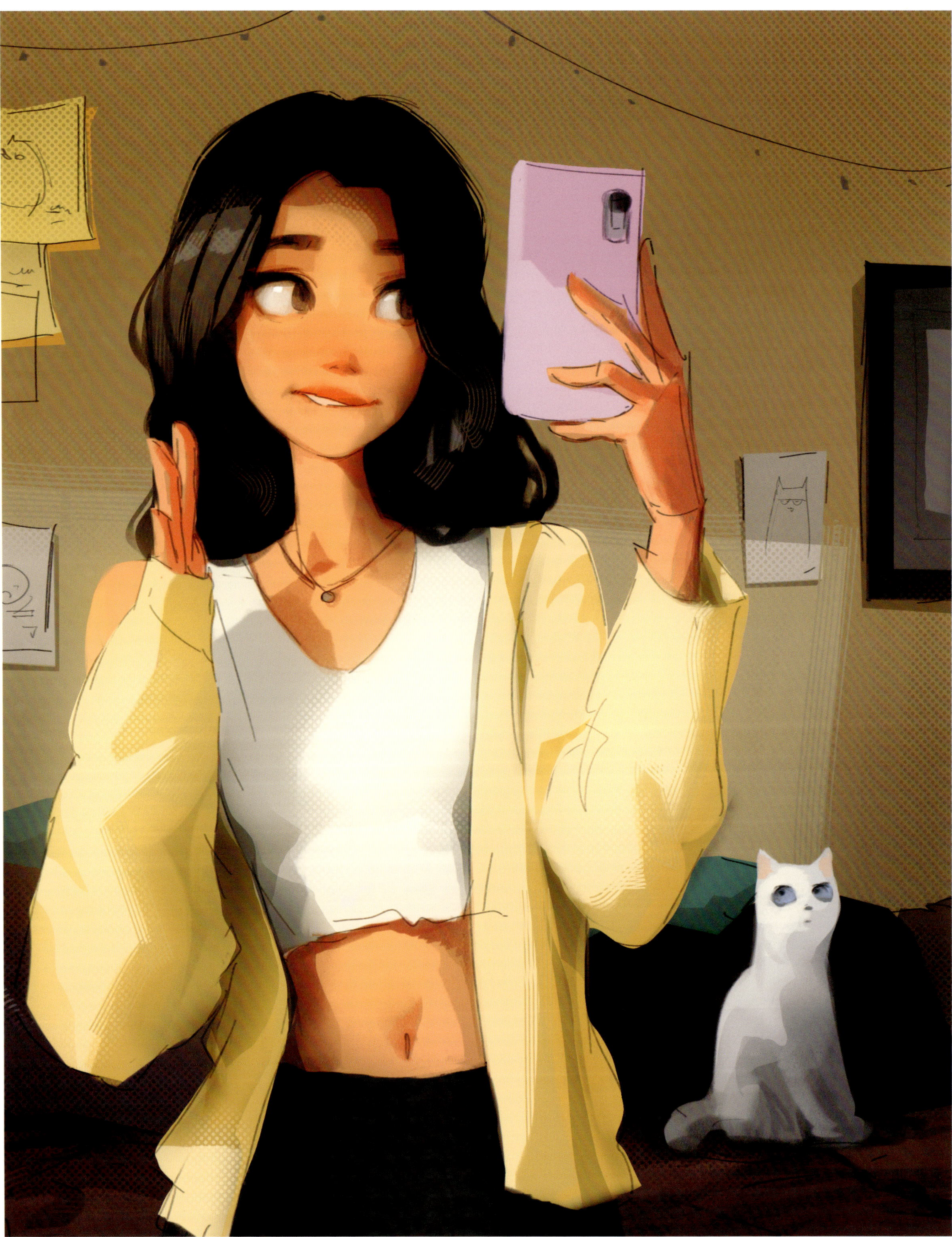

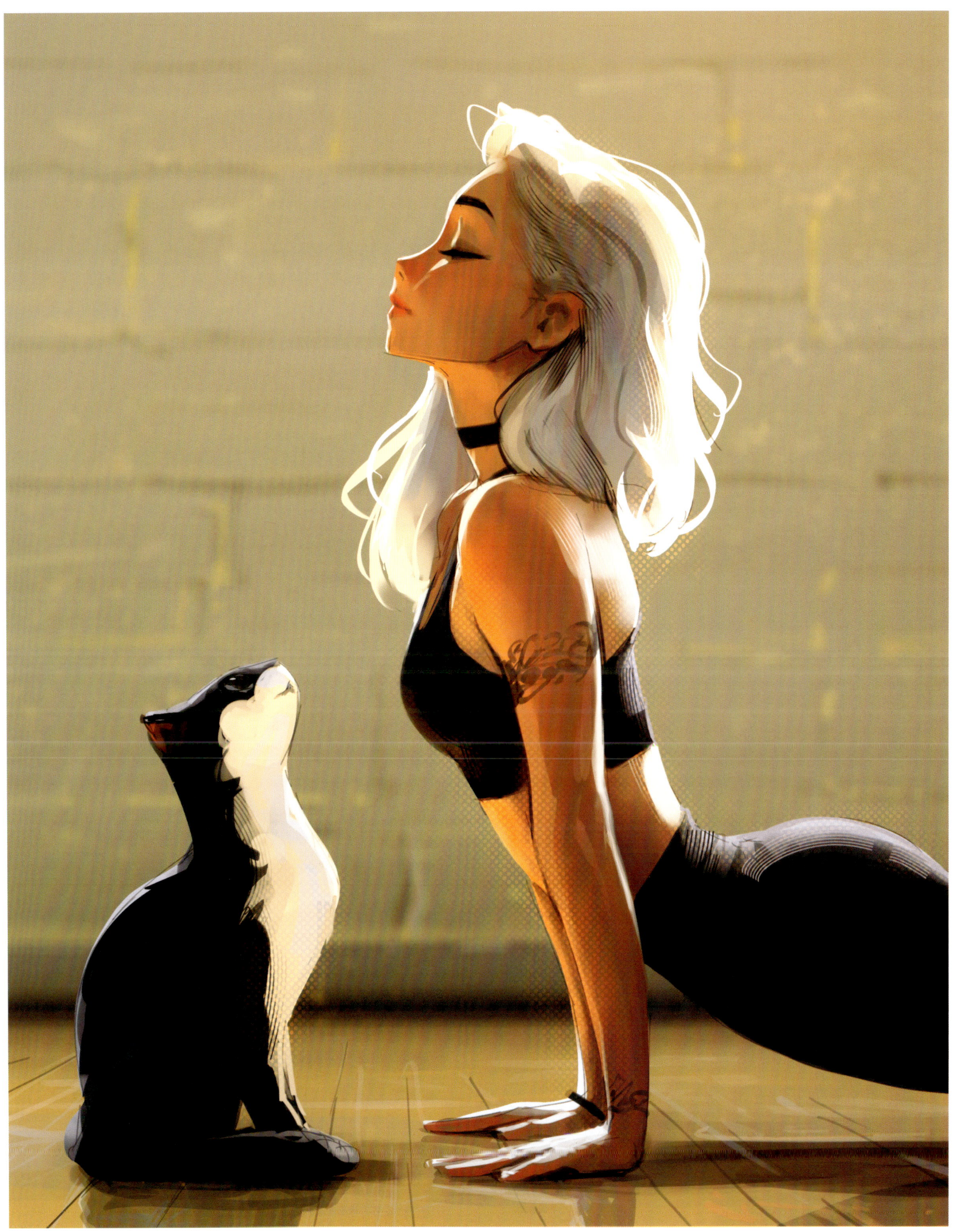

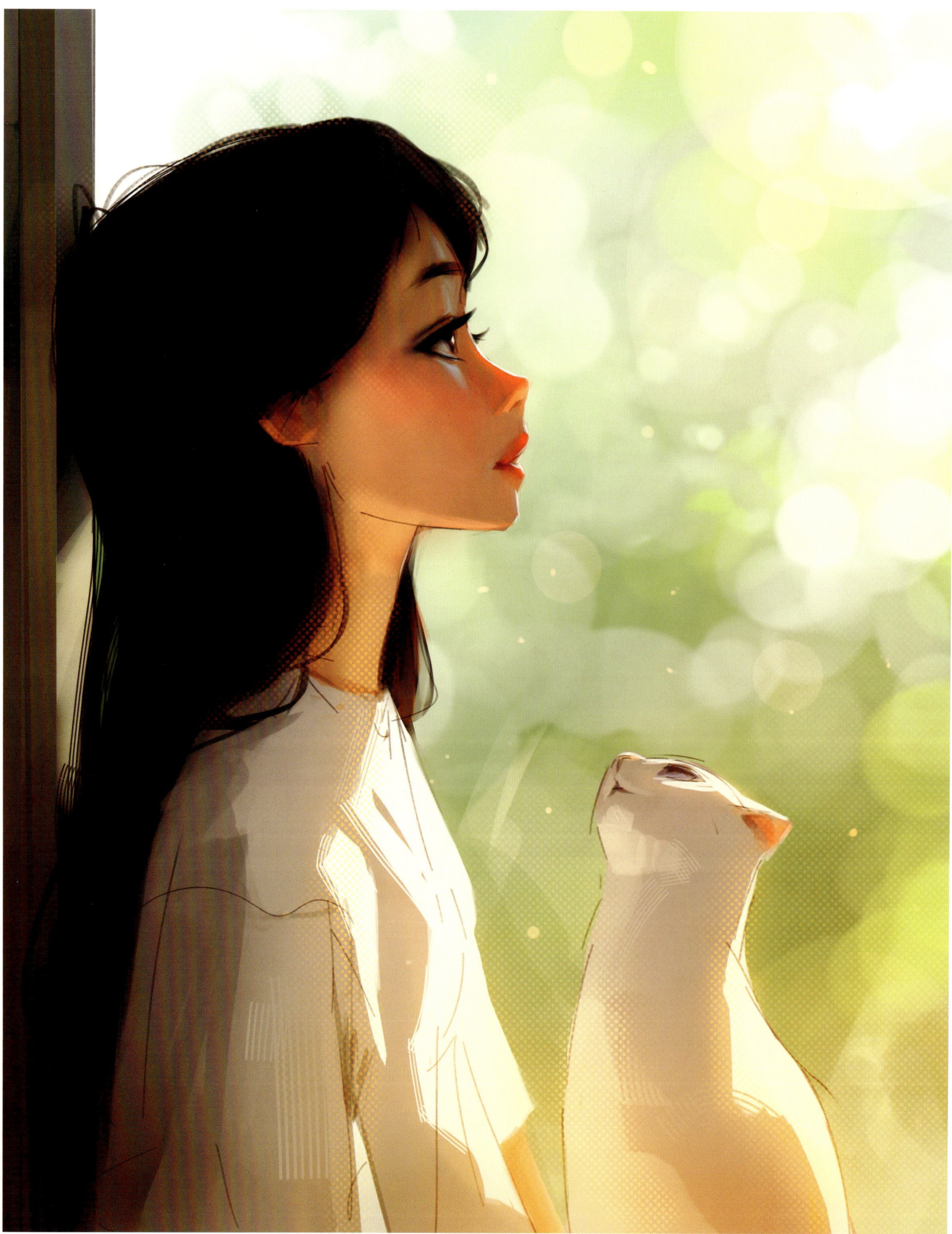

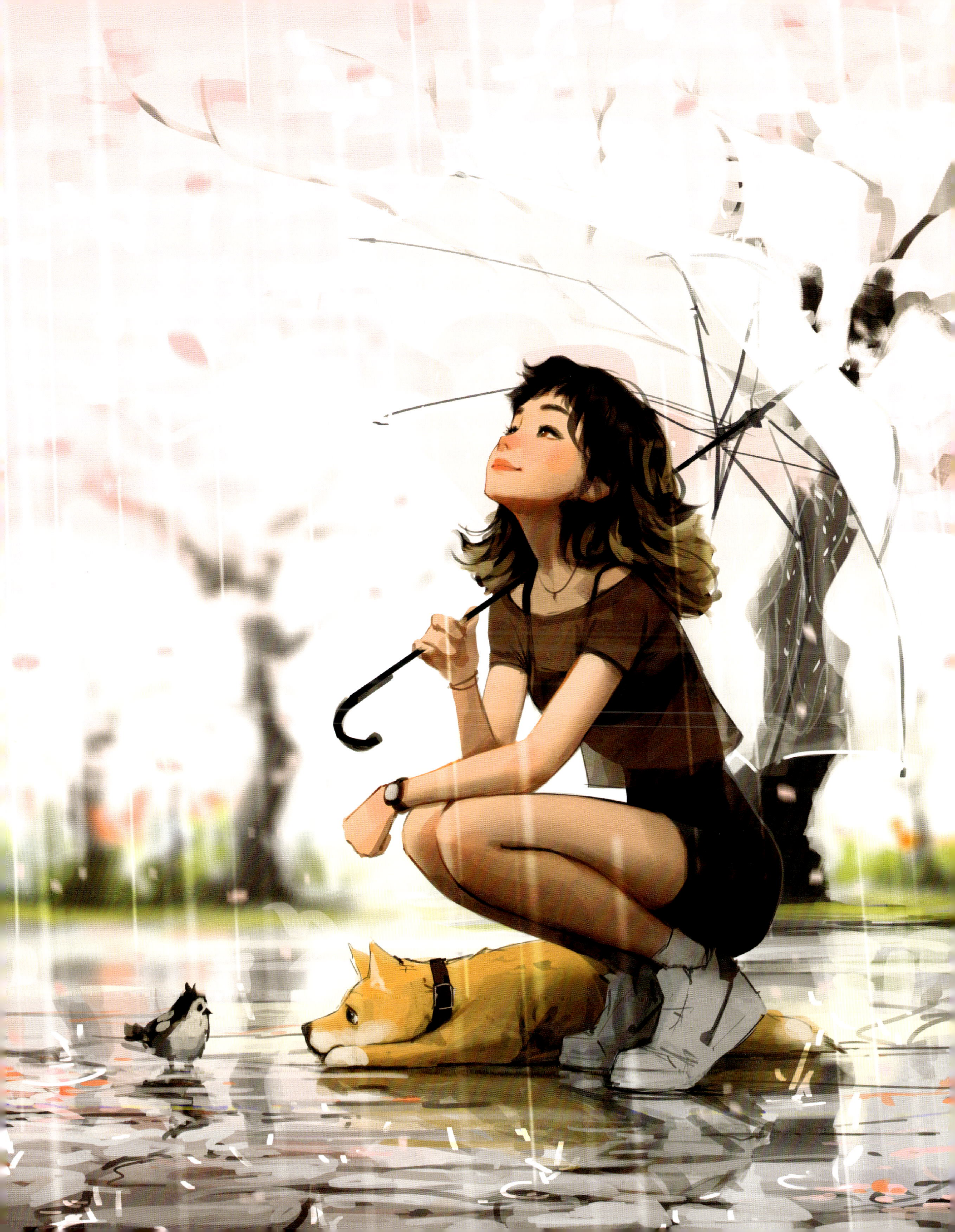

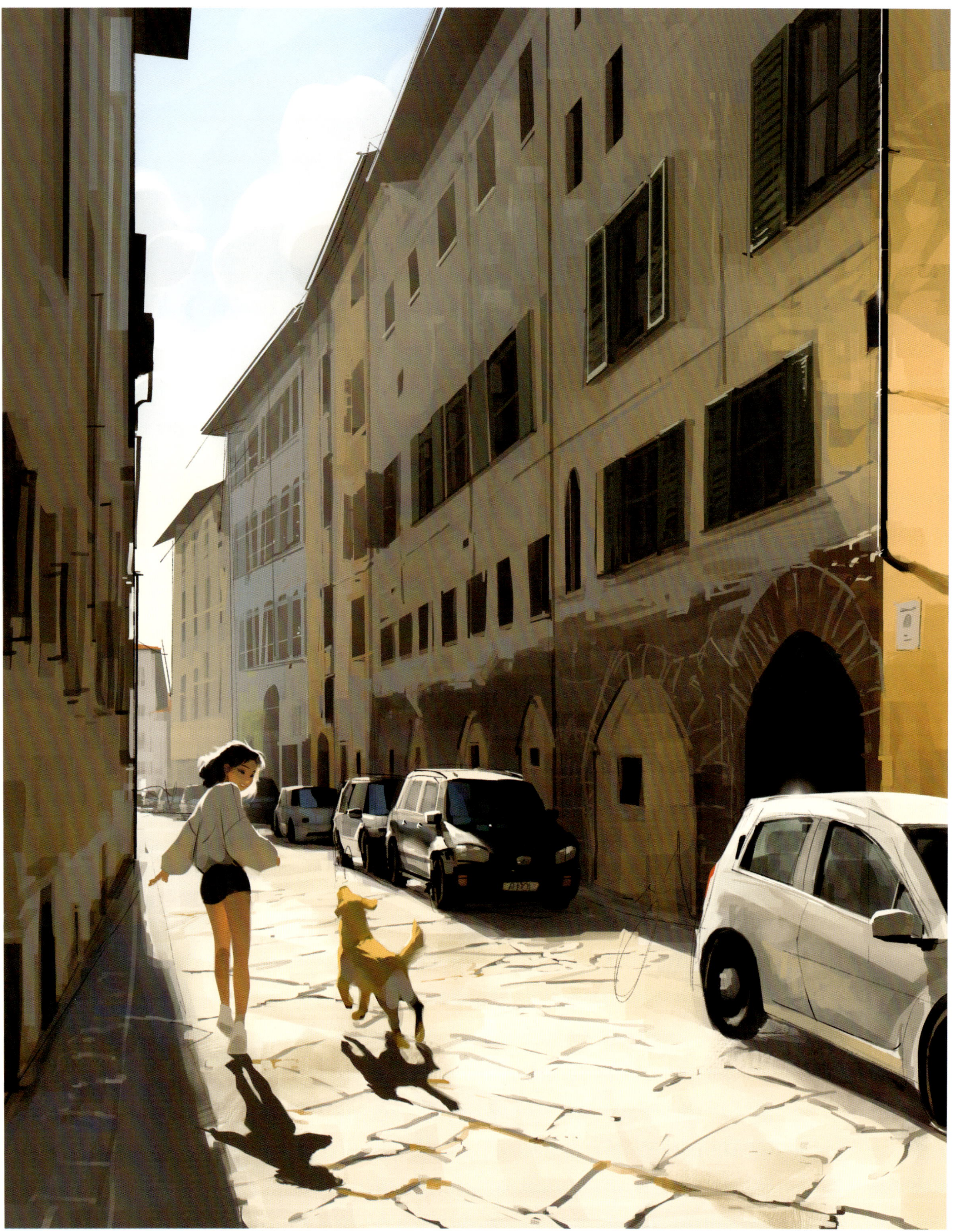

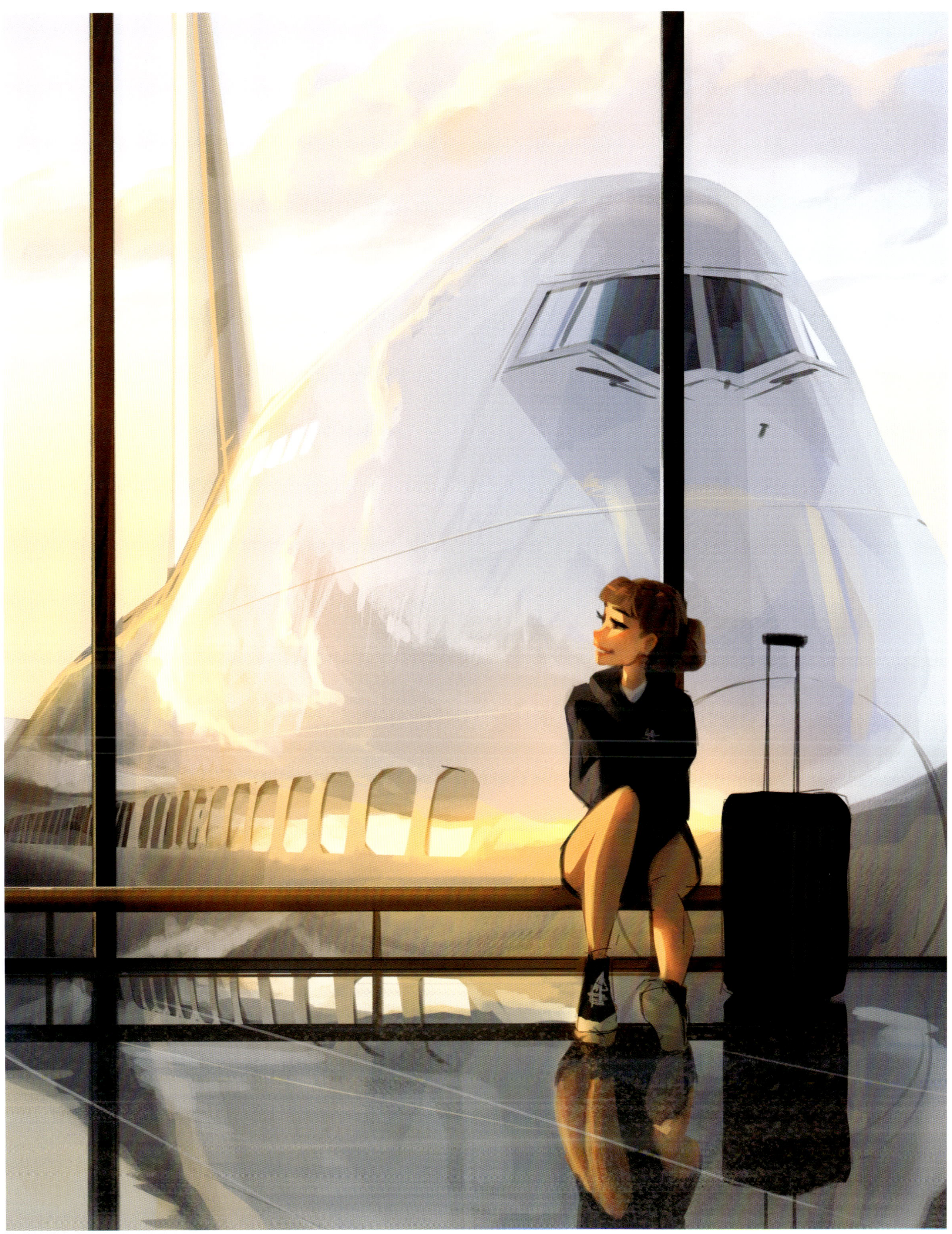

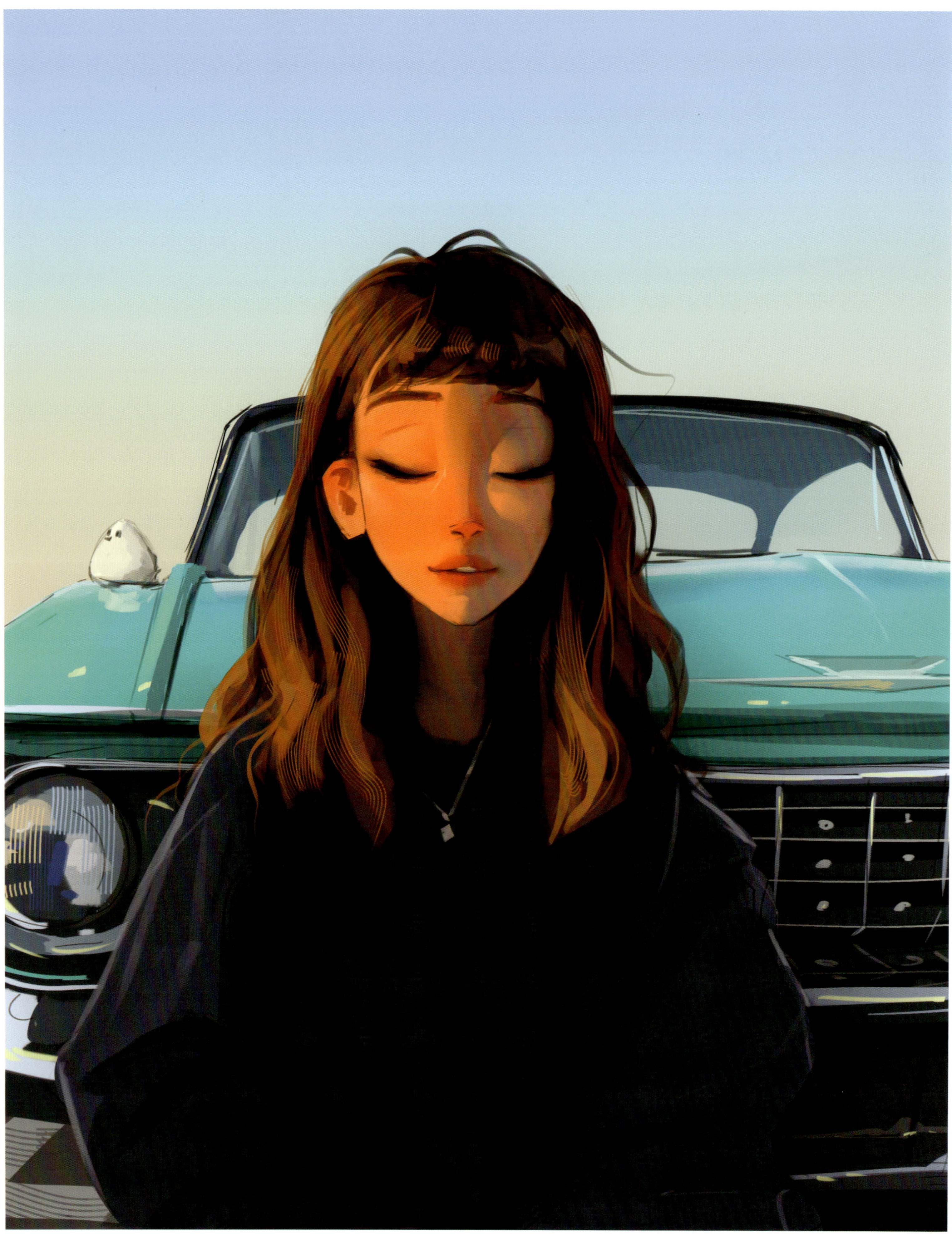

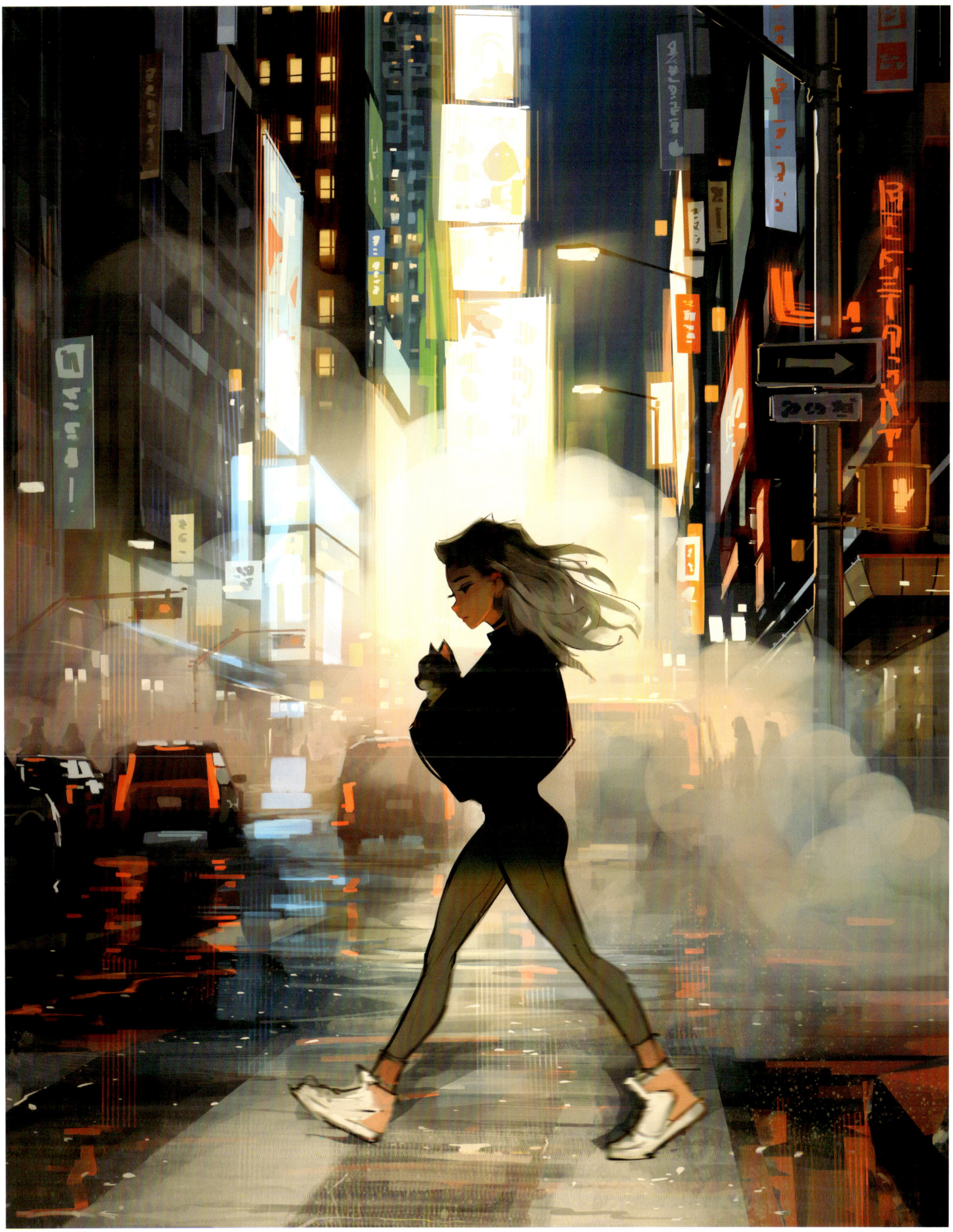

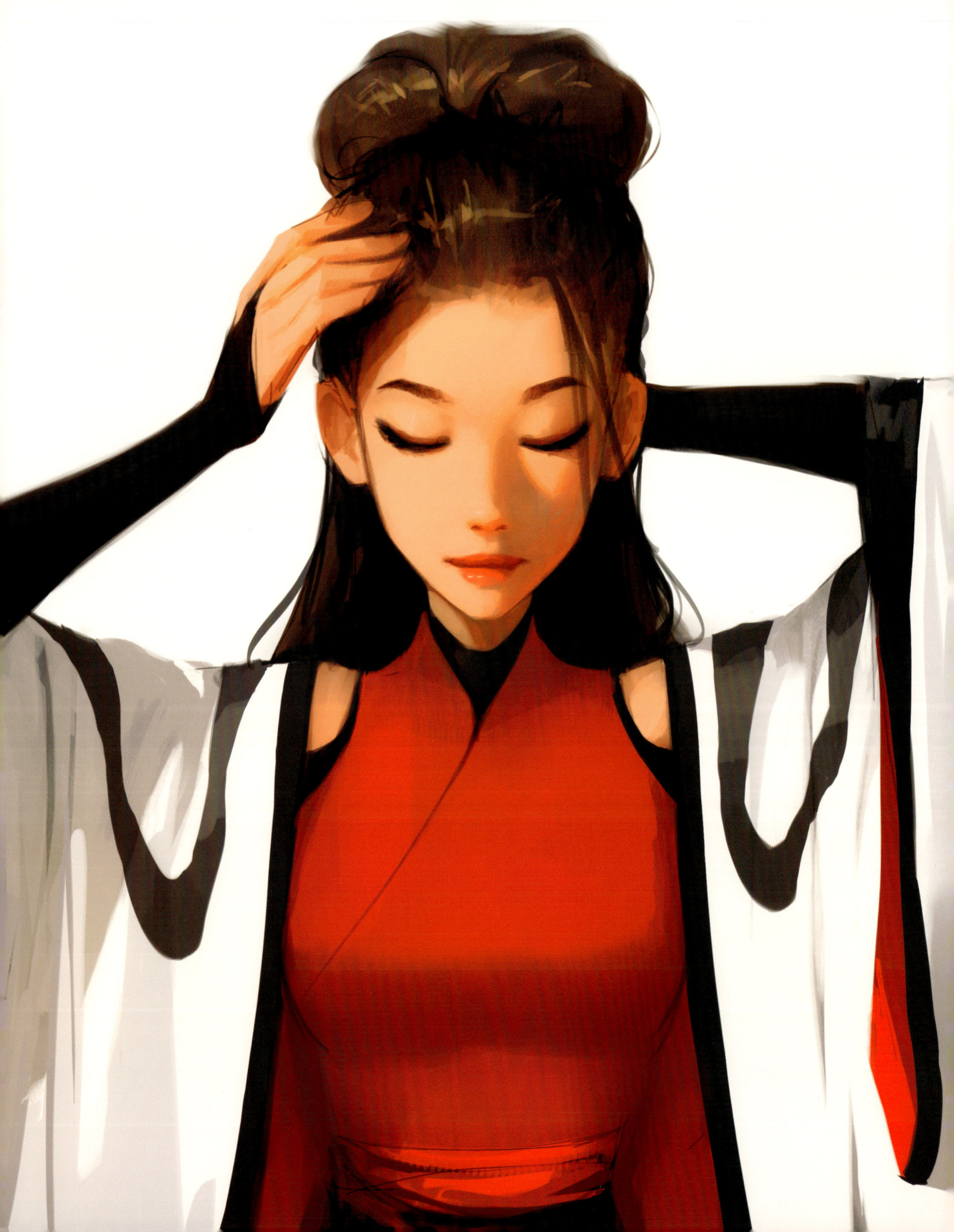

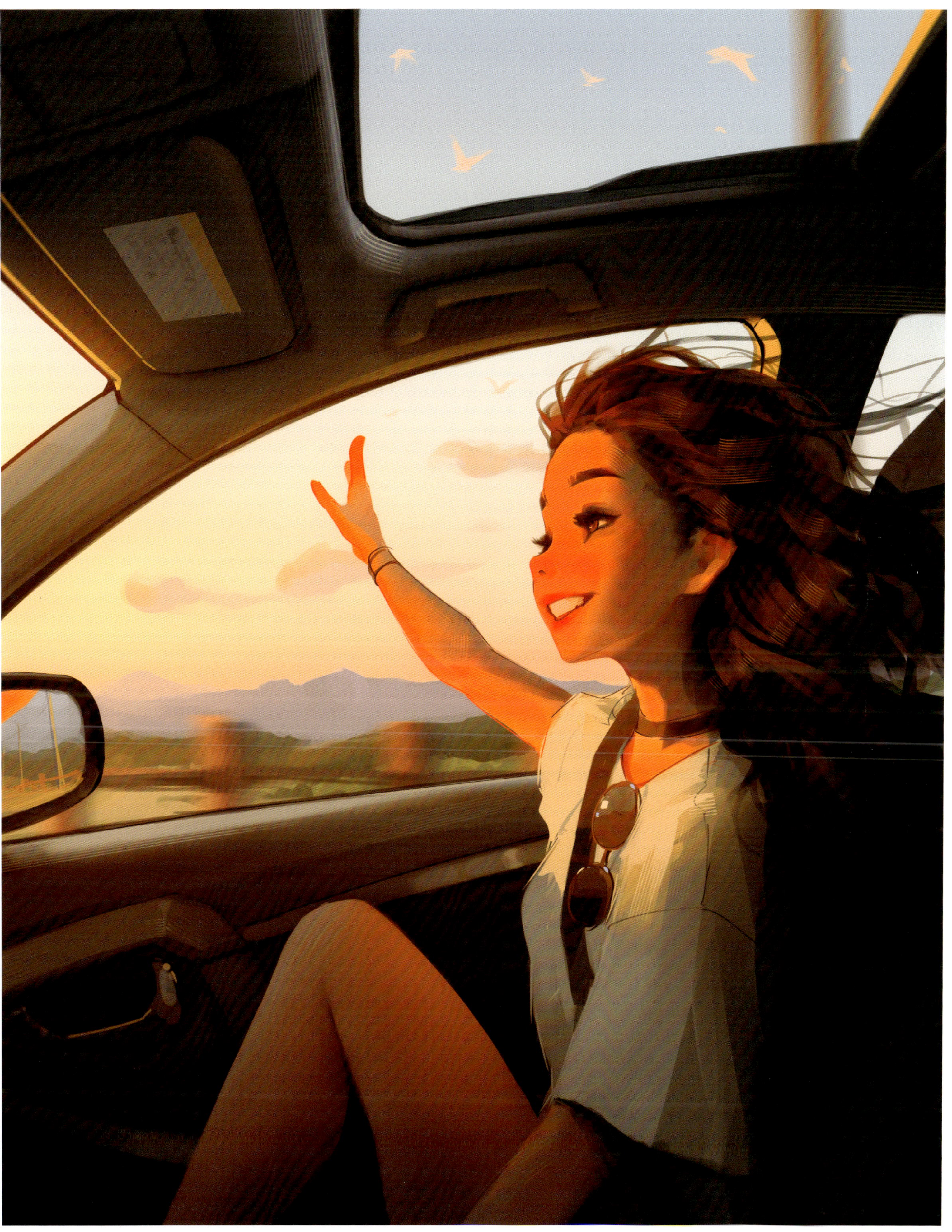

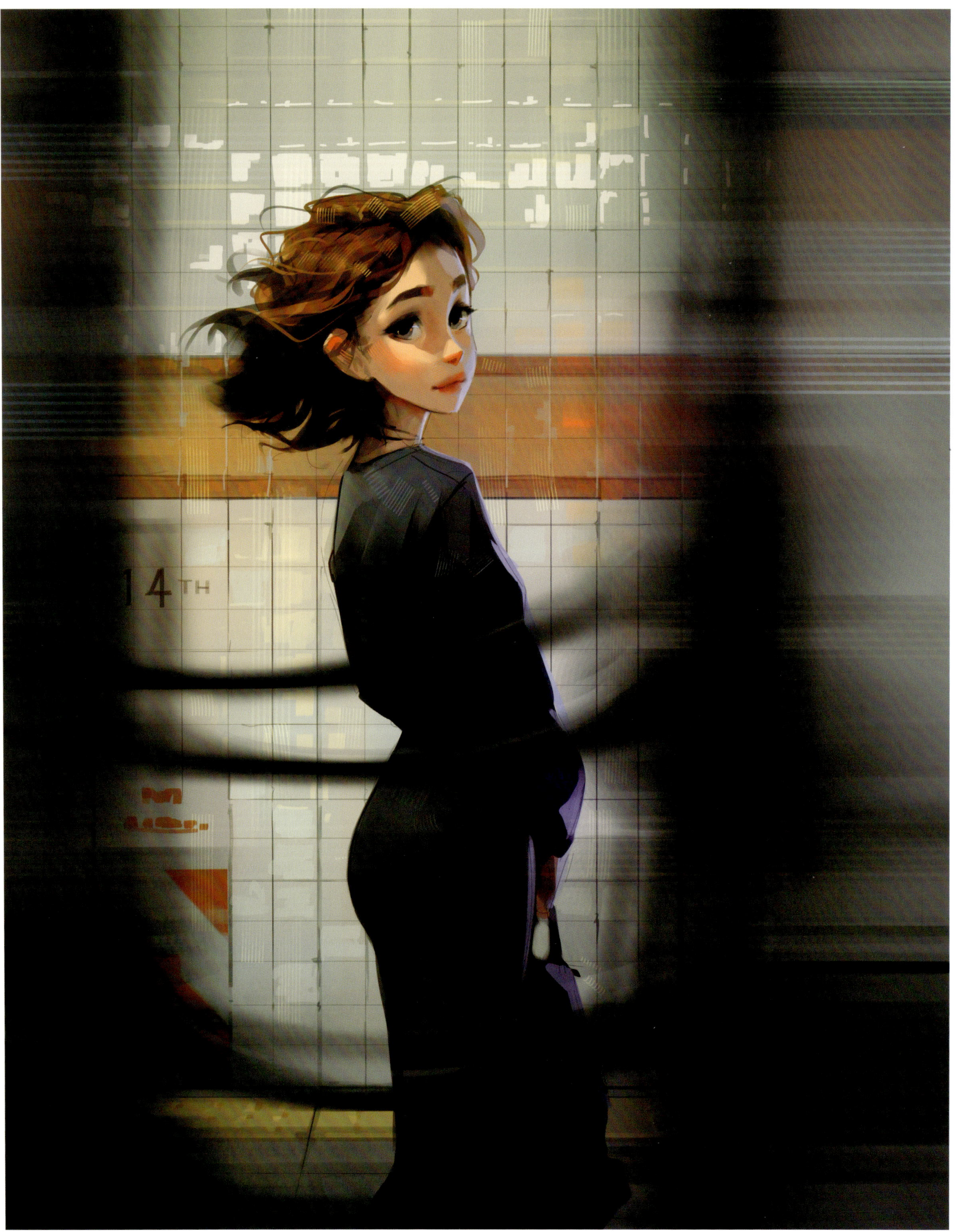
14TH

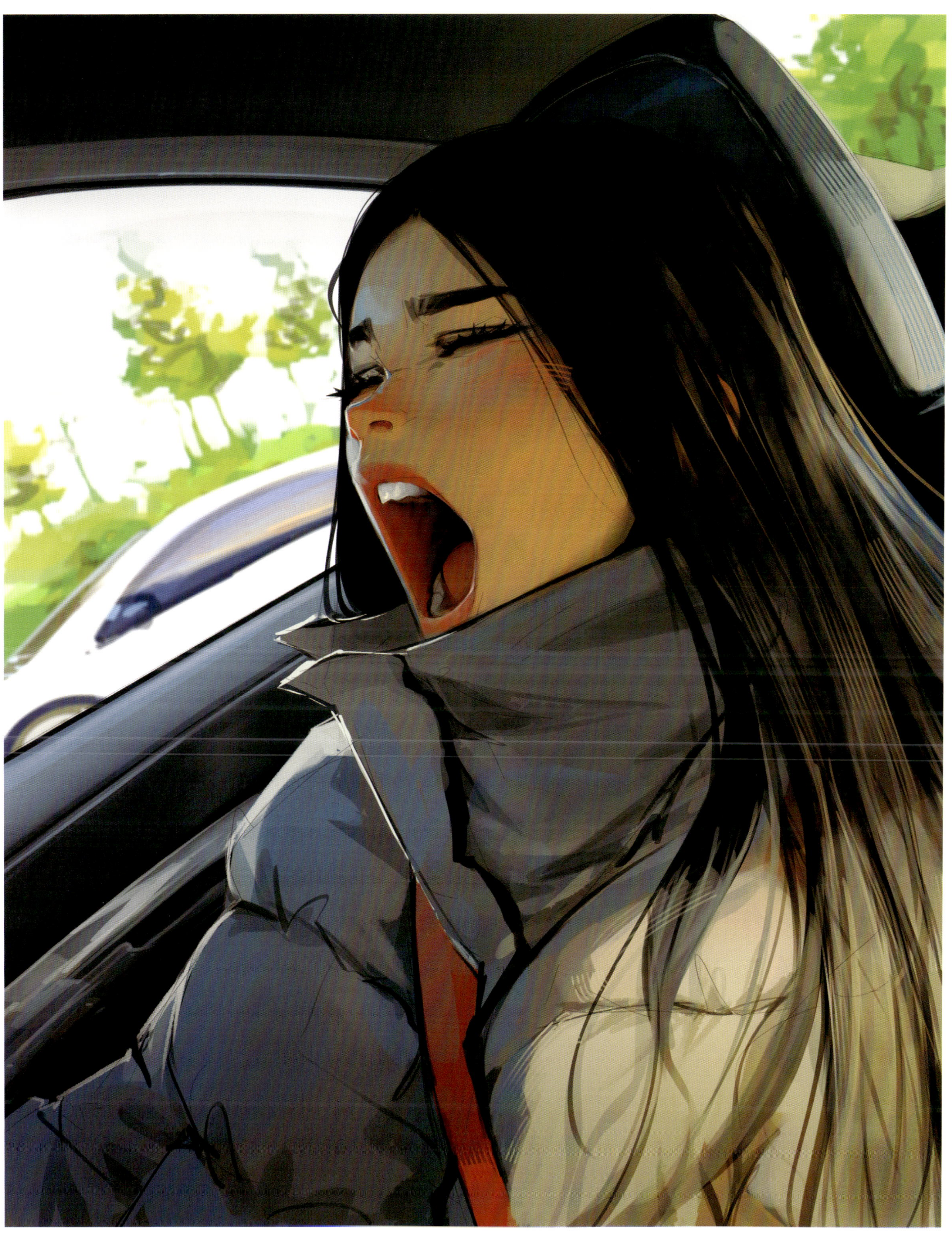

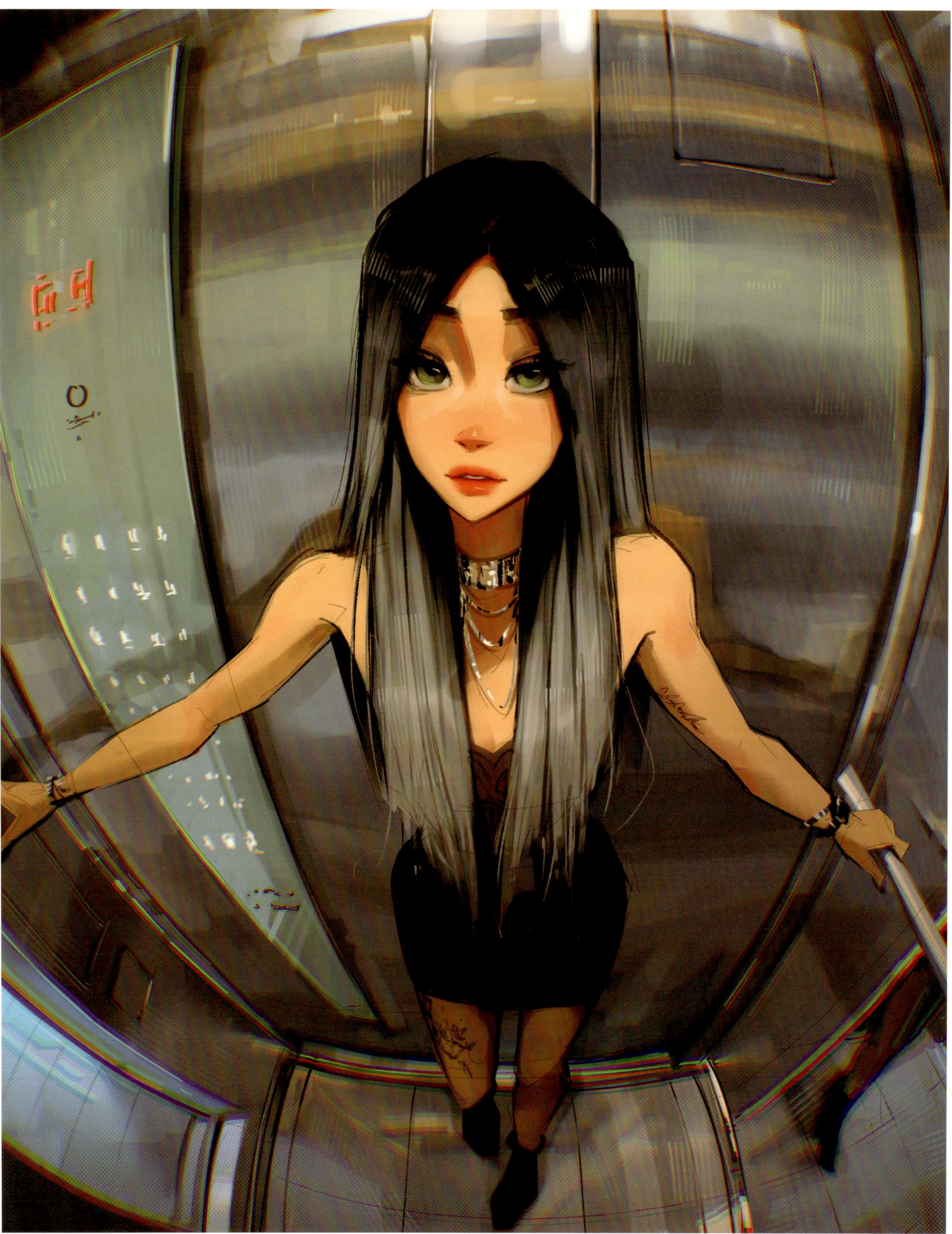

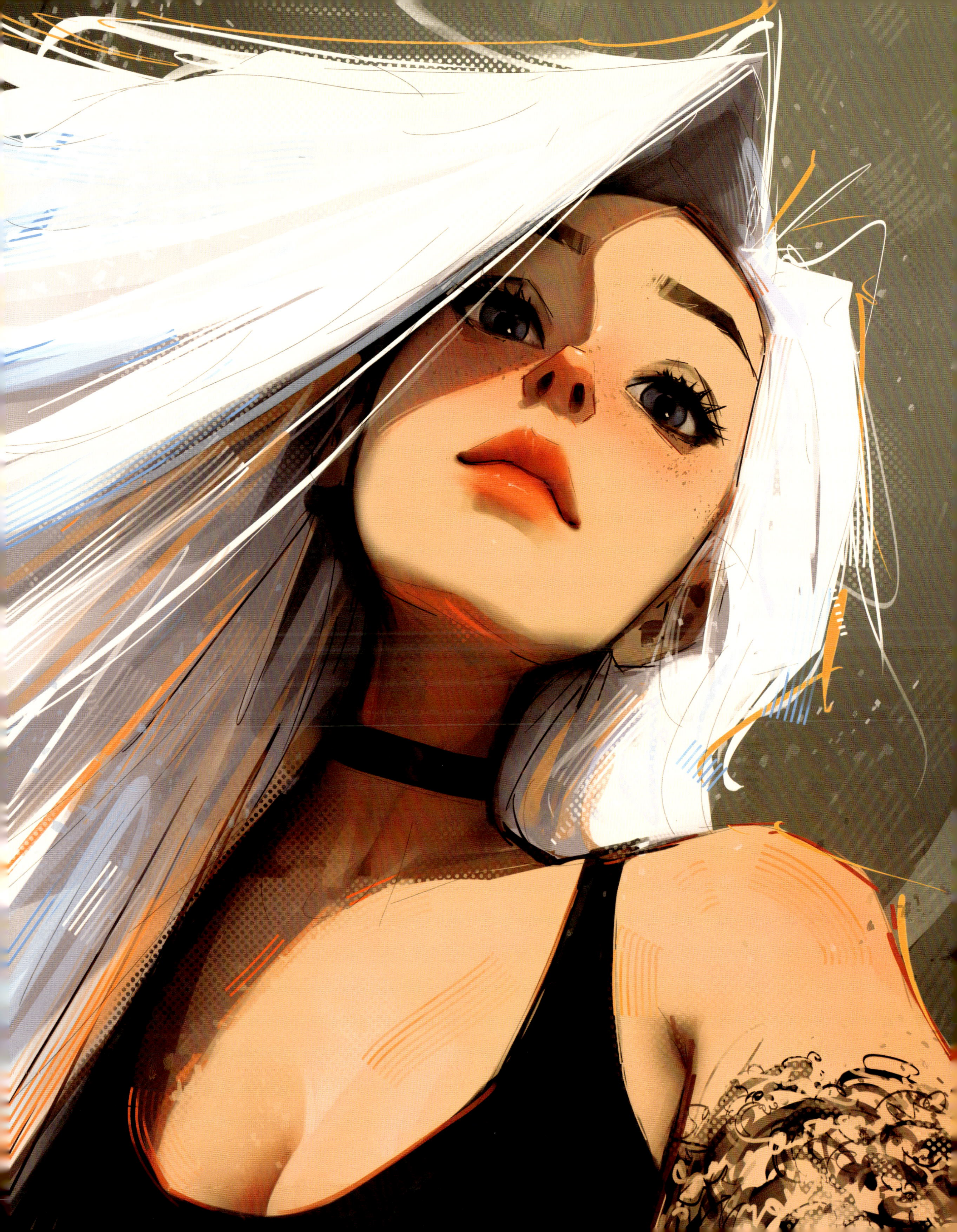

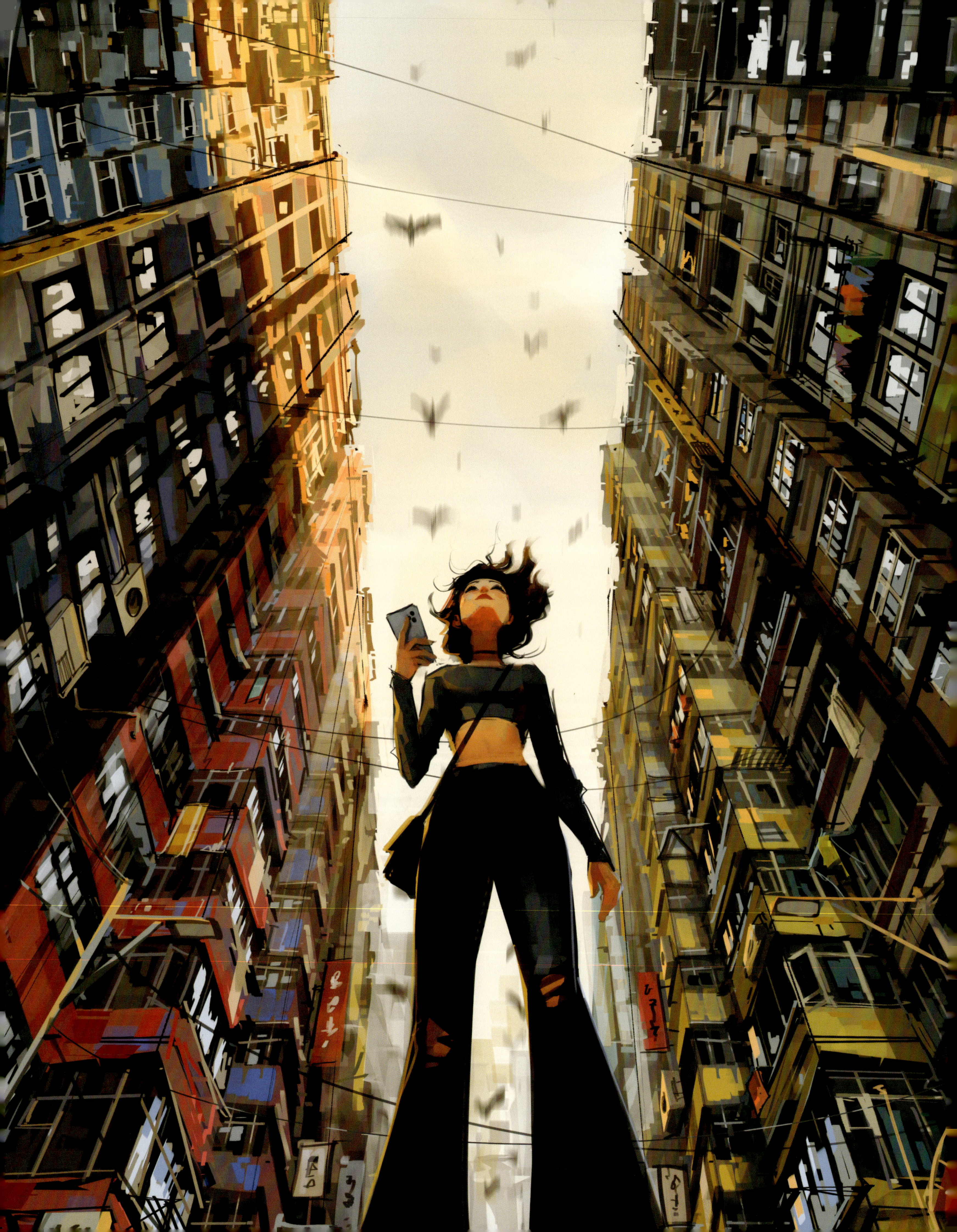

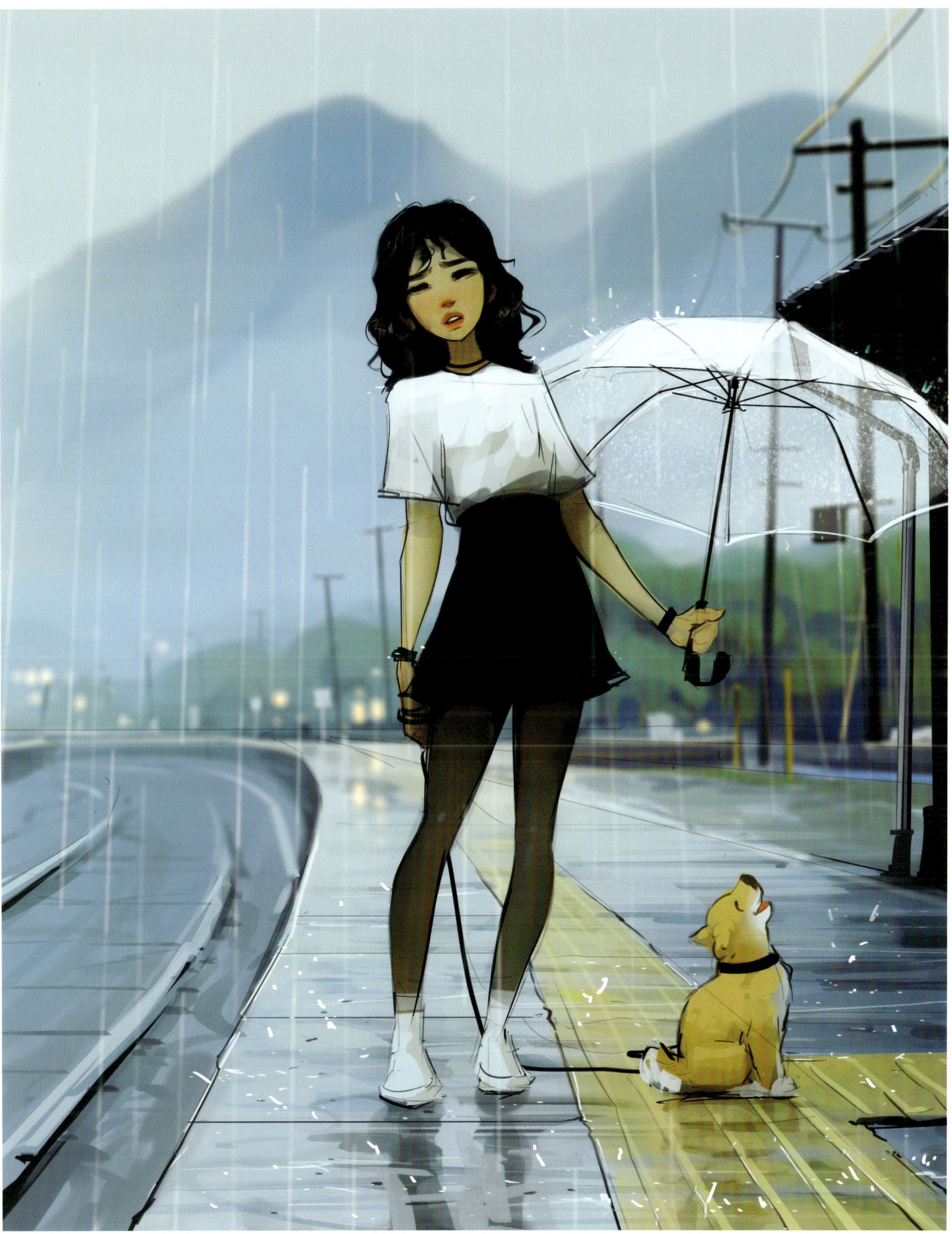

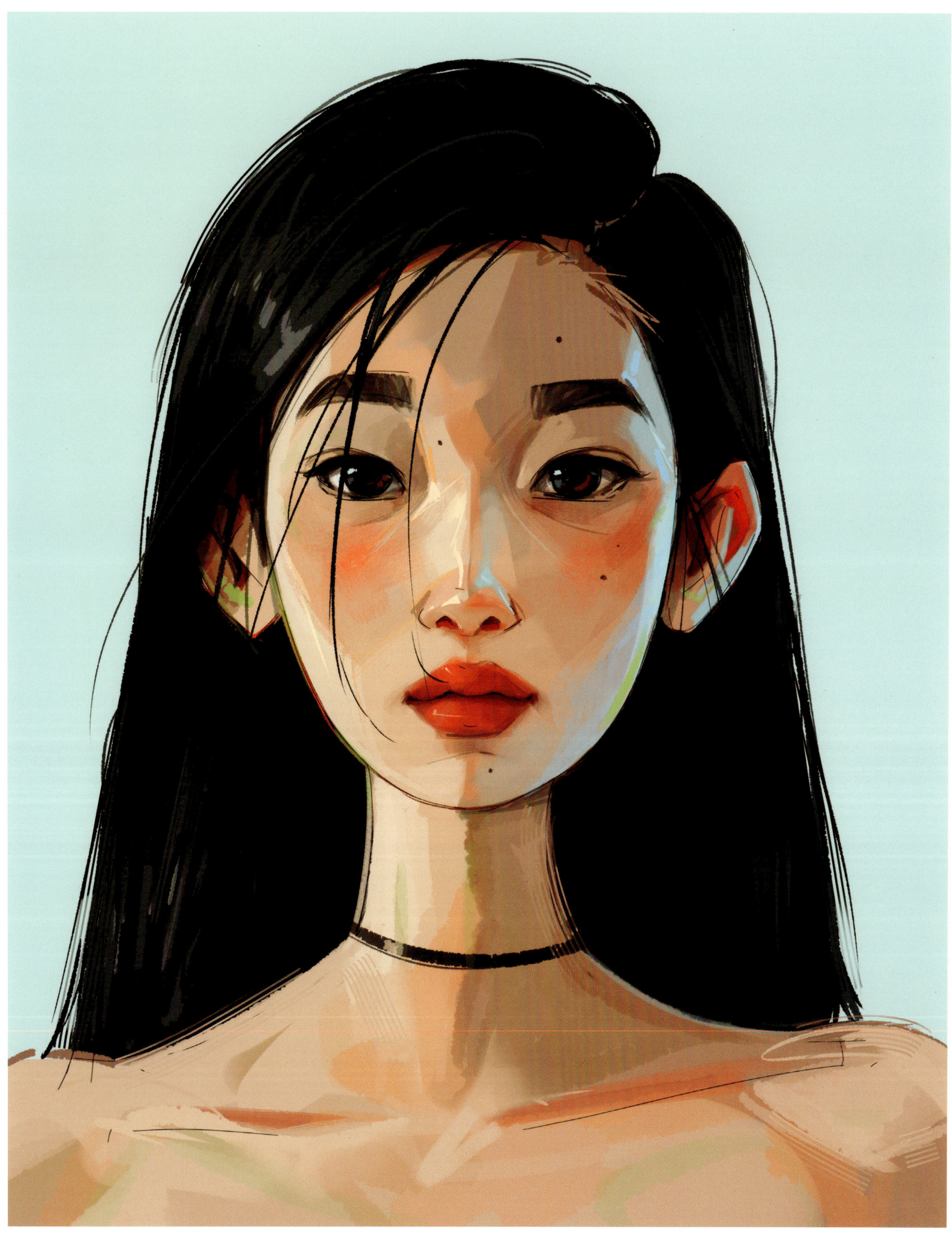

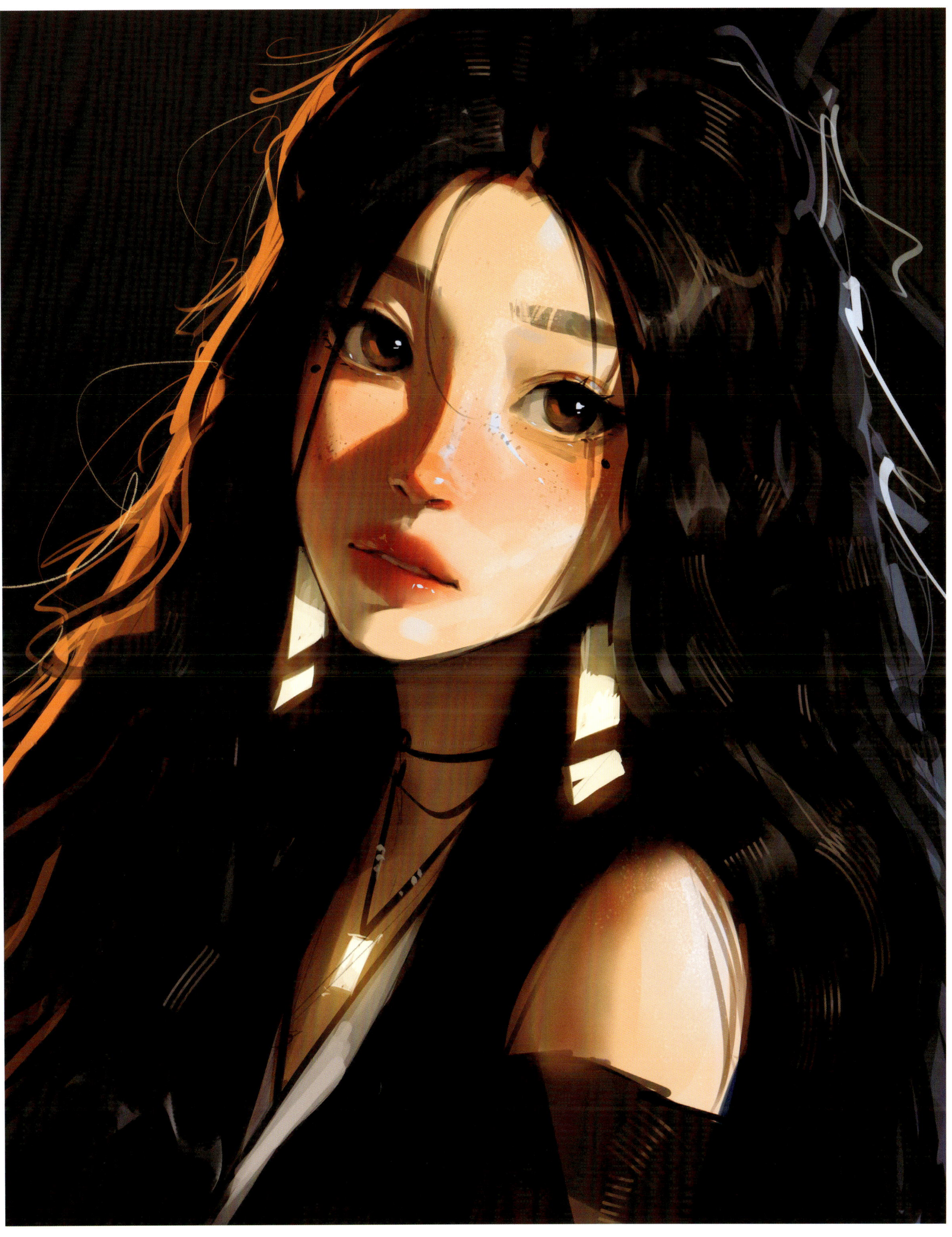

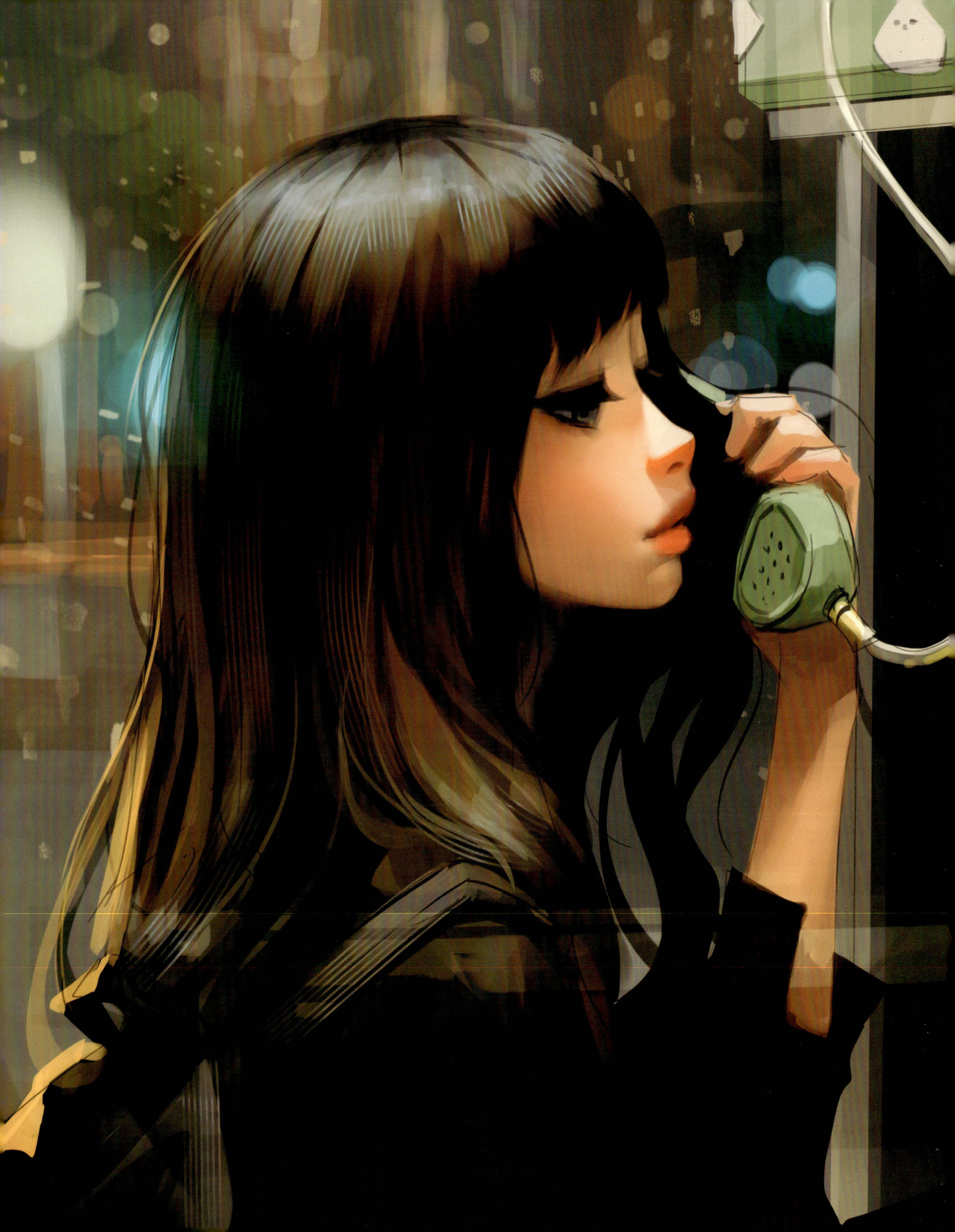

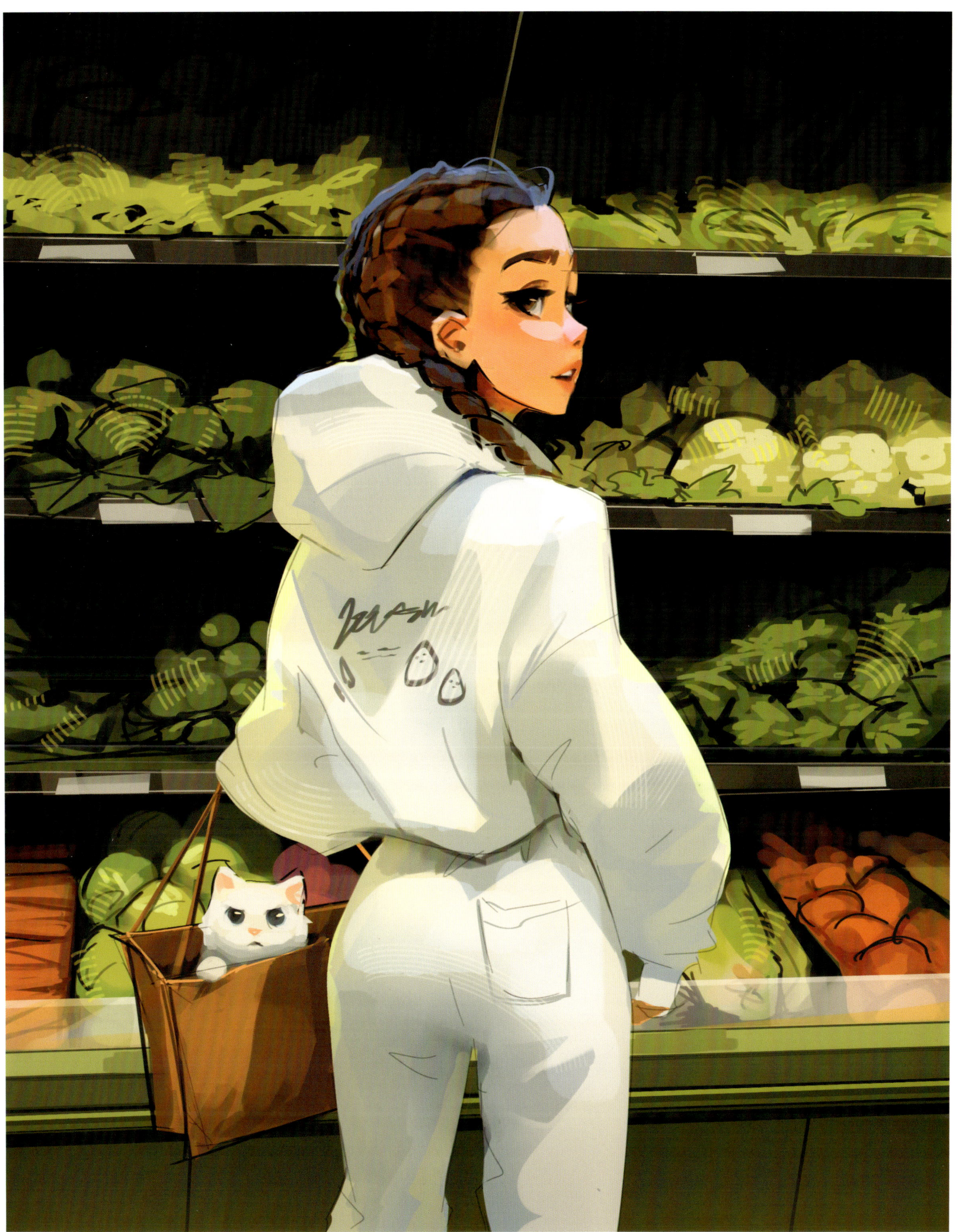

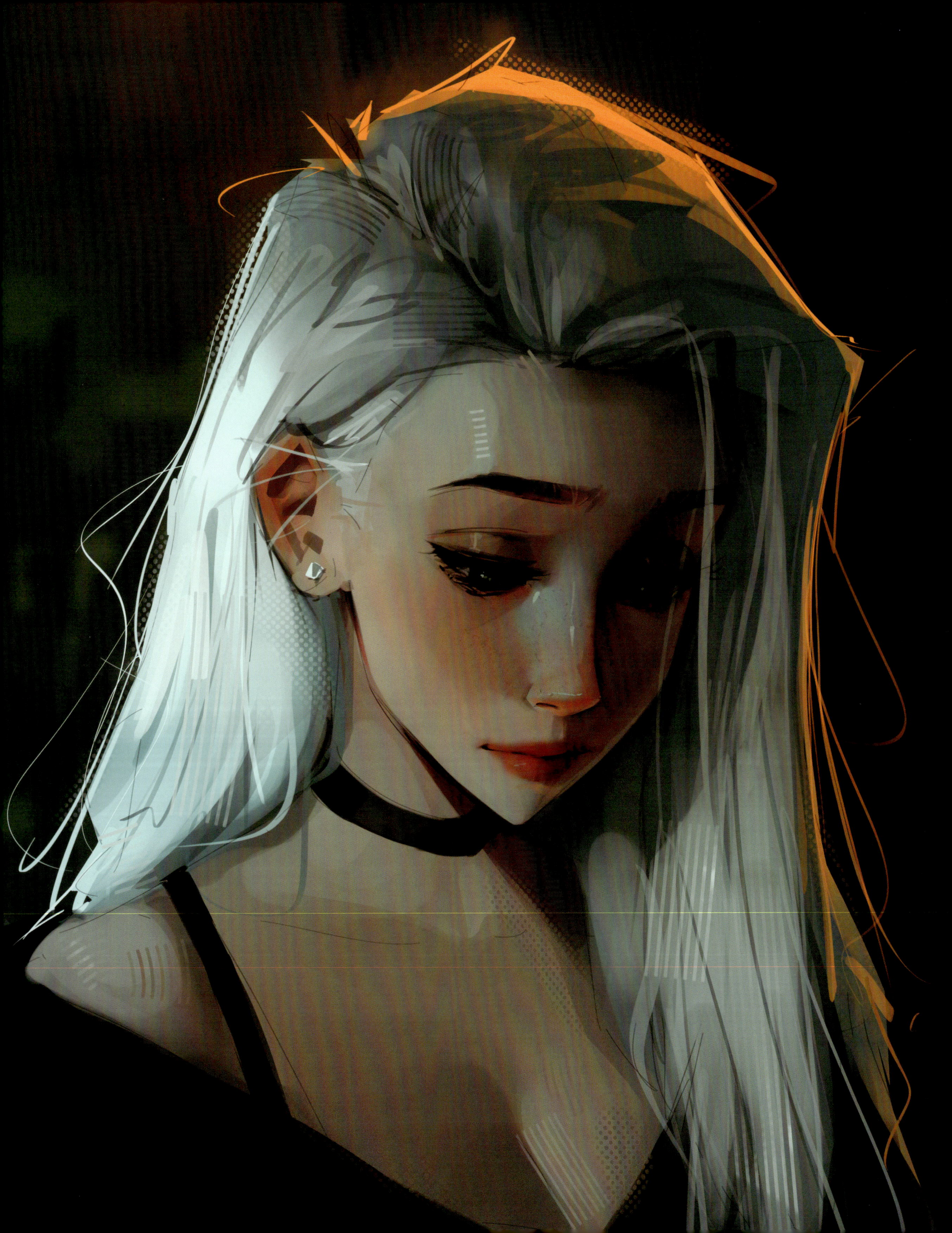

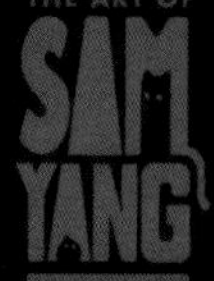

targeted practice

Method & mindset

I usually try to focus on one or two things per piece when it comes to practice. For example, if I feel inspired by the lighting in a reference image, I will concentrate on capturing it and worry less about things such as a character's costume design, shape, or stylization. This is not to say that I entirely forget about other aspects that make up a good painting, but it's a way to direct more energy towards one in particular. In doing so, I find that I'm able to absorb more information about the main subject of study that inspired me in the first place – in this case, lighting.

Sunset Study, August 2022. I placed the focal point on capturing the warmth of the setting sun. The rich orange colours, as seen on the skin of the character and the warm wash on the green grass, conveys the atmosphere of the scene

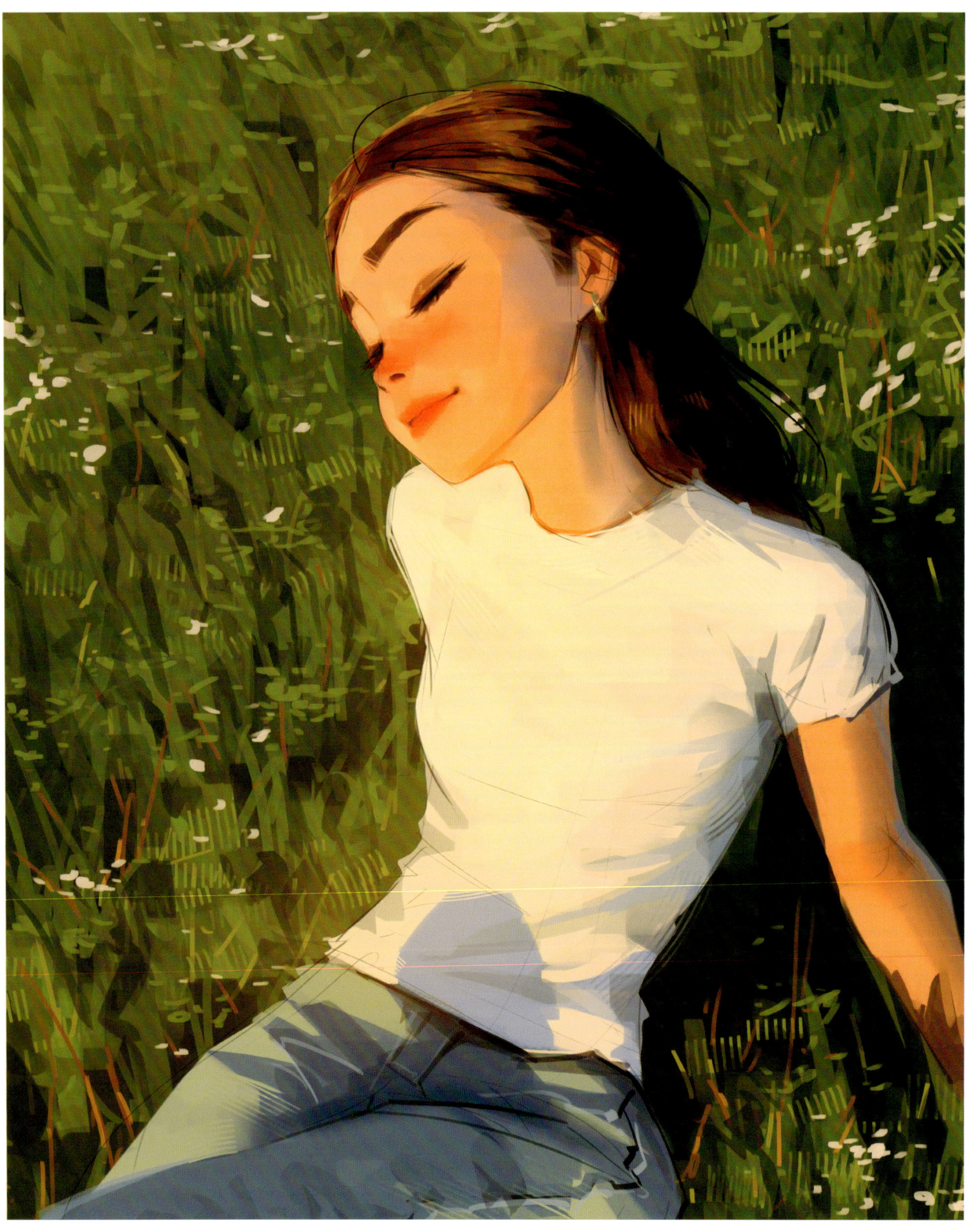

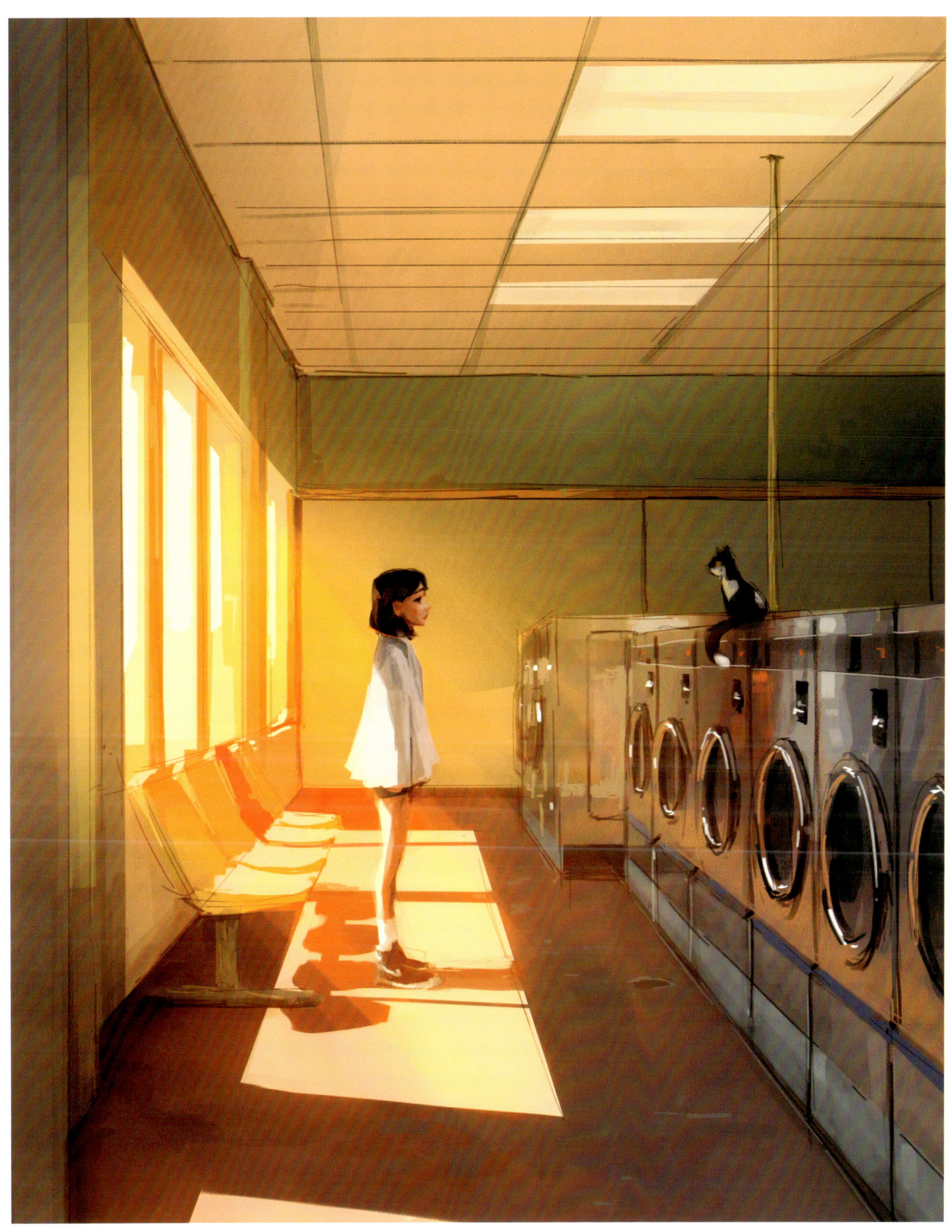

Washers, October 2020.
I focused mostly on capturing the warm light flooding through the windows. I find it fascinating how lighting affects the mood in a painting

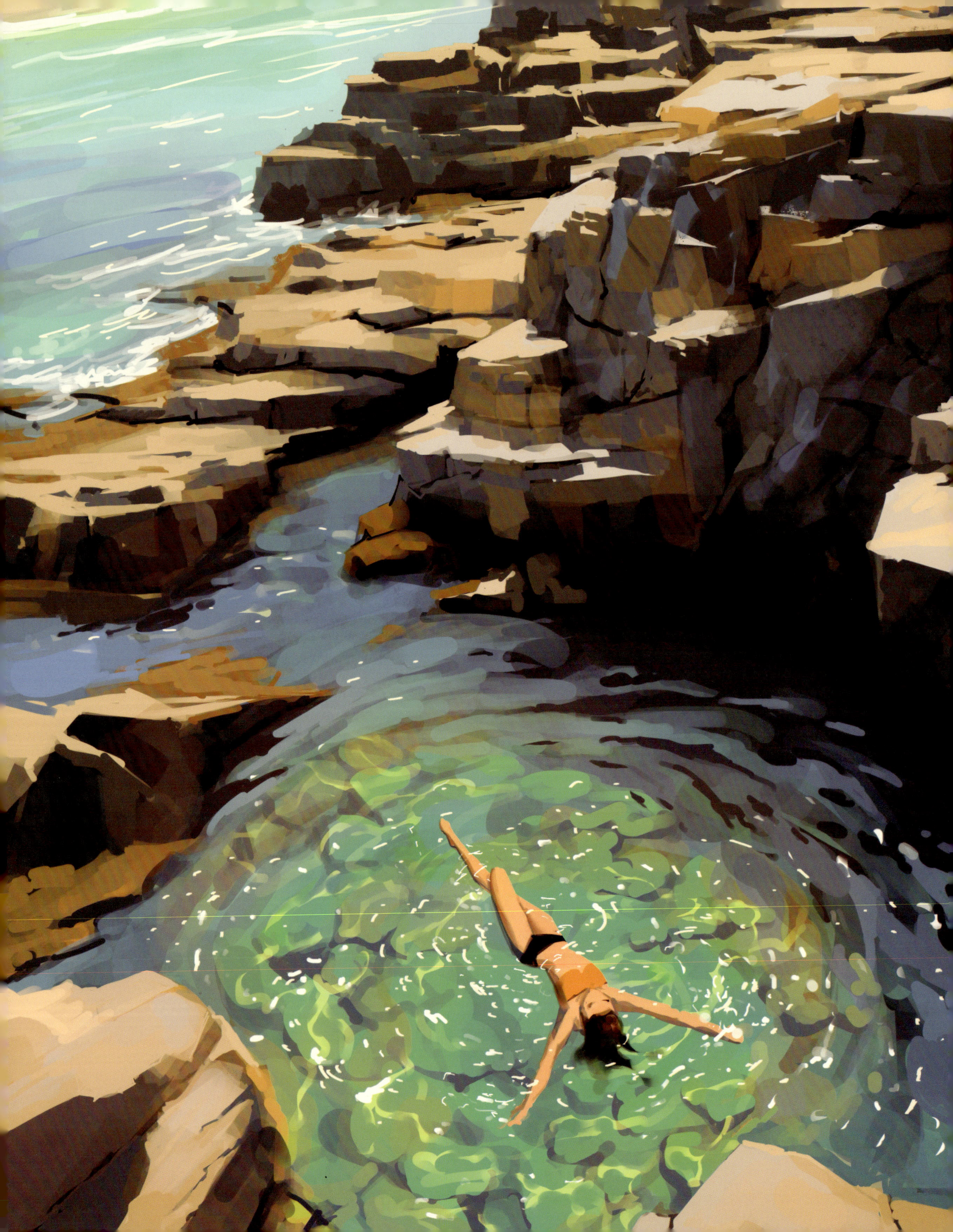

Left | *Reflections*, January 2021.

This piece was a study in which I focused on the colours and reflections of clear water on a sunny day. One of my favourite parts is the blend of teal, yellow, green, and orange as the water transitions from light to shadow

Below | *Water*, August, 2021

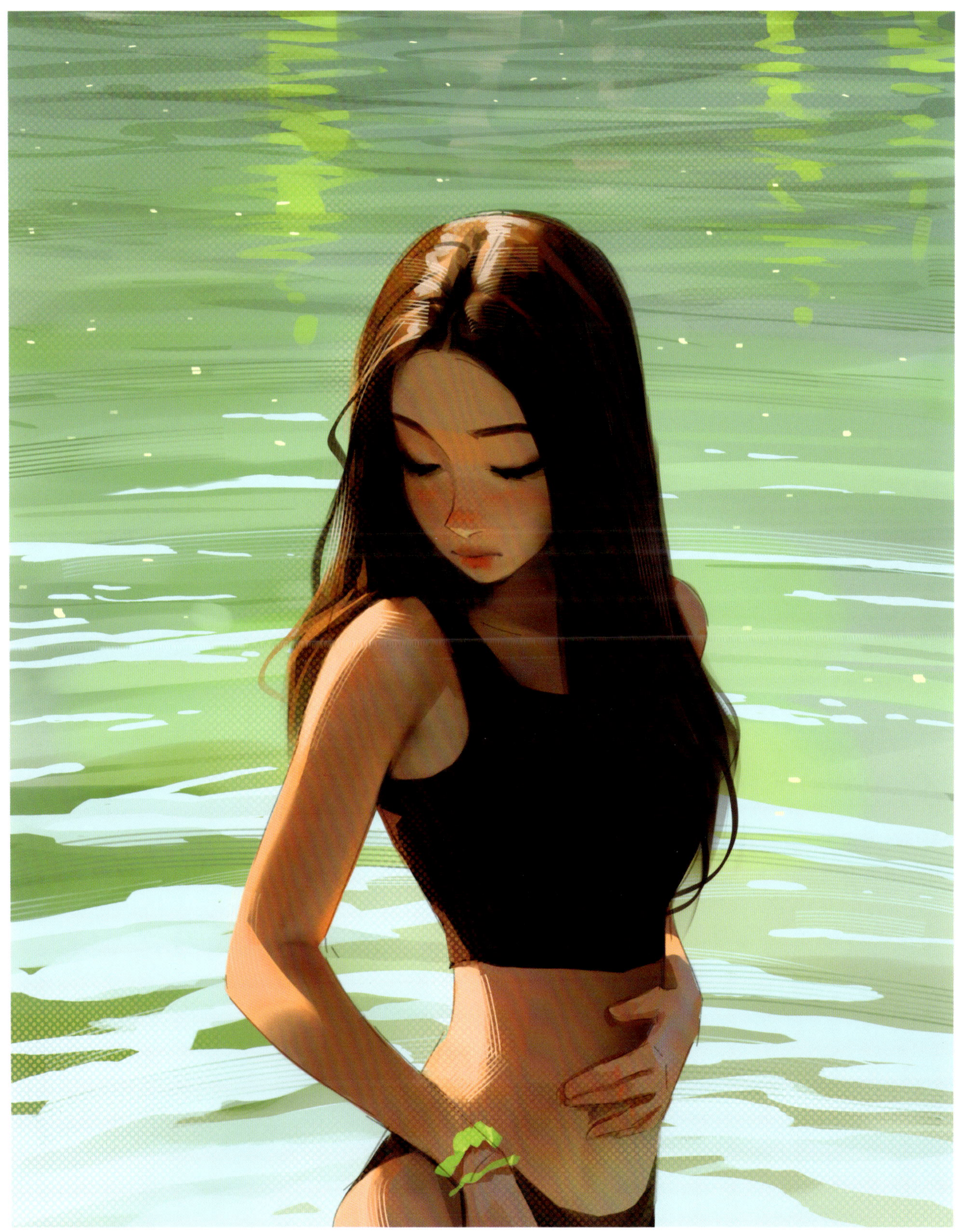

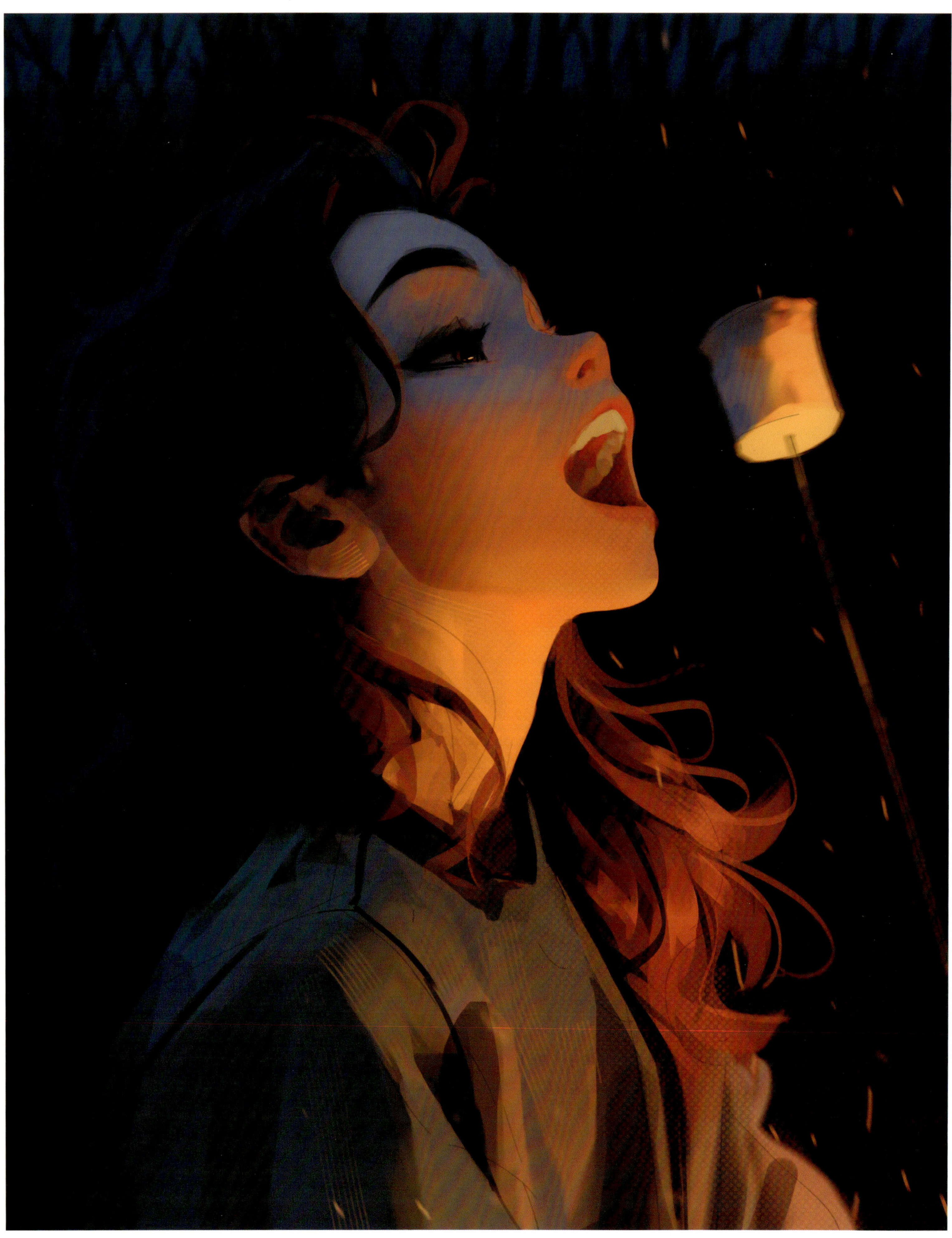

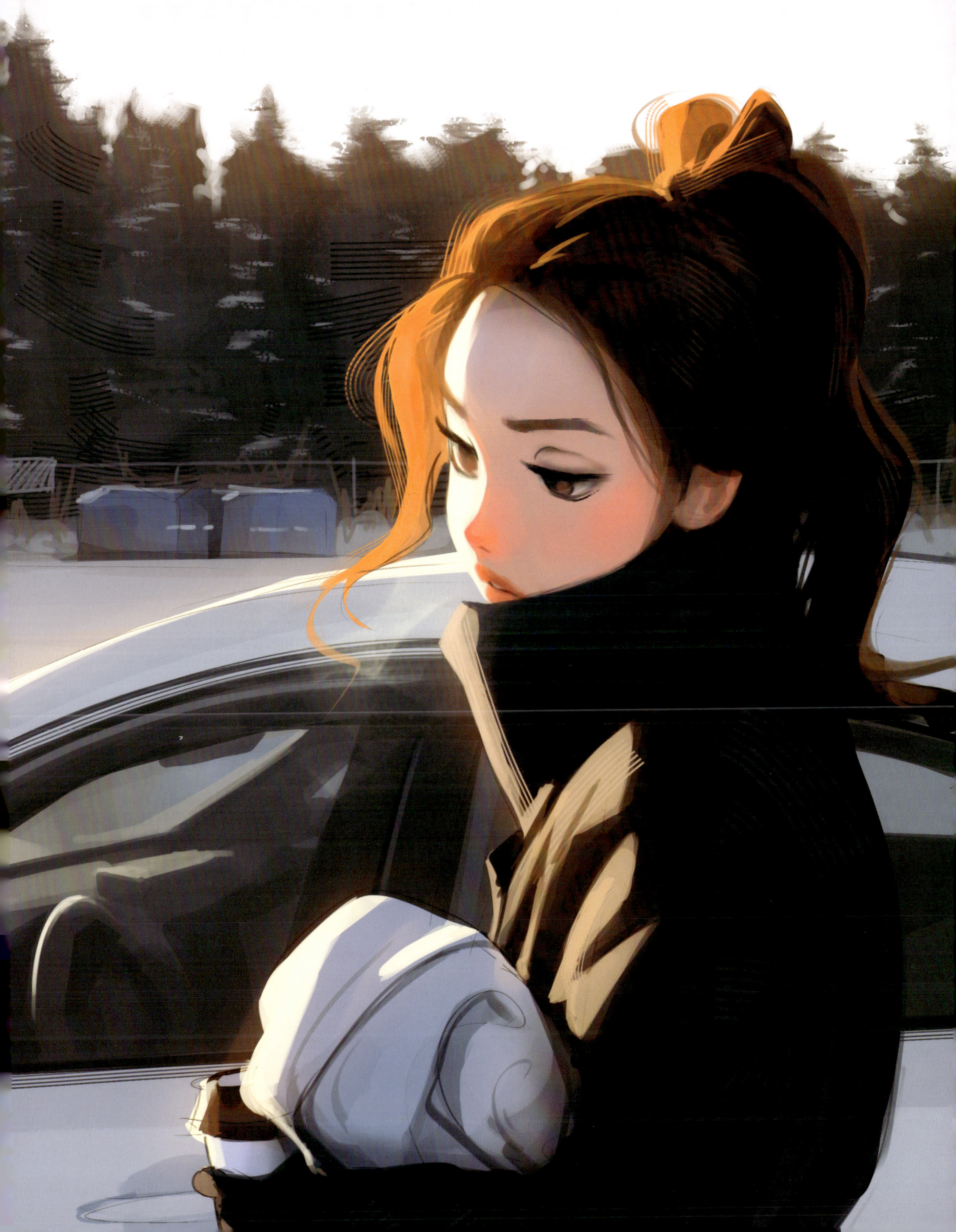

Focusing on one art aspect at a time can be done in a variety of ways. Sometimes, I find beautiful dynamic poses that inspire my study. In this case, the pose itself is the focal point, so things like colour, lighting, and even the appearance of the character performing the pose can be changed completely. I often do this with my original characters; I use them as a vessel to capture the essence of a dynamic pose.

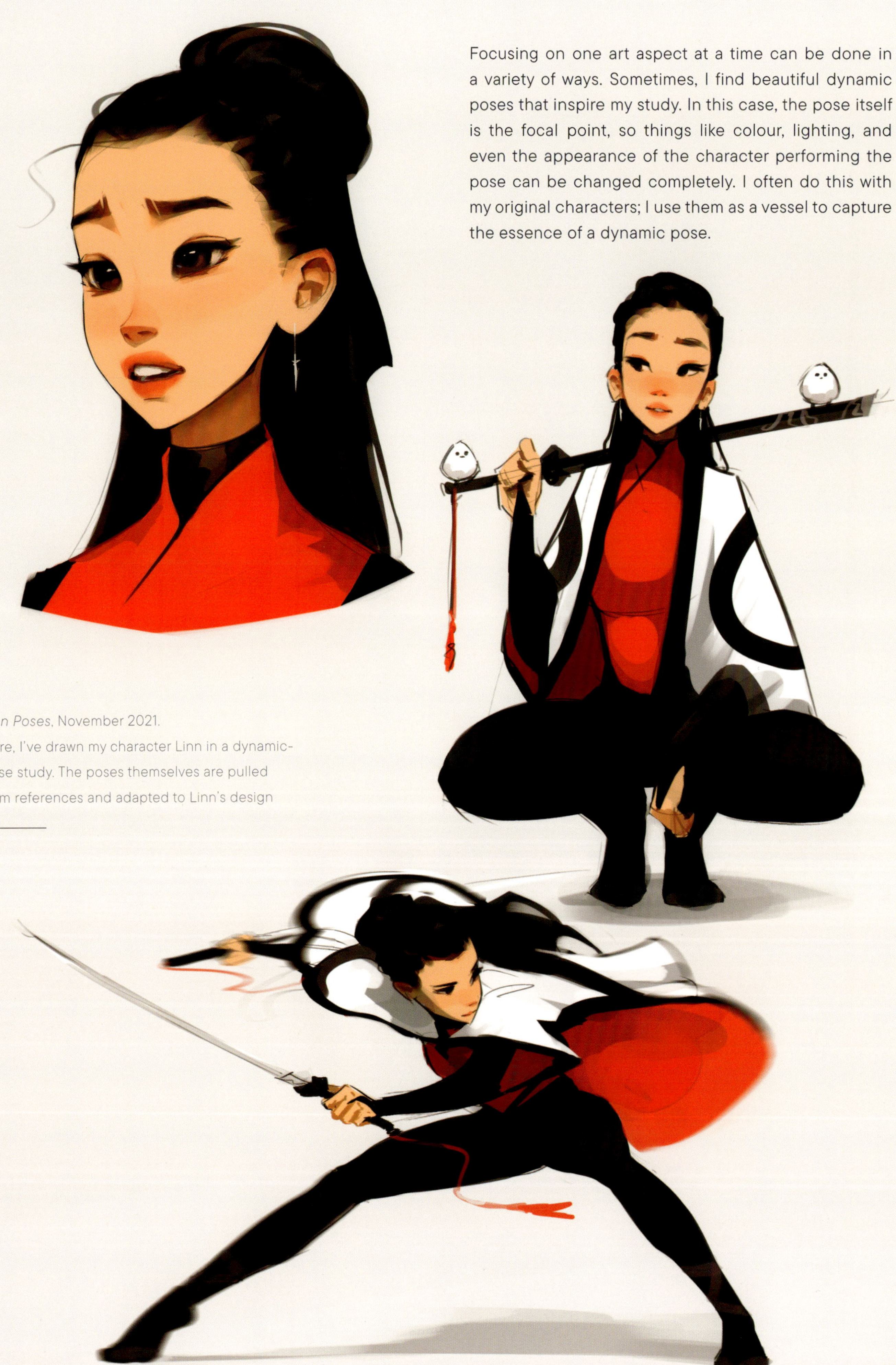

Linn Poses, November 2021.
Here, I've drawn my character Linn in a dynamic-pose study. The poses themselves are pulled from references and adapted to Linn's design

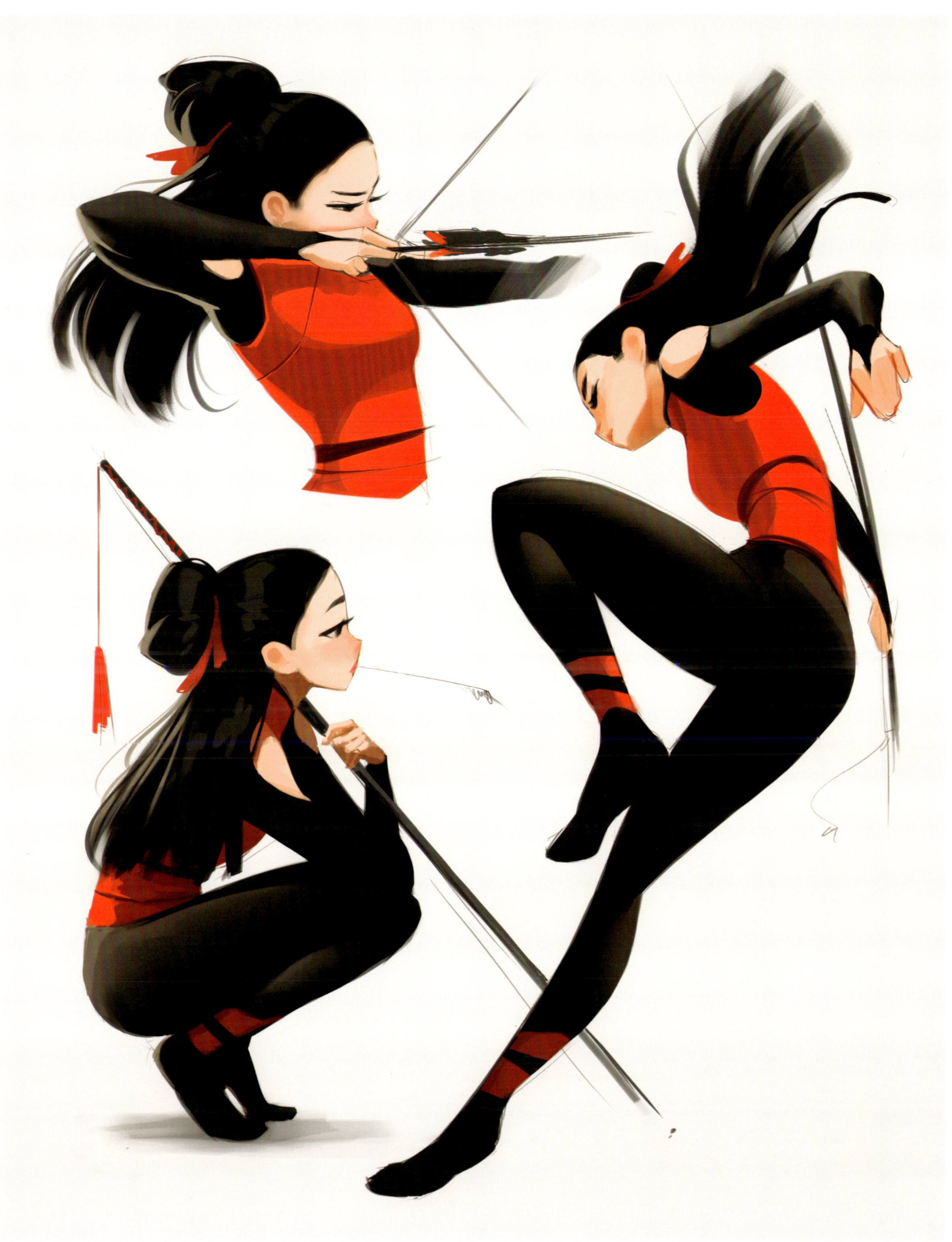

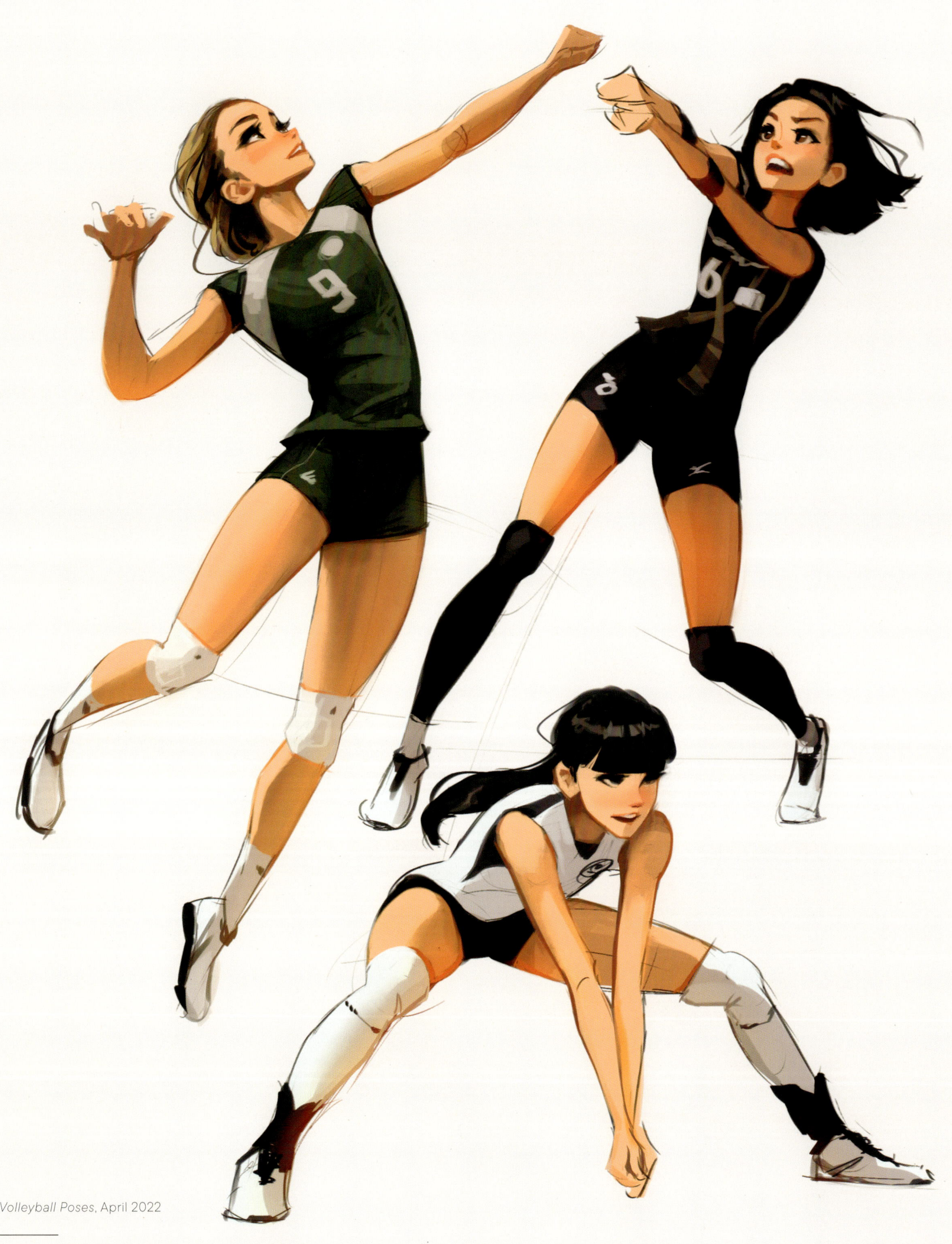

Volleyball Poses, April 2022

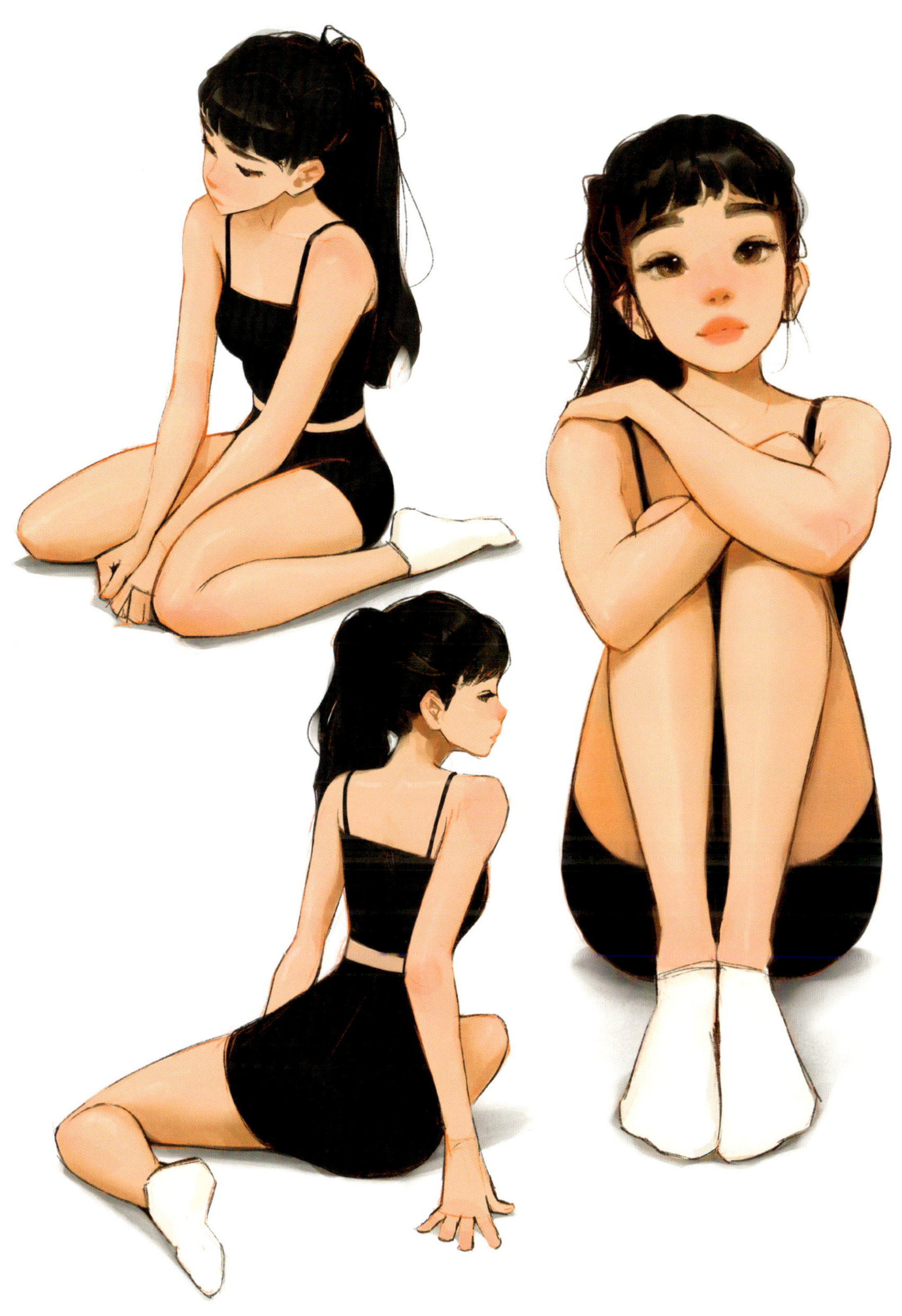

Poses, March 2021.

These pose studies are a great way to get a feel for what characters look like while performing different actions. It's important to not get lost in adding detail and rendering. Our main focus here is the gesture and energy of the action itself. Some poses can convey stillness, while others, such as the volleyball poses, have an explosive energy to them. As seen on pages 130–131 with Linn, pose sheets can also provide much-needed context for your characters, and they're frequently used by animators to showcase a character in action

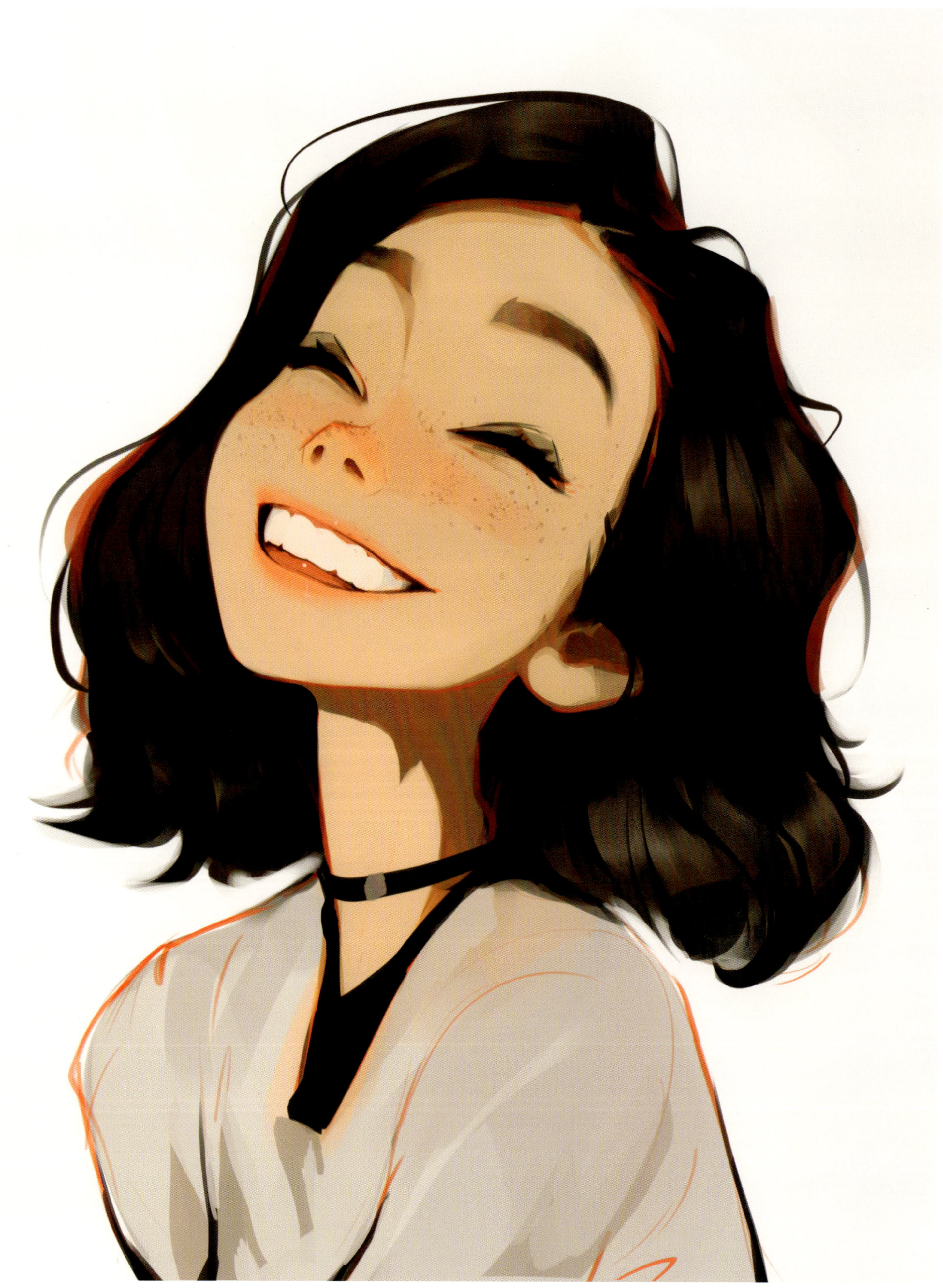

The same could be done with facial expressions as well. If you know that an uptick in the corner of the character's mouth and a raised lower eyelid create a friendly smile, you can easily apply that expression to any face you wish to draw. The ability to translate different expressions onto one of your own characters' faces is not only a useful study method – it's also essential in being able to tell a good story through your visual work.

When thinking longer term, focused practice on a single topic or group of topics could mean dedicating weeks or months to it. An artist has a seemingly impossible amount of information to absorb, so taking on too many things at once could easily become overwhelming.

For many of the pieces in this chapter, I focused on one or two things to learn from, absorbing little bits of knowledge each time and taking them with me to the next piece.

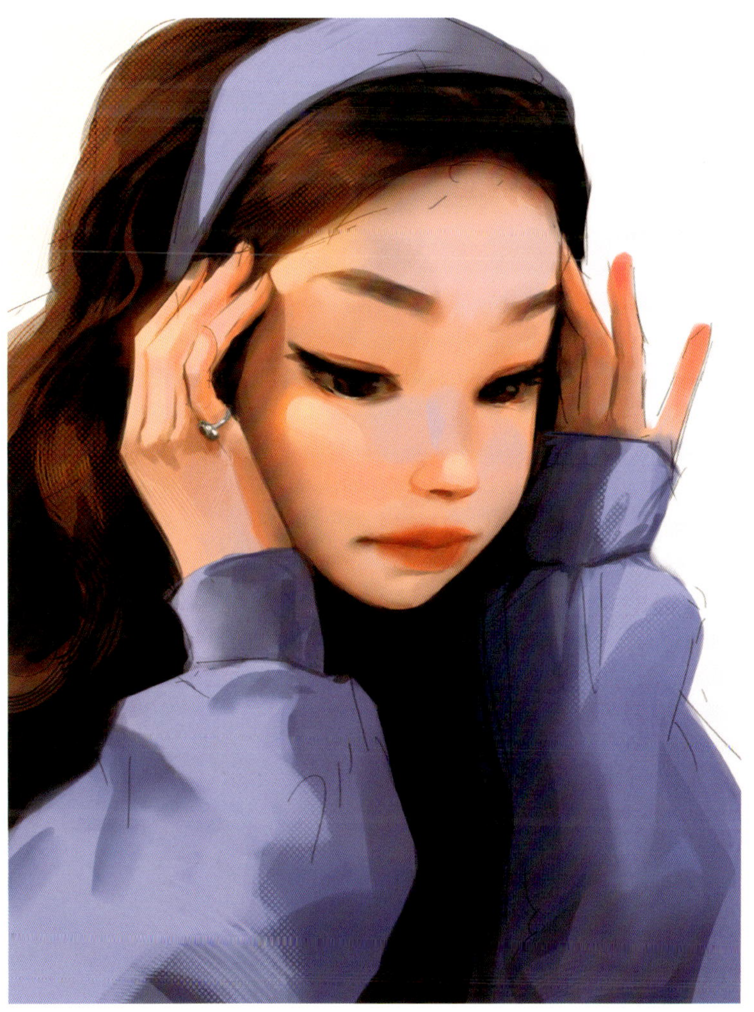

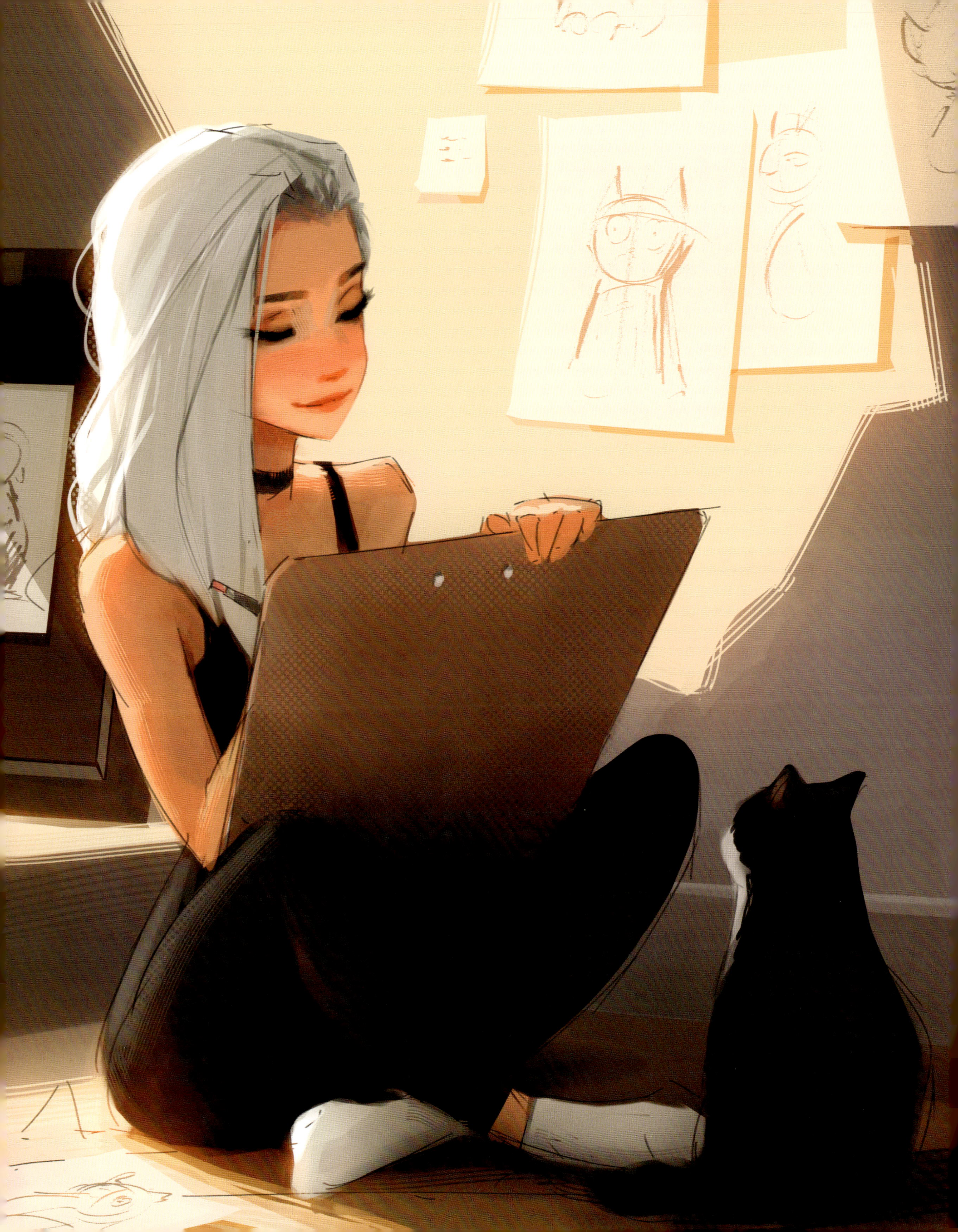

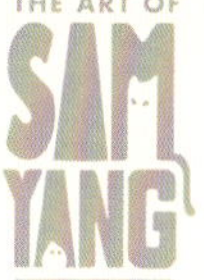

creating characters

Design, story, inspiration

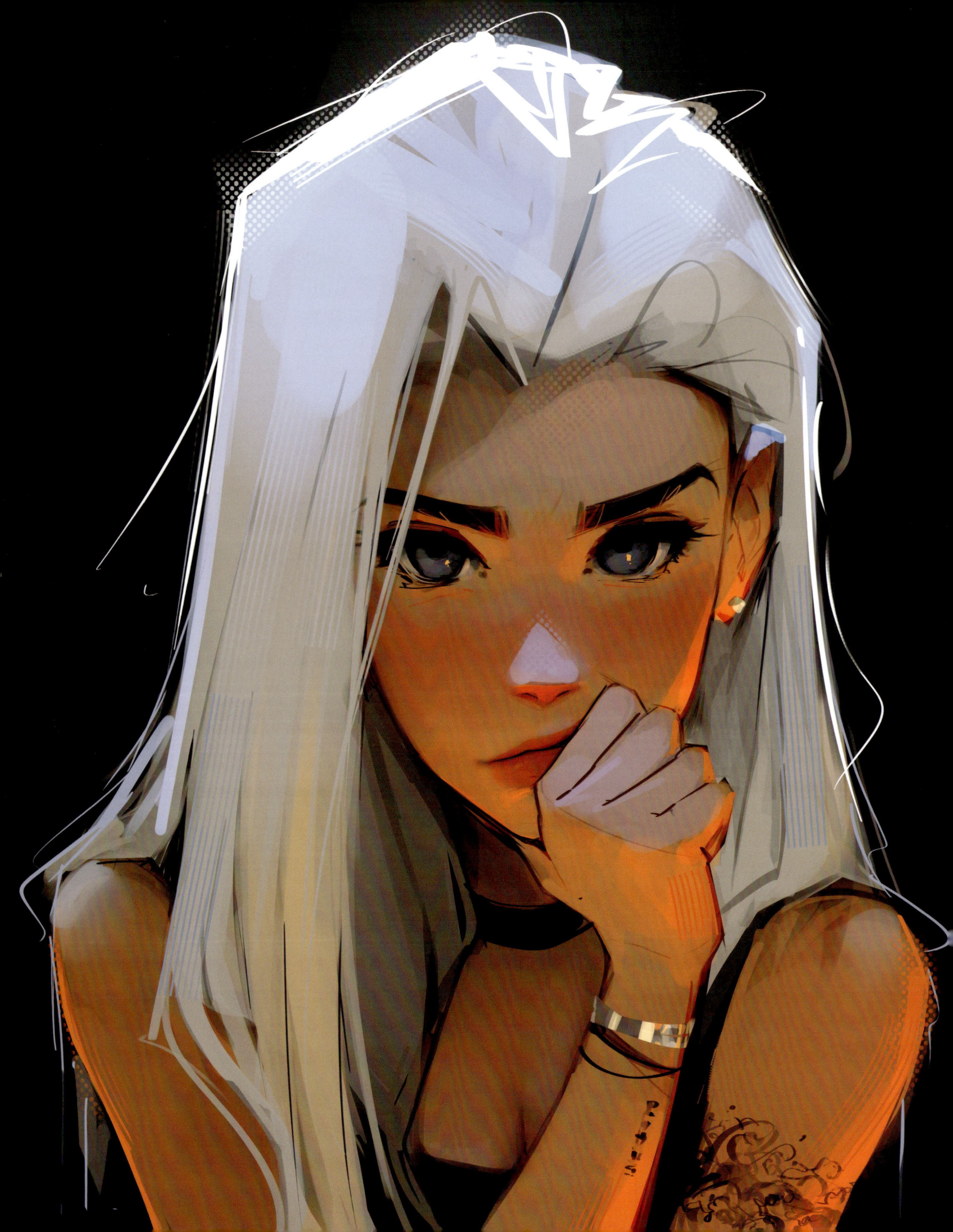

I love the idea of creating your own characters. Among my original characters, or OCs, Kara is the most well known. She is an artist too, and her favourite subject to draw is her cat, Bruce. Kara is kindhearted, good spirited, and you'll generally find her in a good mood, just appreciating the little things in life. Much like everyone else around her, she's just trying to figure out her place in this big confusing world.

Her story doesn't have a beginning or end just yet, but her world is an embodiment of most positive things I find in life. The inspiration I have for my characters mainly stems from feelings and emotions; Kara is a personification of the joy of finding beauty in the smallest, most mundane things. I imagine she struggles and fails quite a bit in her pursuit of art, but she would always try to hold her head up high. She'd learn from her mistakes and make the most of every moment. In a sense, she's also someone who inspires me.

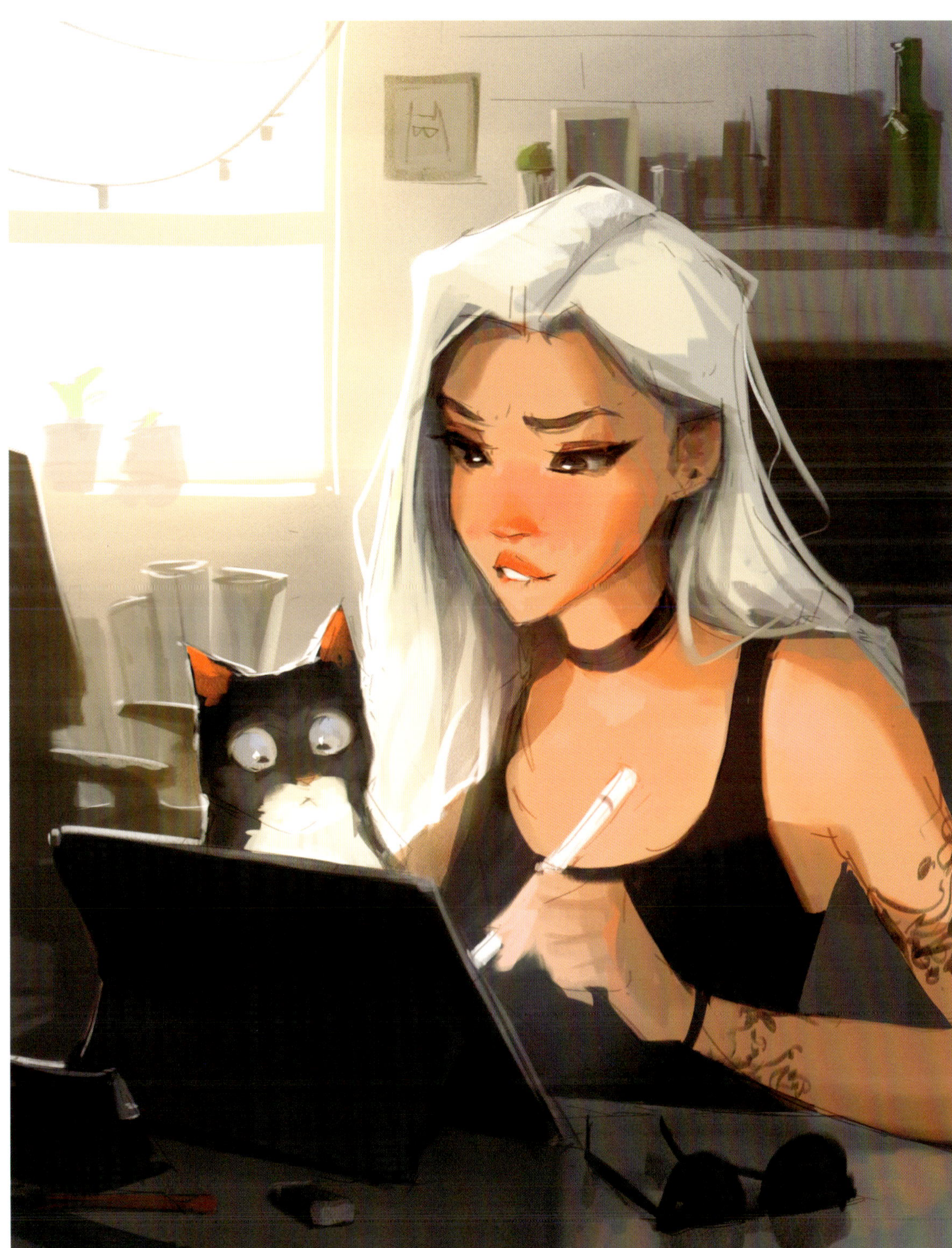

Left | *Kara*, November 2022

Right | *Kara Drawing*, September 2020.
This is one of my earliest drawings featuring Kara and Bruce, as you can probably tell. I wanted to capture a feeling of focus that every artist has experienced. The room in the background was largely drawn with no reference, and you can see some prints rolled up under the window. Those are a throwback to the time when I drew this piece. Back then, I was still printing my own prints and selling them on Etsy, writing my own labels, and mailing them out every weekend

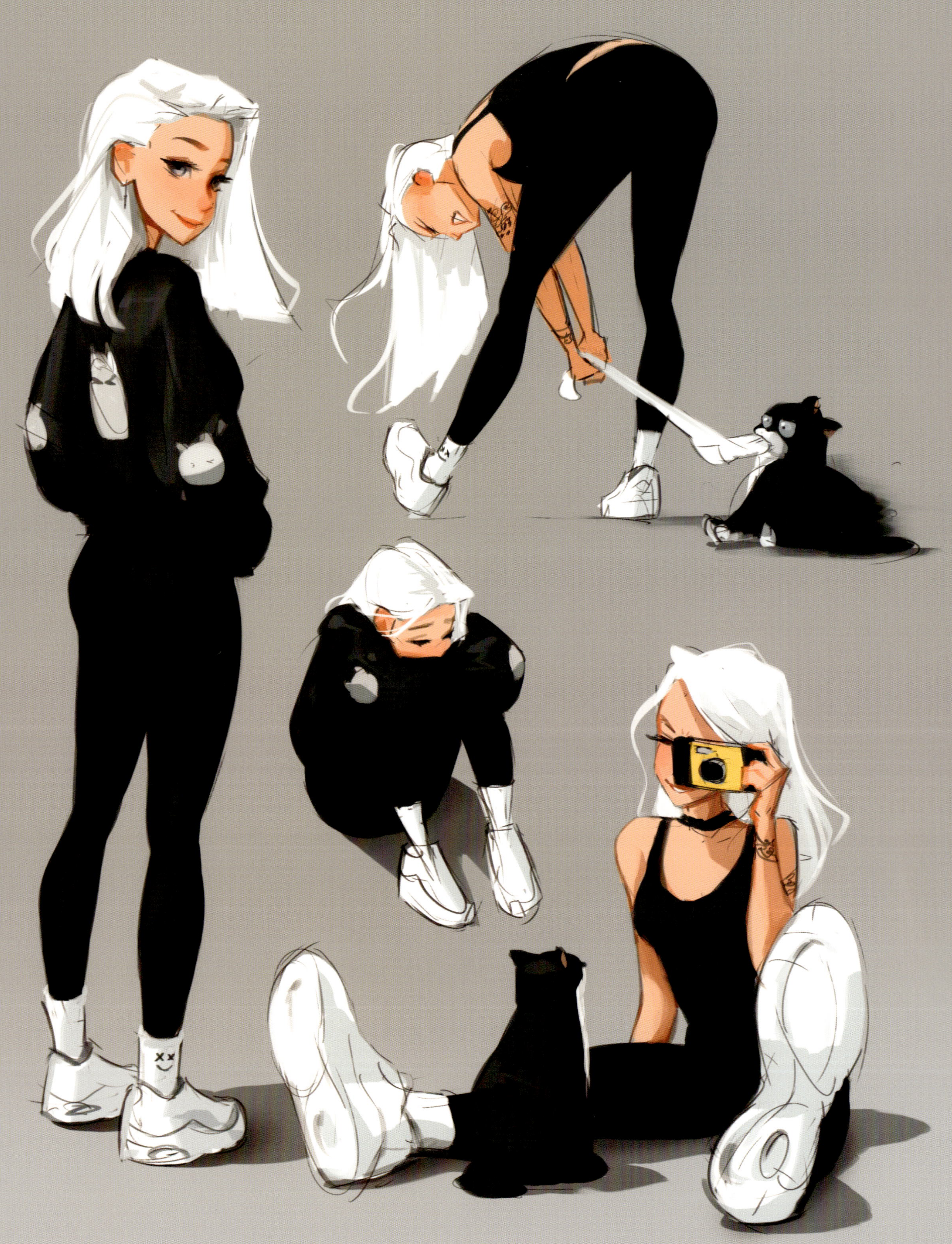

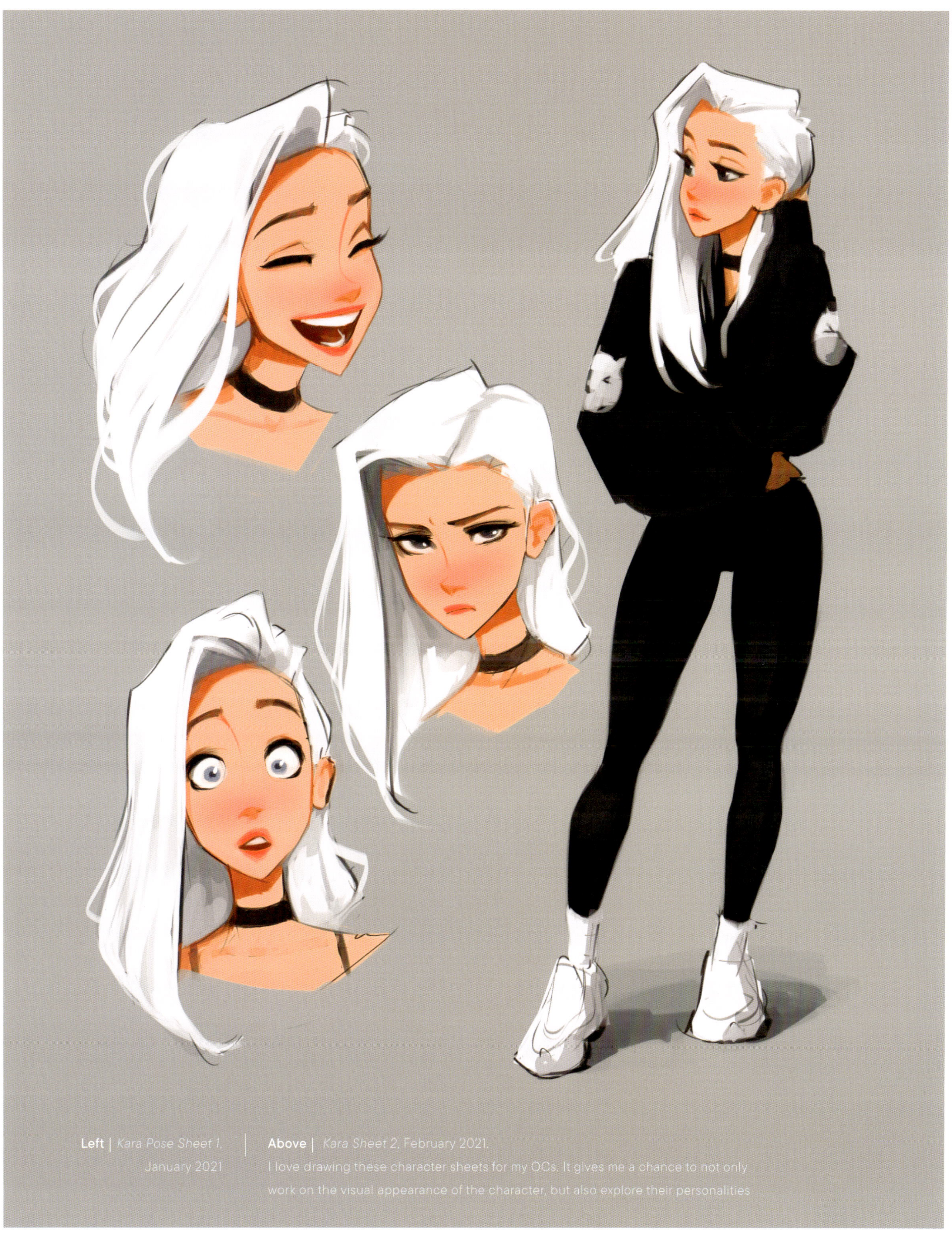

Left | *Kara Pose Sheet 1*, January 2021

Above | *Kara Sheet 2*, February 2021.
I love drawing these character sheets for my OCs. It gives me a chance to not only work on the visual appearance of the character, but also explore their personalities

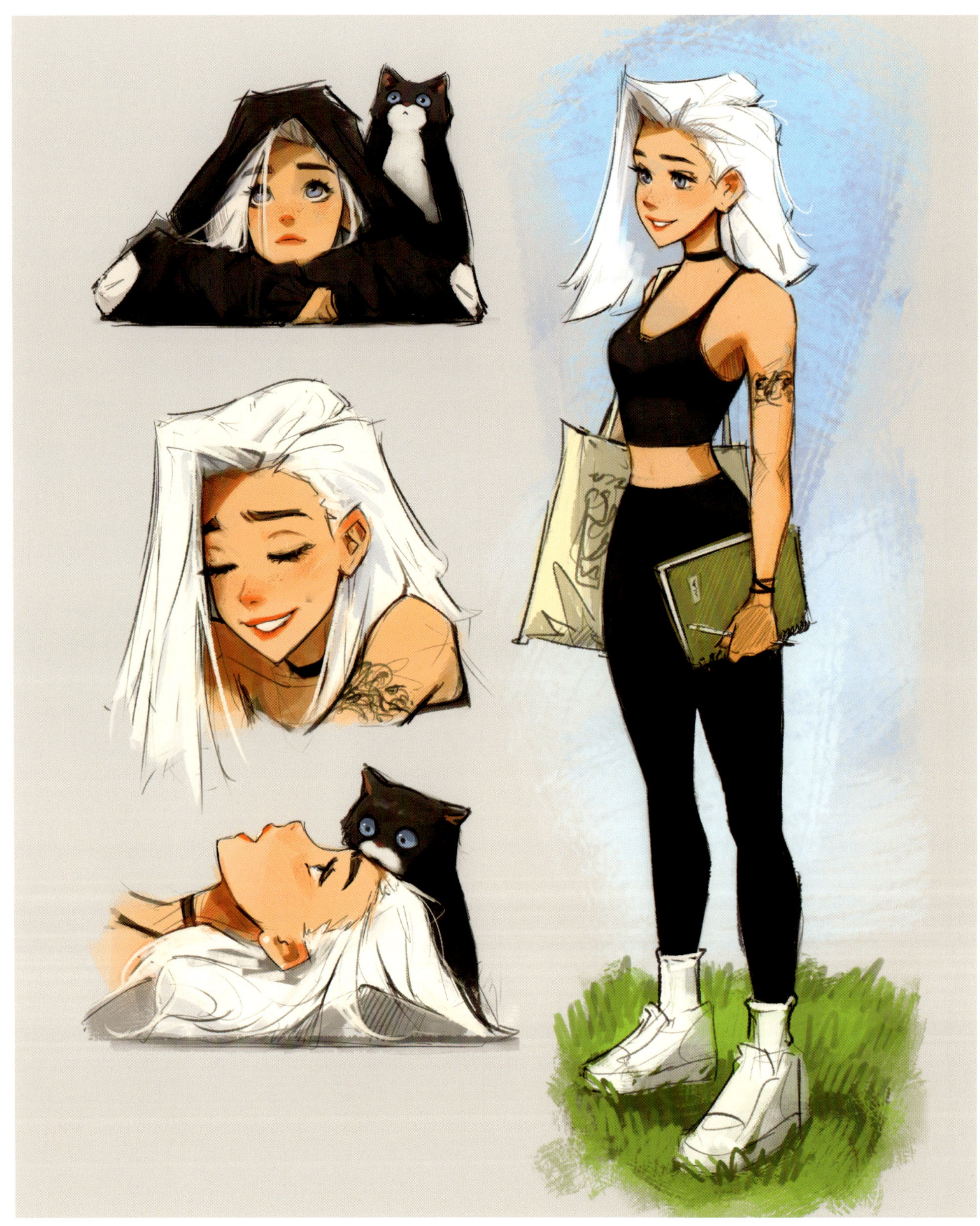

Above | *Kara Design*, May 2023.

Expression sheets are an integral part of effective character design. They establish a range of emotions for your character, and based on the way each emotion is depicted, they can also speak volumes of the character's personality. It's quite important to keep these simple. When our goal is to capture an expression, other things, such as lighting and minor insignificant details, can take a back seat. Simplicity works wonders here. Often, you'll find that more rendering and detail can actually work against you

Right | *Light – Full*, March 2022

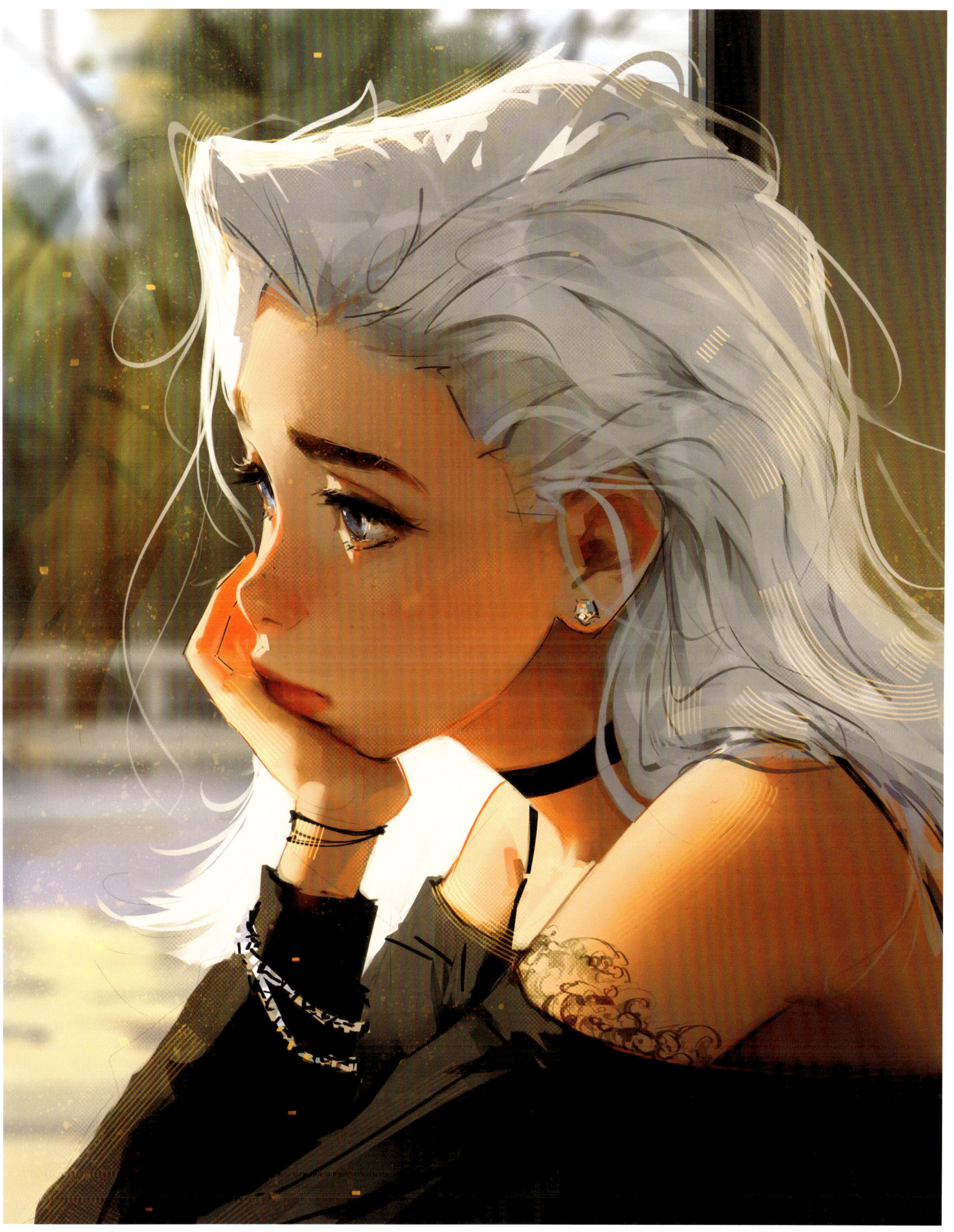

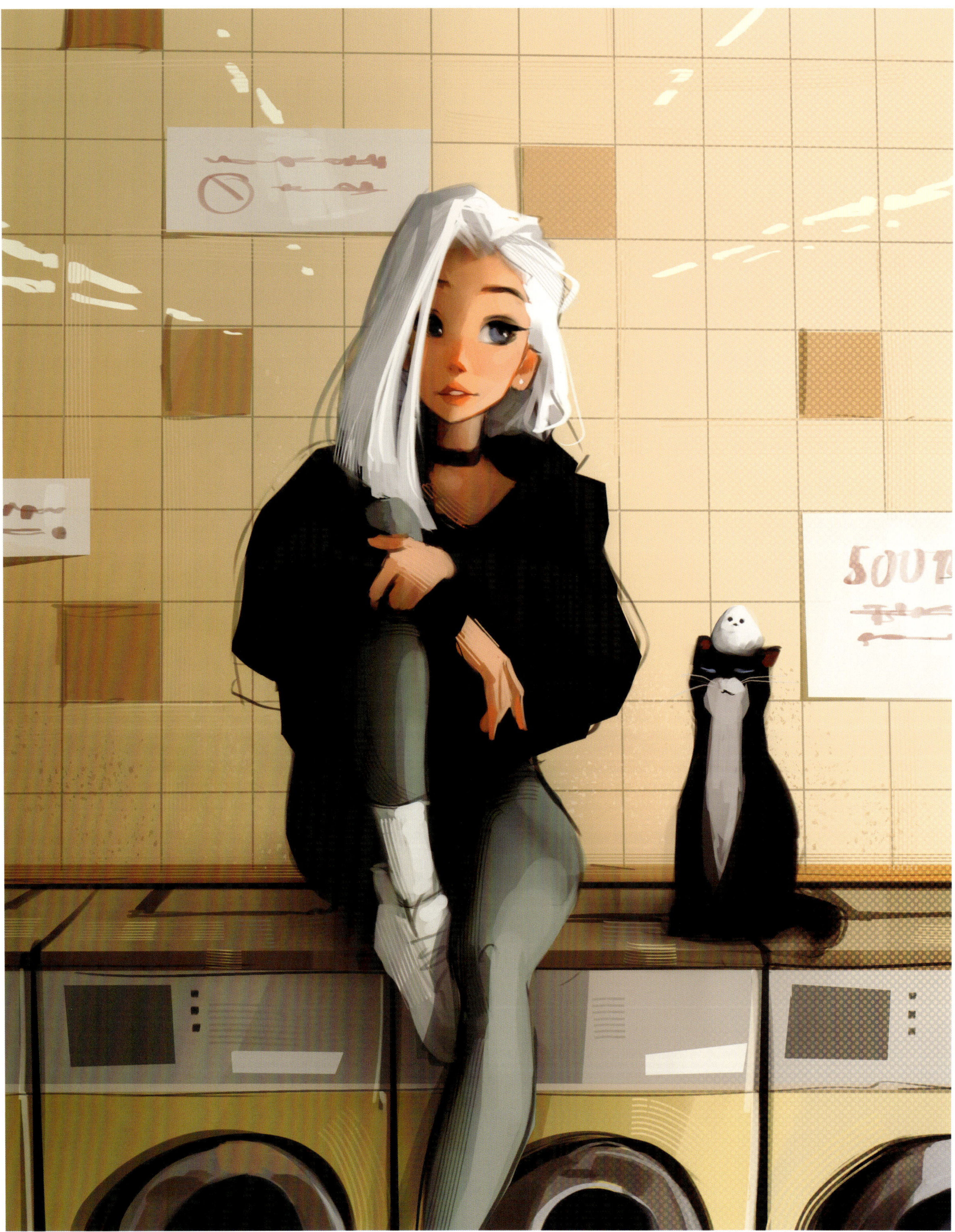

Kara's design carries a sense of confidence. The combination of black and white generates a simplified, graphic look that is easily recognizable, especially in the context of my more colourful rendering style. No wild, flashy colours or complementary combinations, just plain old values at the opposite end of the spectrum coming together to create a beautiful look. The simplicity also reflects her personality, finding beauty in the mundane. I think there's something wonderful about simple designs that are instantly recognizable, and Studio Ghibli legend, Hayao Miyazaki, is someone I greatly admire for achieving it.

Left | *Laundro*, February 2021

Below | *Angry Kara*, May 2022

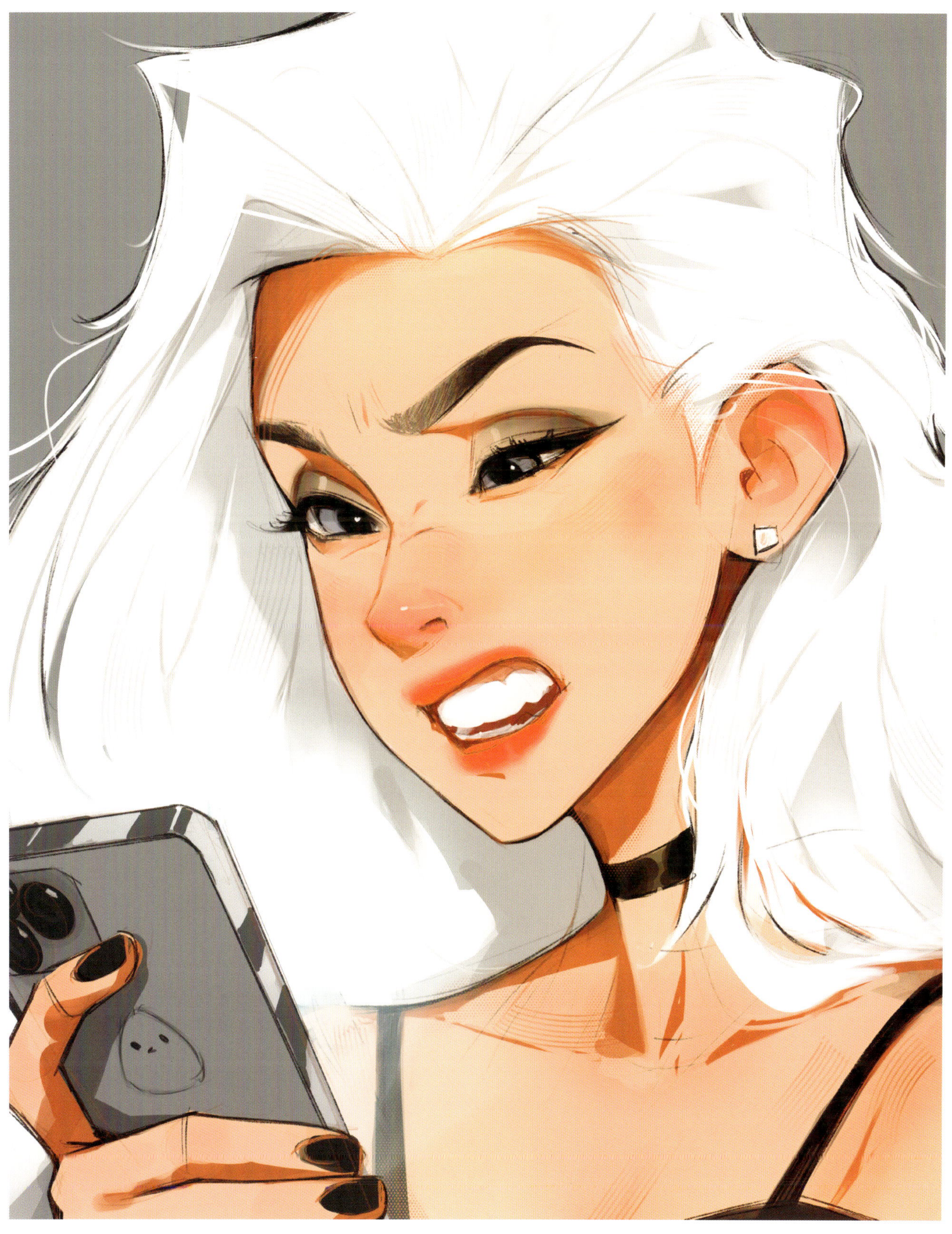

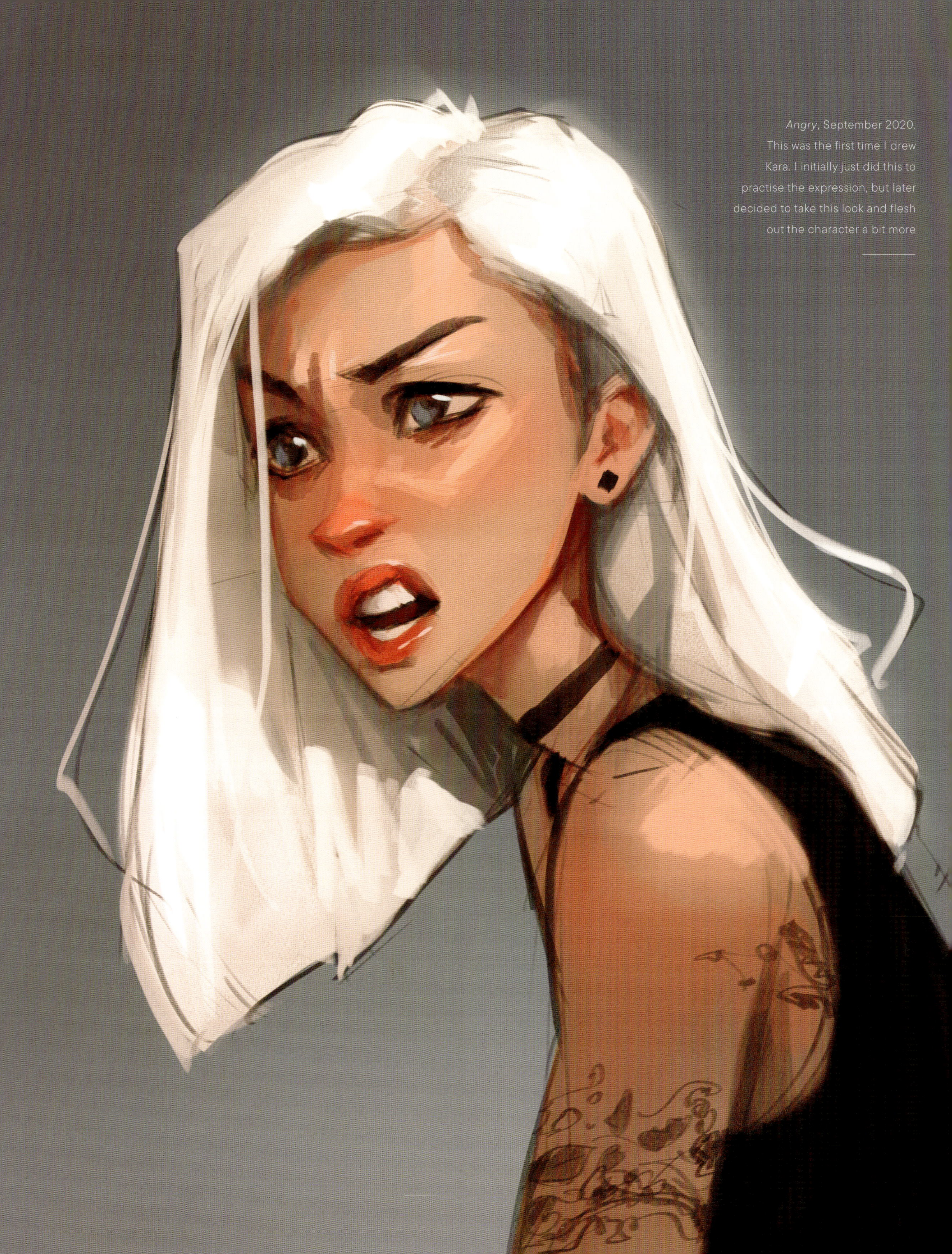

Angry, September 2020. This was the first time I drew Kara. I initially just did this to practise the expression, but later decided to take this look and flesh out the character a bit more

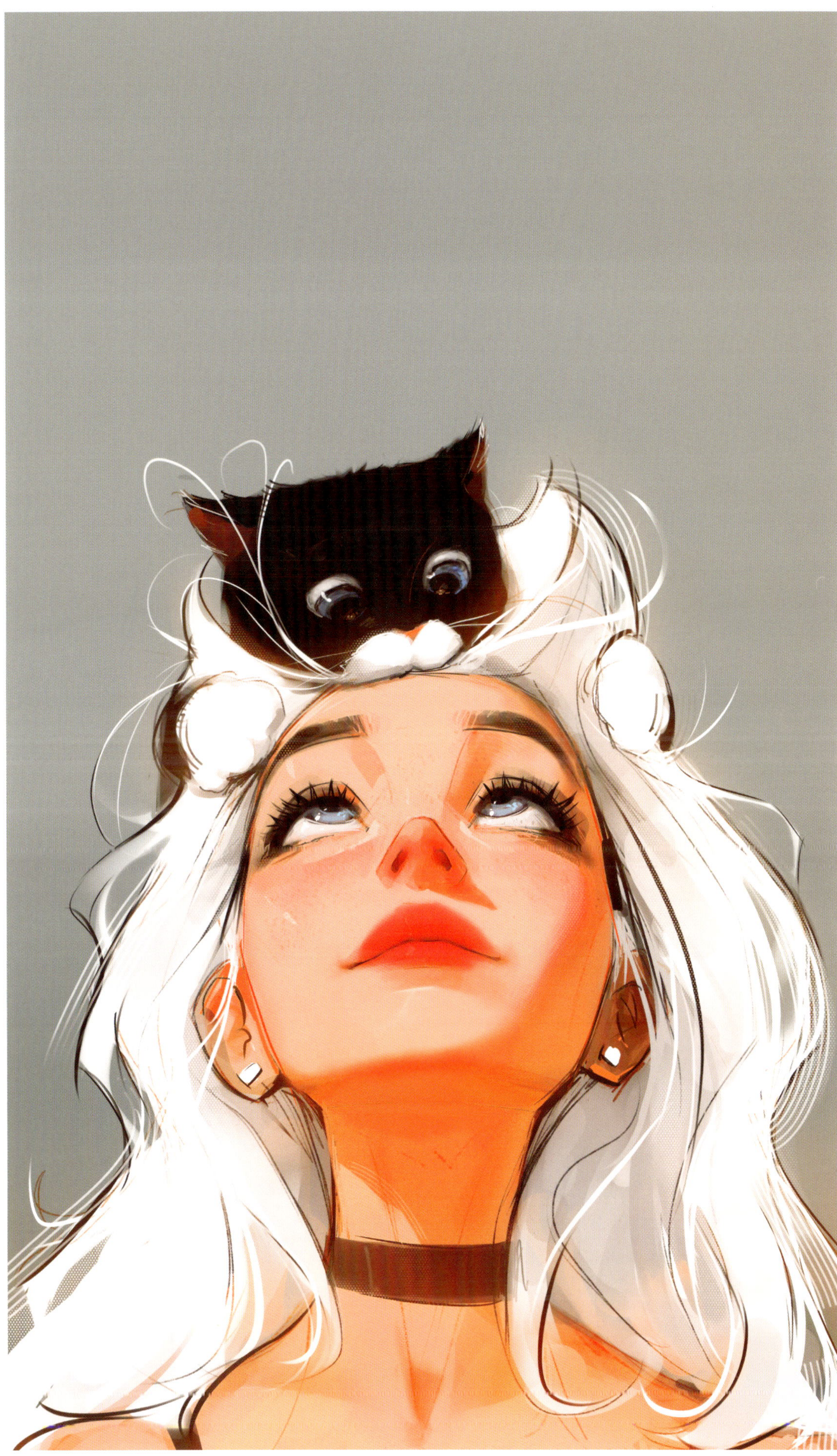

The types of clothing Kara wears are also great portrayals of simplicity: plain tank tops, hoodies, leggings, and white shoes. At a glance, she appears to be someone you might see walking down the street. Her tattoos consist of ocean waves wrapping around her upper-left arm and right wrist. Tattoos usually tell you a lot about a person – it's a way of expression, after all. Kara's waves give us an insight into her mentality: going with the flow and being at peace with where the current takes her.

Kara's cat, Bruce, is also black and white. He gets his name from the little white pattern on his mouth and belly which makes him look like Batman. His colour scheme is designed to complement Kara's own, just like how he complements her in everyday life. Bruce often has no thoughts behind his eyes, but Kara still appreciates him for being there.

Full, January 2023

My favourite way of creating an OC is to base them on something I've felt or experienced in some way. A character you feel a true connection to will no doubt be a great way for you to express yourself through your art. It could be an aspect of their personality, or perhaps their story that fuels that connection. Maybe their path in life is a metaphor for something you've been through that had a remarkable impact on your life. If you can find such a connection, your character's personality will surely materialize in time.

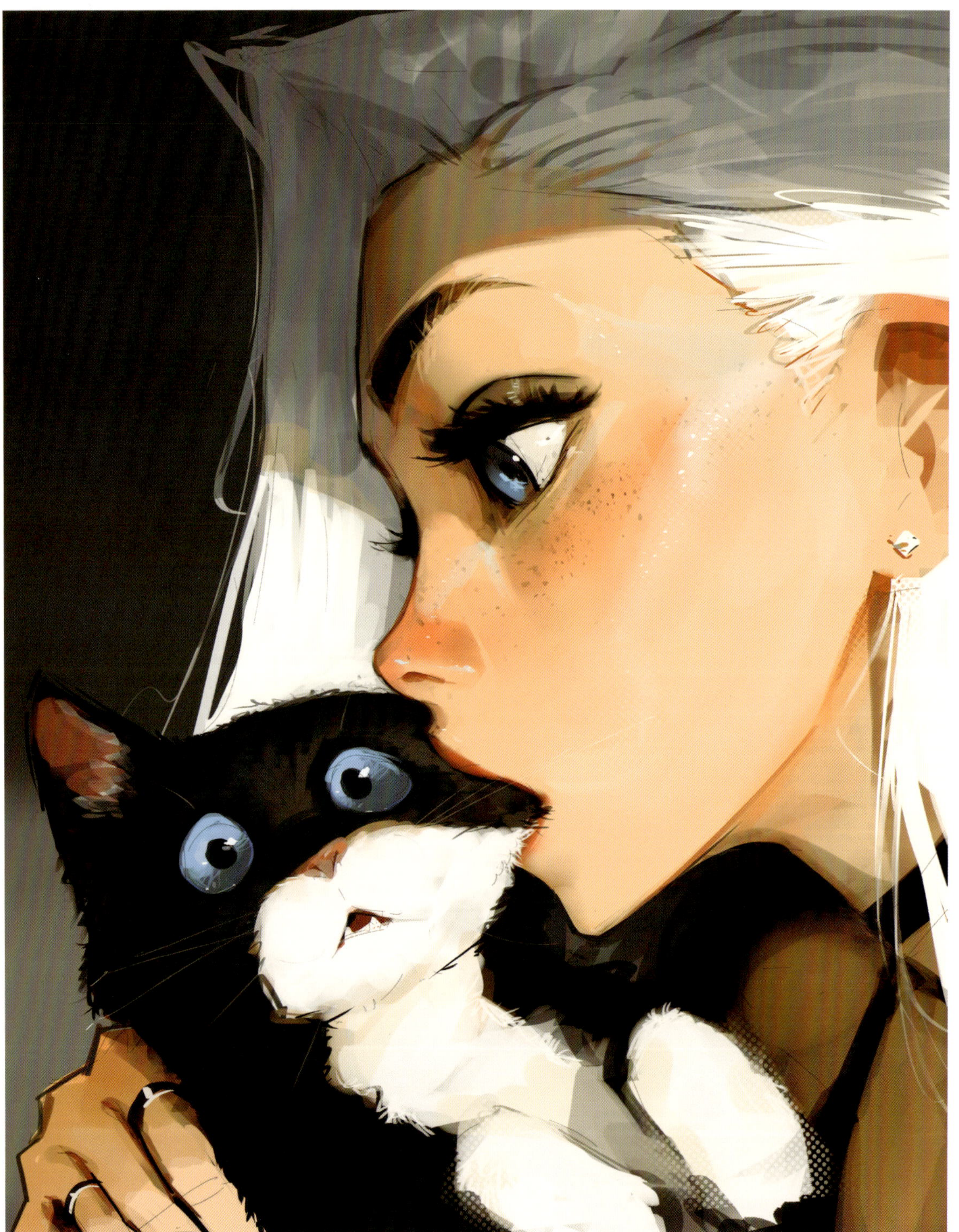

Left | *Chomp*, January 2023

Right | *DTIYS*, February 2023. Kara and Tessa from my *Draw This In Your Style* challenge. If you're looking to connect with other artists in the community, a good way to do this is to participate in art challenges hosted by individual artists. I did this quite a bit when I was first starting out. It's a great experience, especially if you feel art-blocked and don't know what to draw next

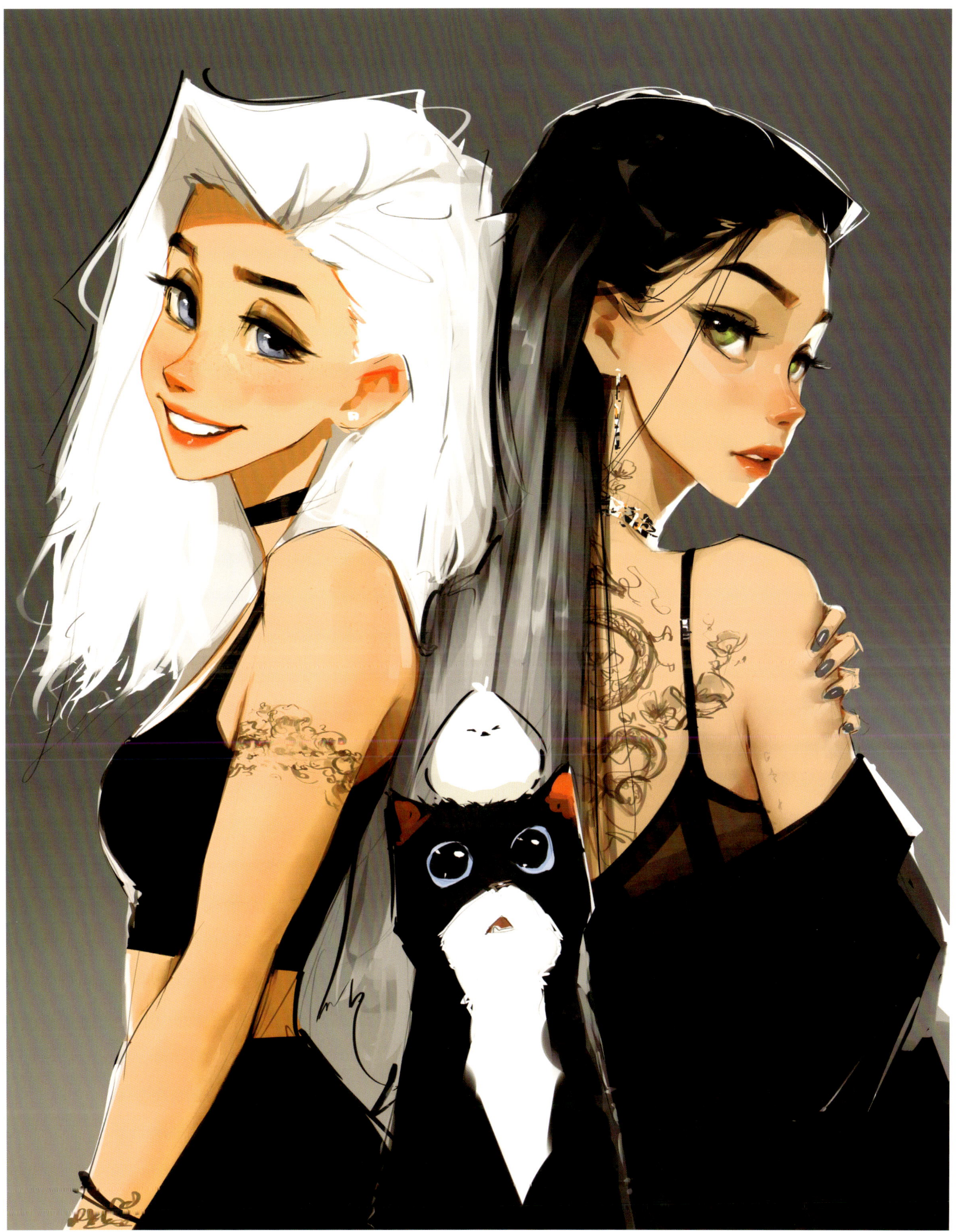

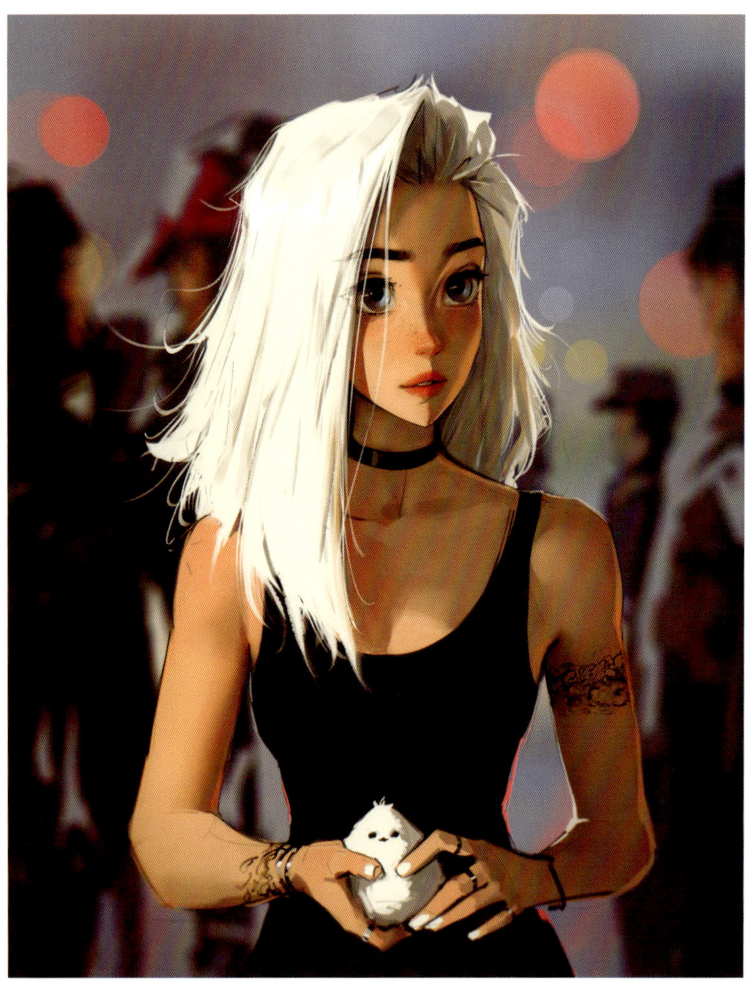

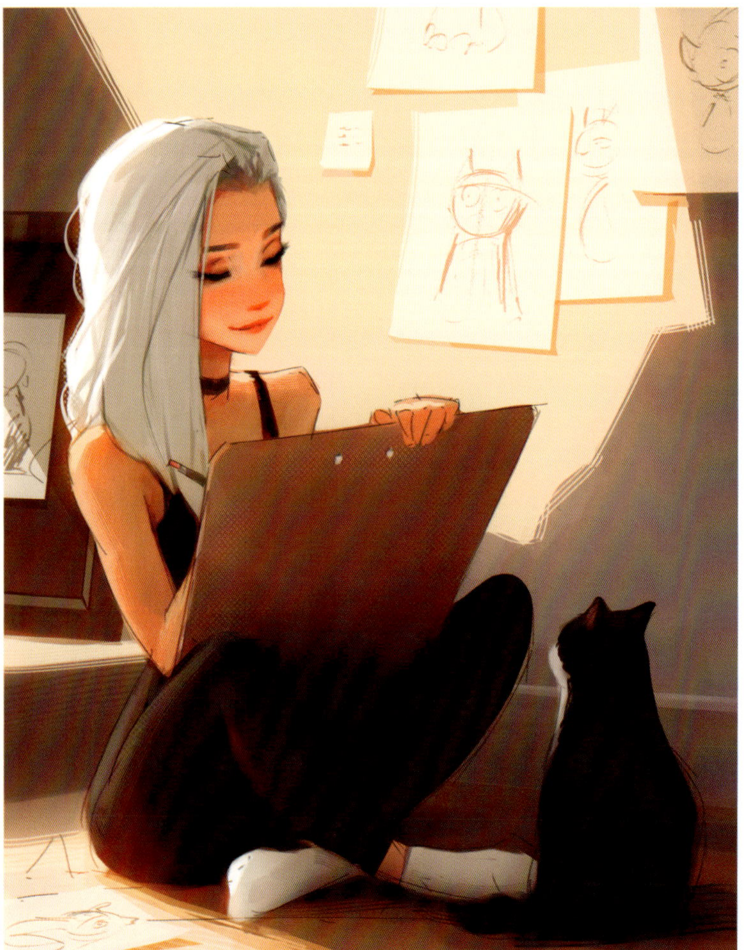

Above | *Kara and the Birb*, January 2021

Right | *Kara's Study Session*, January 2021.
Here is another example of a repaint I made of Kara and Bruce. The updated version is on the opposite page

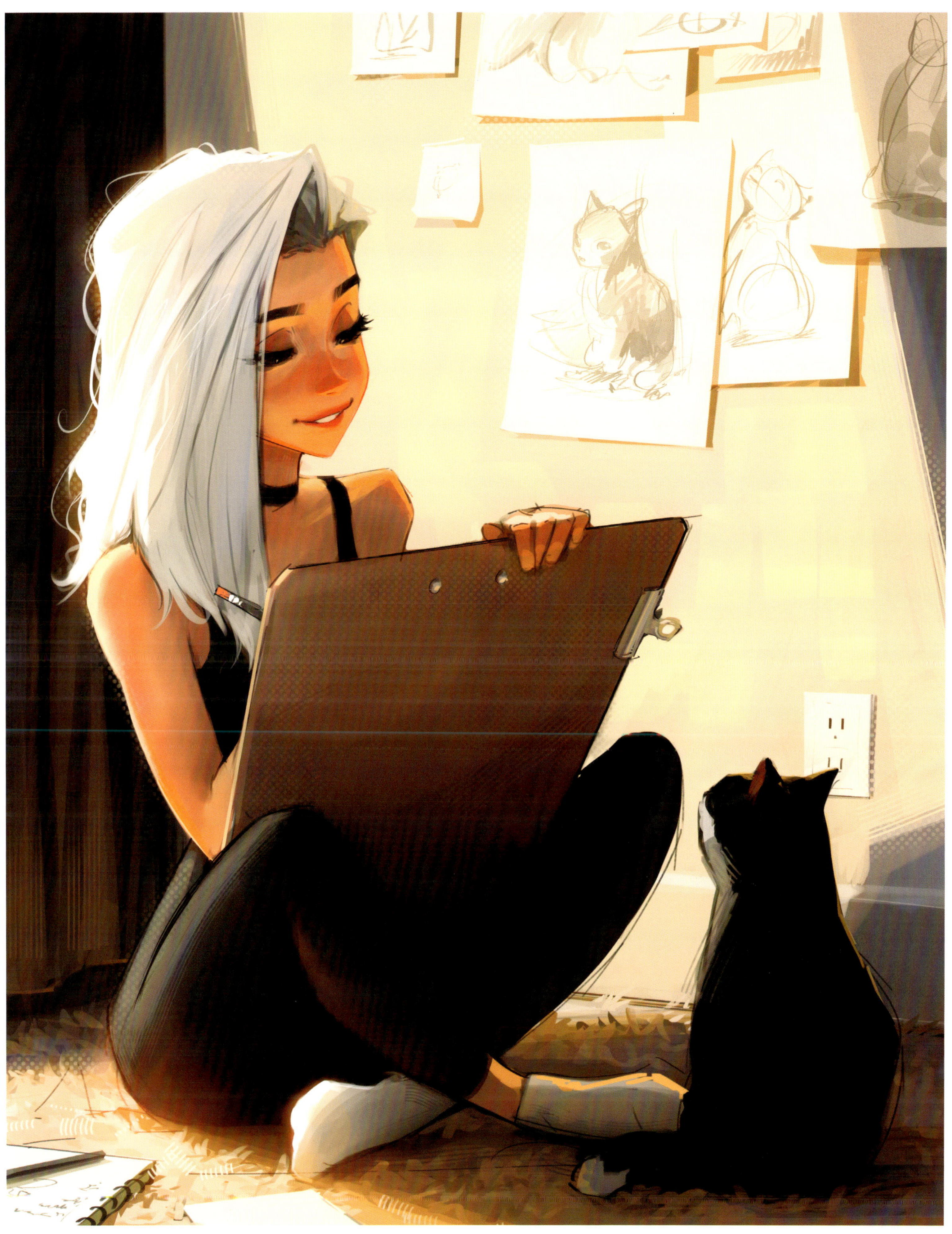

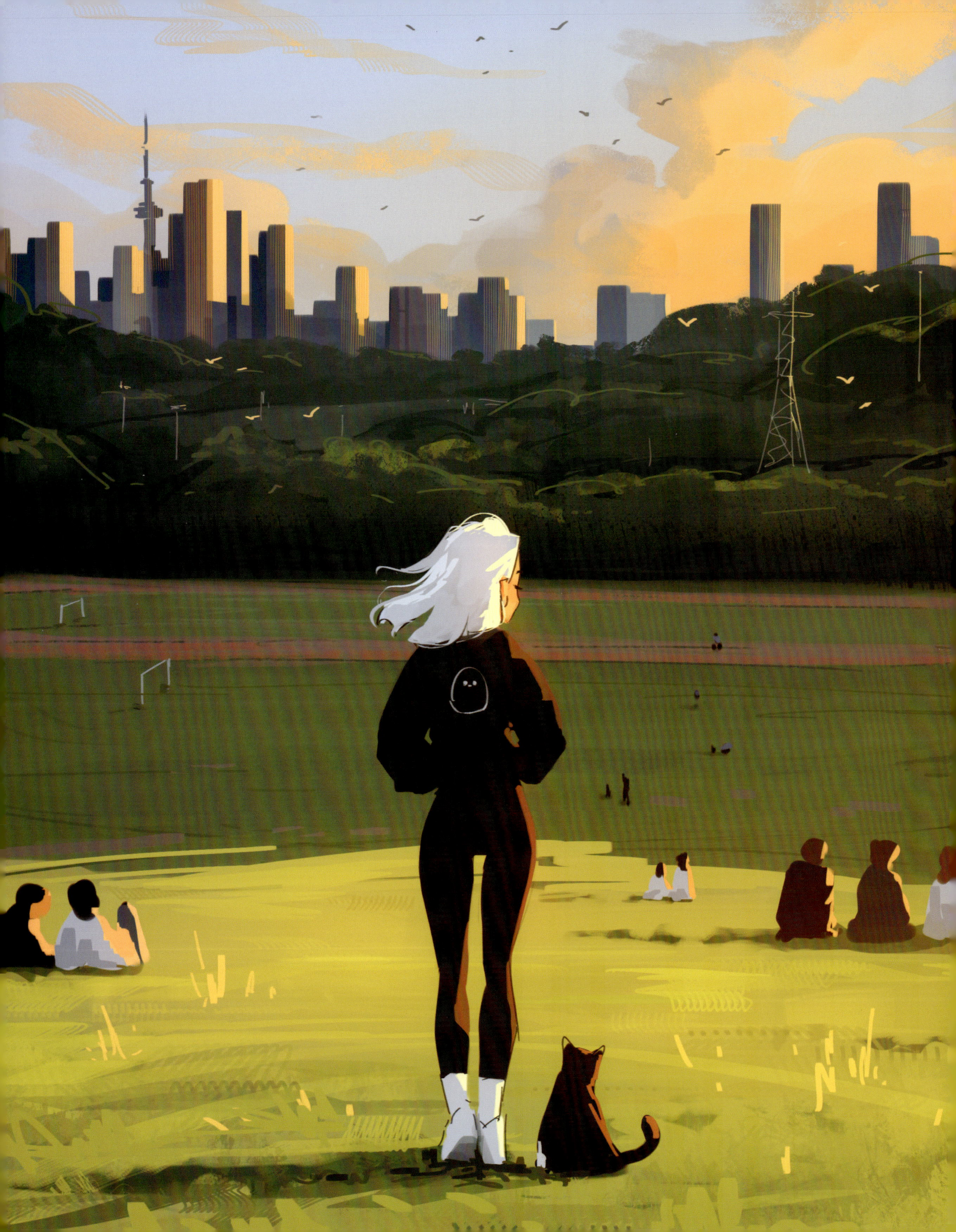

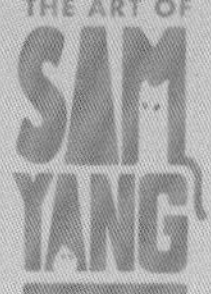

the art community

Taking the first step, building a community

Part of my job also involves creating videos for YouTube and Patreon. I use these video platforms to create content that will entertain and educate, but really, I just want to reach more people and hopefully inspire others to take up art as a hobby or career.

Art is fundamental to human nature. I'm a nerd for history and culture, and I find human traditions and artistic expression absolutely fascinating. Historically, each society has its own unique identity and much of that is expressed through the visual language of art. From magnificent Ancient Egyptian reliefs to awe-inspiring Renaissance frescoes, the importance of art is felt everywhere you look. But in my experience, growing up in this fast-paced world where everything changes at the speed of light, it seems less and less like we hold on to the practice of making art as we age. When we were younger, everyone drew. We didn't always make the best drawings, but our younger selves never let lack of skill stand in the way of our imagination. Life inevitably gets busy. Things start to get in the way of our hobbies and passions, and no one can be blamed for not having the energy to draw after a long day at school or work. I've seen a lot of peers from school, who were quite gifted, leave art behind altogether as they grew into adulthood. It's a pity.

I hope sharing my work gives newcomers the encouragement to try out drawing for themselves. Maybe it'll even inspire people who have fallen out of love with art to pick up their pencils and start doodling again. I want to share the things I've learned and show people through videos how fun the process of creation can be; and in doing so, I want to build a community of people who share the same passion. In the art community, there's always more to learn from those around us. There is a tremendous wealth of knowledge and information out there to help new artists find their footing, including many free resources found by using simple searches on YouTube. There are also tons more intensive, paid courses offered by schools or individual artists. As art is so accessible nowadays, I hope to help more people incorporate it into their lives and contribute to the growth of the amazing visual-art community. However, it's not just up to me or other well-known artists – as soon as you share something you made with the world, you could be the source of inspiration who helps someone else rediscover their love for art.

I think that's the beauty of being so interconnected in today's world. It has never been easier to find a community of like-minded people. A great artist will always learn from their peers; so if you're on an art journey, whether it's a career or a hobby, remember to pay attention to the beautiful artworks being made all around you. There's something you can learn from almost everyone if you look closely enough!

My first few posts on YouTube were simple timelapse process videos. I thought that would be as much as I'd ever put onto that platform. But after a few uploads, some viewers wanted me to explain the process and provide step-by-step walkthroughs – so I did! I still remember clumsily recording my voice for the *Cookie* process video. When I played it back through my editing software, I was absolutely mortified at how I sounded, but I didn't let that stop me. The video went up anyway and can still be found on my YouTube channel to this day. After gaining over one million views, it seems YouTube loves to push old, embarrassing content ...

Not too long after my first voice-over video, I was approached by a drawing-tablet company to review one of their products. That was the first time I had to set up a camera and point it at myself while speaking, which was such an uncomfortable experience. I had to then rewatch myself speaking awkwardly on camera as I guided myself through the editing process. Needless to say, it was not my most flattering moment, but it did open new doors for me. Taking that first step had such far-reaching effects for my career's trajectory.

Many aspects of what I do today, including YouTube, Patreon, selling prints, making this book, and the decision to get better at drawing, all emerge from simply taking that first step. It's a sentiment that is demonstrated in everyone's artistic journey. Sure, it opens the door to the repeated pain of failures, but also to a wealth of knowledge that can be gained from that experience. I urge you to take your first step towards something, no matter how small, and see what blossoms as a result.

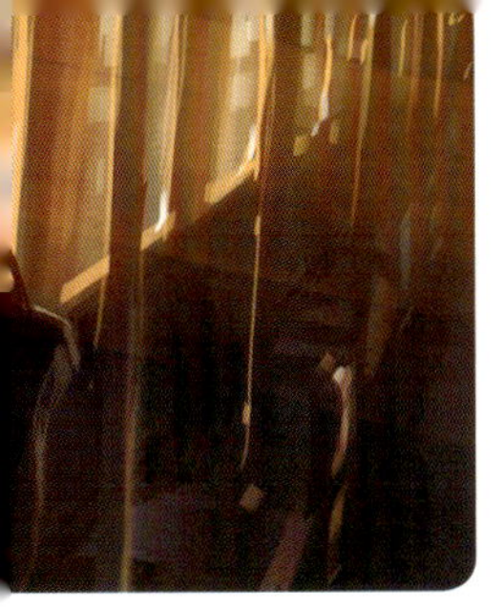
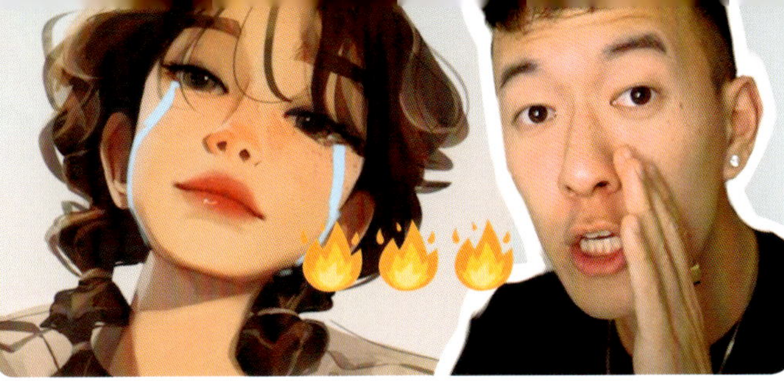
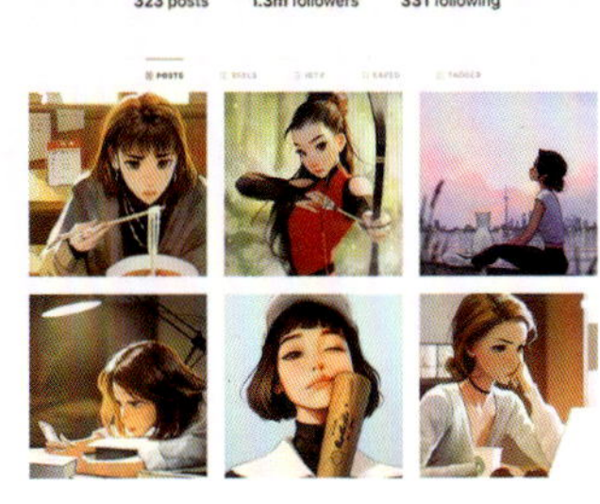
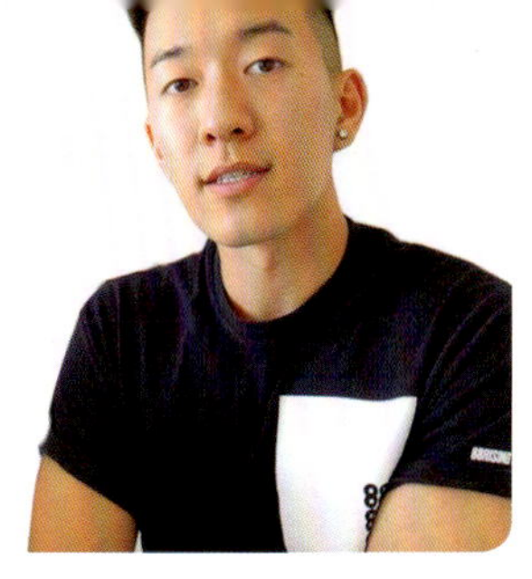
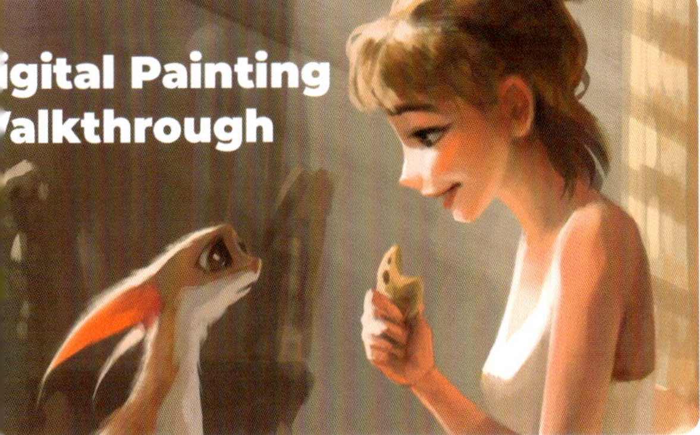

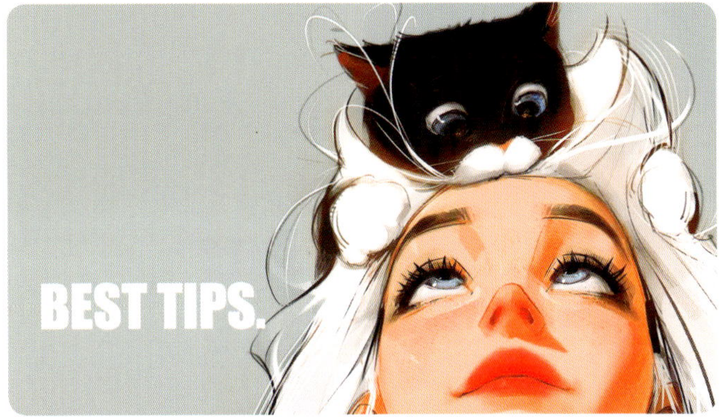

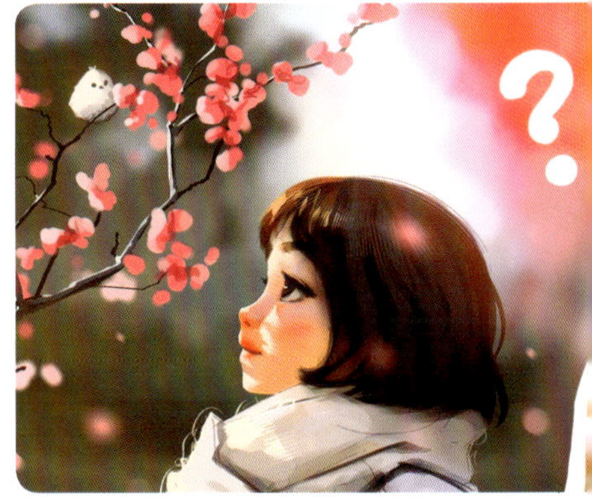
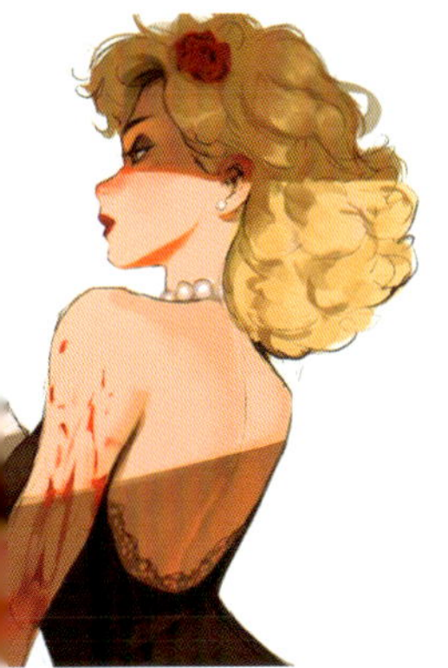
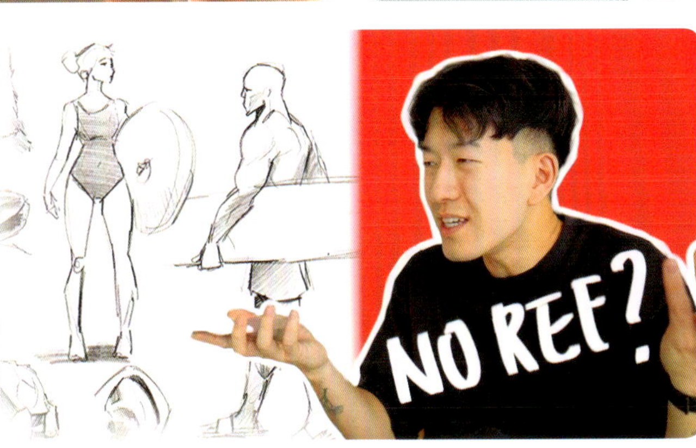

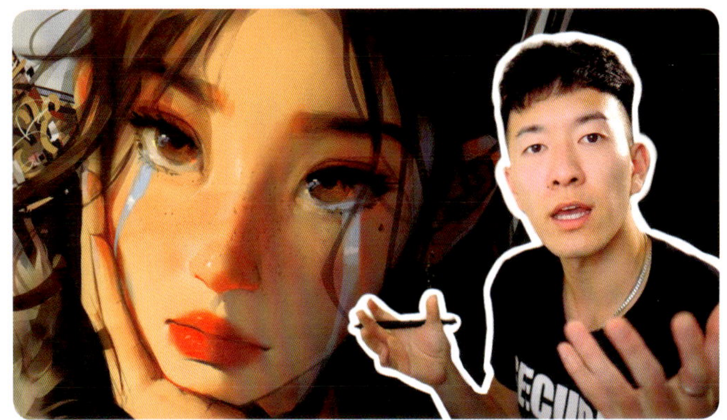
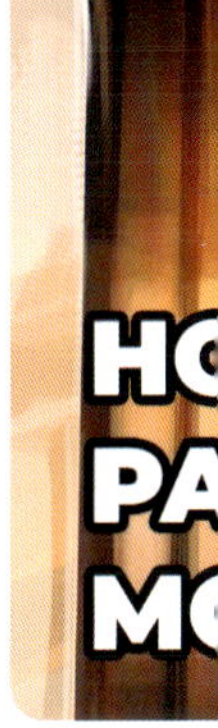
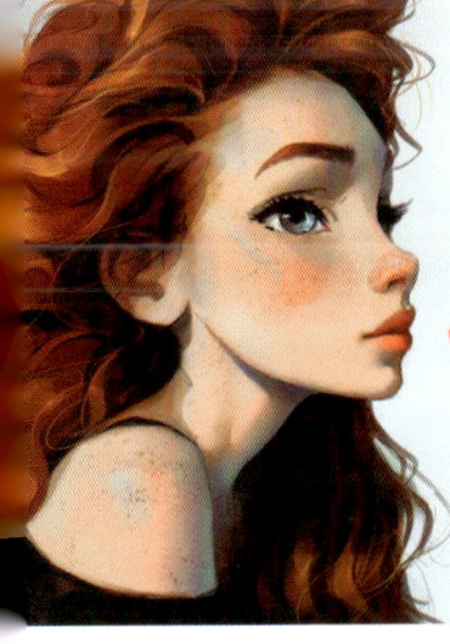
STOP.
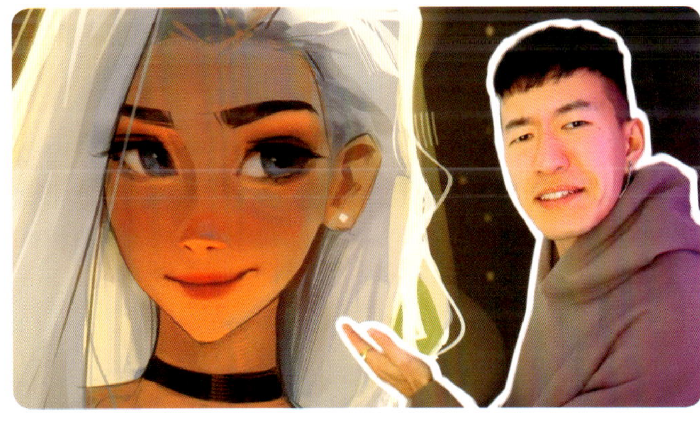
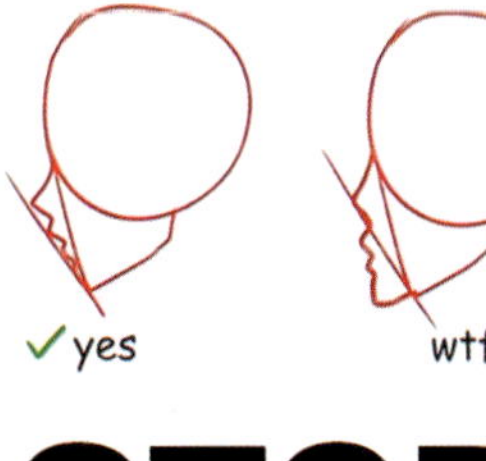

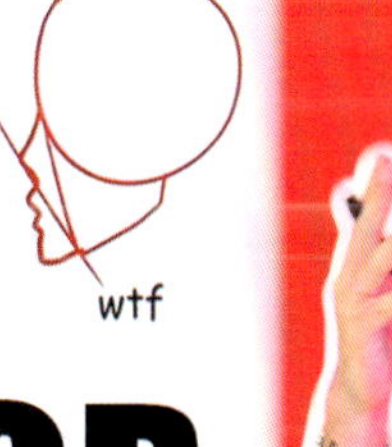

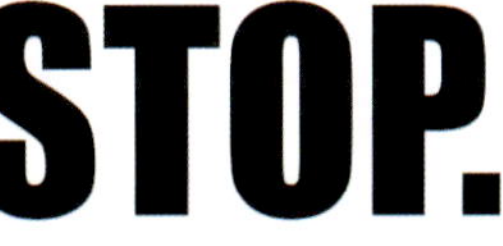

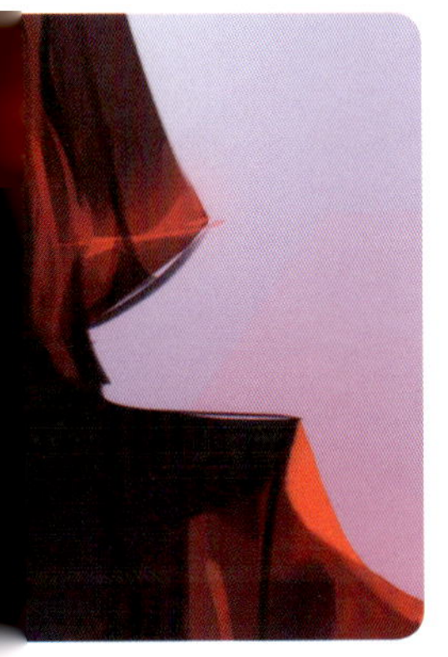
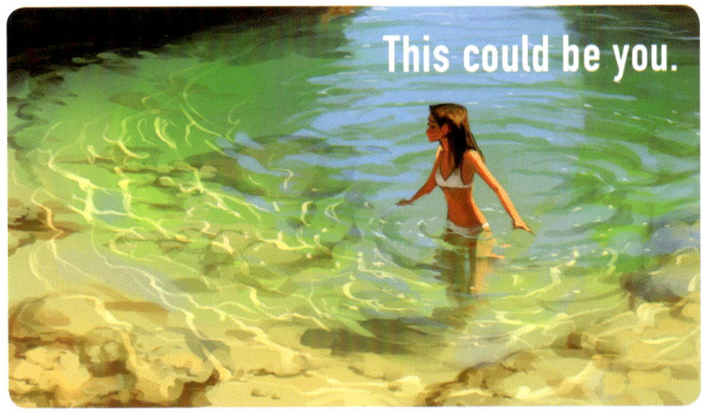

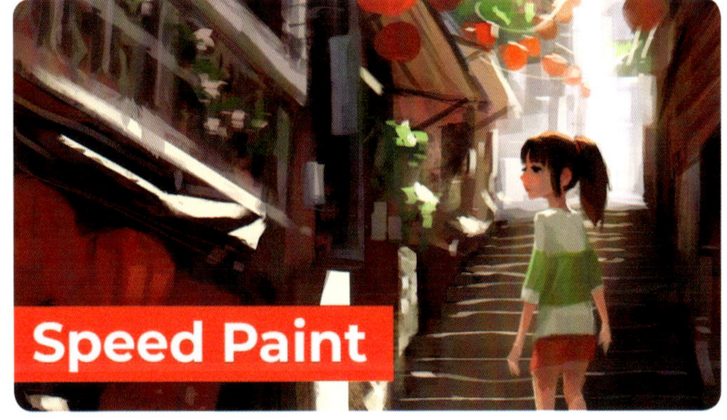

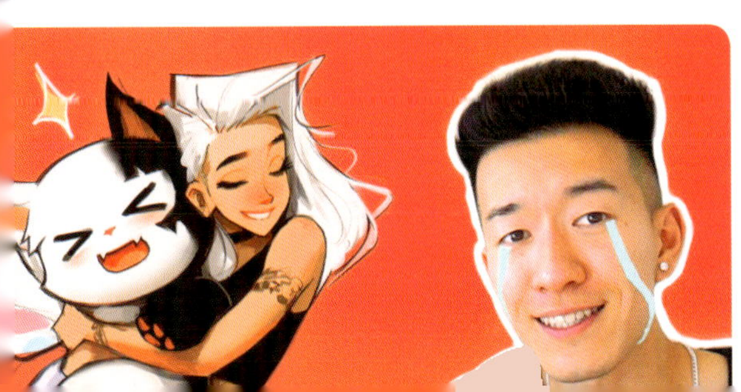
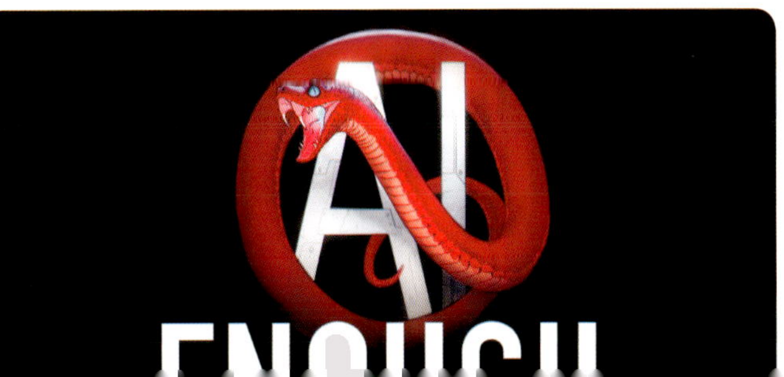

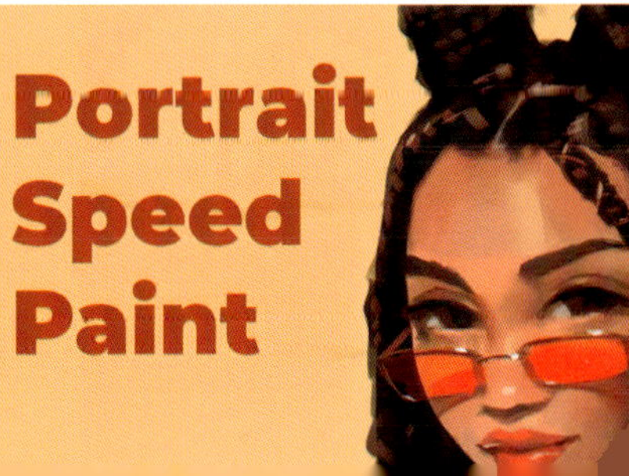

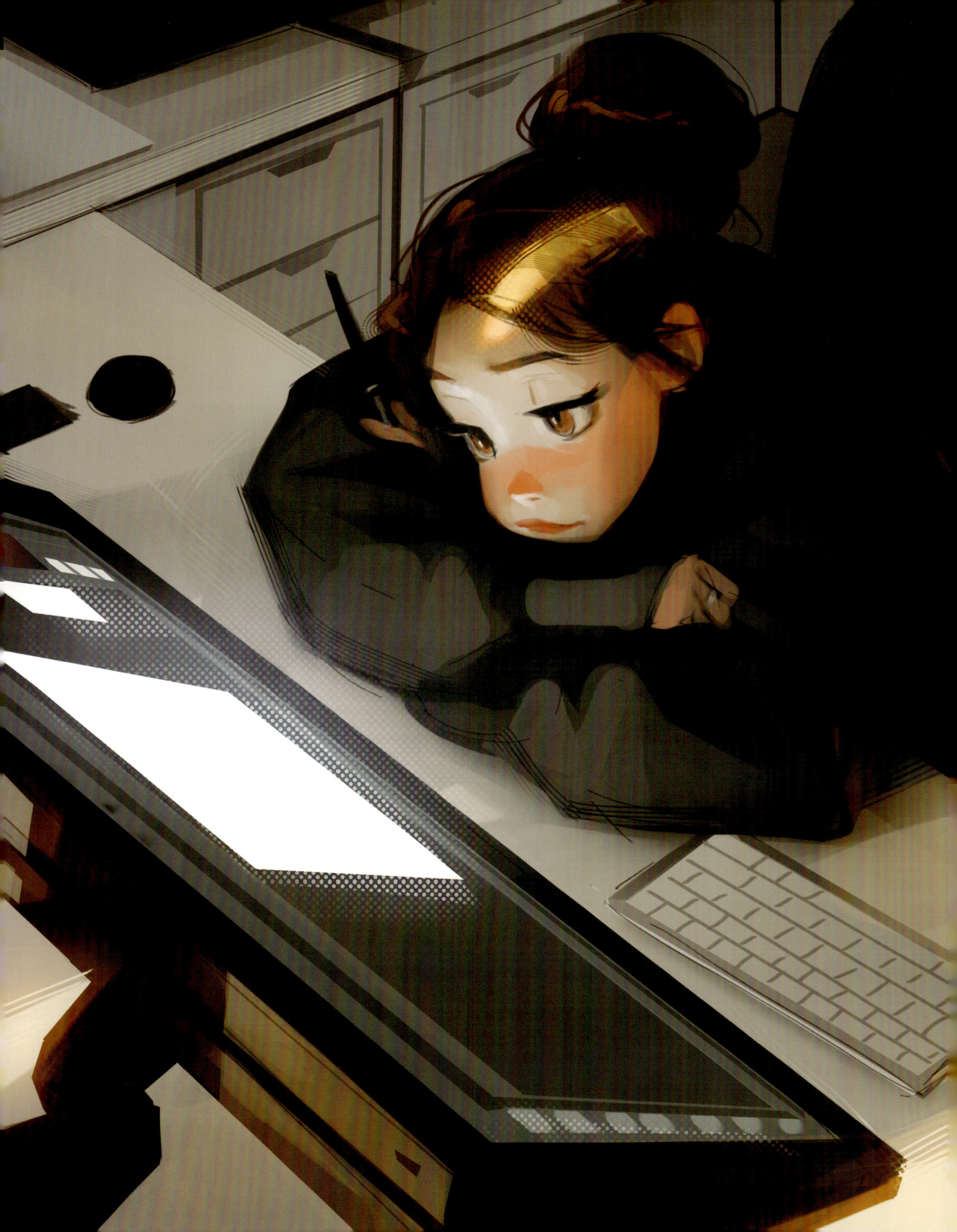

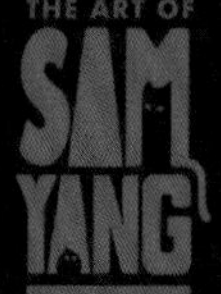

how I work

Methods & insights

FUNDAMENTALS

Remember that fundamentals are irreplaceable. Many creators nowadays try to teach 'shortcuts' and 'hacks' to instantly make your art good, but anyone with experience would tell you that foregoing the hard work is not an option. In order to draw environments well, it's important to understand perspectives; in order to draw heads from different angles, you have to know the anatomy and structure of the face; in order to create an appealing scene, you need to know compositions. Basic fundamentals can be boring, and it can seem like an overwhelming number of things to learn, but I find it helpful to focus on one topic at a time. Set some goals and work backwards from there.

For example: want to improve the way you capture lighting? Well, you need to know that light travels in straight lines and takes the path of least resistance. You have to study and understand different types of light, such as direct, ambient, bounce, and rim lighting. You might also need to brush up on your colour theory in order to understand the colours of light and shadow, and how they transition into each other.

It might sound like a lot for one simple goal, but when you break things down and work on one thing at a time, those smalls steps can add up to truly significant results. For a goal like this, you can take a week or more just studying how light casts itself onto shapes in greyscale, taking note of where surface and cast shadows form. Once you're comfortable, you can add in colour and practise lighting scenarios for the following few weeks. After that, you can study and break down different lighting scenarios on portraits, such as direct or bounce light, focusing on just a couple at a time. For me, segmenting studying in this way and levelling up one small step at a time is the best way to learn. However, you can also mix it up in any way that suits you. I get bored when I focus on one topic for too long, so I tend to mix things up between studies.

LIGHTING

Lighting is a crucial skill to have if you wish to venture beyond line art and flat colours. It's one of the hardest aspects to grasp because you can't directly see rays of light travelling through the environment around you; to make things even more confusing, it's often entangled with colour theory.

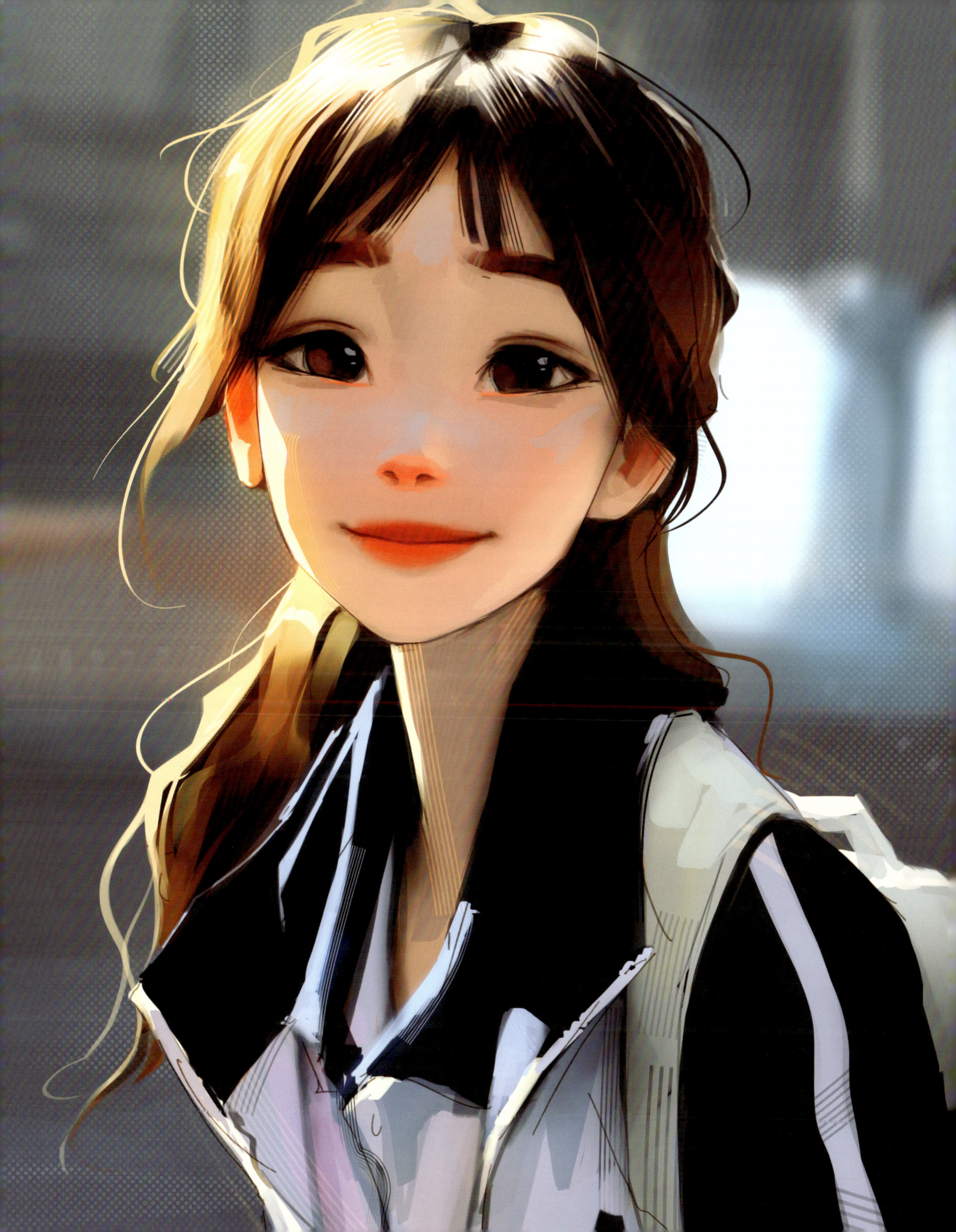

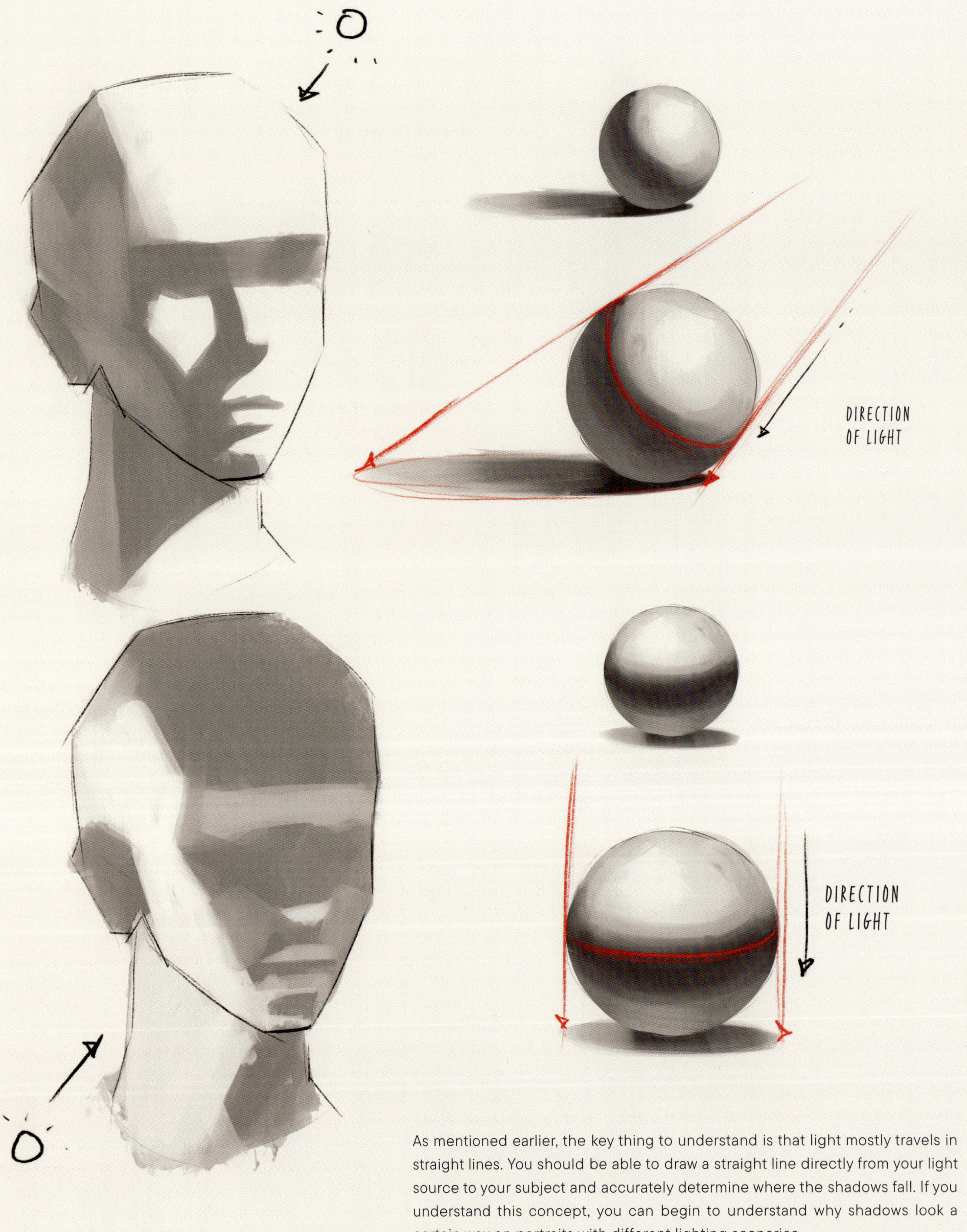

As mentioned earlier, the key thing to understand is that light mostly travels in straight lines. You should be able to draw a straight line directly from your light source to your subject and accurately determine where the shadows fall. If you understand this concept, you can begin to understand why shadows look a certain way on portraits with different lighting scenarios.

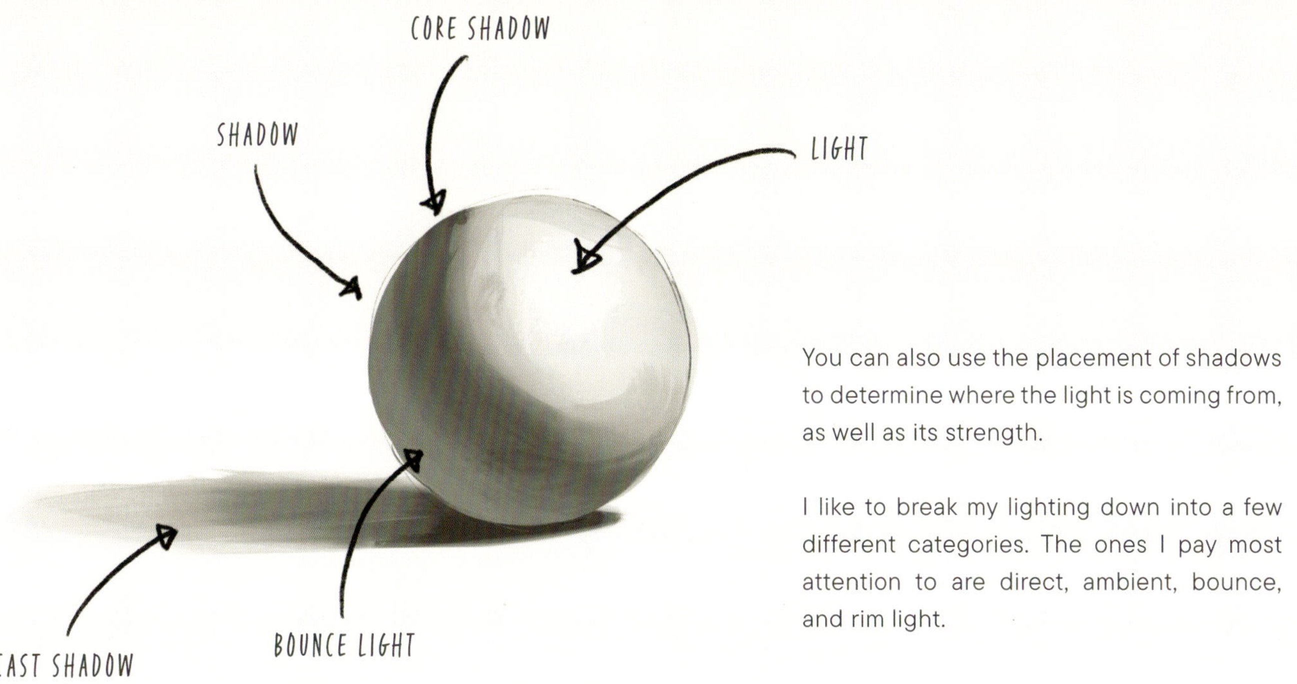

You can also use the placement of shadows to determine where the light is coming from, as well as its strength.

I like to break my lighting down into a few different categories. The ones I pay most attention to are direct, ambient, bounce, and rim light.

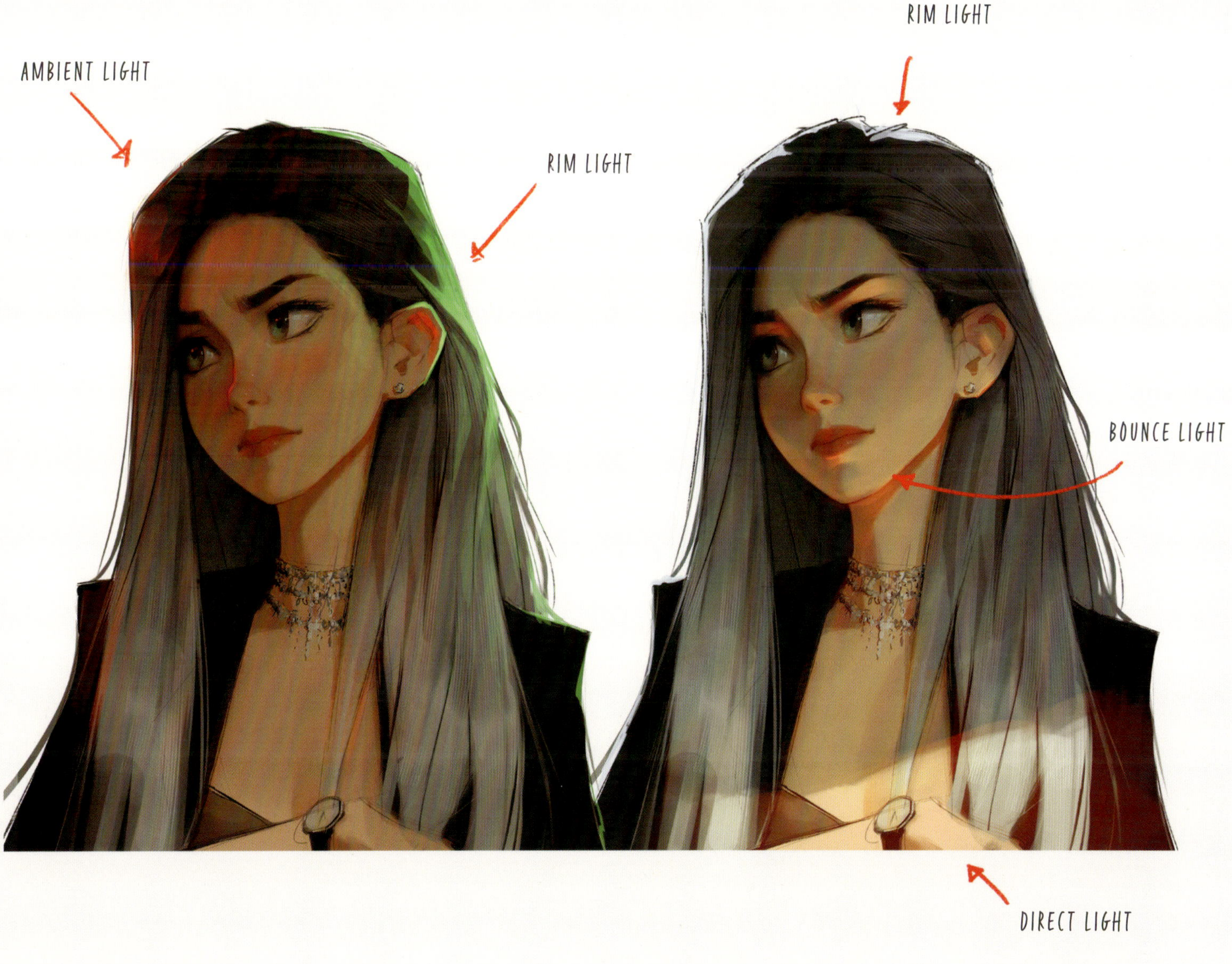

AMBIENT LIGHT

RIM LIGHT

RIM LIGHT

BOUNCE LIGHT

DIRECT LIGHT

DIRECT LIGHT

The definition can be found in the name. Direct light is usually the primary light source hitting the subject head on. It's essentially what allows you to see the subject with clarity. In my work, you'll see this most often in the form of sunlight or bright artificial light.

On this page, you may notice harder, more defined shadows with a clear distinction between light and dark. This is also the most important light source for conveying believability in terms of your subject's physical form. Simple lighting-practice pieces are a great way to study how direct light affects your subject. Use greyscale to focus on shapes and add in colour once you're comfortable with how lighting works.

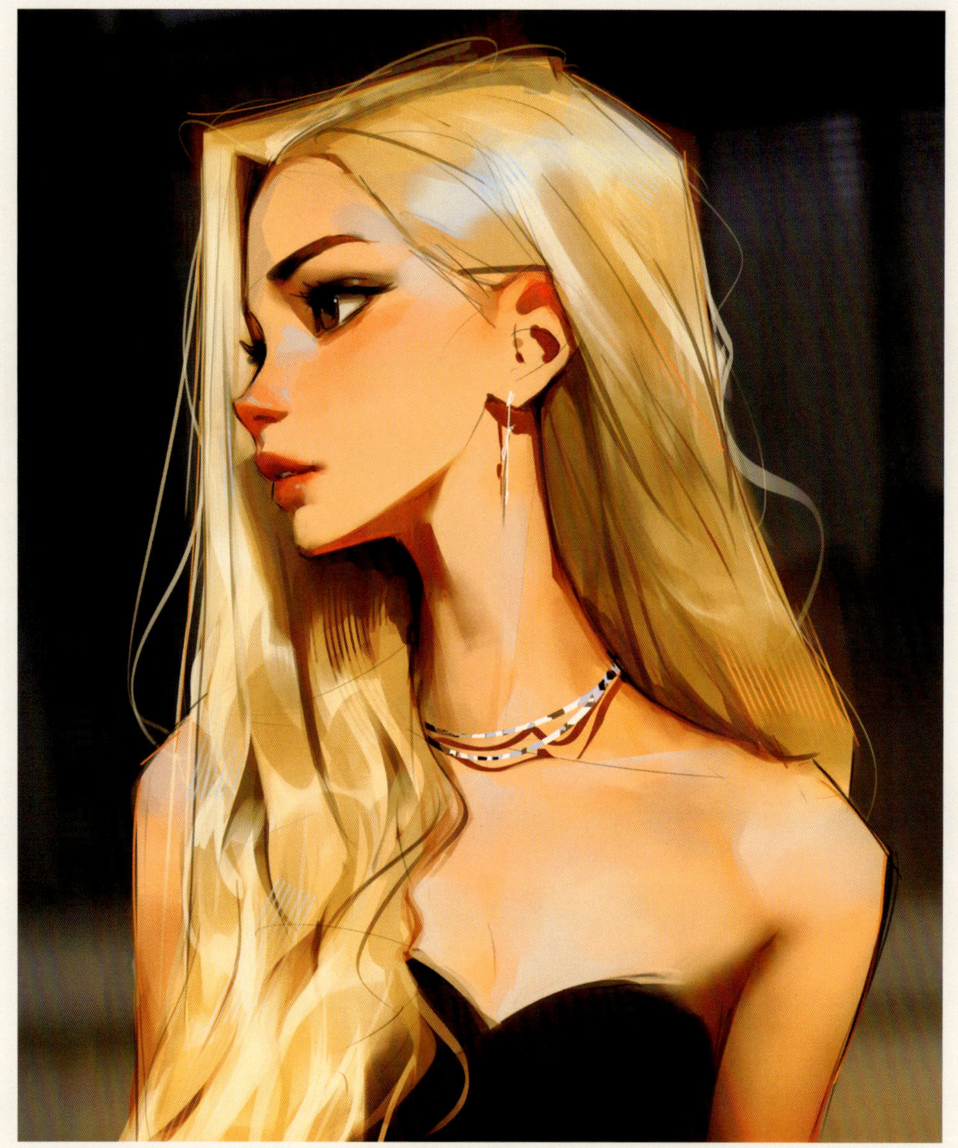

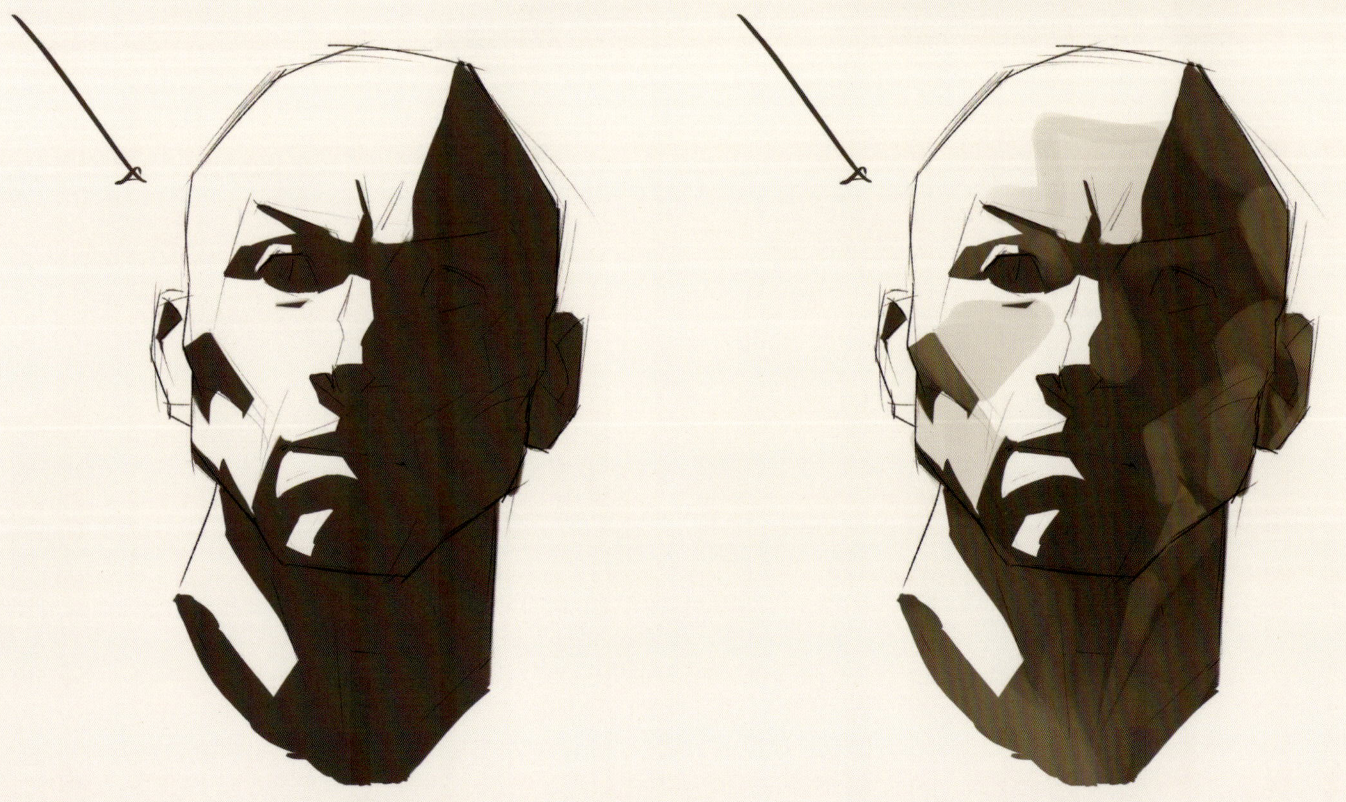

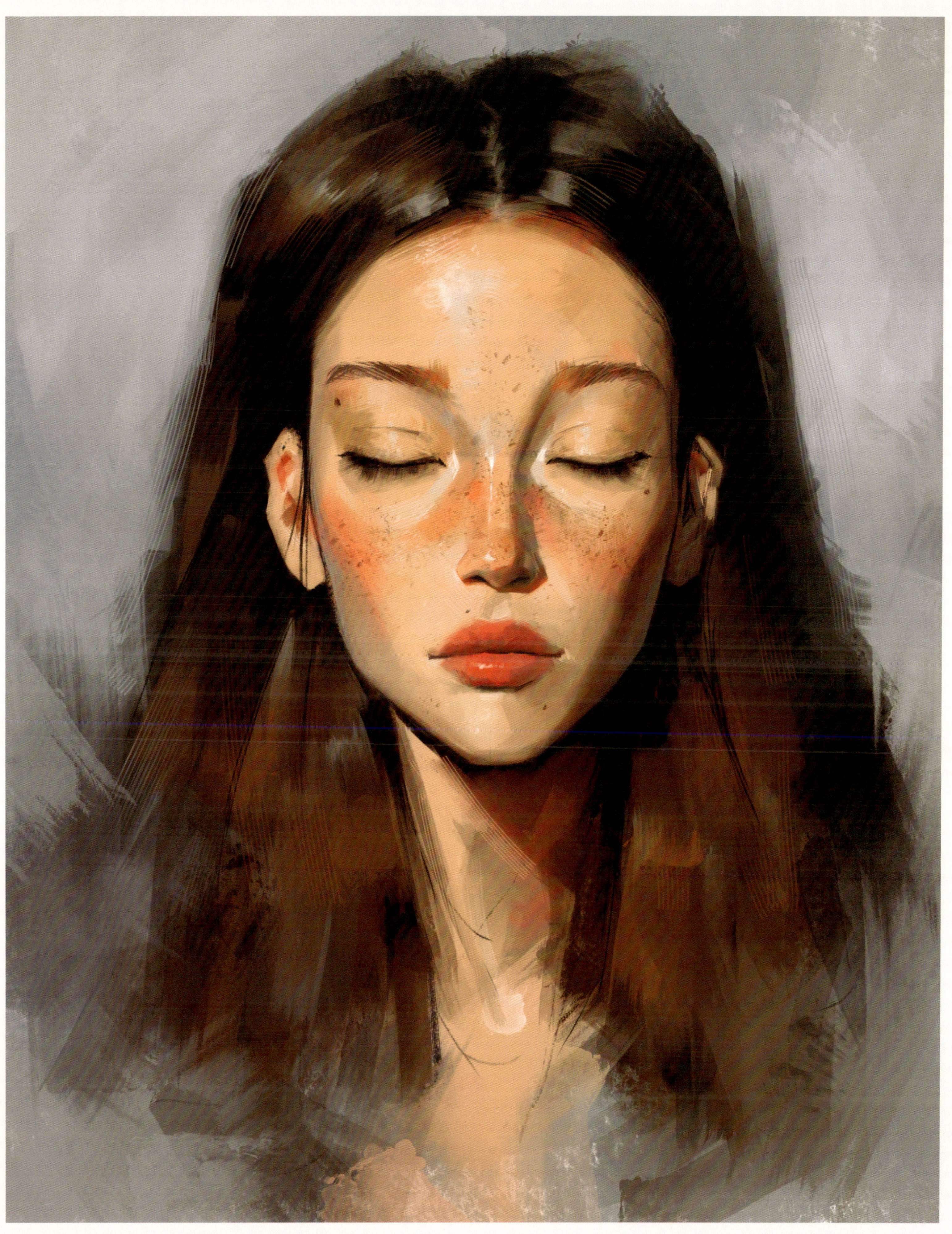

AMBIENT LIGHT

Ambient light is a weaker, softer light. I mostly use ambient lighting as a secondary light source. It usually gives colour to your shadows. When observing subjects in real life, you'll notice that shadows are rarely completely dark and void of colour. Instead, the colour of the shadow is most often determined by the ambient light in the environment.

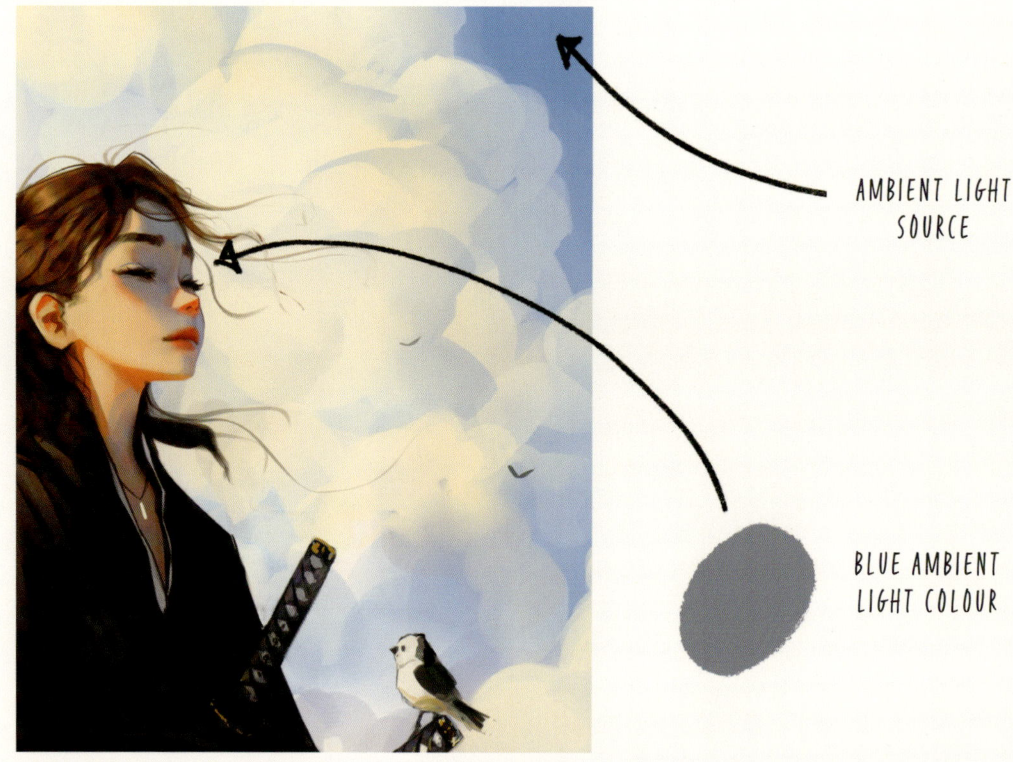

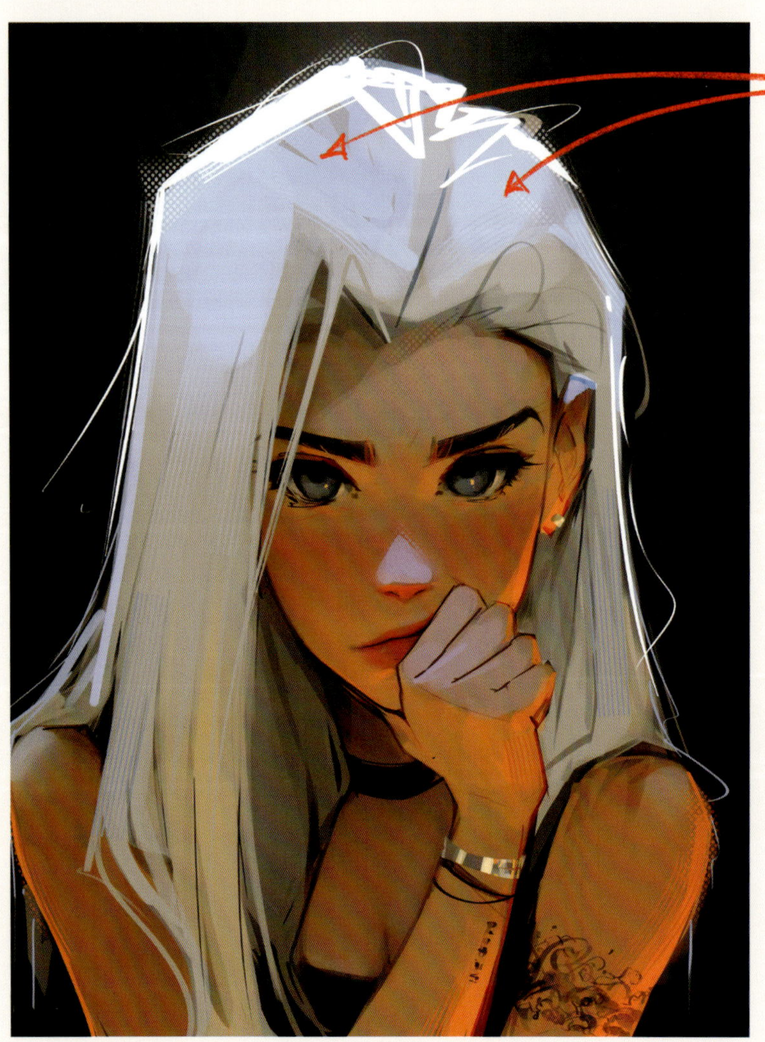

For example, the ambient light on a sunlit portrait outside is most often a soft-blue tone because it's affected by the blue ambient light from the sky above. It's a very soft light, but it definitely affects the colour of your subject.

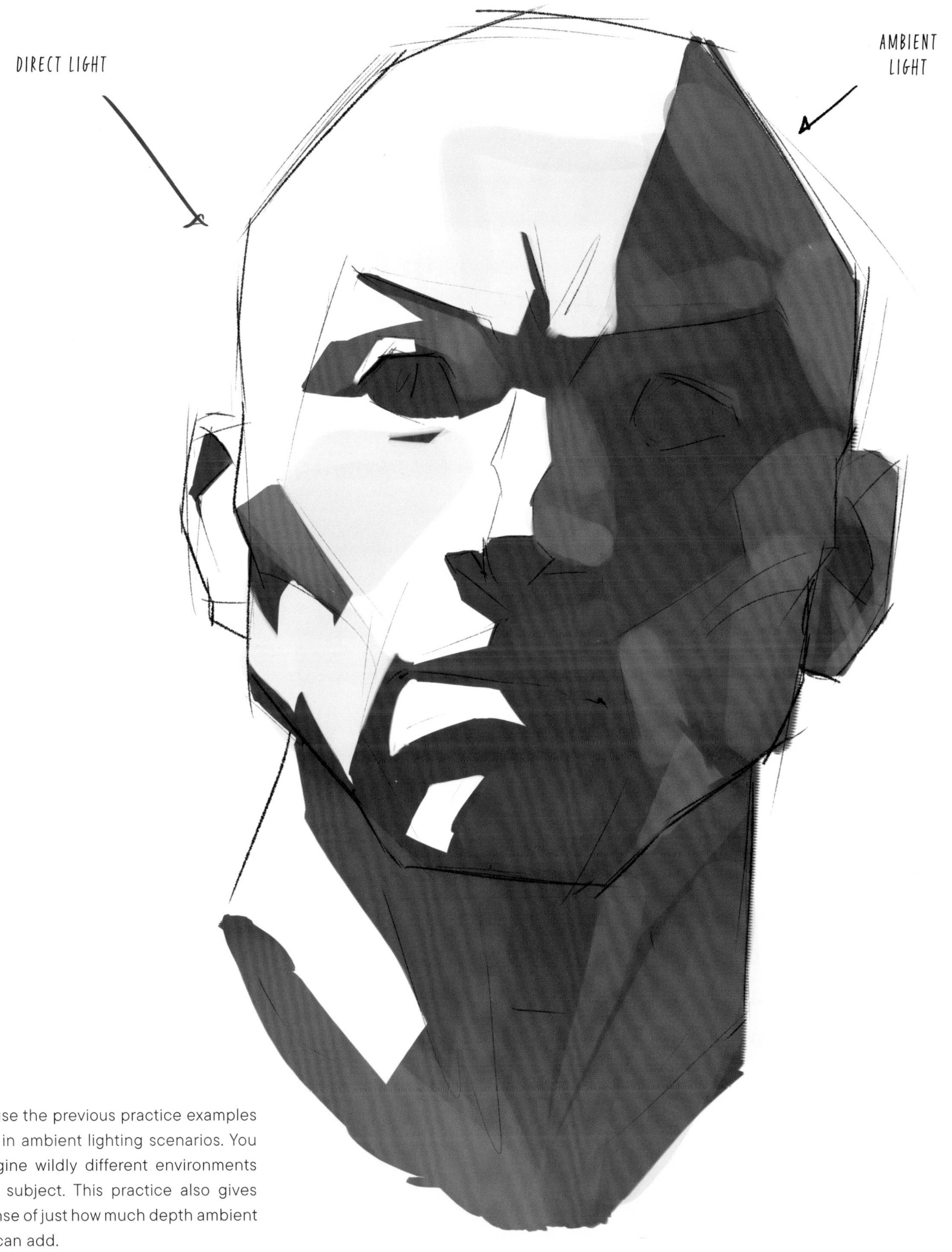

I like to use the previous practice examples and add in ambient lighting scenarios. You can imagine wildly different environments for each subject. This practice also gives you a sense of just how much depth ambient lighting can add.

BOUNCE LIGHT

Bounce light refers to light rays that come in contact with a surface, bounce off that surface, and then hit other surfaces in the scene. This is one of the properties of light that can instantly make your paintings come to life, if it's done correctly.

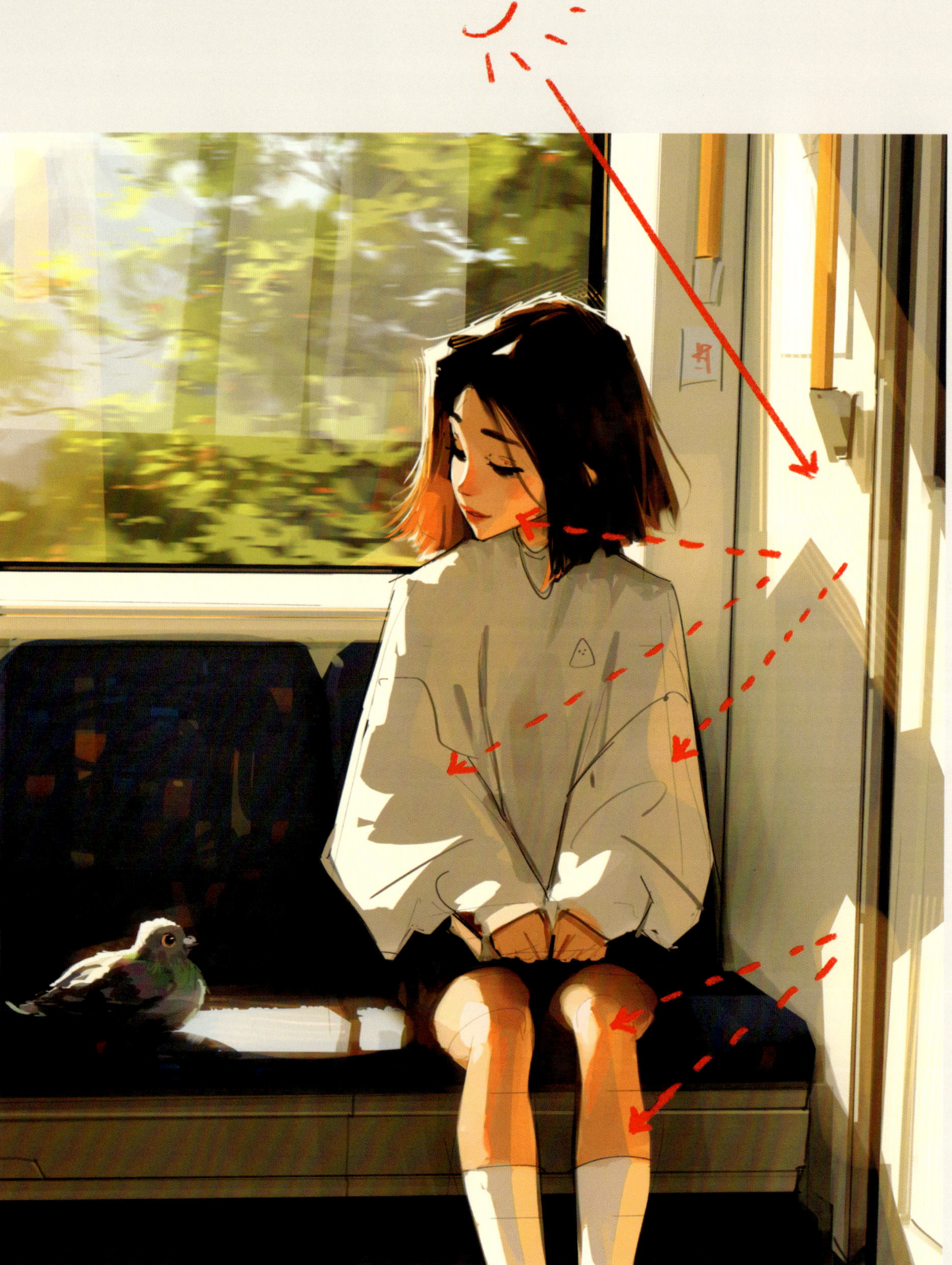

When there is a strong light source in a scene, such as sunlight, you'll often find bounce light present too. When sunlight hits a surface like the ground, some of it will bounce back up, hitting your subject at an upwards angle.

When light bounces off a surface and hits another surface, some of the colours of the initial surface will be transferred onto the next surface the light ray touches. When sunlight makes contact with a grassy field and bounces back up, the bounce light will have a green hue. Similarly, when a spotlight meets a red floor, the bounce light will have a red hue.

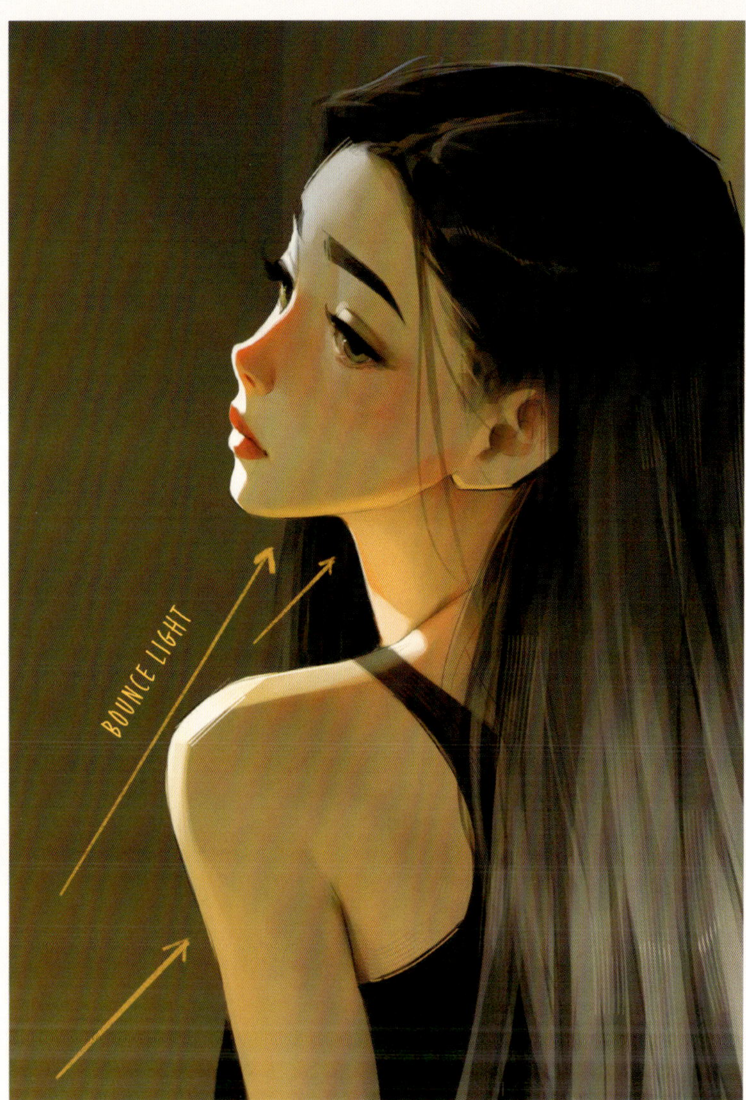

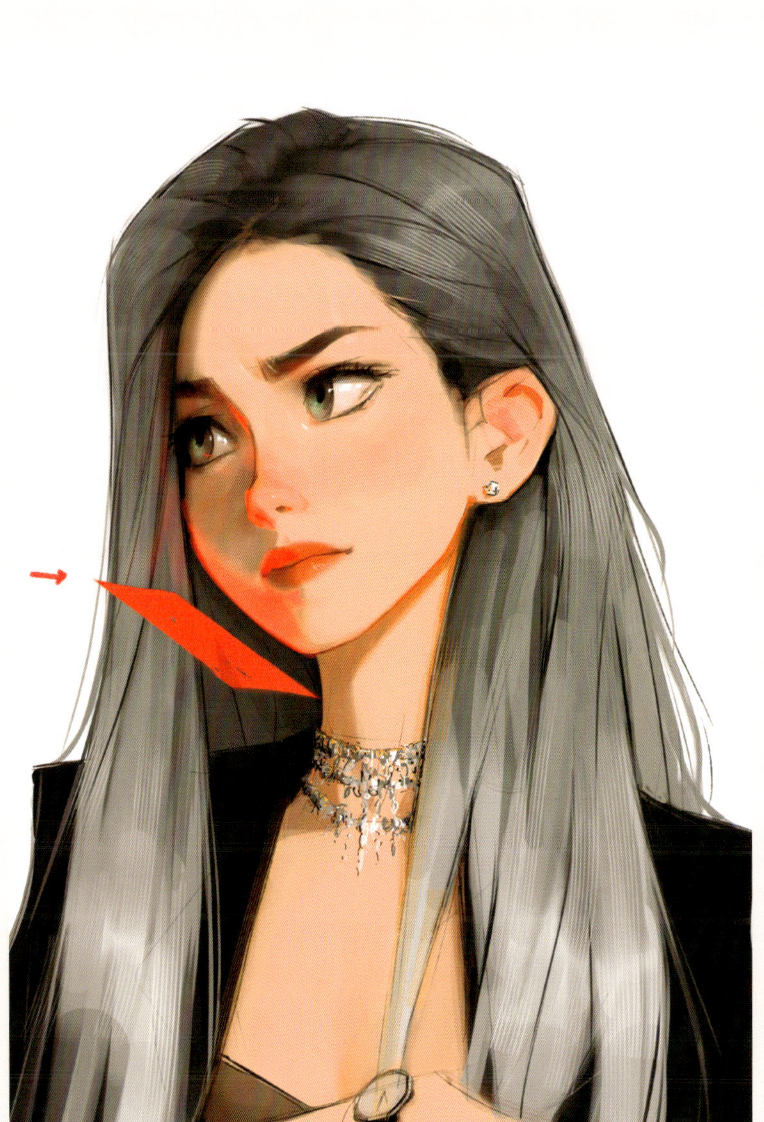

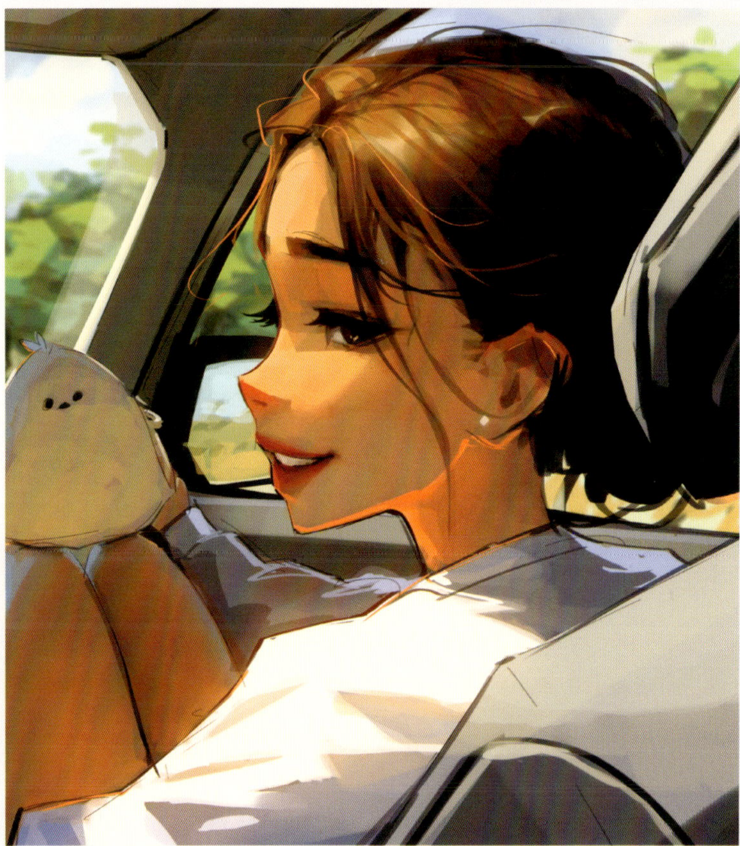

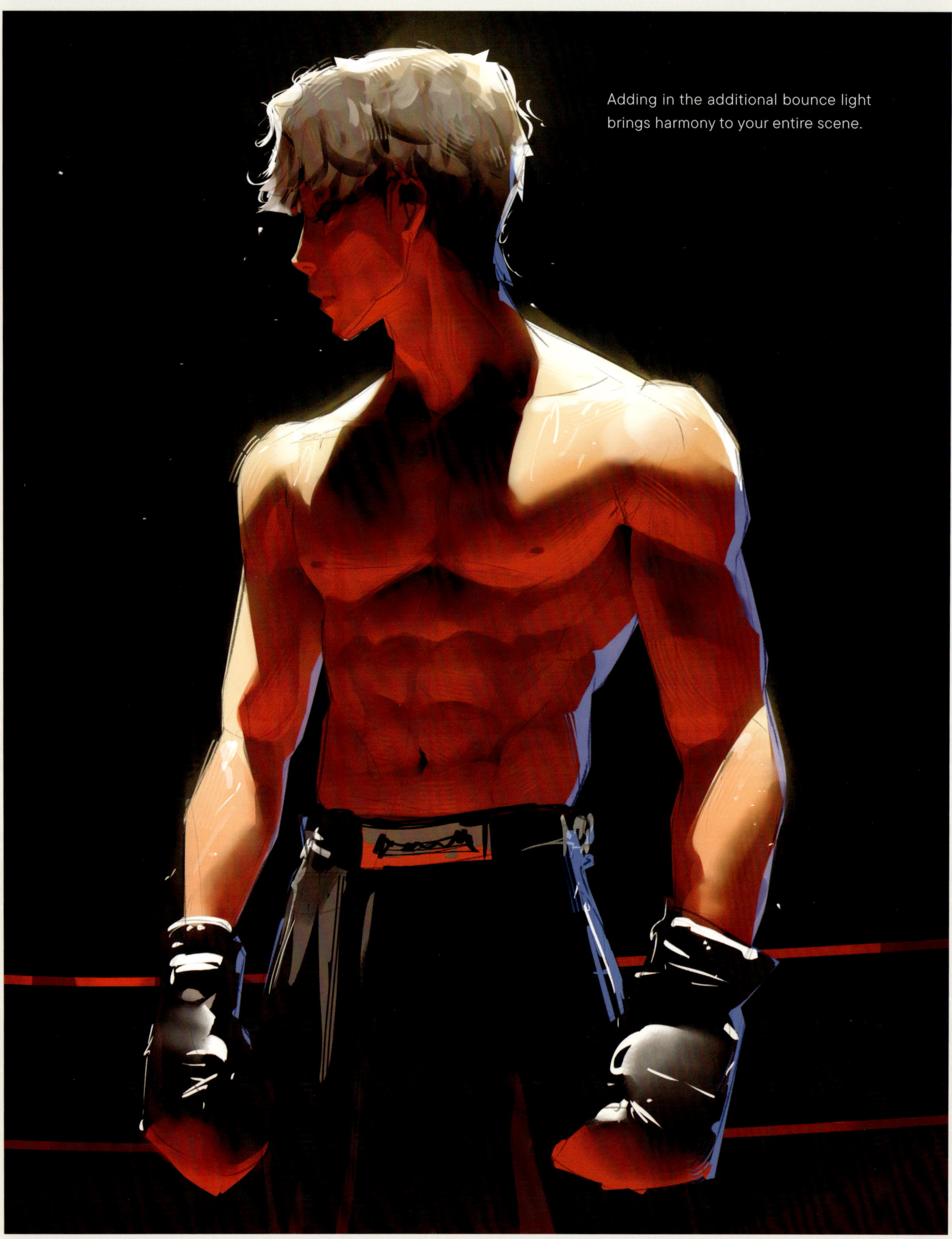

Adding in the additional bounce light brings harmony to your entire scene.

RIM LIGHT

Rim light occurs when the direct light is somewhere behind your subject. Instead of illuminating the surface of the subject facing you, it illuminates the other side facing away from you. This scenario is extremely useful in creating contrast and drawing attention to a silhouette.

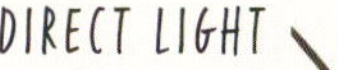

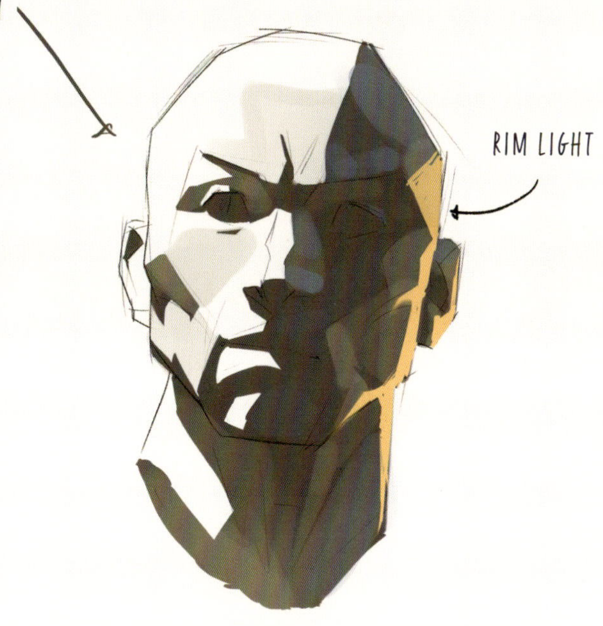

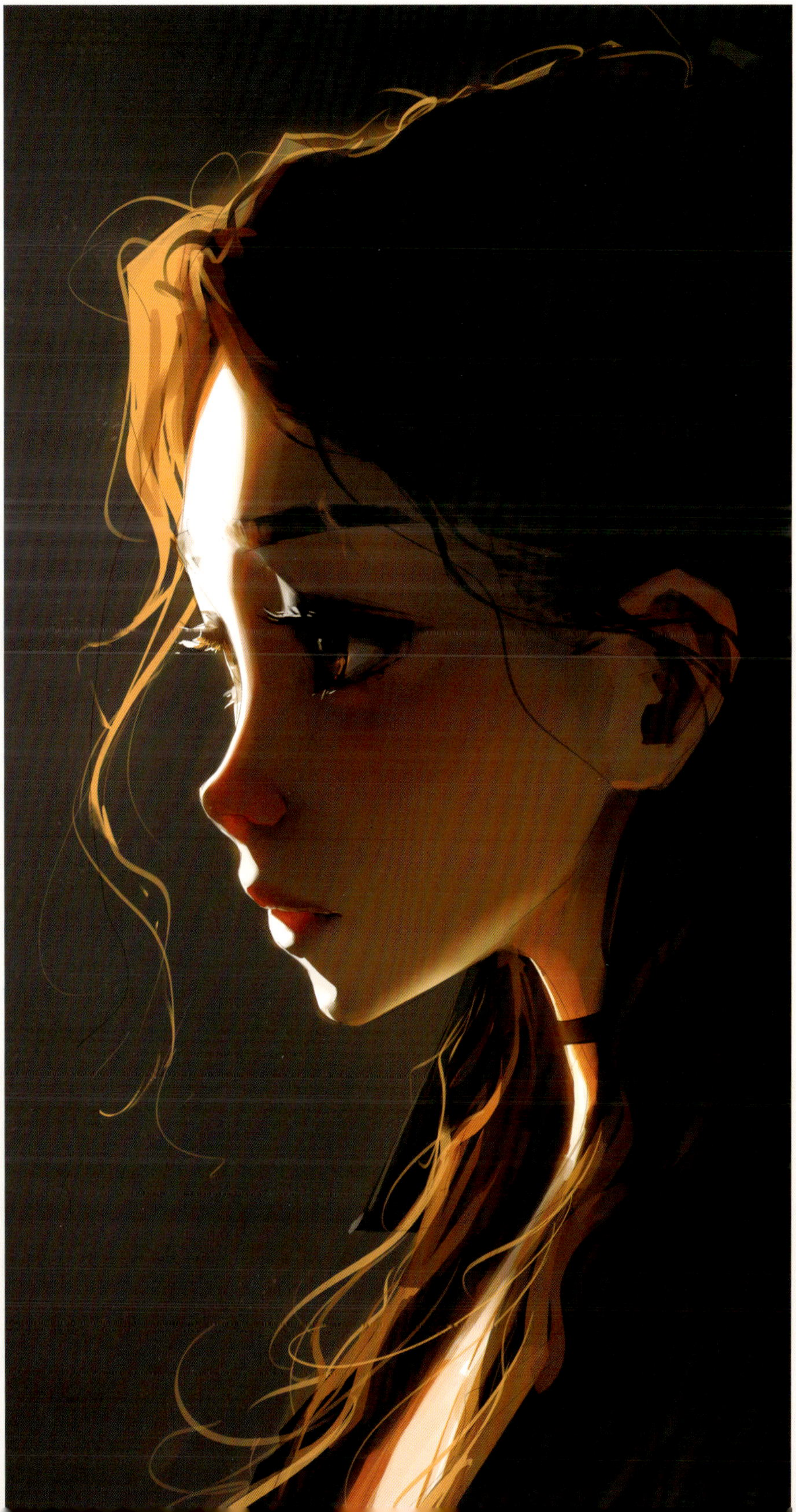

Keep in mind that this light is not an evenly distributed rim along the silhouette of your character. It will actually interact with the many planes and surfaces you'll find on your subject. There will be areas where the rim light is strong and thick, and others where it becomes so thin that it's barely perceptible.

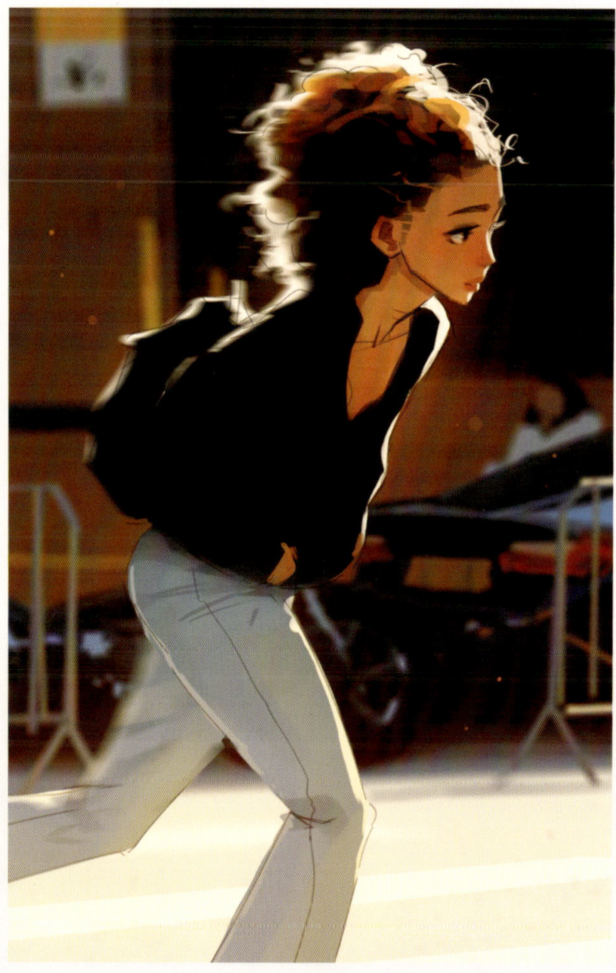

EXPRESSIONS

Expressions really breathe life into your characters. I've always had a hard time with expressions and still struggle to this day. I don't think that will ever go away. But to me, expressions are one of the most fun things to draw.

I studied a lot of animation character designs and film stills to better understand how I could simplify expressions to make them readable. There are artists I look up to for this, such as Glen Keane; his work on the Disney animated film *Tangled* is a great example of his mastery of simplified and expressive characters. Studying from another artist can often show you things that you may not think of on your own, such as how much you can stretch a face or exaggerate focal points like the eyes.

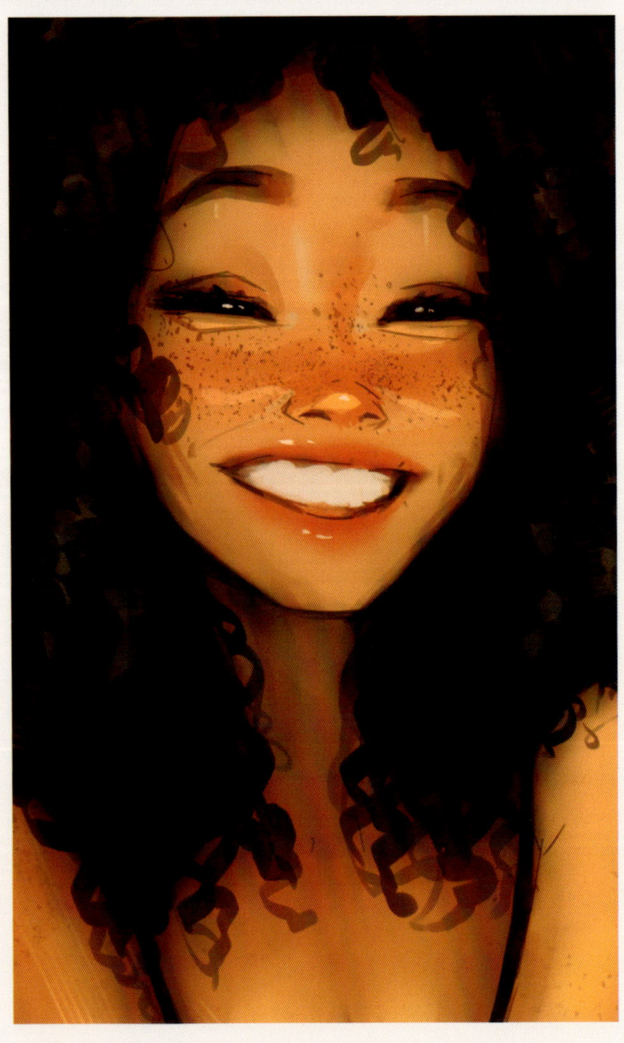

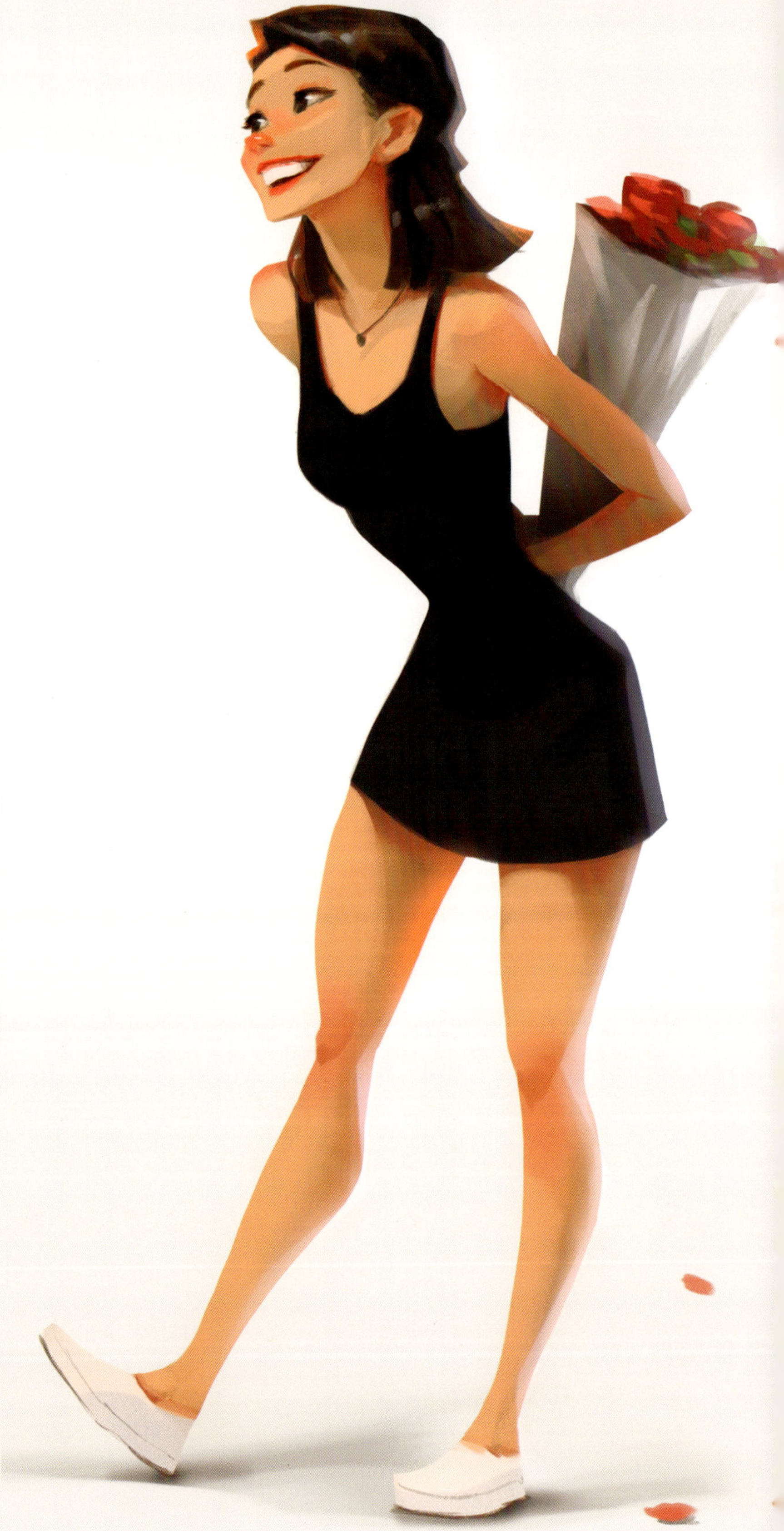

I've found that there are certain elements of the face that make a really big difference to how a character's expression is perceived. These include the brows, eyelids, and mouth. But just before we dive into that, there are some important fundamentals to keep in mind.

In real life, the majority of faces are divided into three equal vertical portions: the first is the forehead, the second is the nose, and the third is the mouth and chin.

There are always exceptions to these rules, but you can use them as a general guide. In more expressively stylized drawings, you may find that artists allocate a larger portion of the face to the nose segment, which contains the eyes. This is because it's in our nature to focus on another person's eyes when looking at their face, and the eye area can often contain a significant amount of information.

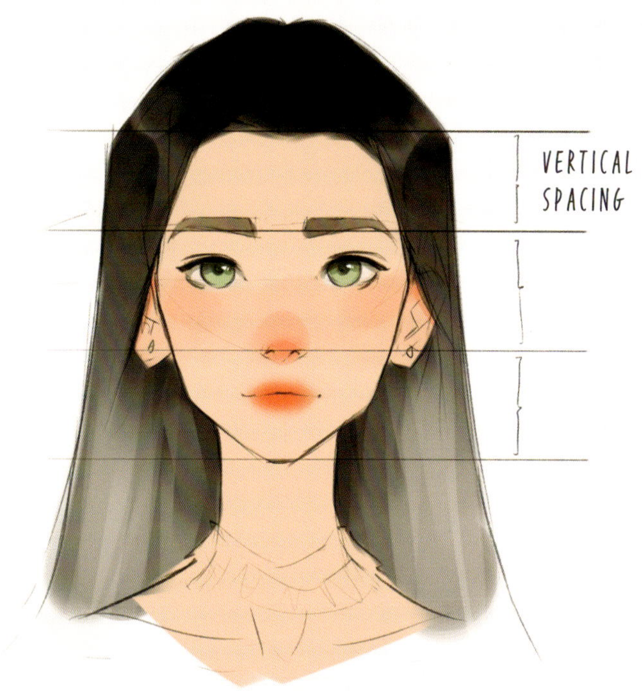

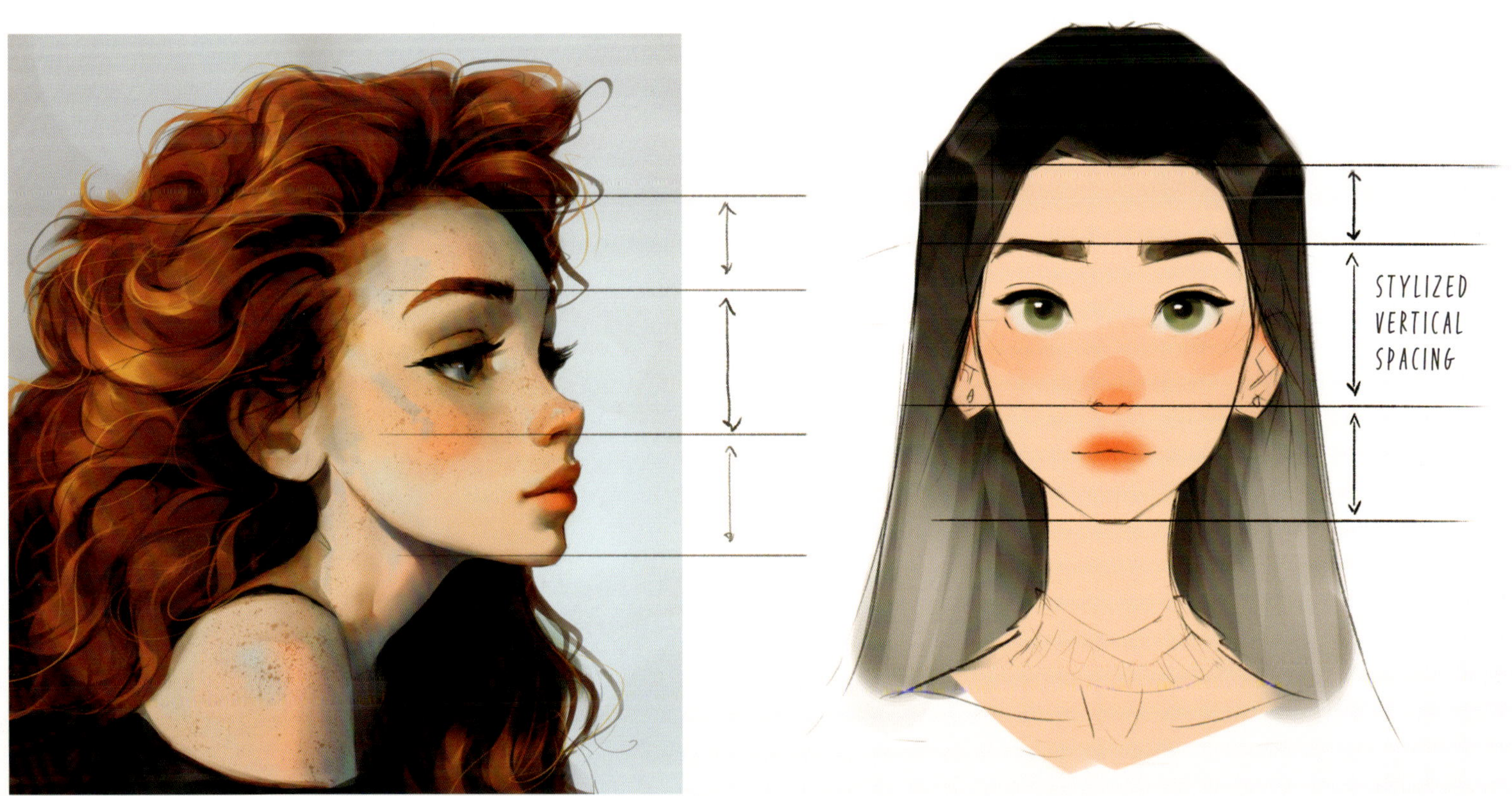

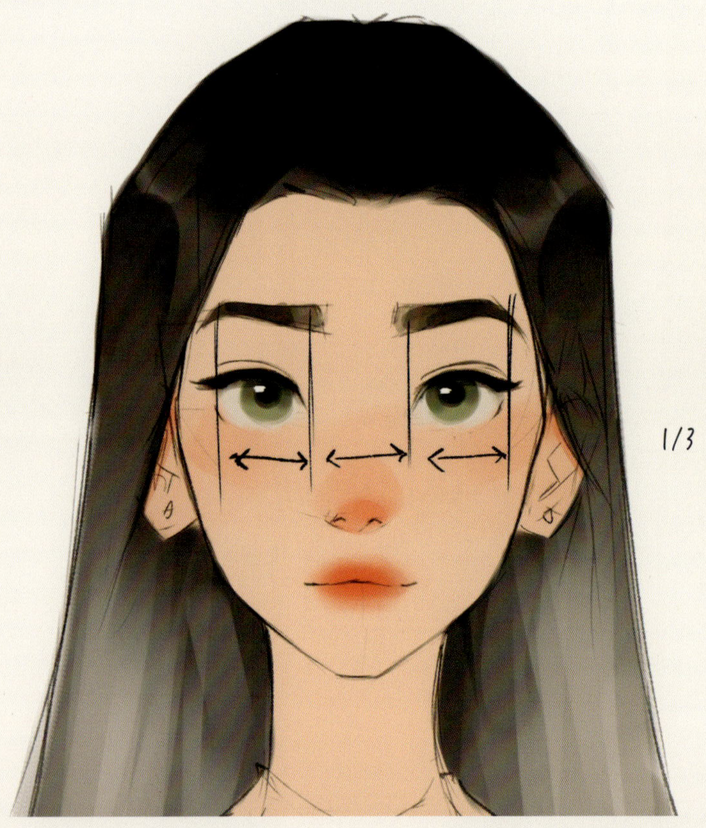

The second set of measurements are the horizontal measurements of the eyes. Remember that the space between the eyes is most commonly equal to the length of one entire eye. Again, there are exceptions to this in real life; however, it's a very valuable rule to keep in mind.

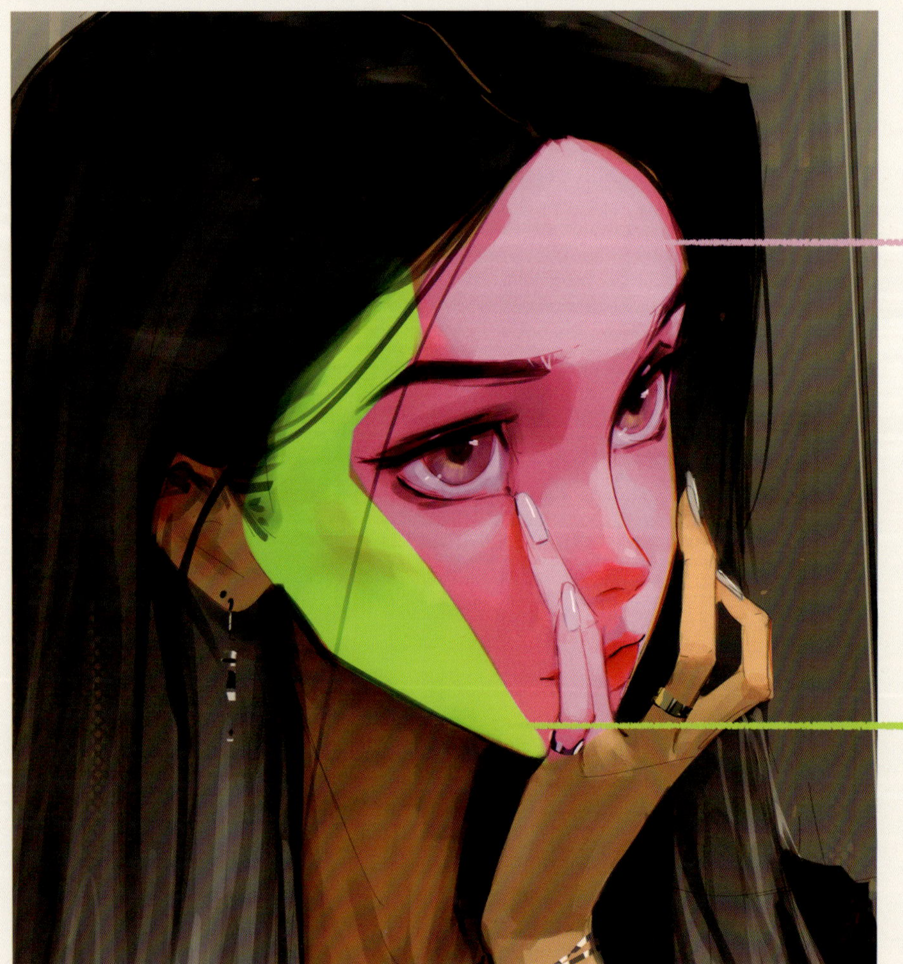

FRONT PLANES

Lastly, always make sure your character's face doesn't melt off the front plain. No matter what angle or expression, your character's facial features should sit on the same front plain of the face. One of the most common mistakes made by beginners is allowing the eyes, or the corner of the mouth, to slip onto a side plane.

SIDE PLANES

BROWS

The brows are relatively straightforward. They can convey certain expressions on their own. For example, when both brows are pointed down in the middle, we interpret this as an angry expression. When both brows are raised in the centre but dip at the side, this could represent a sad expression.

The brows can also convey more nuanced expressions depending on the type of movements on the other parts of the face. The overall expression depends on a combination of different types of movements in the brows, eyes, and mouth. An 'angry' or lowered brow combined with a smiling mouth can communicate a sense of evil intent or determination. However, when it's combined with a frowning mouth, it can suggest pure discontent.

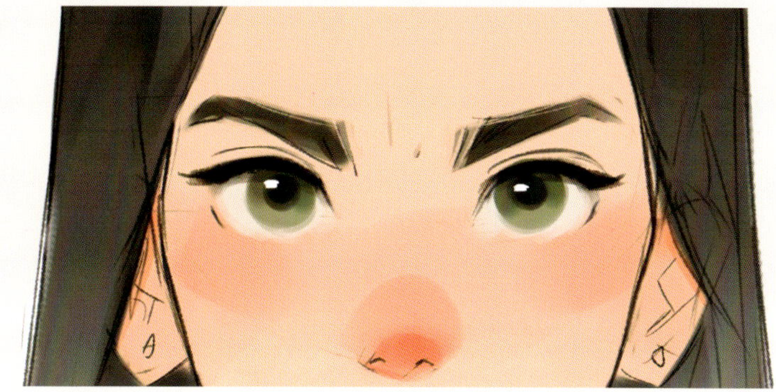

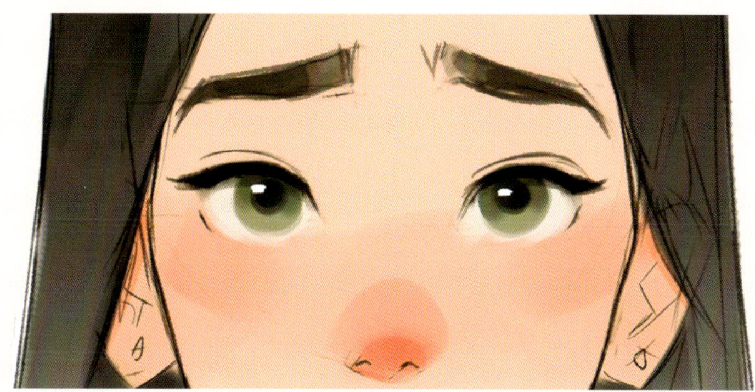

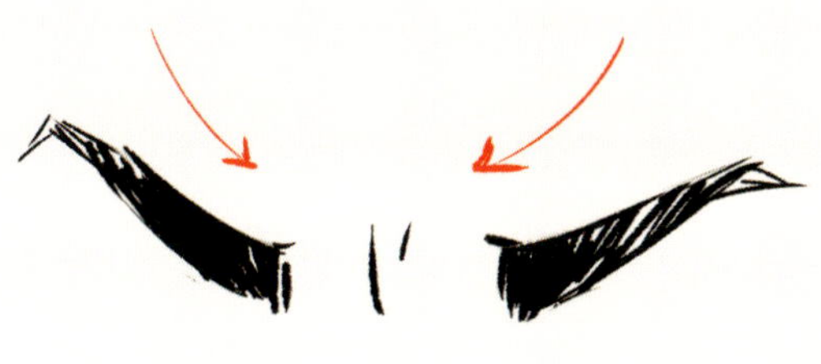

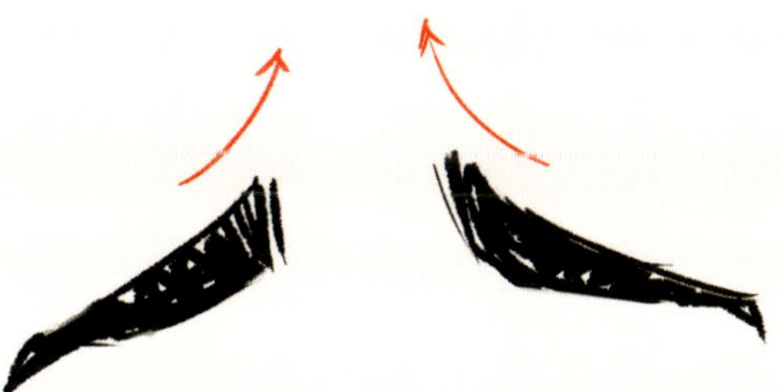

The brows can also move independently of each other. One raised brow and one lowered brow gives us the feeling of confusion or mischief.

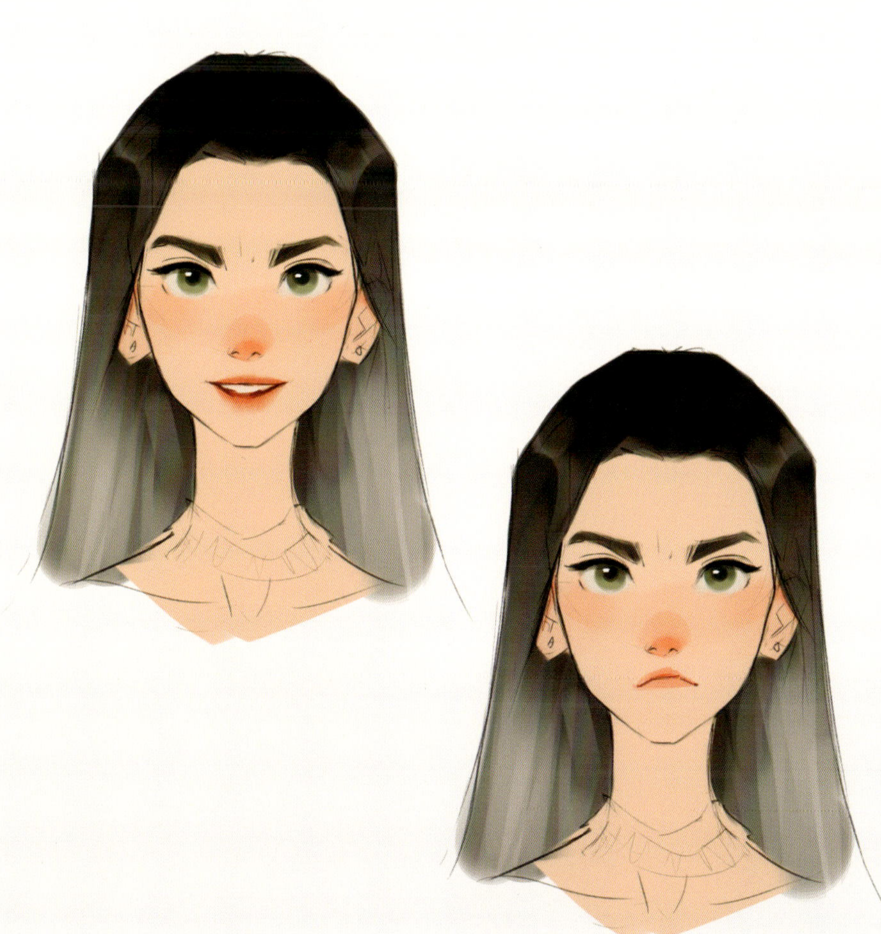

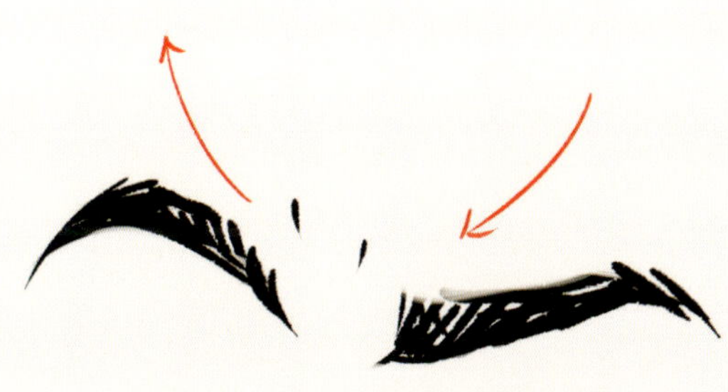

EYES

The eyes are powerful tools that can be used to sell an expression. Eye movements are often subtle, but can contain the majority of emotional weight.

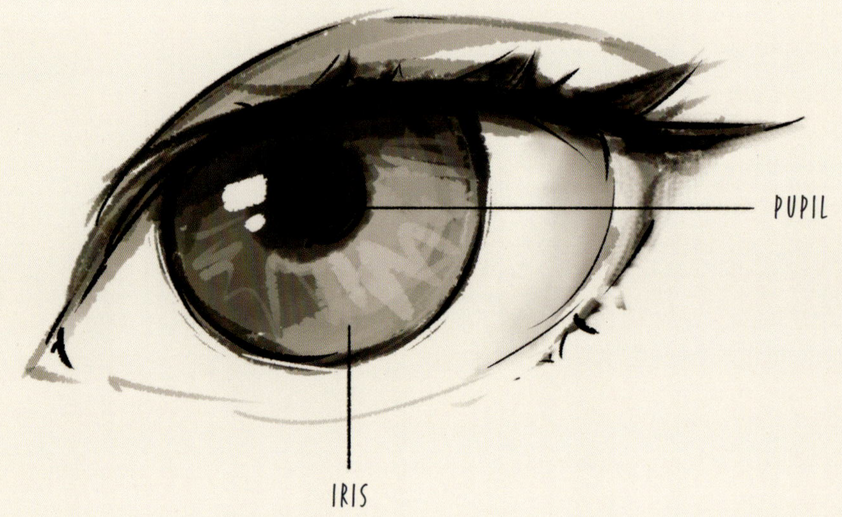

IRIS POSITION

The first thing I like to consider for the eyes is the positioning of the iris. The iris is the round disc shape in the centre of our eyeball. Our pupil sits in the centre of the iris. This part of the eye is an aperture that allows light to flood into the eye, hence why it is the darkest part.

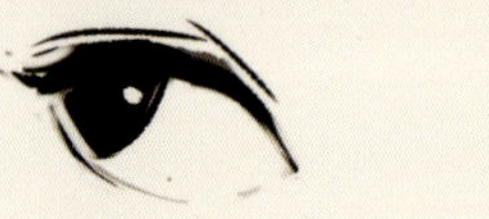

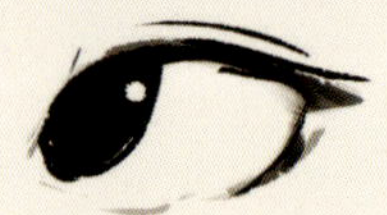

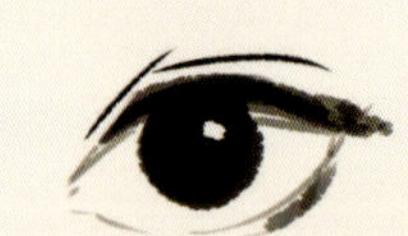

The position of the iris within the opening of the eyelids tells us where a character is looking. In terms of storytelling, getting your character to look in the right direction is crucial, and you have to ensure that both eyes appear to be looking in the same direction.

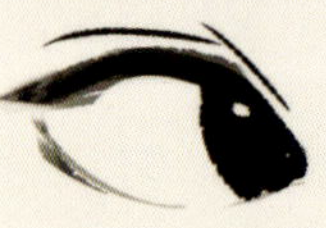

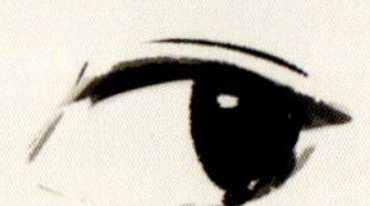

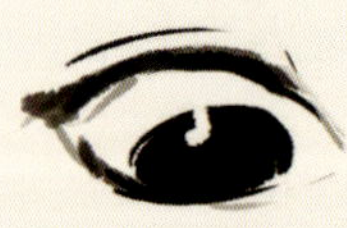

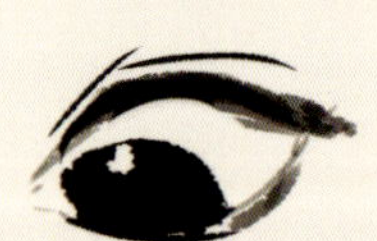

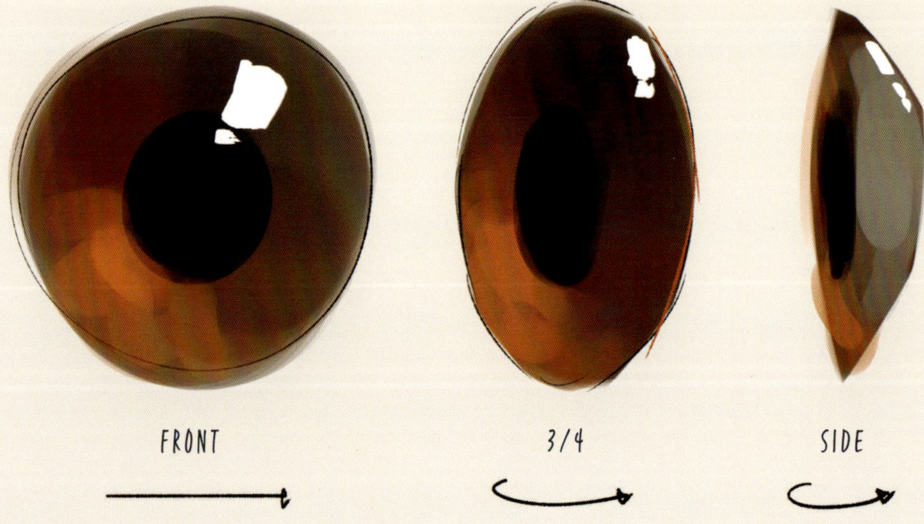

Remember that from straight on, the iris is a perfectly round disc. But as the eye moves to one side, the iris will appear more oval in shape. This occurs because of a simple distortion in perspective. If you take a 2D circle and start to turn it, the surface you see will appear slimmer the further you turn.

HOW MUCH OF THE IRIS CAN YOU SEE?

Once you've determined the placement of the iris and the direction your character is looking, the next step is to figure out how much of the iris you can see.

If part of the iris's top half is obscured, this means your character's top eyelid is hanging down over the eye in a more neutral position. This is a very common resting position for most eyes. You also have to pay attention to how much of the top half is covered. If almost all of the top half of the iris is covered, your character may look tired or apathetic. In contrast, if the top portion of the iris is visible, this might imply a sense of excitement, shock, or fear. Our top lids only reveal the top of the iris when we are triggered by some external factor. If the entire iris is visible and the eyelids don't cover any of it, your character is certainly experiencing some sort of excitement or surprise. Or they could just be drawn to look a little strange.

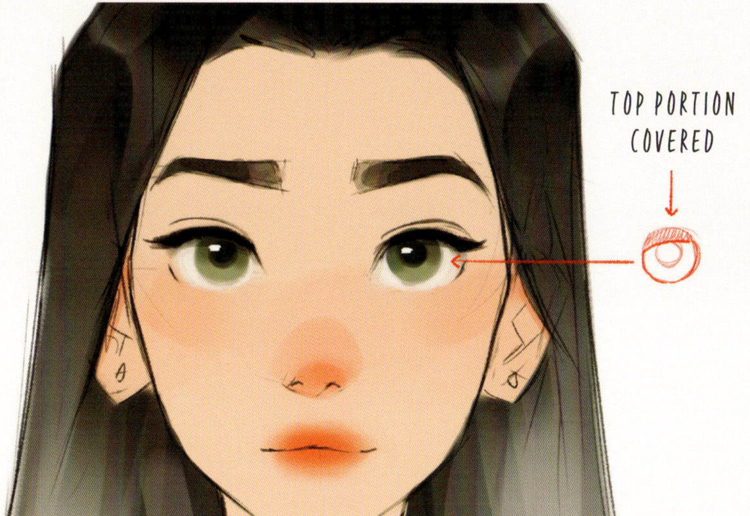

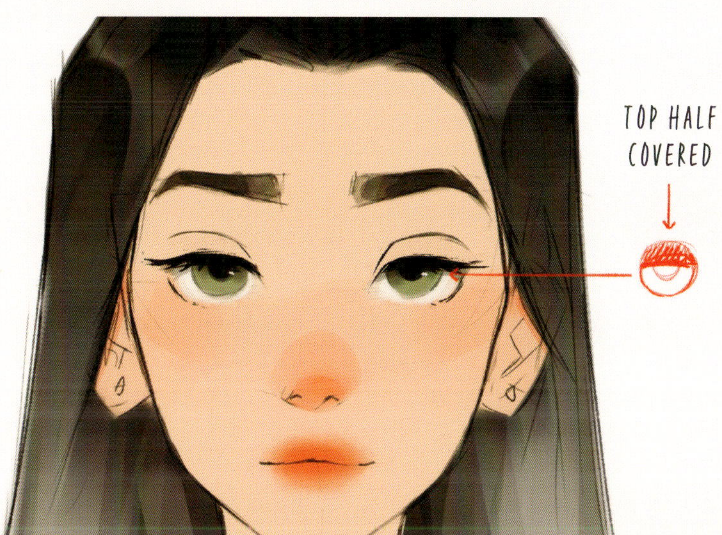

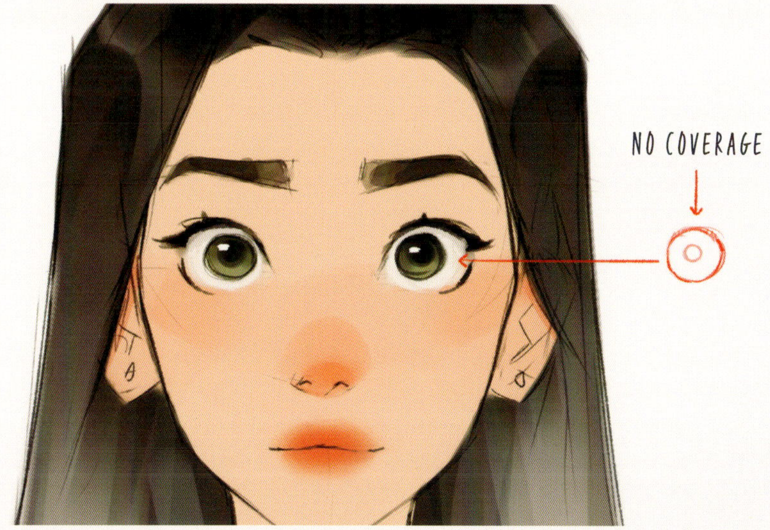

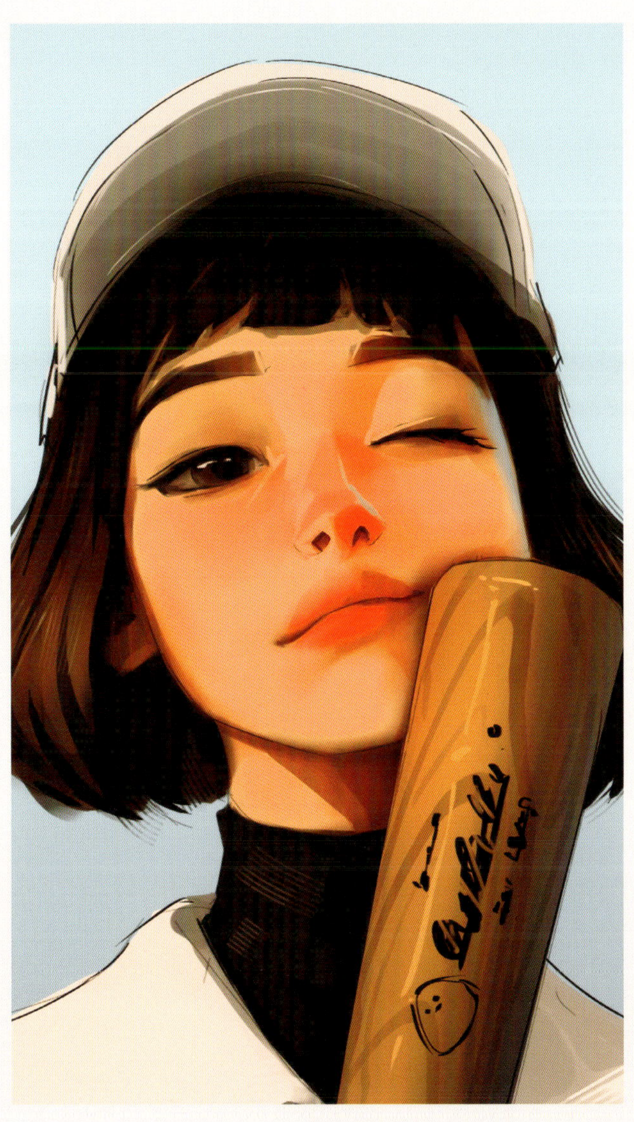

Of course, these are general rules, and depending on the art style in question, there will be exceptions to these rules. This is simply what I've learned and what works best for me.

MOUTH

When it comes to the mouth, you'll mostly examine the corner positionings in relation to the centre, as well as its overall shape and whether it's opened or closed.

When the mouth is spread wide and the corners are pulled back to the sides, we read this as a smile. A smile always brings the corners of the mouth outwards from the centre. Depending on the individual, you may notice different heights for them. Some people may have more curved smiles, while others may have flatter smiles.

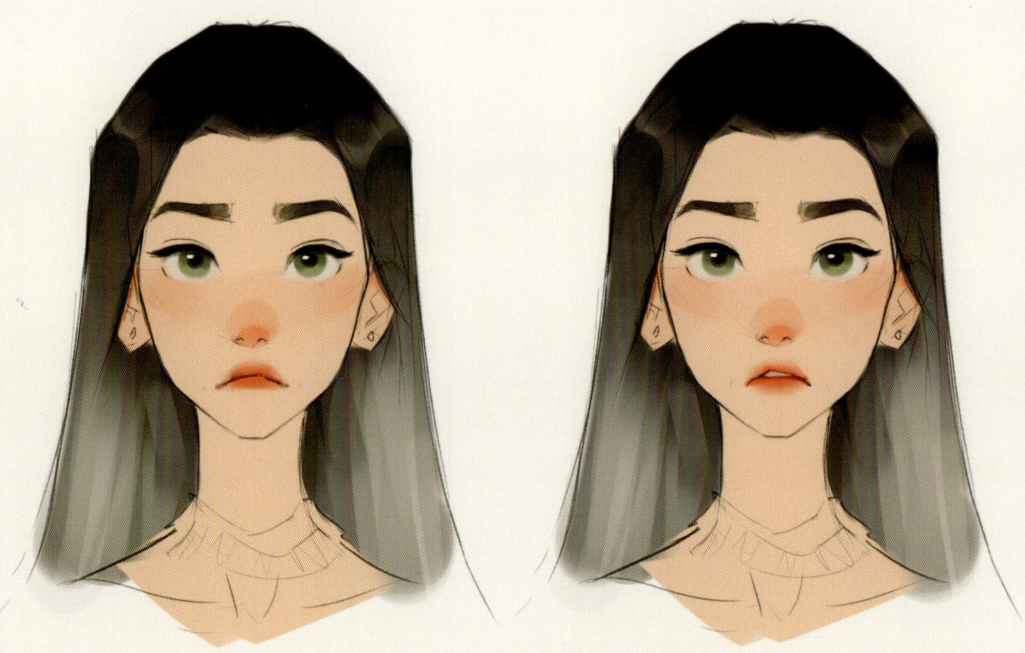

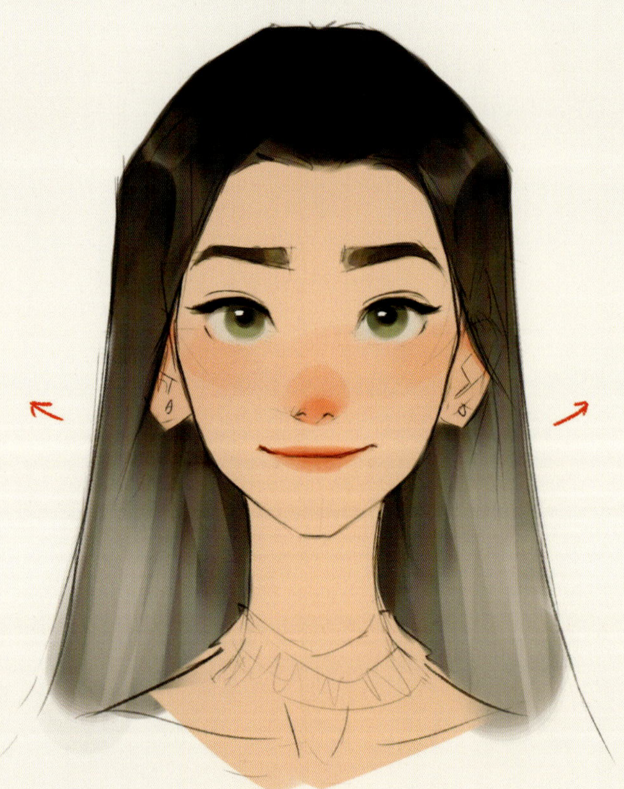

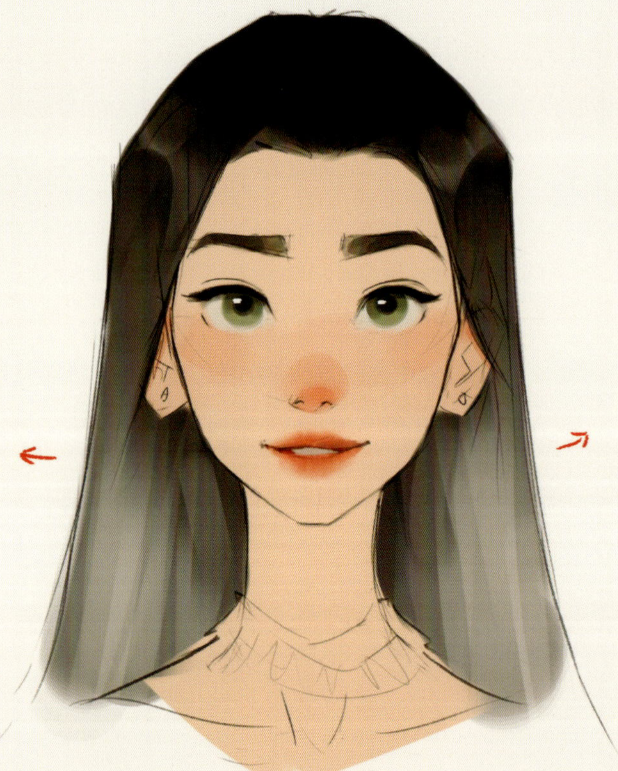

When the corners of the mouth are dragged downwards, that's a frown. This is most often a sign of displeasure; it could be anger or sadness, but sometimes it could also be a face of approval or deep consideration. I'll touch more on this in the final section.

Another thing to look for is the opening of the mouth and how much of the character's teeth you see. Do you see the teeth at all? Is the top row of teeth more visible than the bottom row?

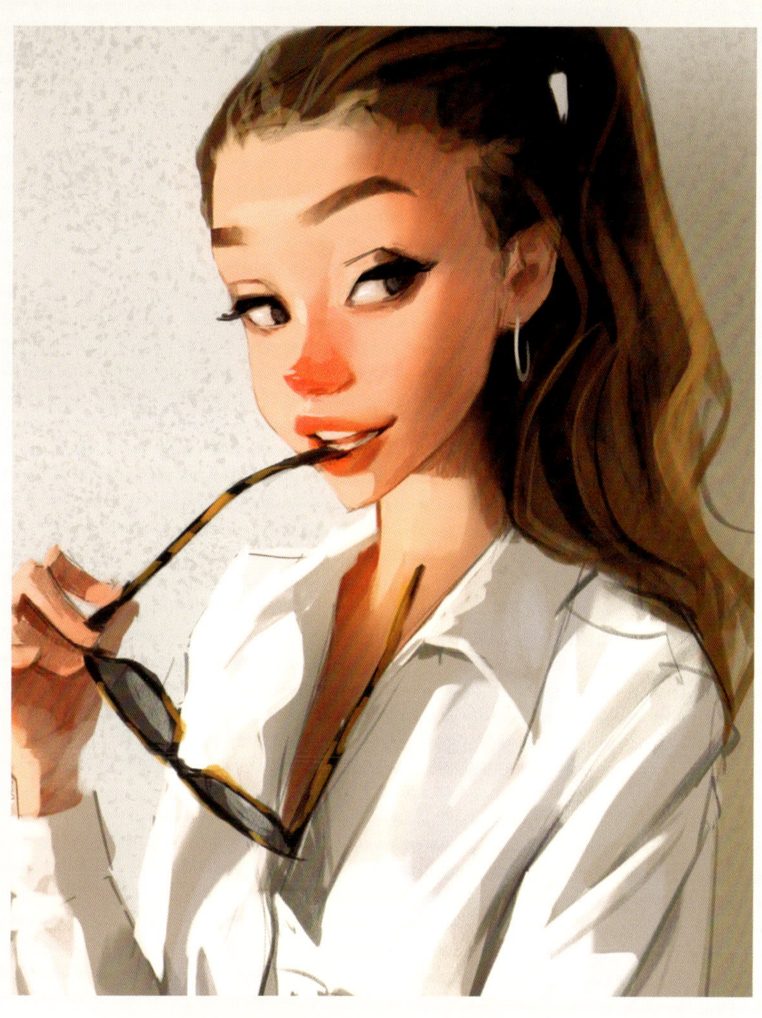
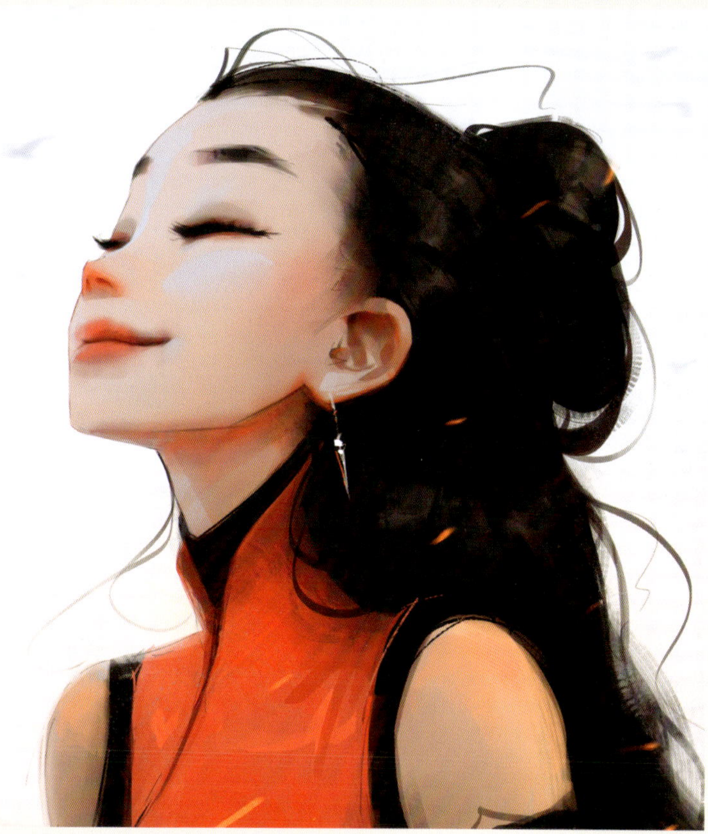
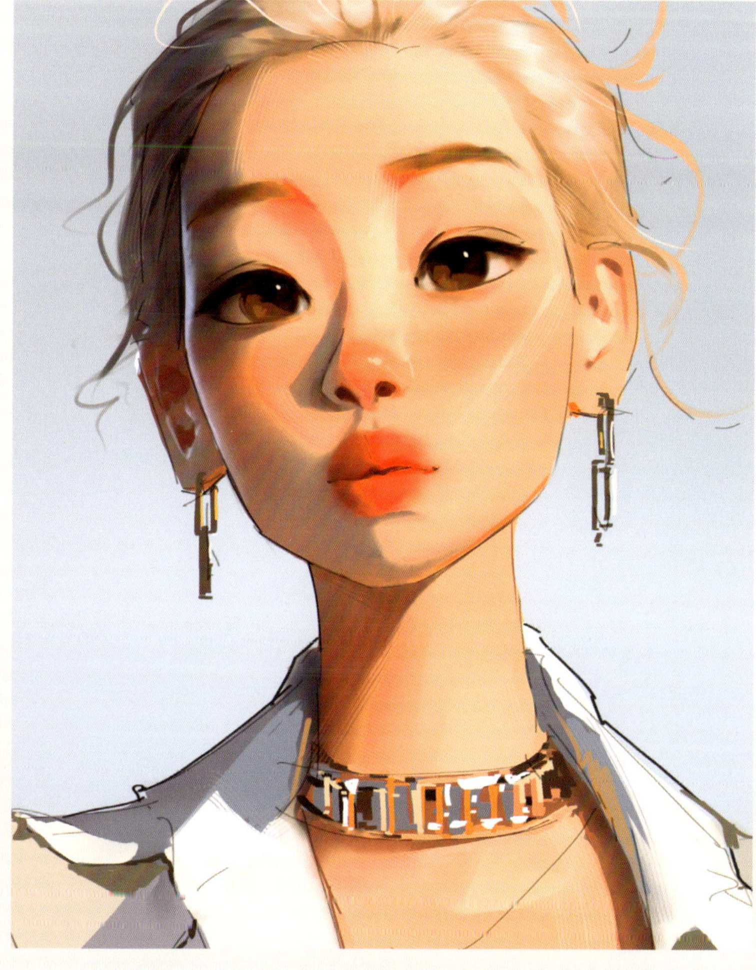
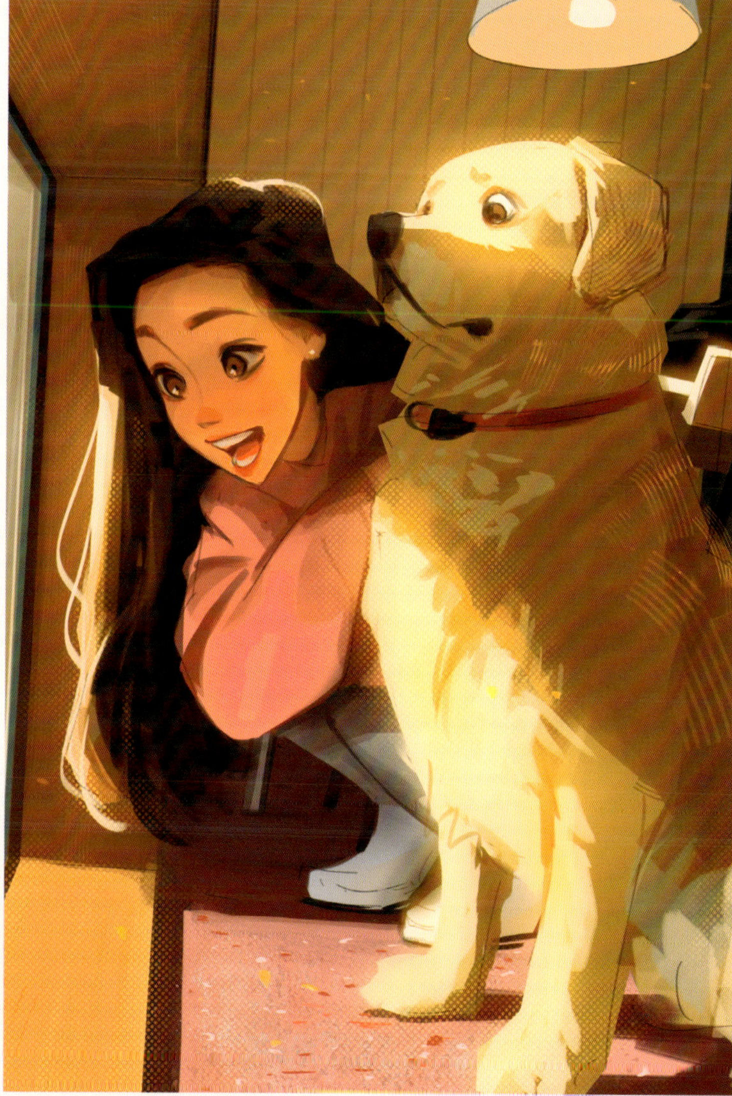

HOW TO DRAW COMMON EXPRESSIONS

NEUTRAL

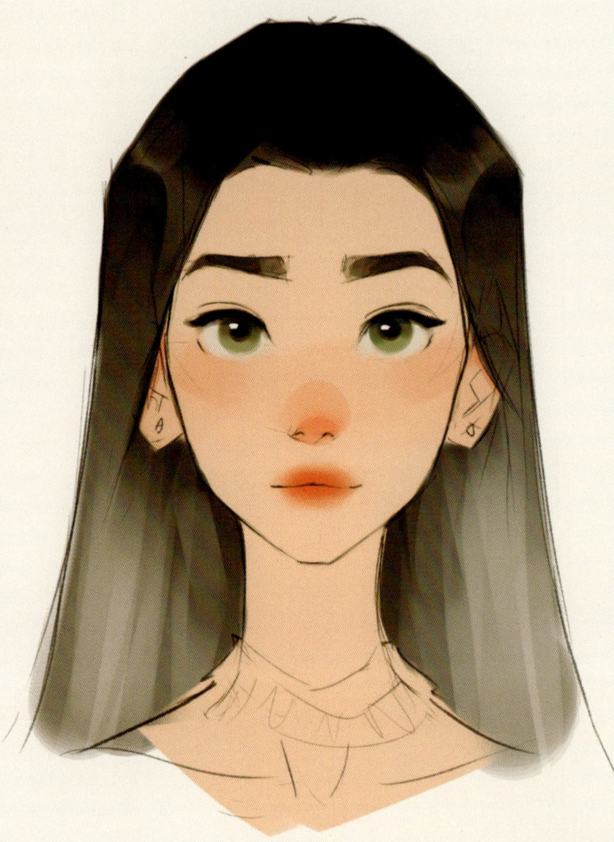

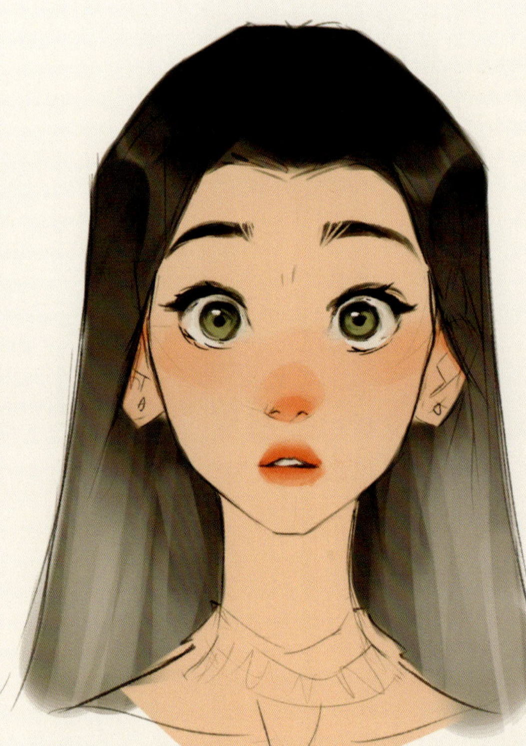

- Raised inner brow
- Raised upper lids
- Lowered mouth corners

SURPRISED

When a character is surprised, you'll often find their eyes wide open; the entire iris will be visible and their pupils may be smaller as a result of their eyes letting in more light. They may also have a slightly opened mouth or a closed neutral one depending on the situation they're reacting to.

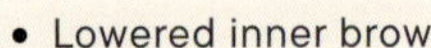

- Lowered inner brow
- Tense lower lid
- Downturned mouth

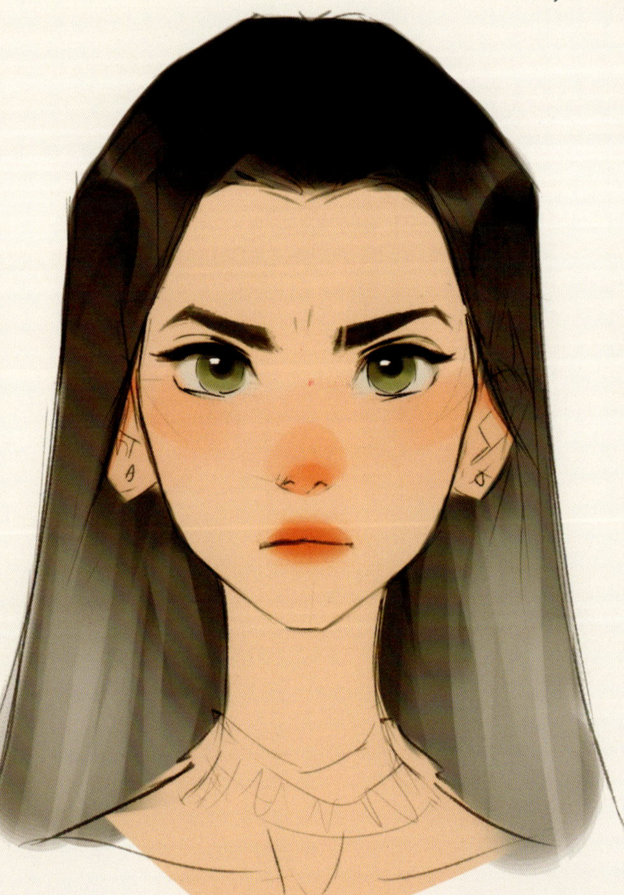

ANGRY

Anger implies tension. When a character is angry, their facial features usually reflect this. The brows will be pointed downwards in the centre, and the iris may be covered, either at the top or the bottom. There will be wrinkling in the skin around the top of the nose ridge, and the mouth will commonly be frowning. Depending on the situation, the mouth could also be open.

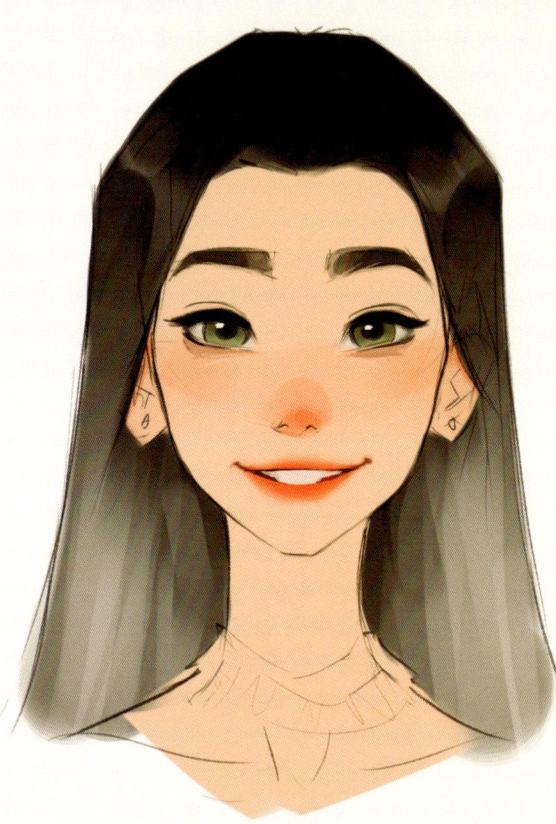

HAPPY

When your character is happy, the corners of their mouth will pull back to the sides, and depending on the scenario, they may reveal teeth. Usually, you'll find that their cheeks will rise up to push against the lower eyelid. You can try this right now: smile and feel your cheeks move upwards as your lower eyelid compresses. This commonly results in the lower half of a smiling character's iris being covered by the lower lid. When smiling, a character's brows could also be slightly raised, communicating a sense of openness.

- Raised brows
- Pulled mouth corners
- Raised lower eyelid

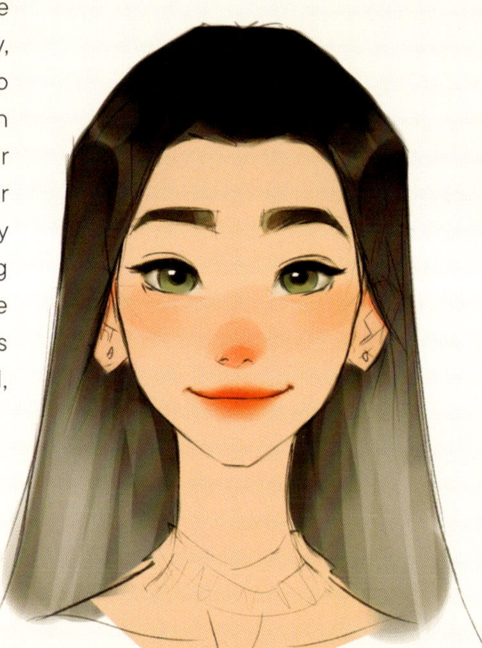

SAD

Here, the brows will raise in the middle and droop down towards the tapered ends. Sadness will sap the energy out of someone, so imagine that the facial features no longer have the strength to hold themselves up. The top lid will often droop down to cover more of the top half of the eye. The mouth corners will either remain the same, or be pulled downwards into a frown.

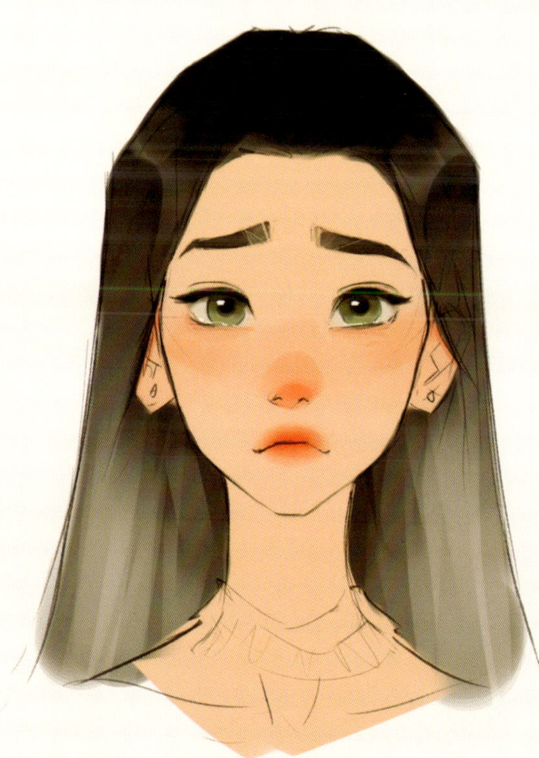

- Lowered inner brow
- Tense lower lid
- Downturned mouth

RELATIVITY

Once you've learned the basic expressions, you can use the various facial feature placements in different combinations. For example, you can try to combine 'sad' eyebrows with a happy smile, or 'angry' eyebrows with a wide, opened mouth. As you practise and get better, you'll be able to create a nuanced expression that may communicate more than one feeling.

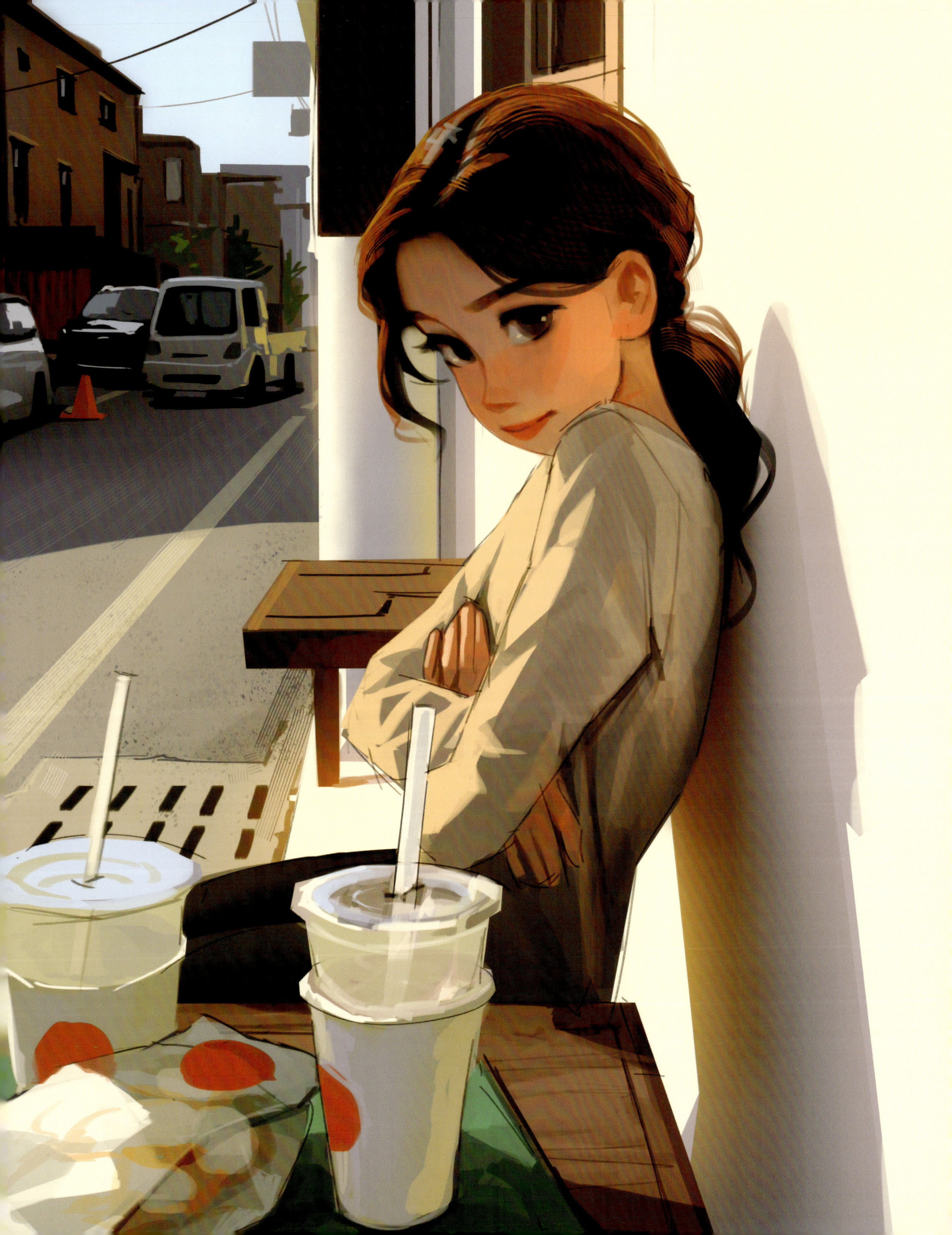

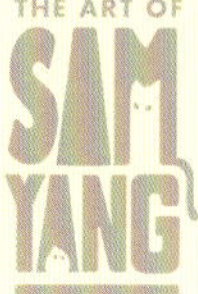

gallery 2

Selection of works from my portfolio

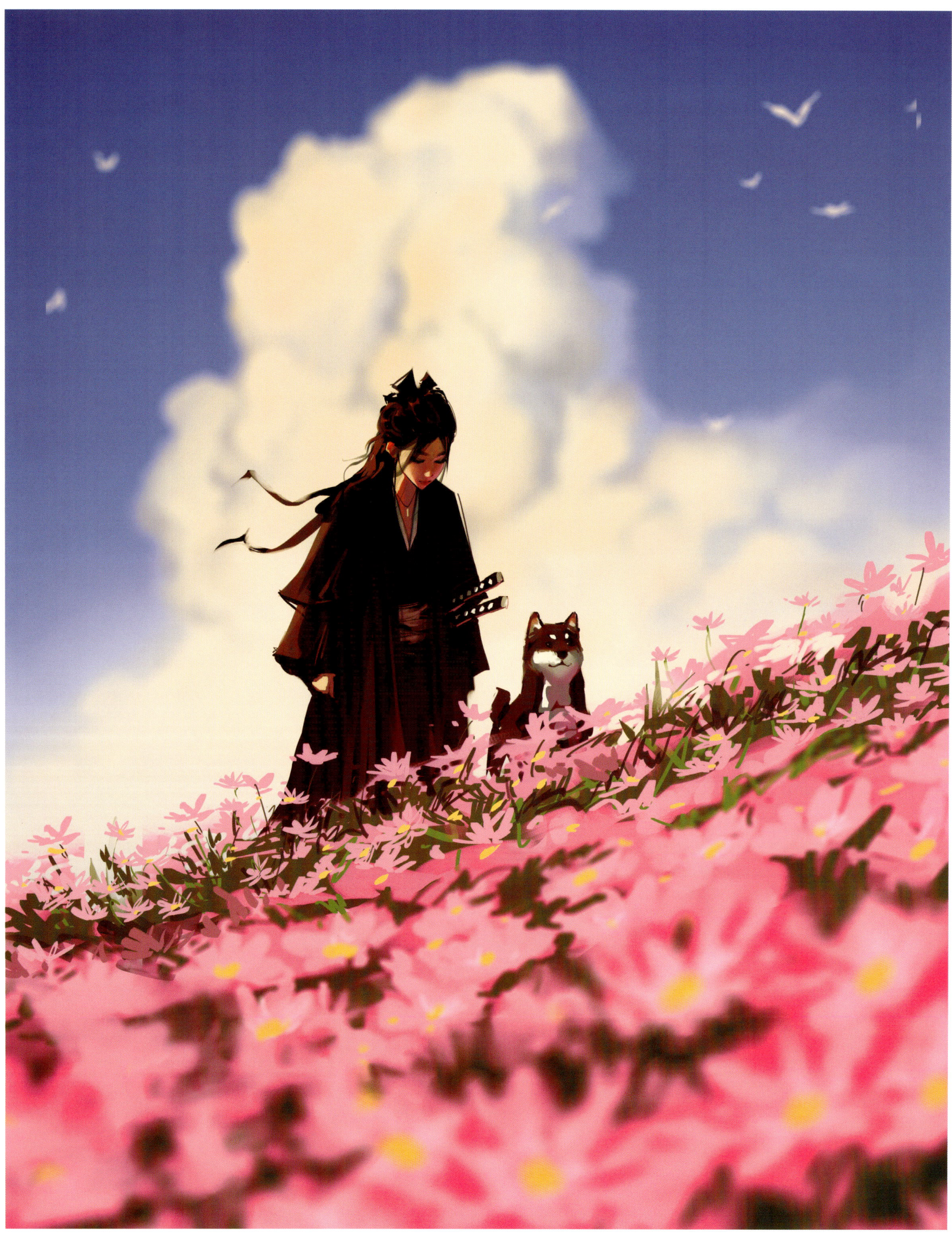

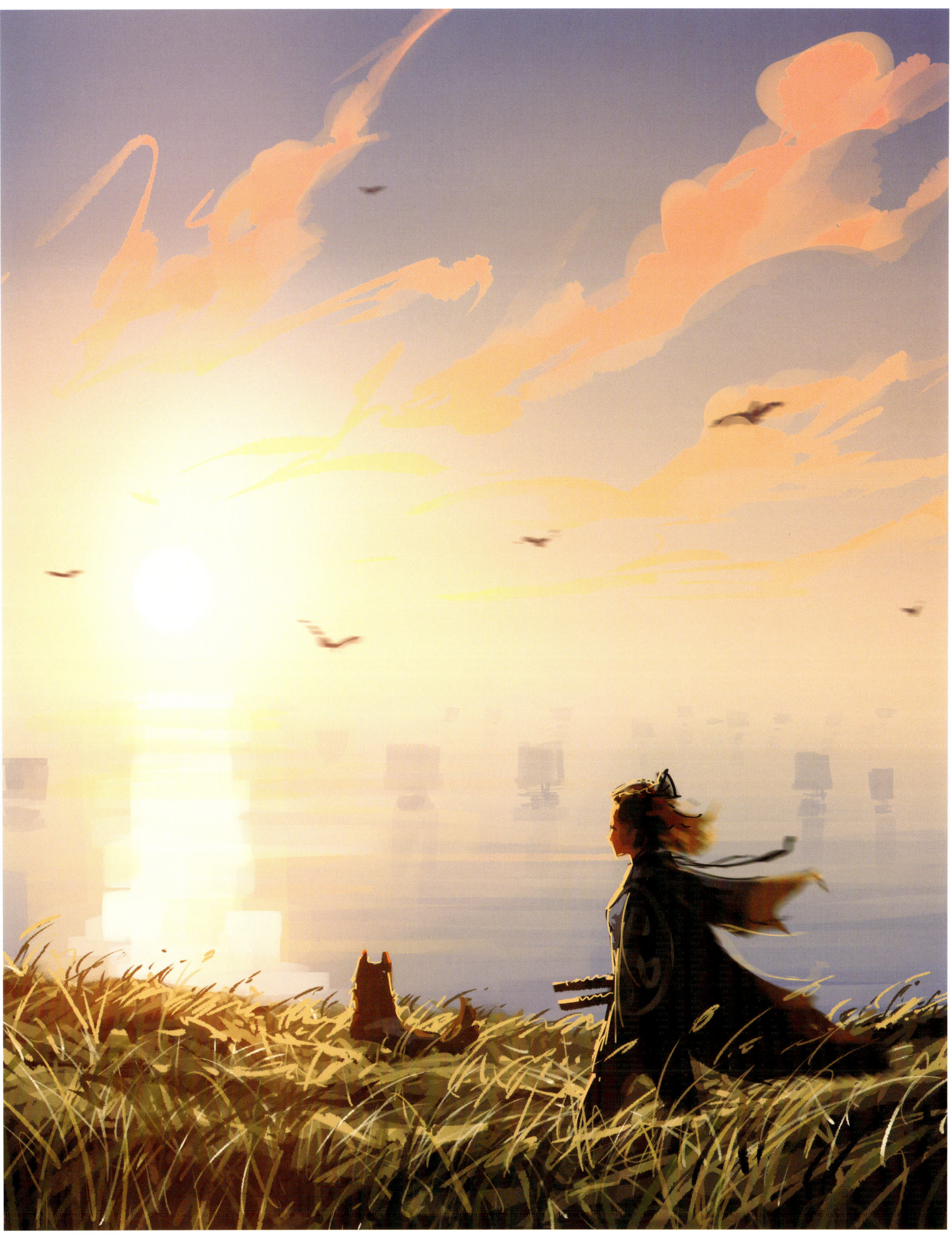

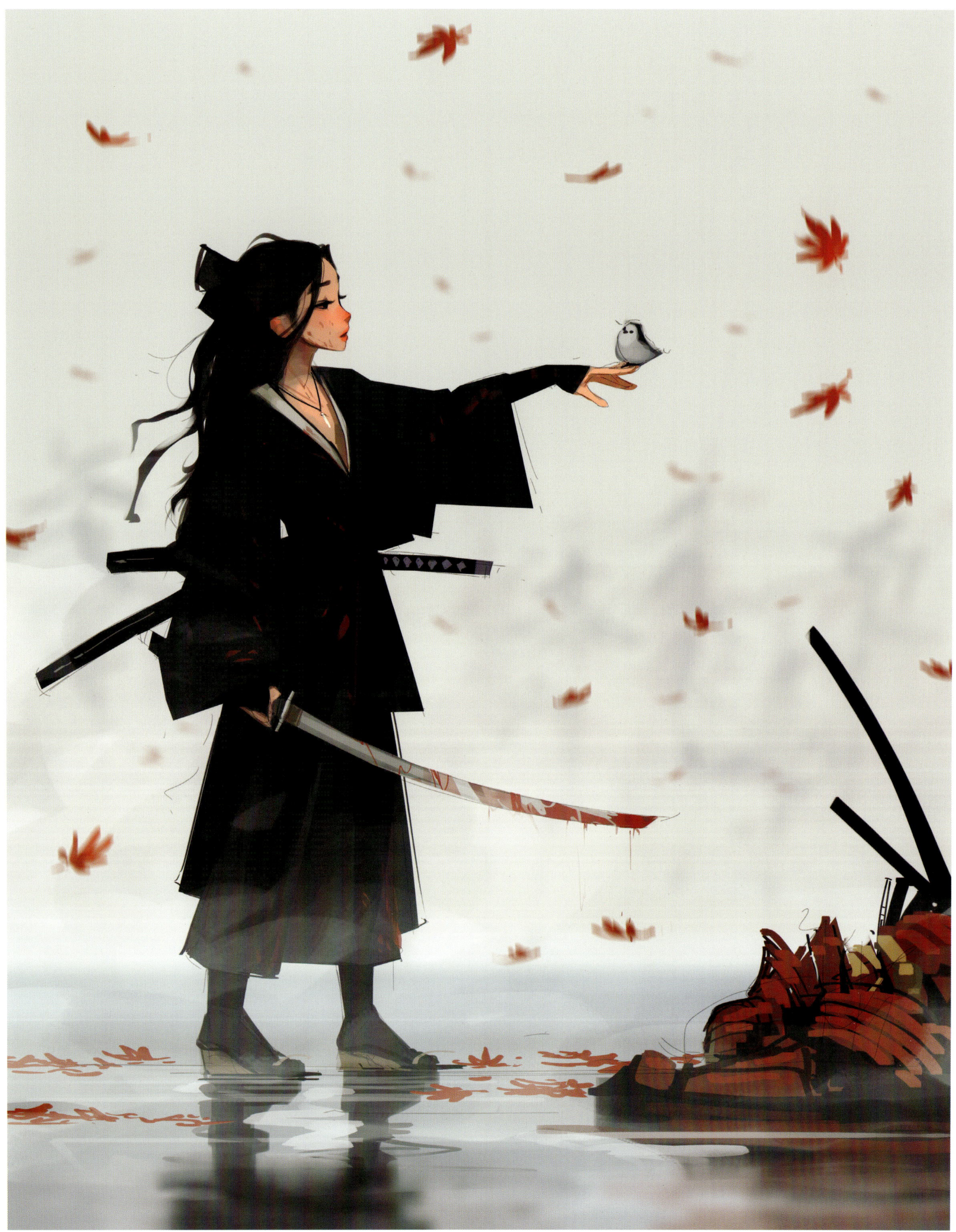

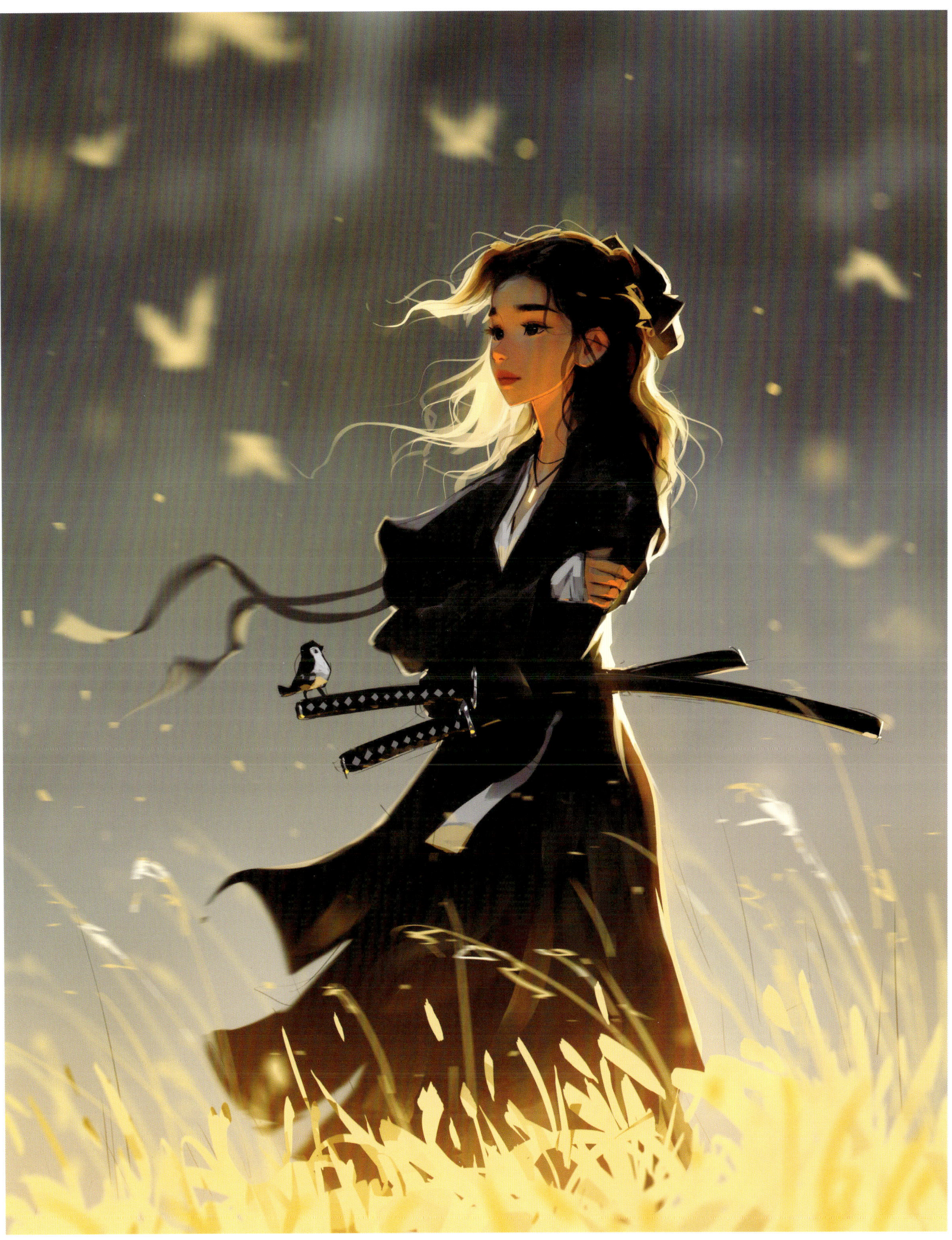

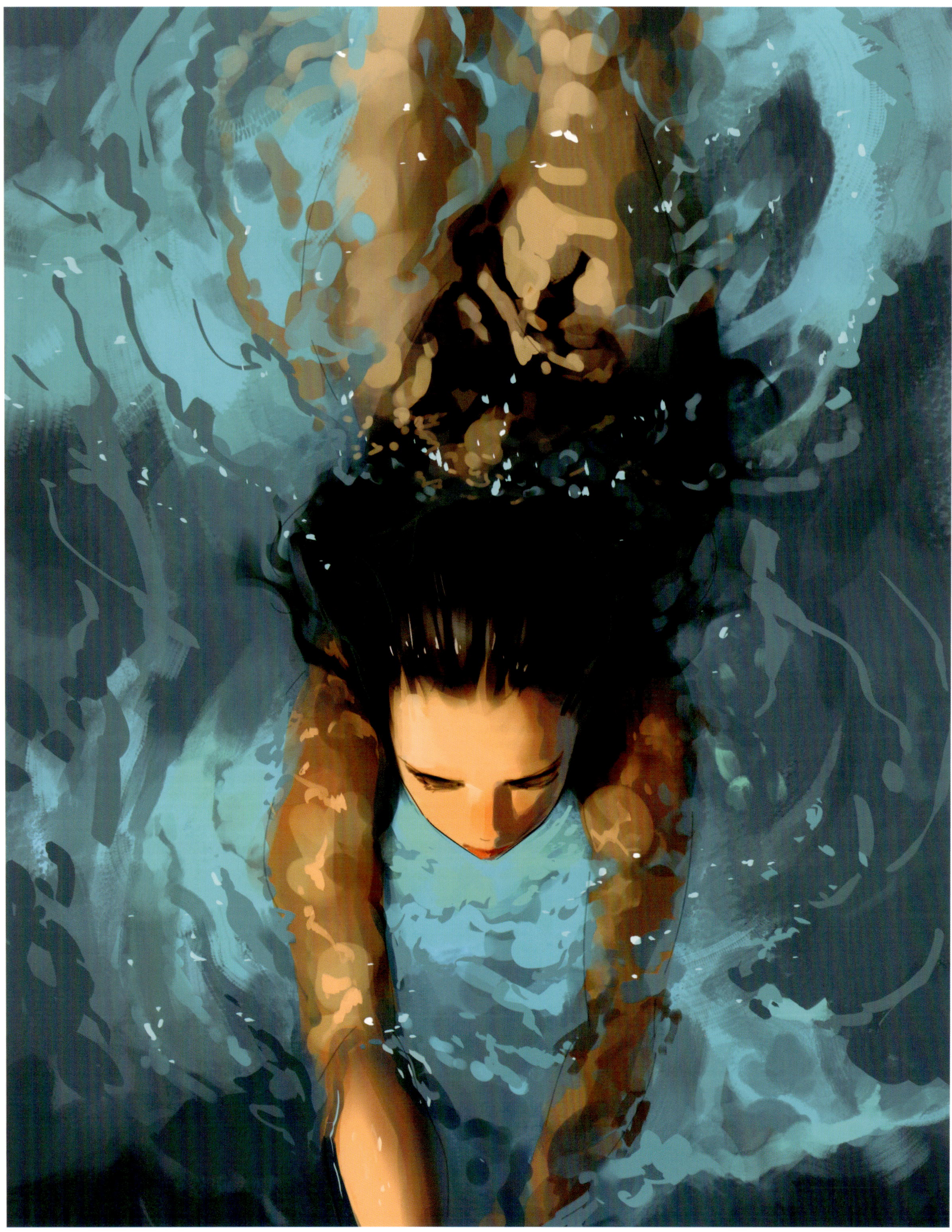

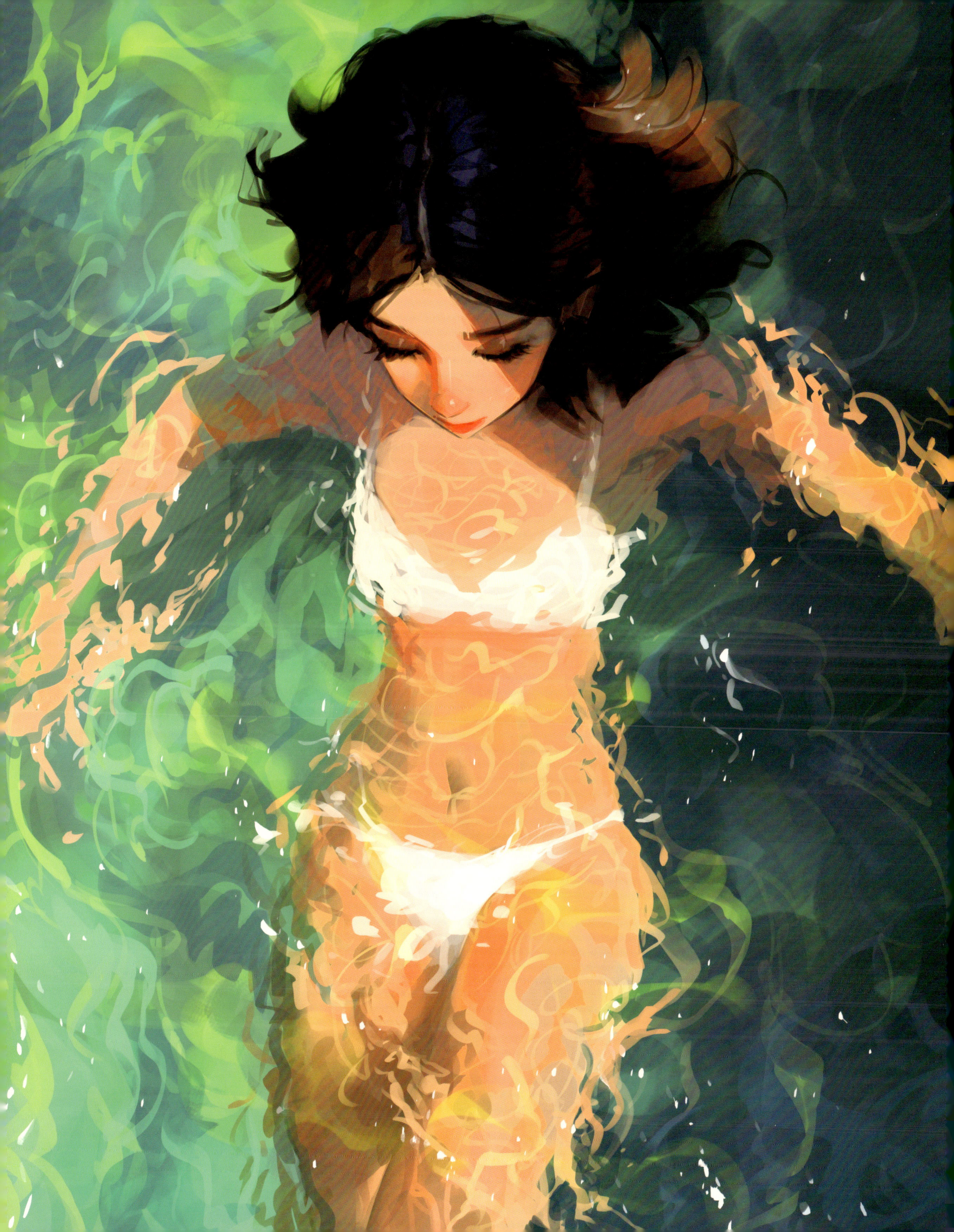

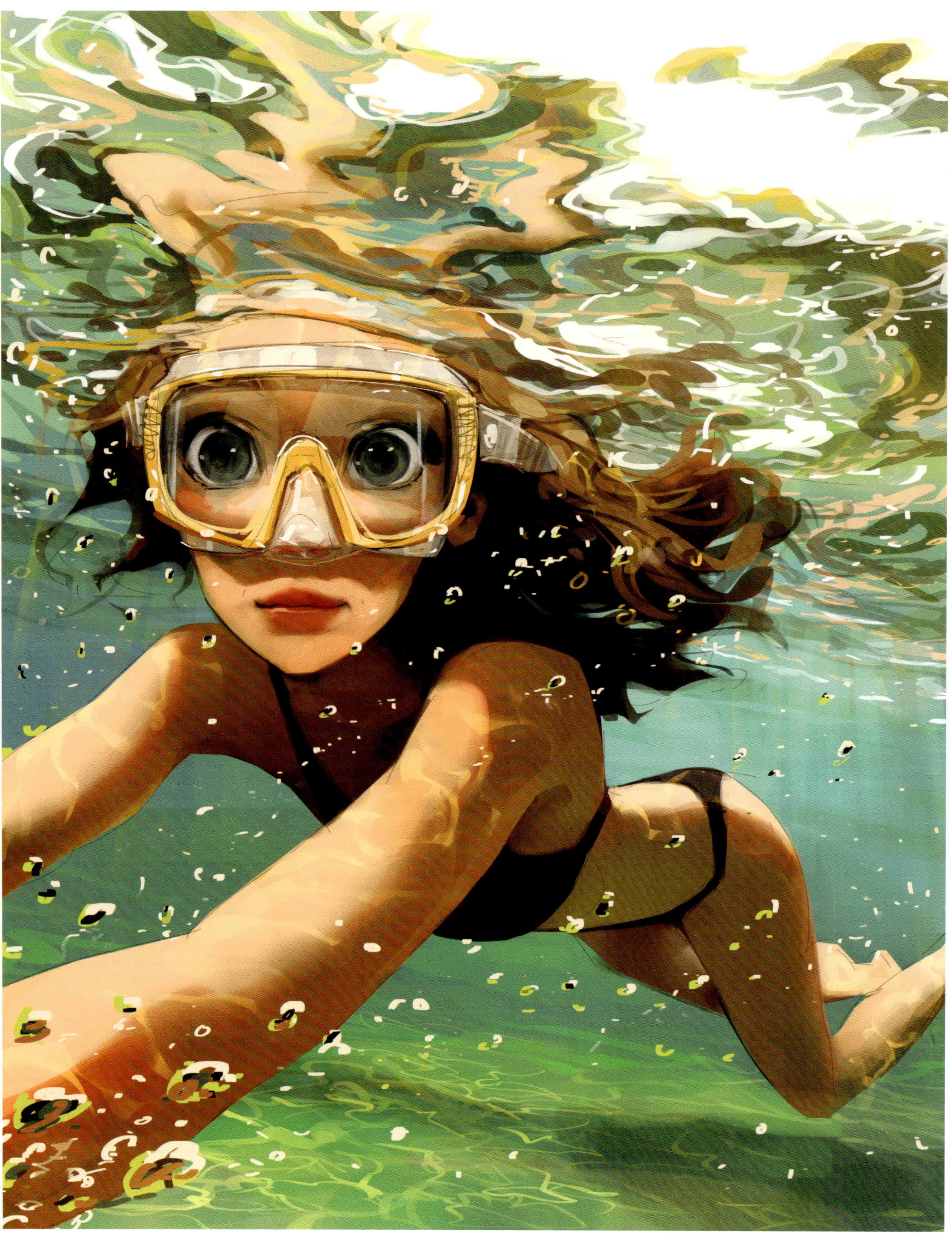

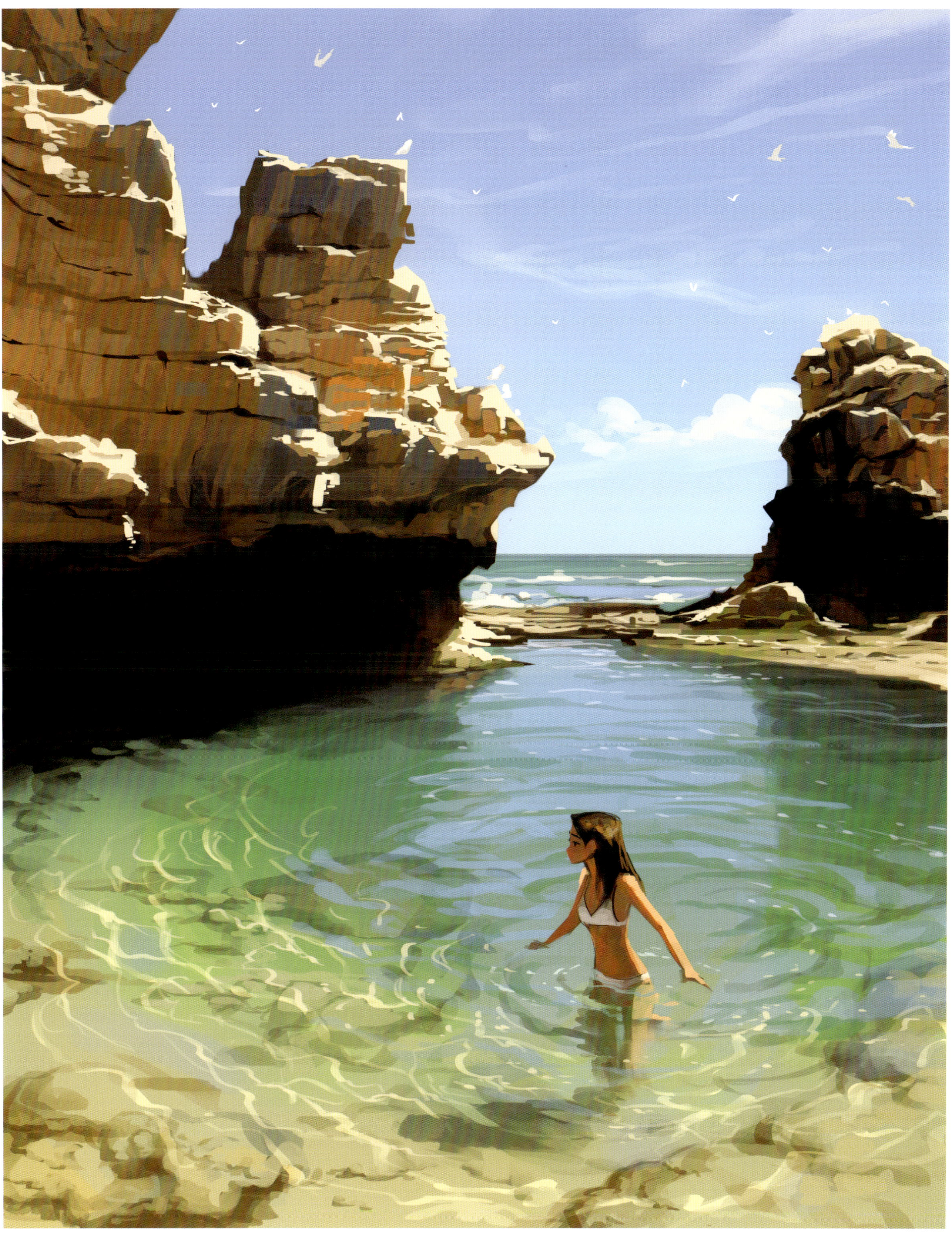

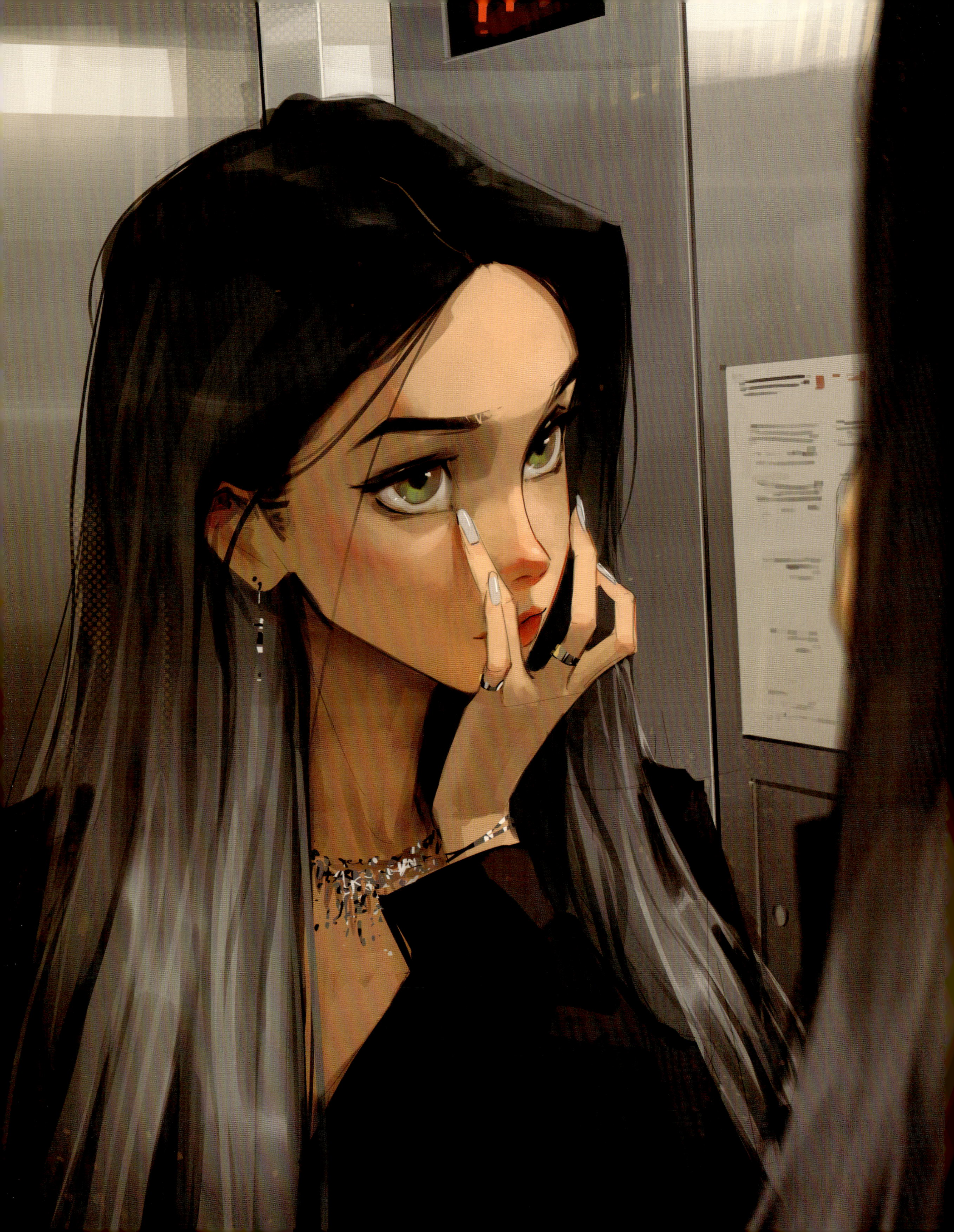

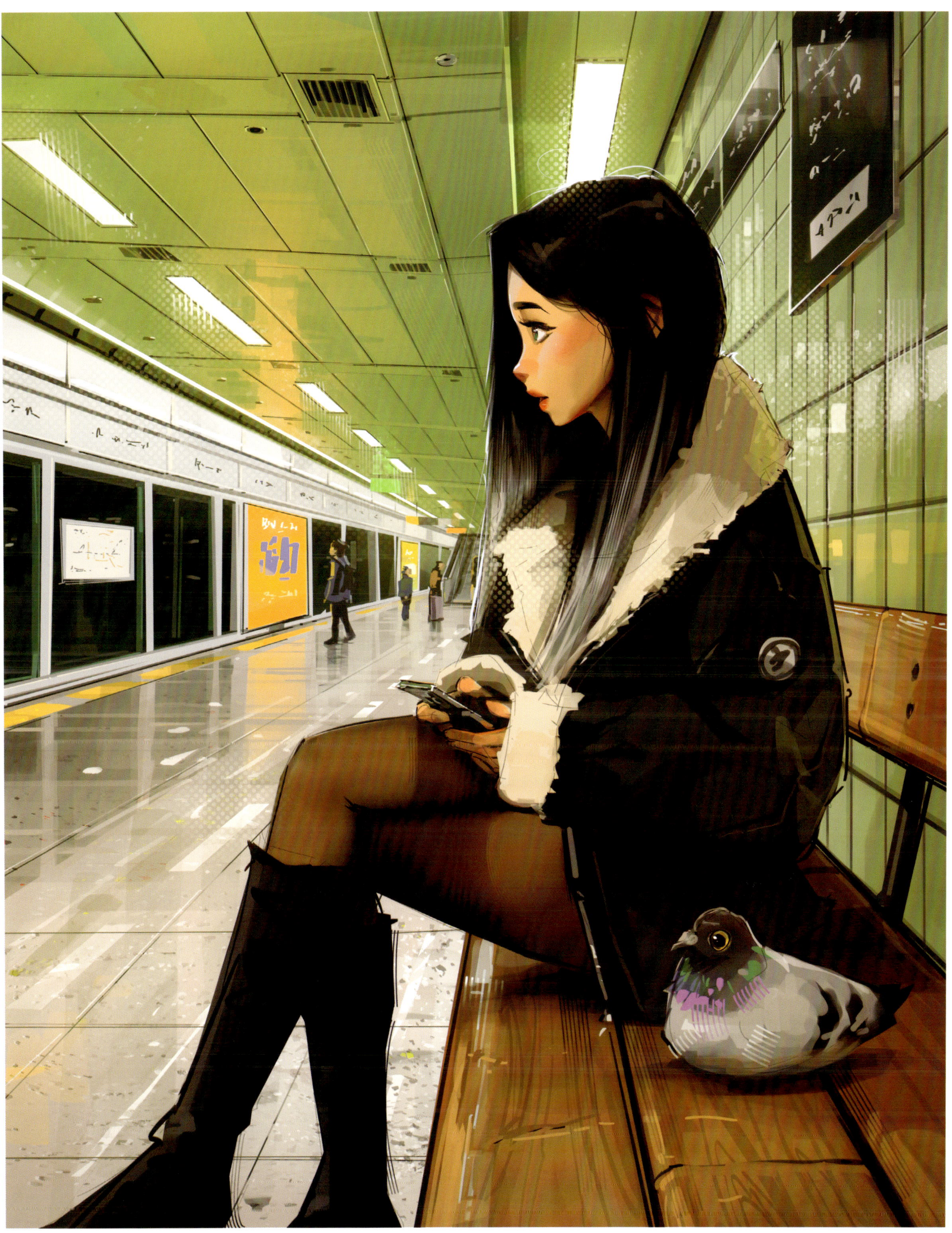

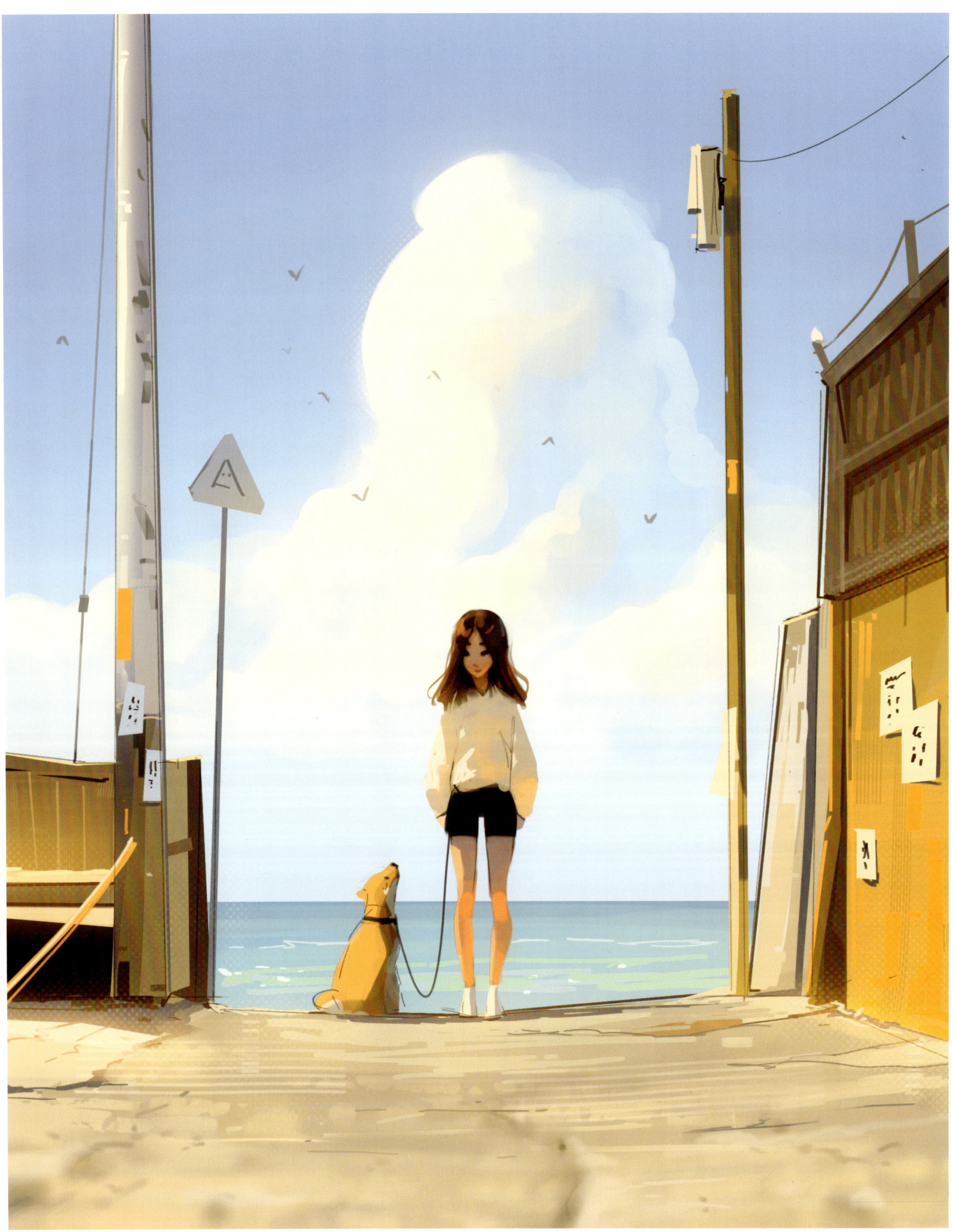

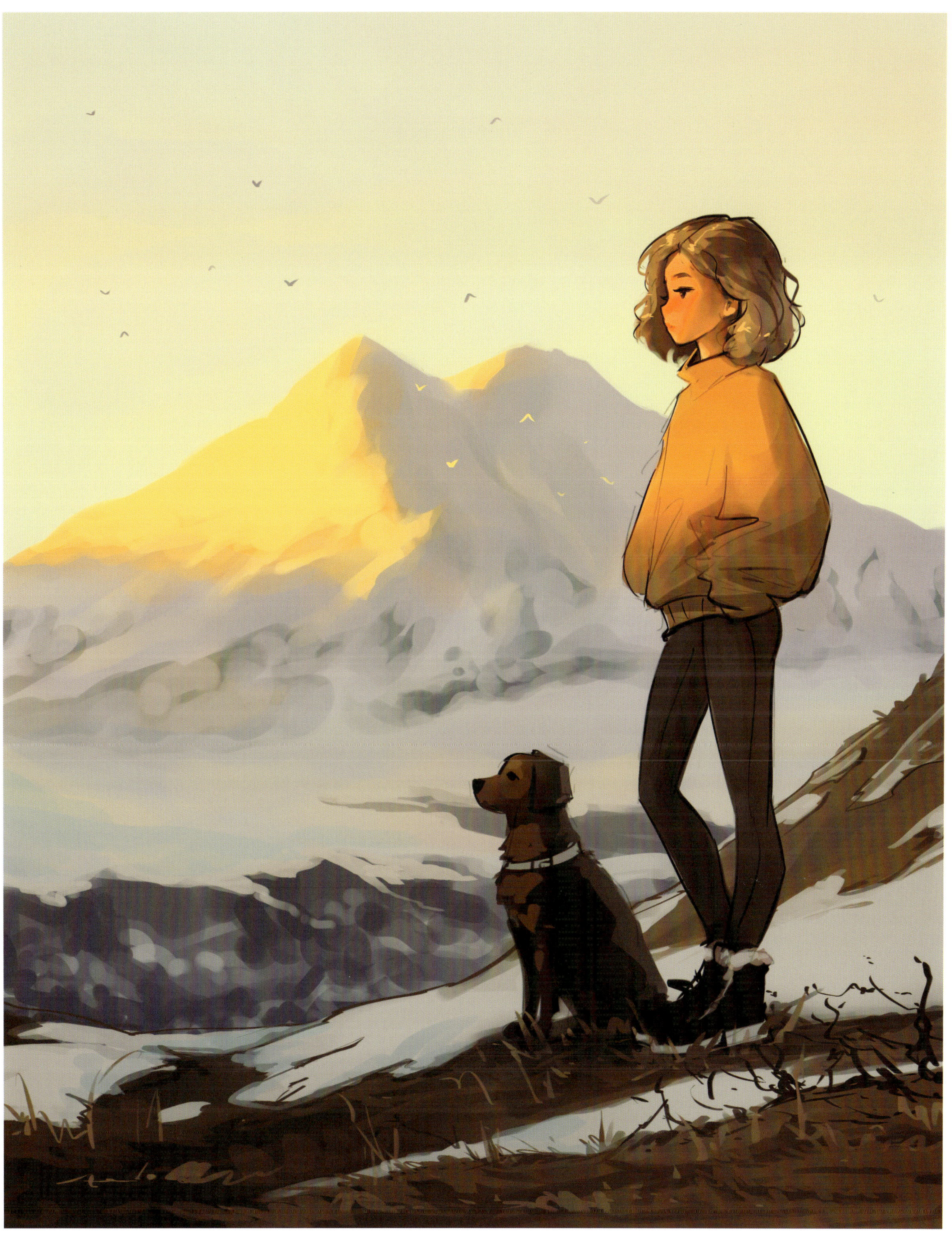

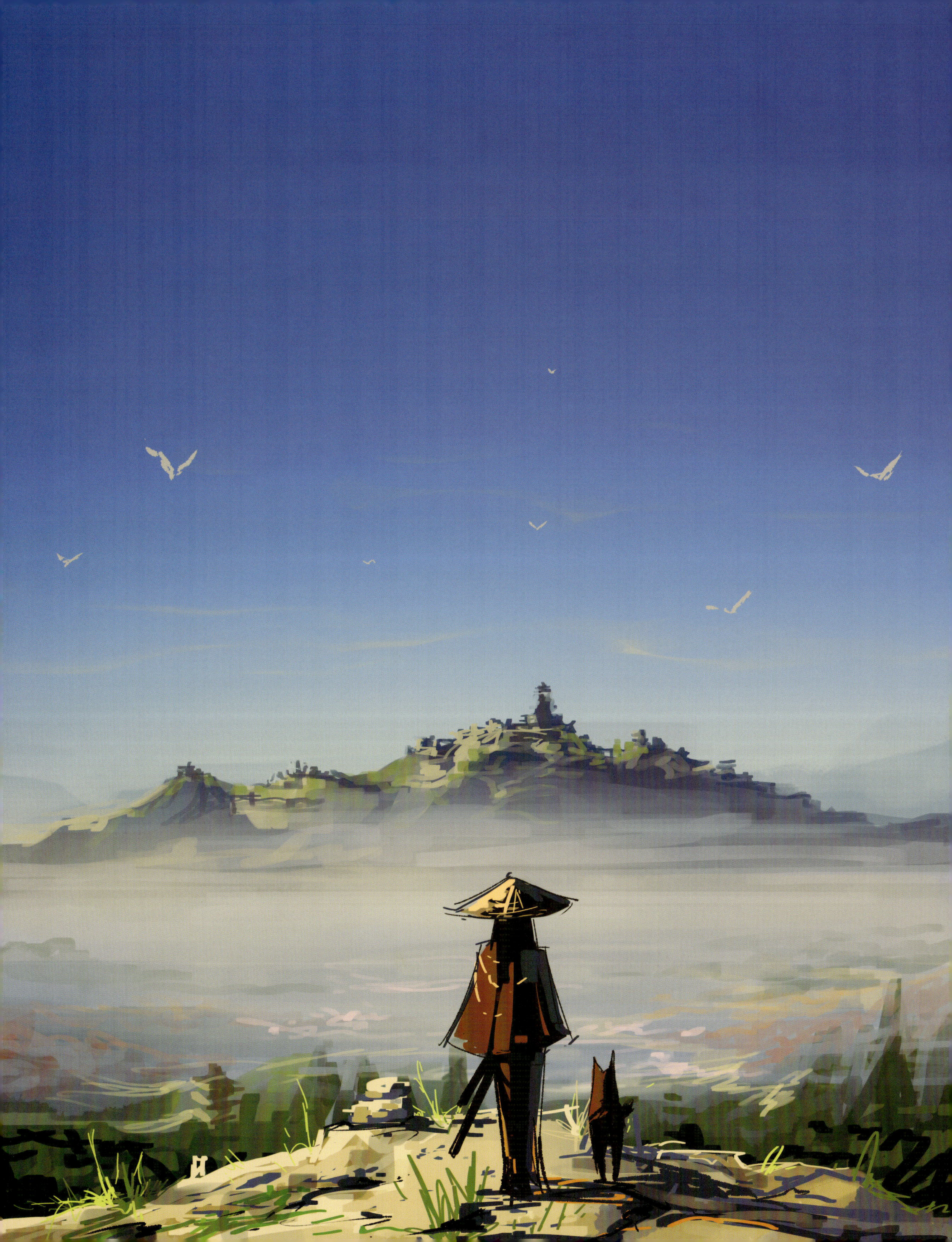

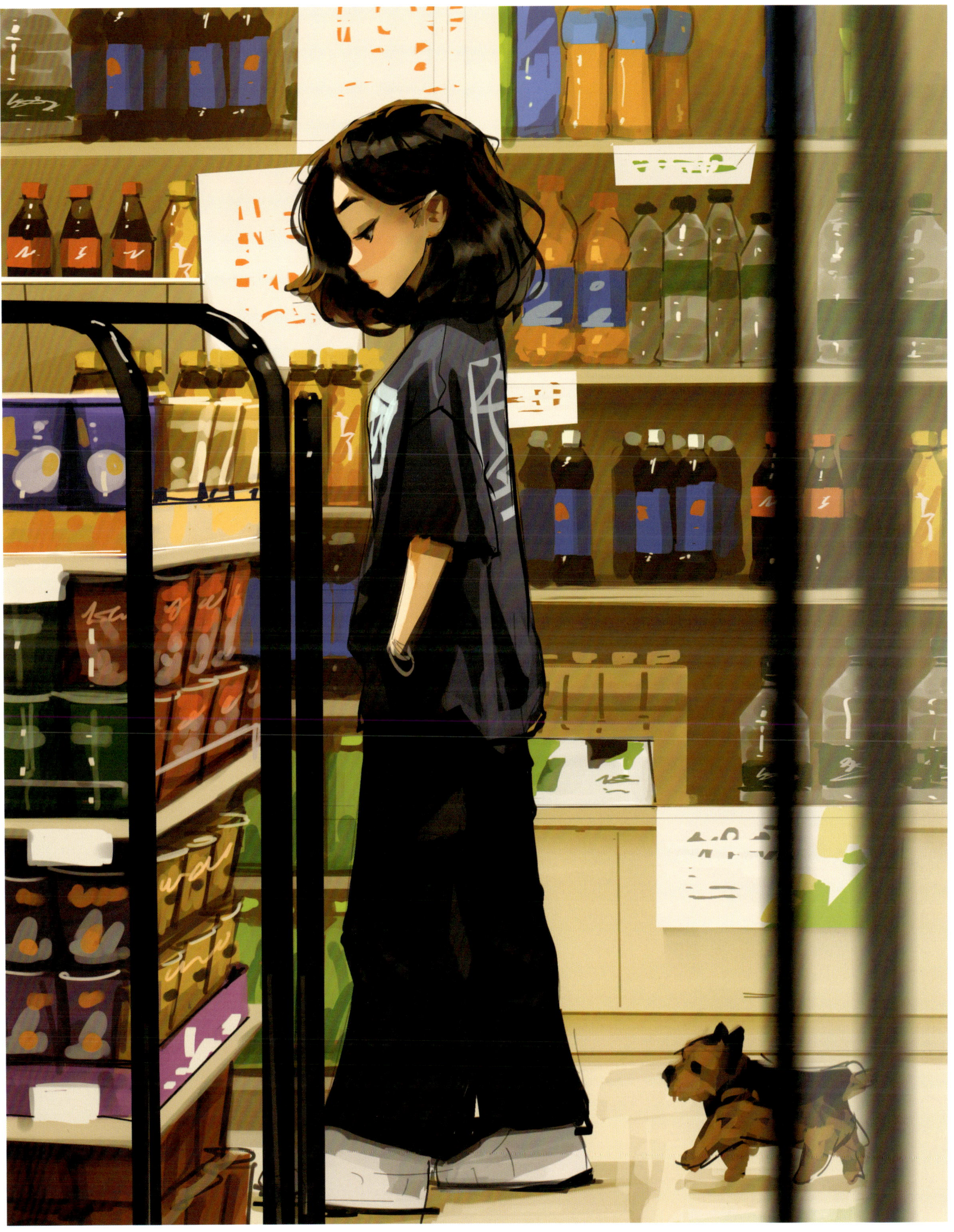

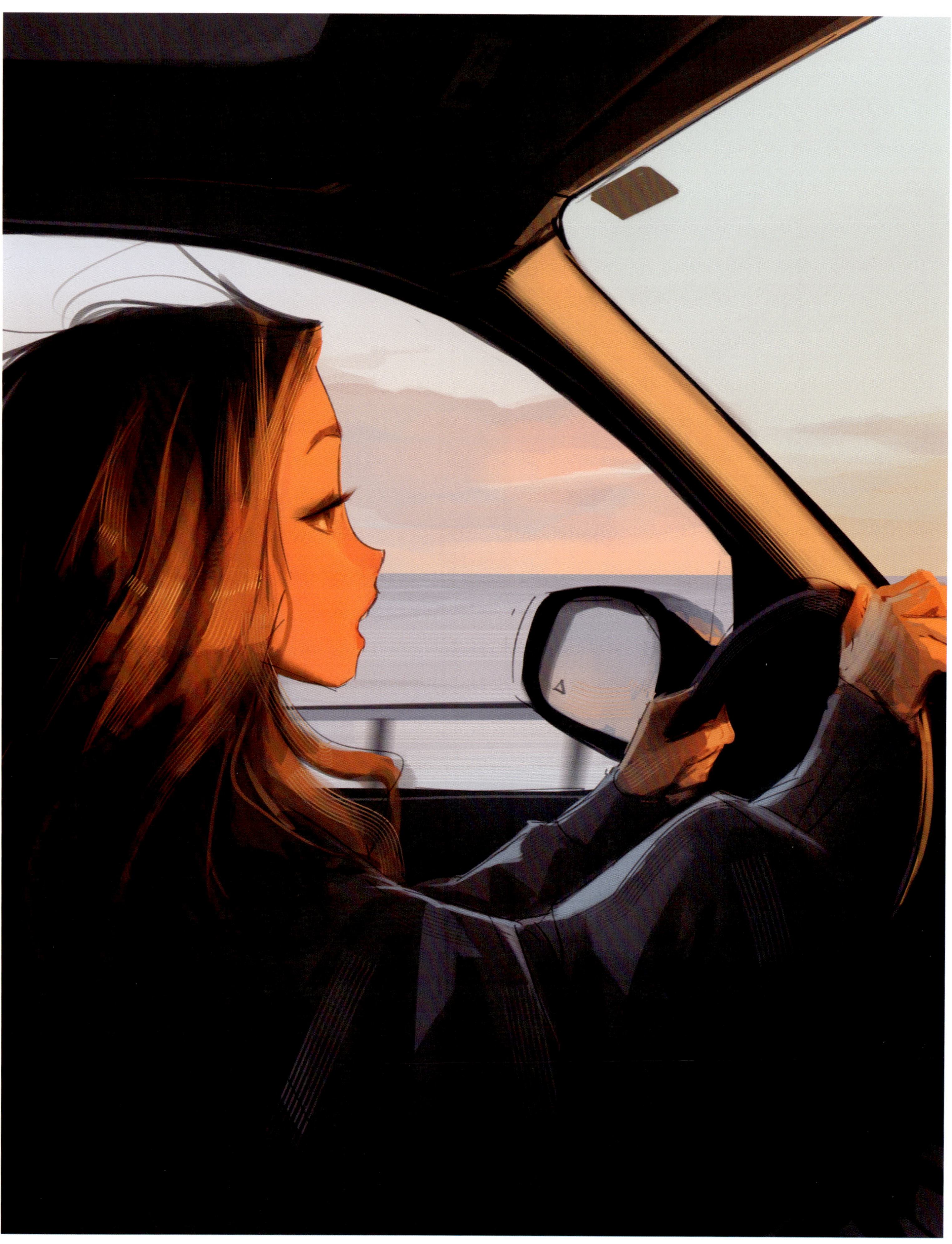

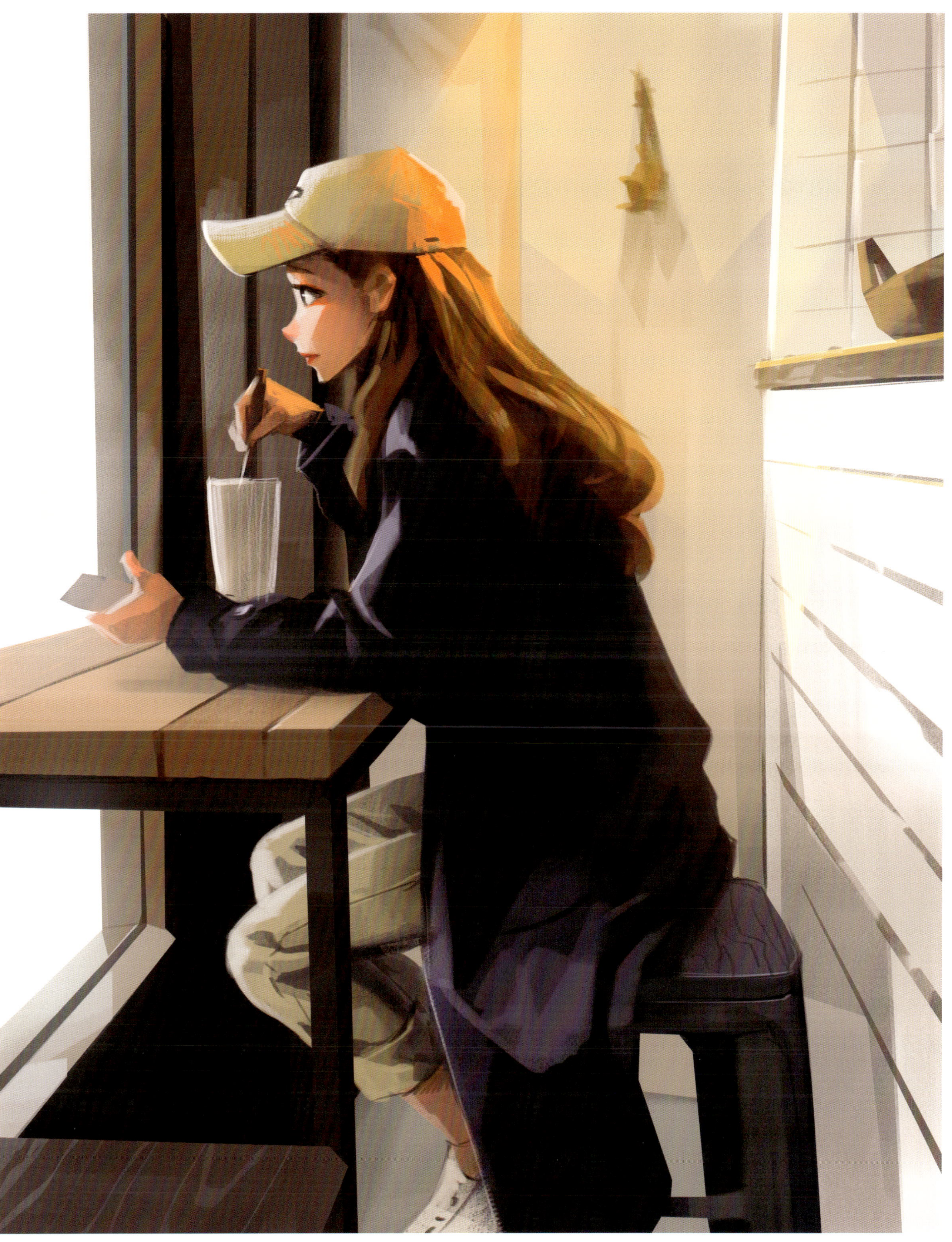

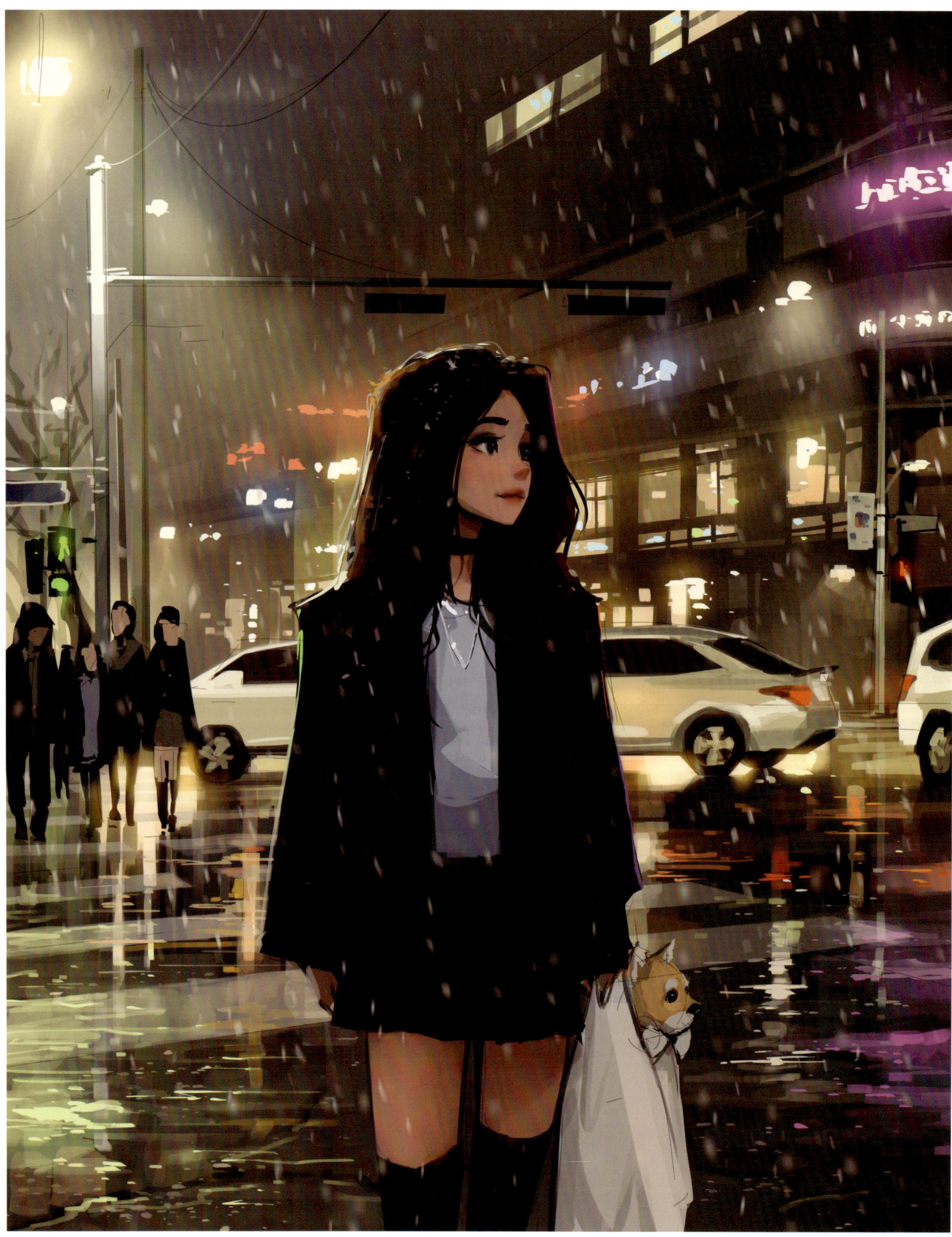

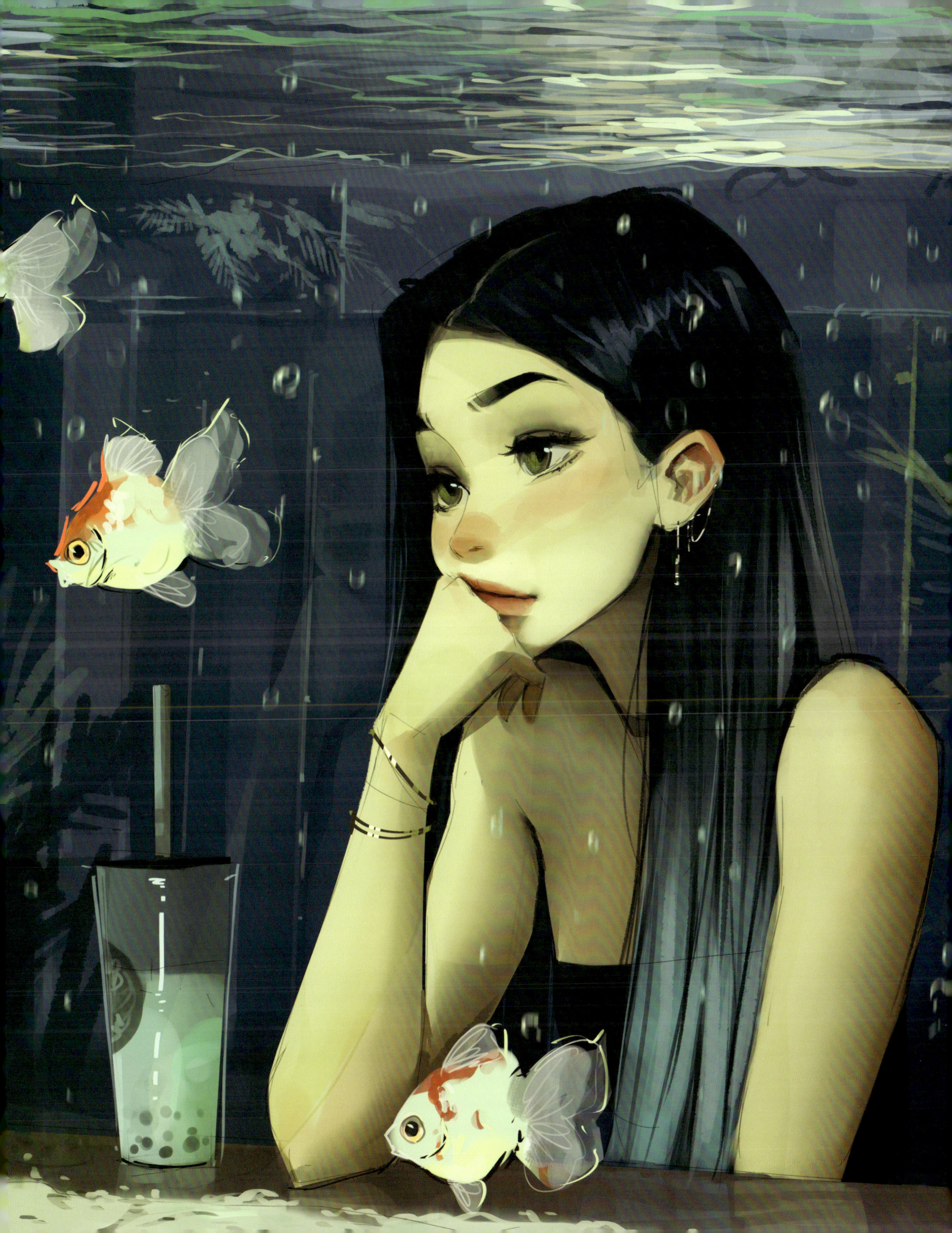

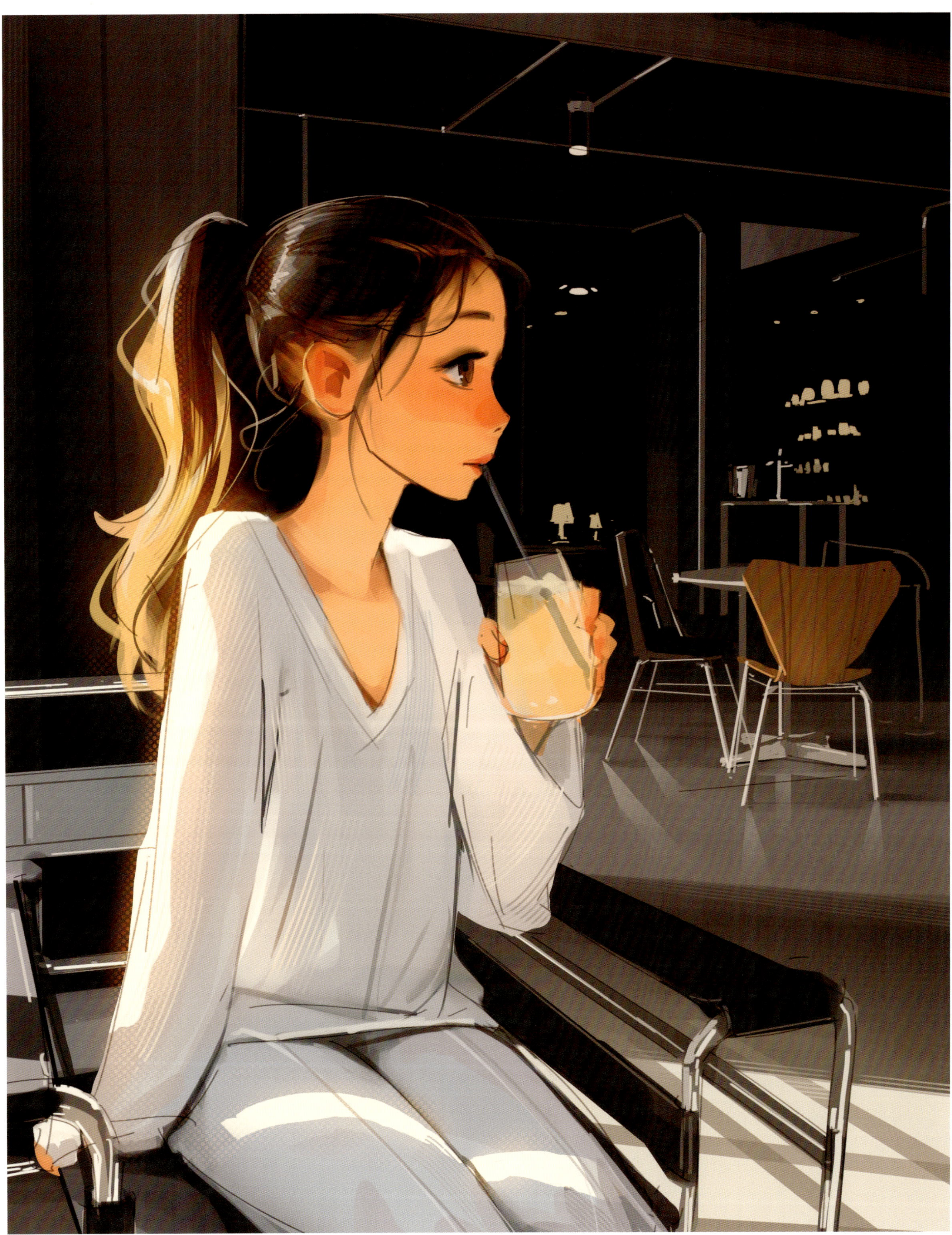

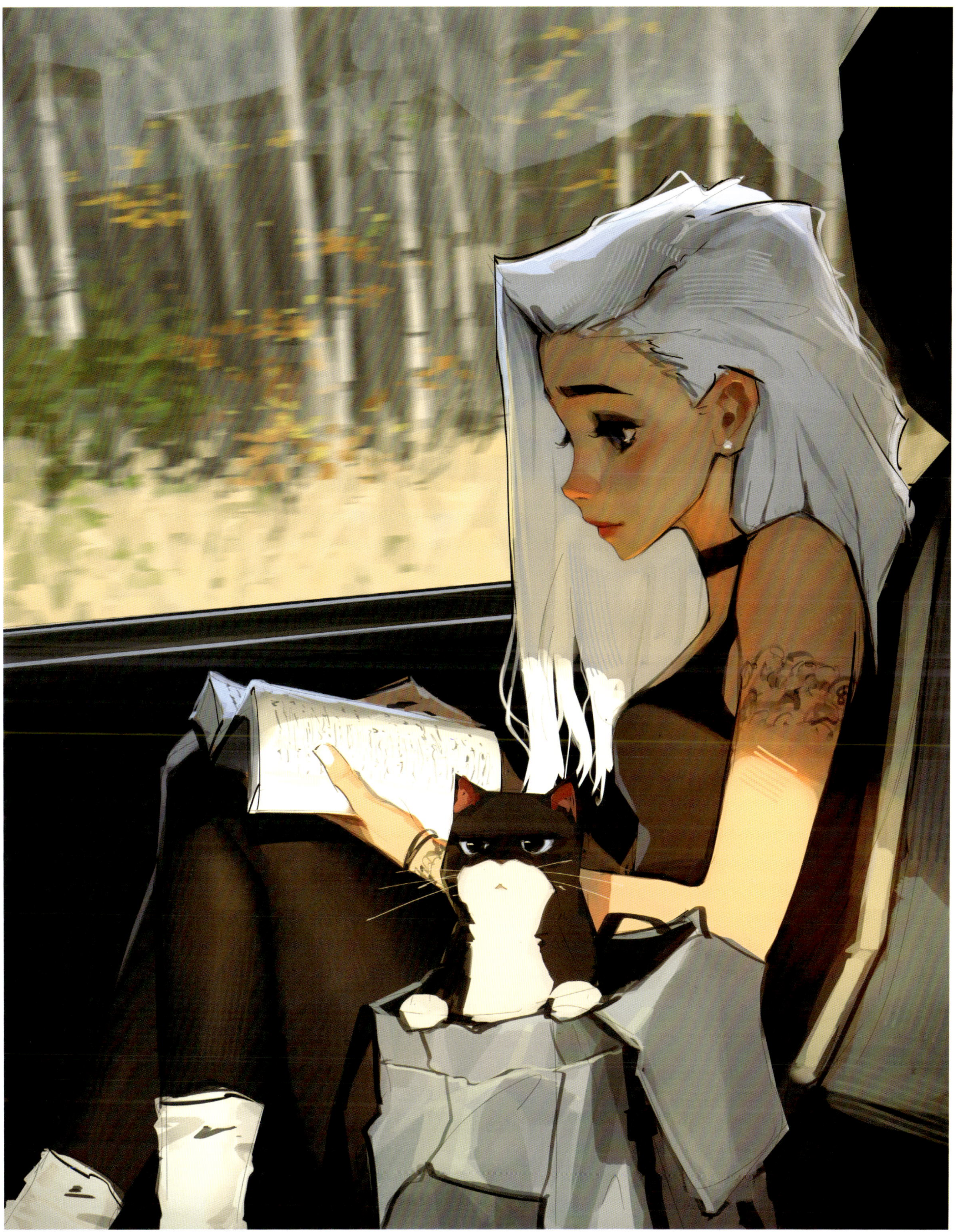

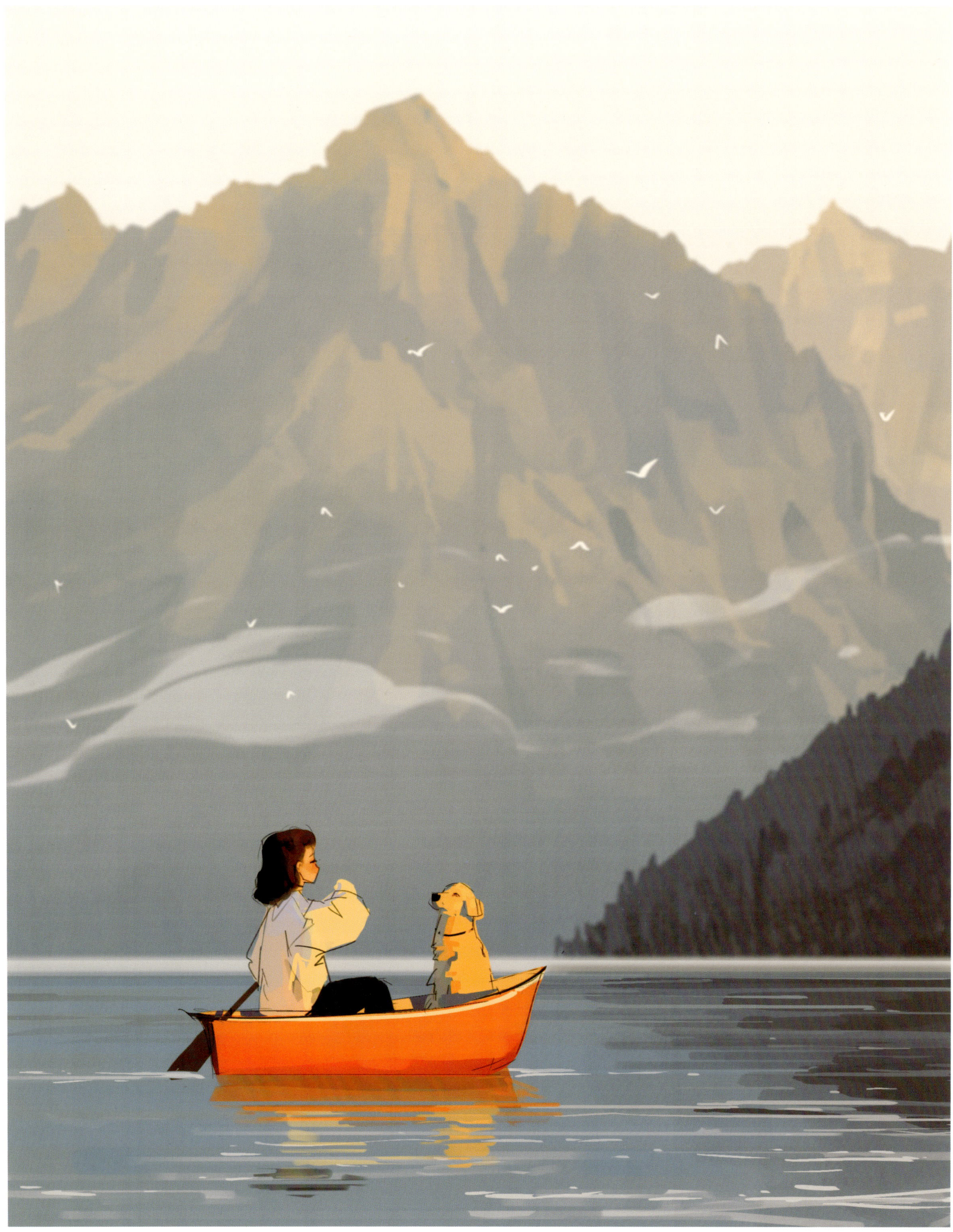

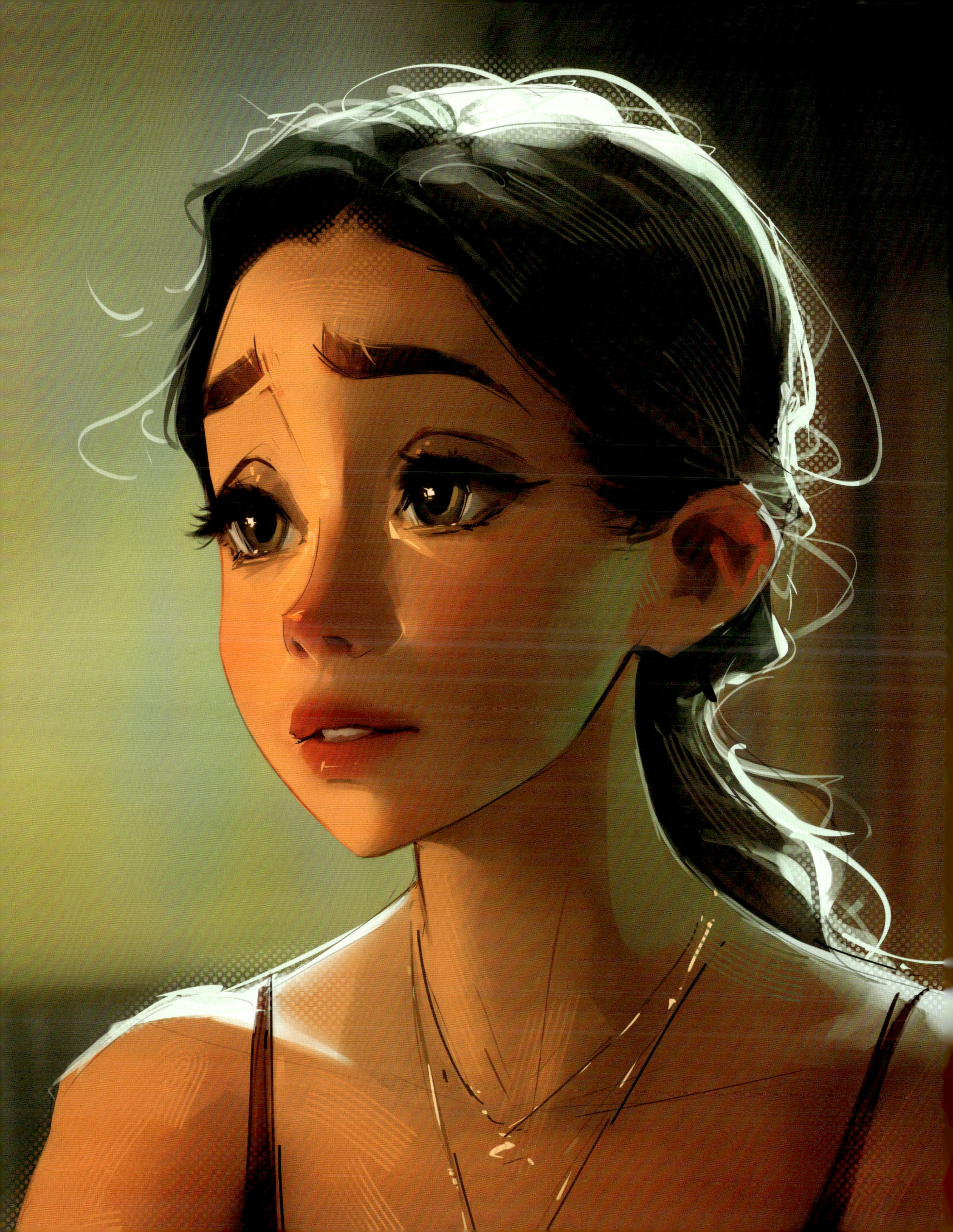

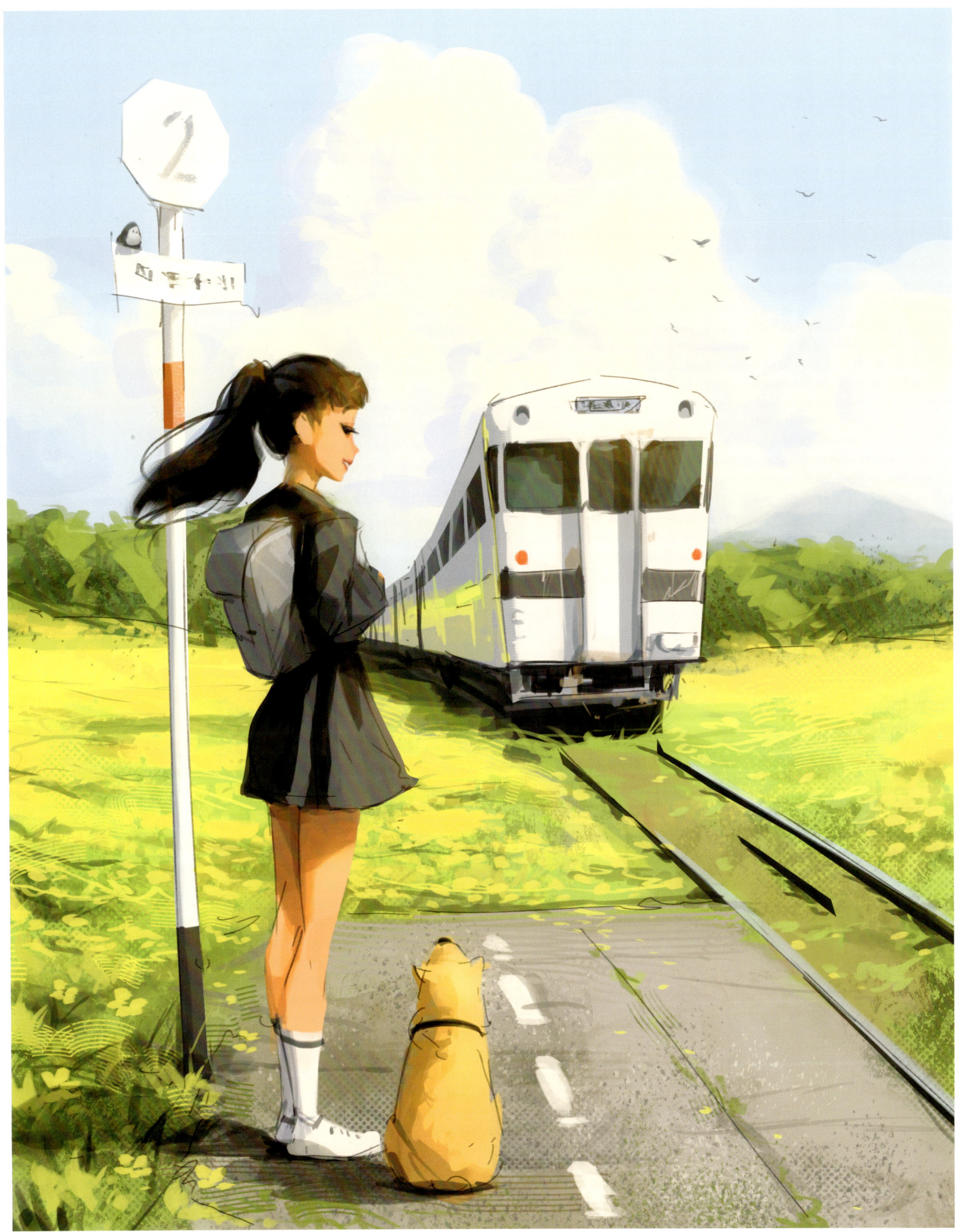
2

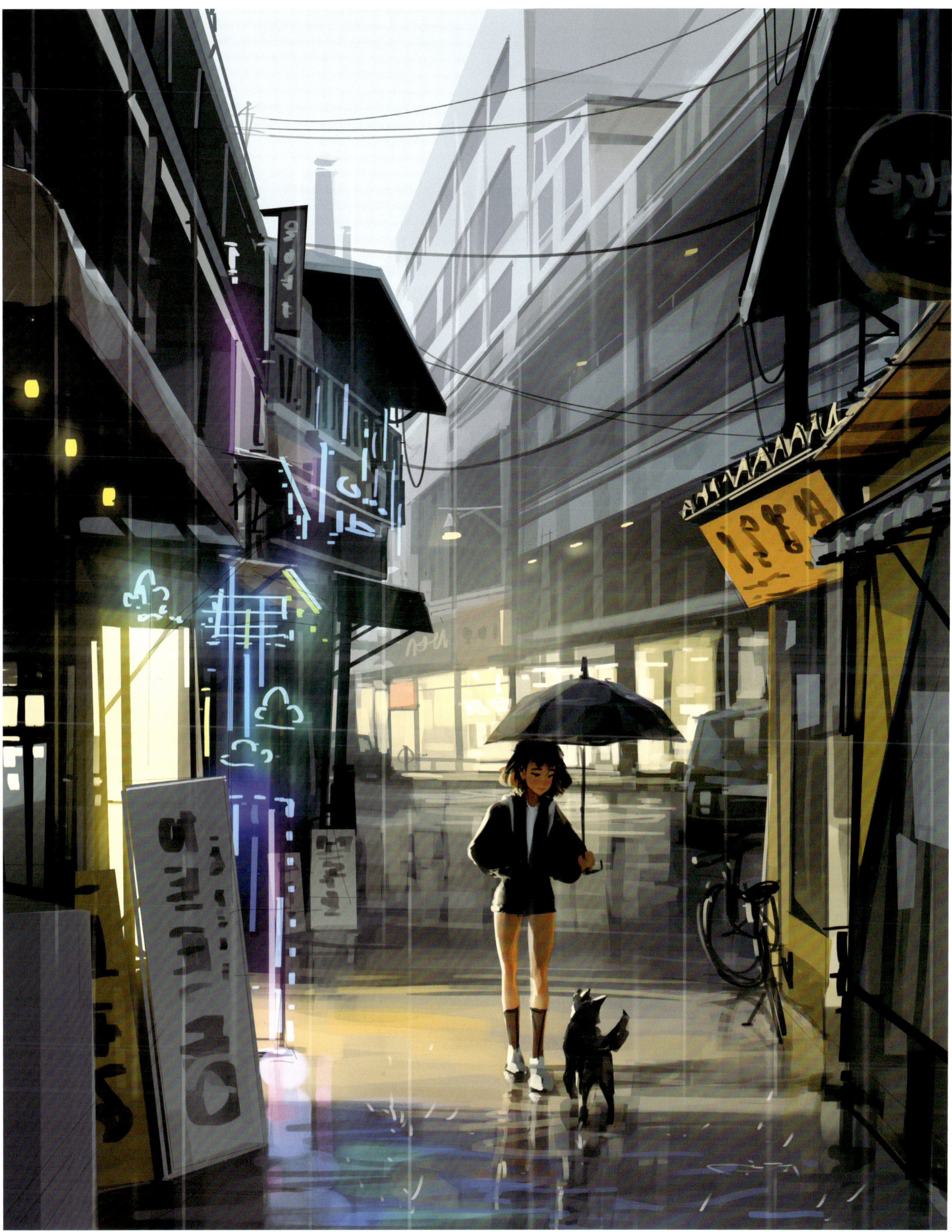

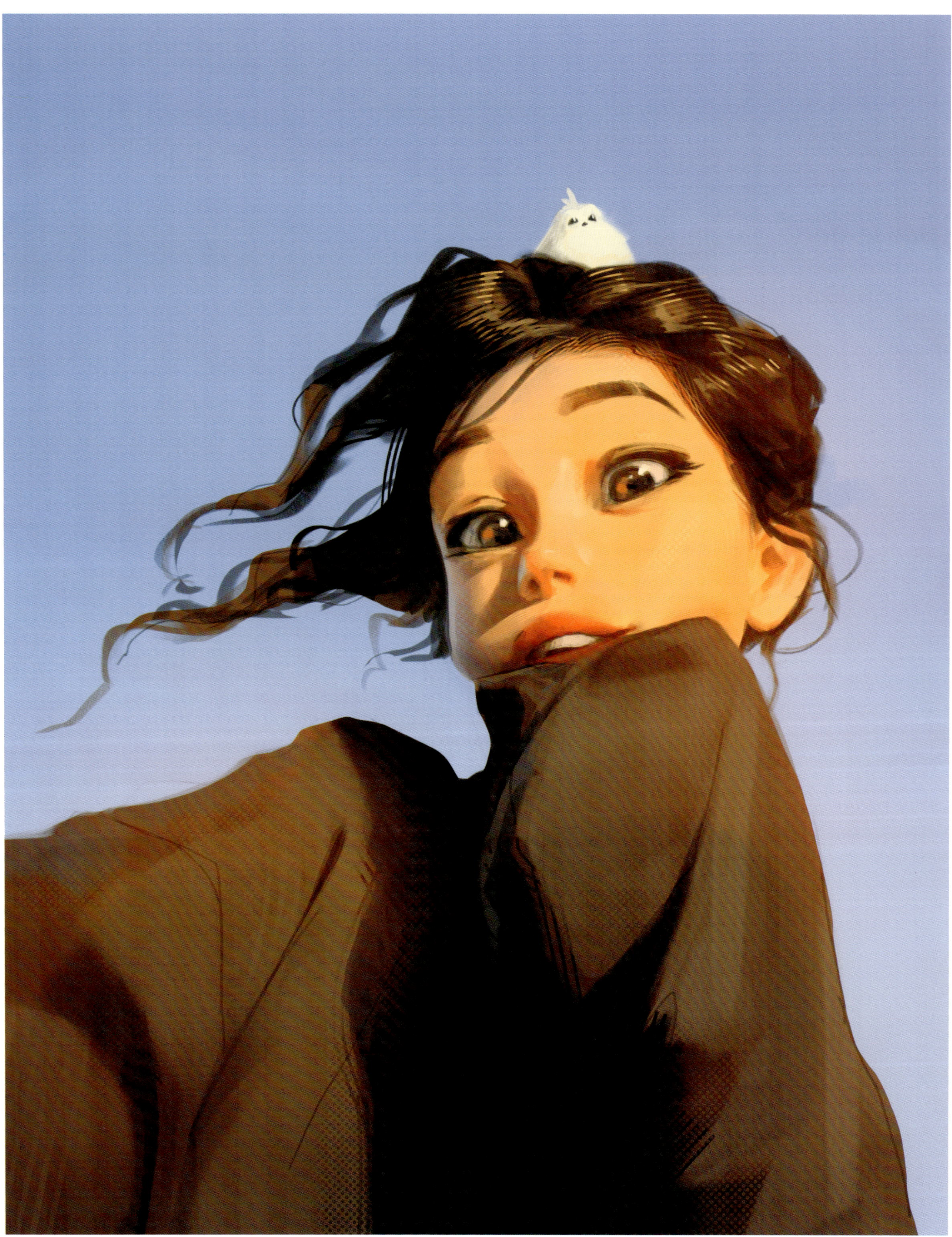

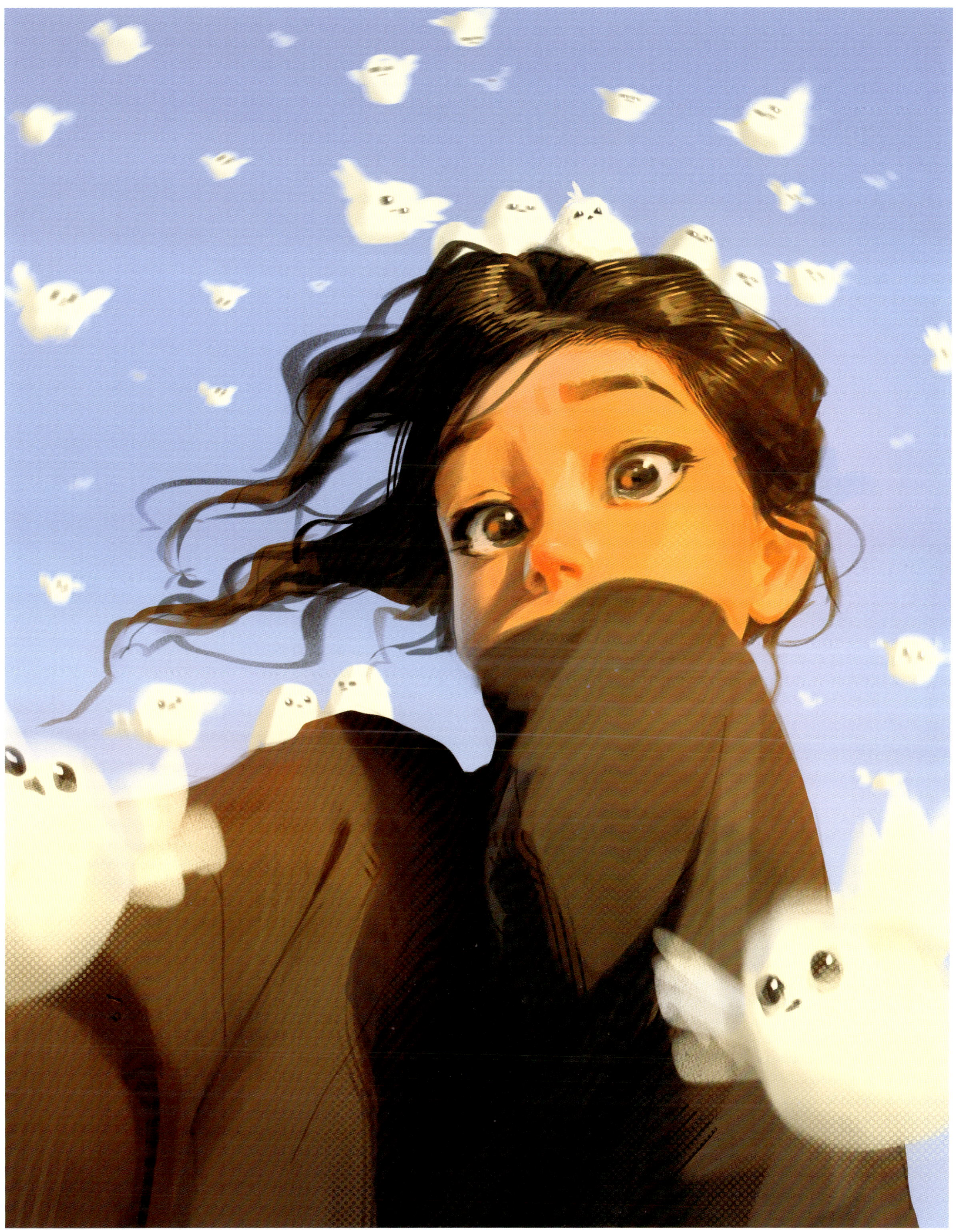

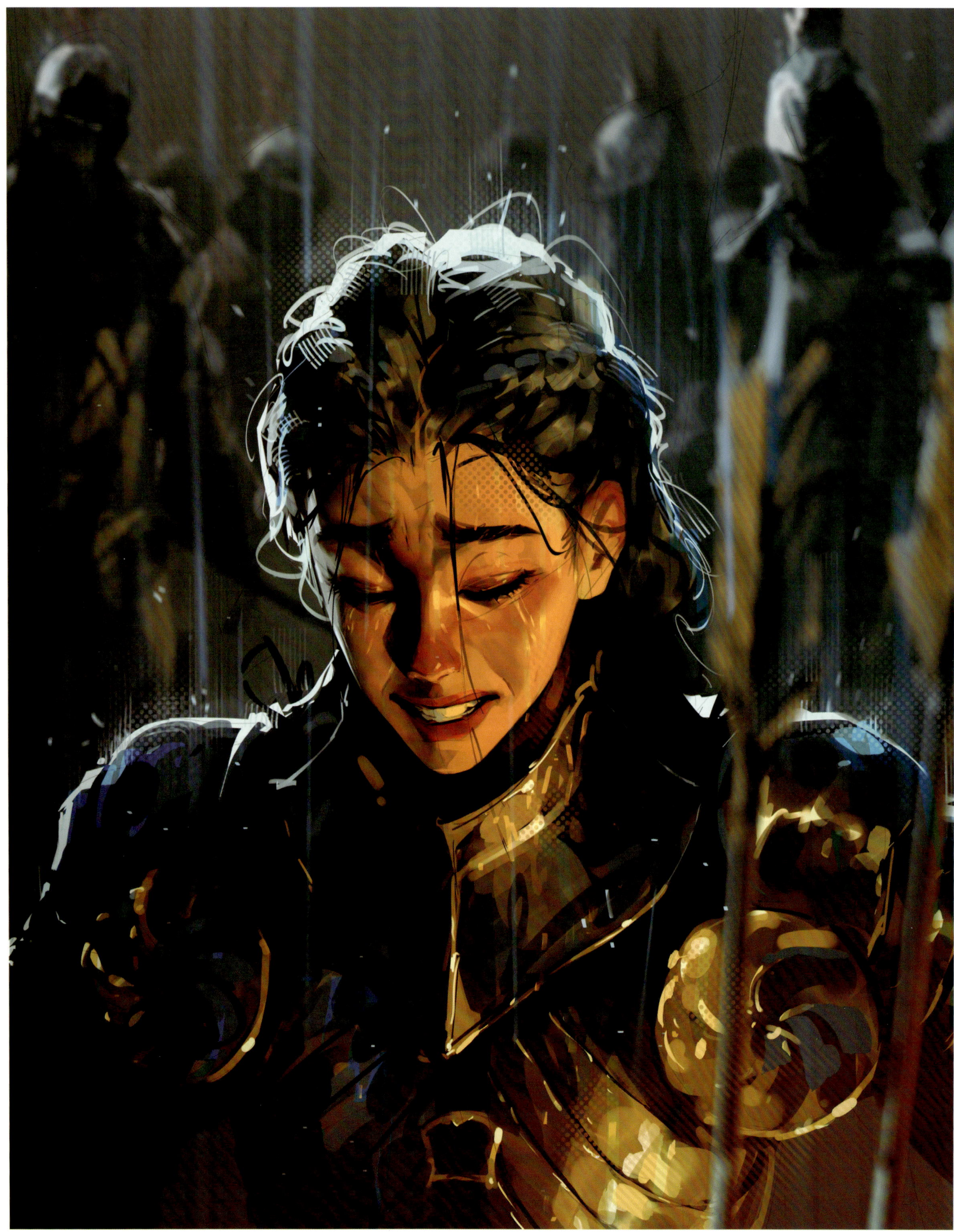

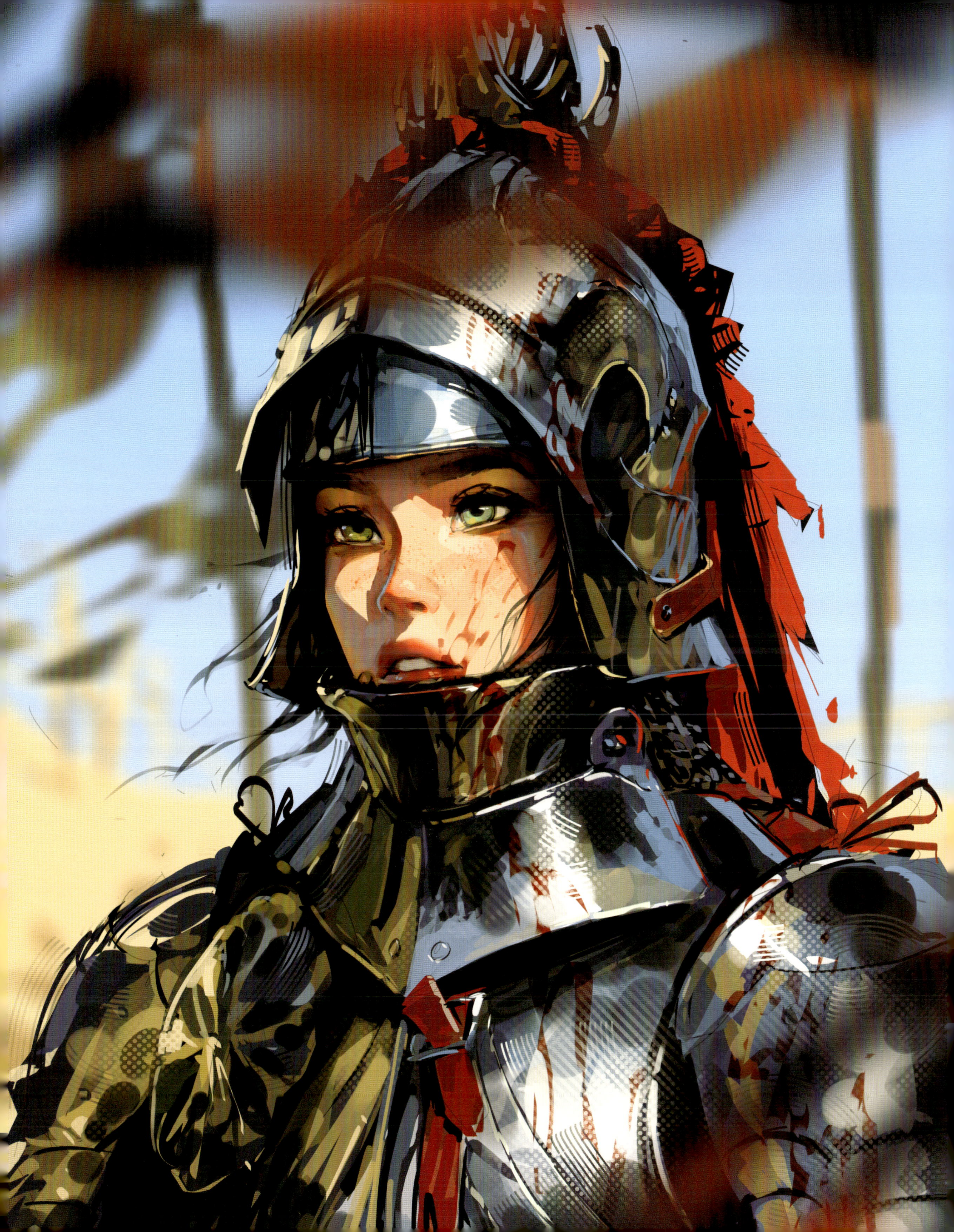

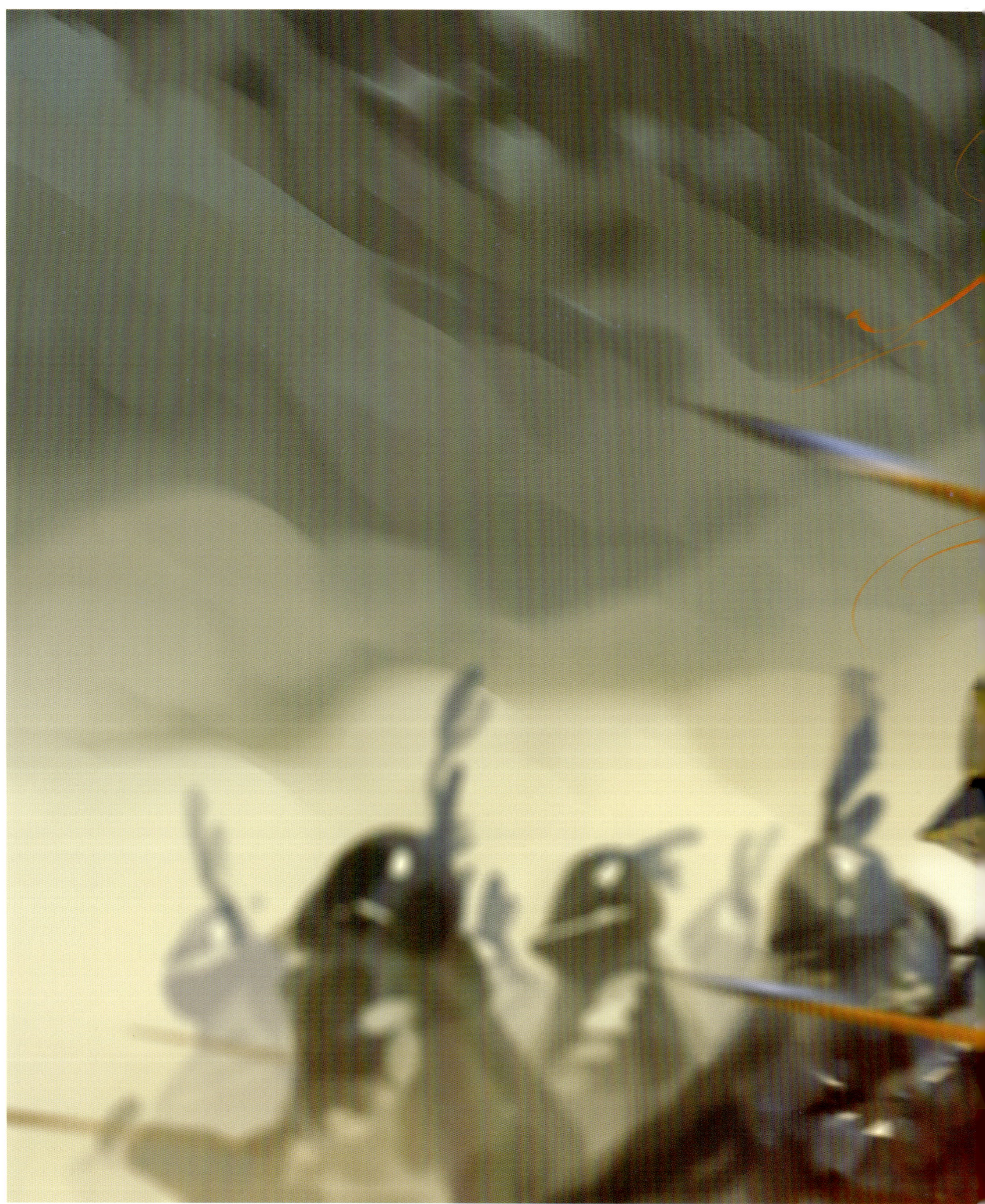

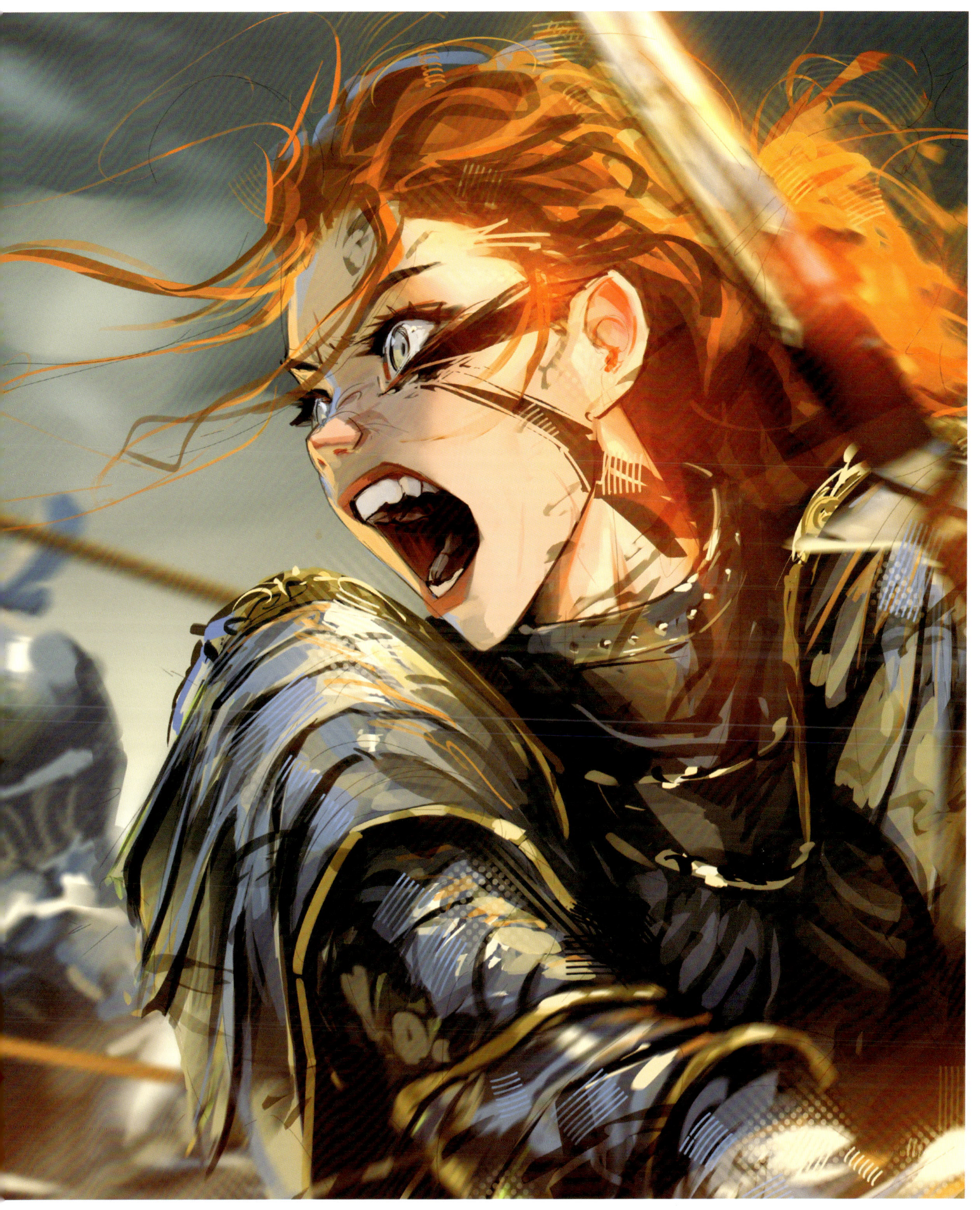

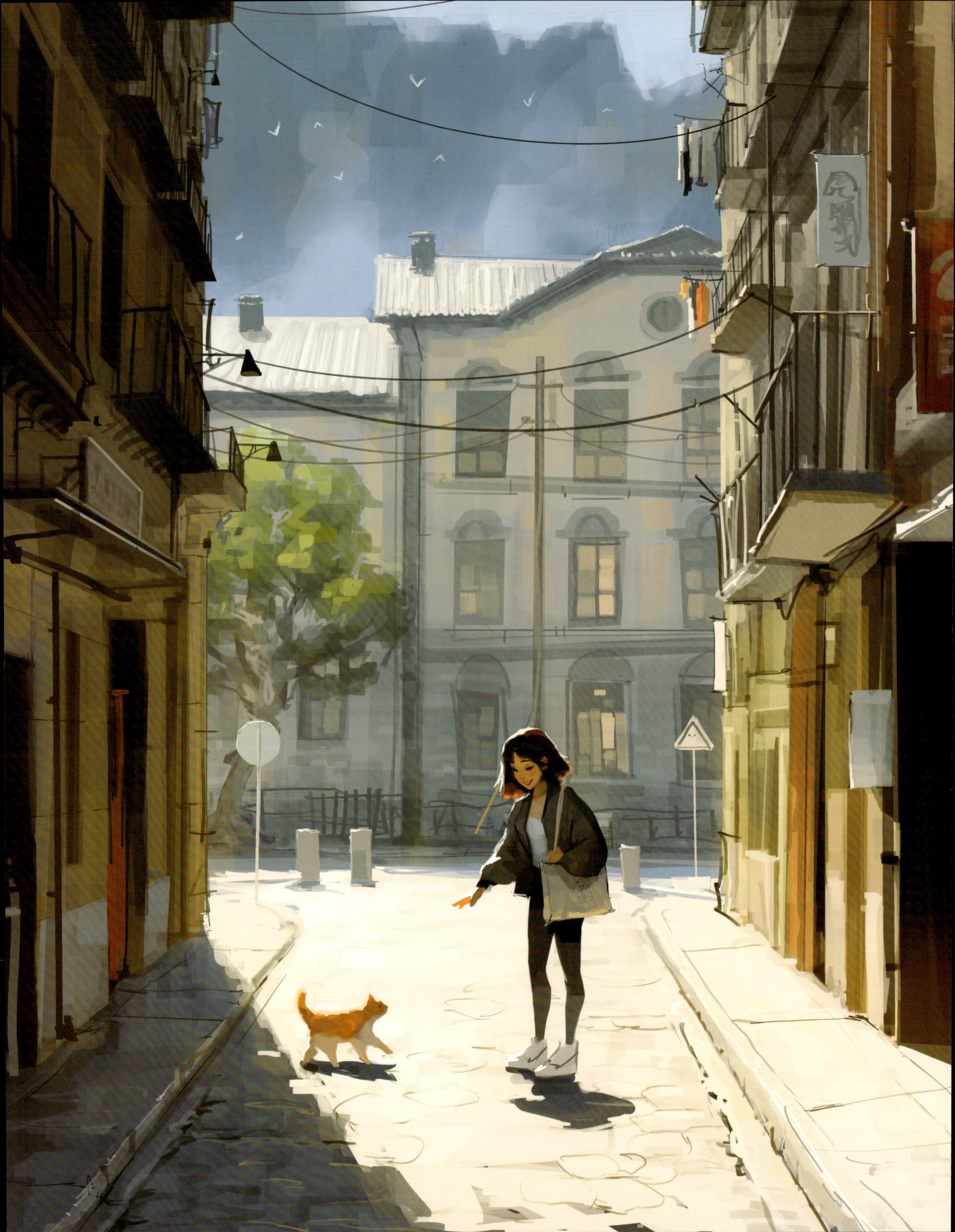

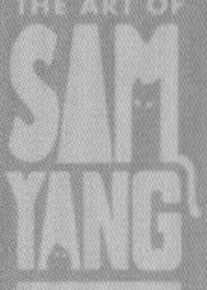

looking ahead

While my art has come a long way, I believe there's still a long way to go. I'd like to dedicate more of my time in the future to learning and improving my work. Eventually, I'd love to be able to draw and tell stories using less effort. I'd like to use my work as a medium to share experiences, feelings, and beauty with the world.

Stylization, anatomy, and environments are just a few things on my mind at the moment. I don't know if they'll ever become easy for me, but I'll try to continue taking steps in the right direction. As I've said before, the beauty of art is that we're never really finished learning. And I'll continue to do so alongside you in this wonderful community.

Thank you for taking the time to read this book – it means the world to me.

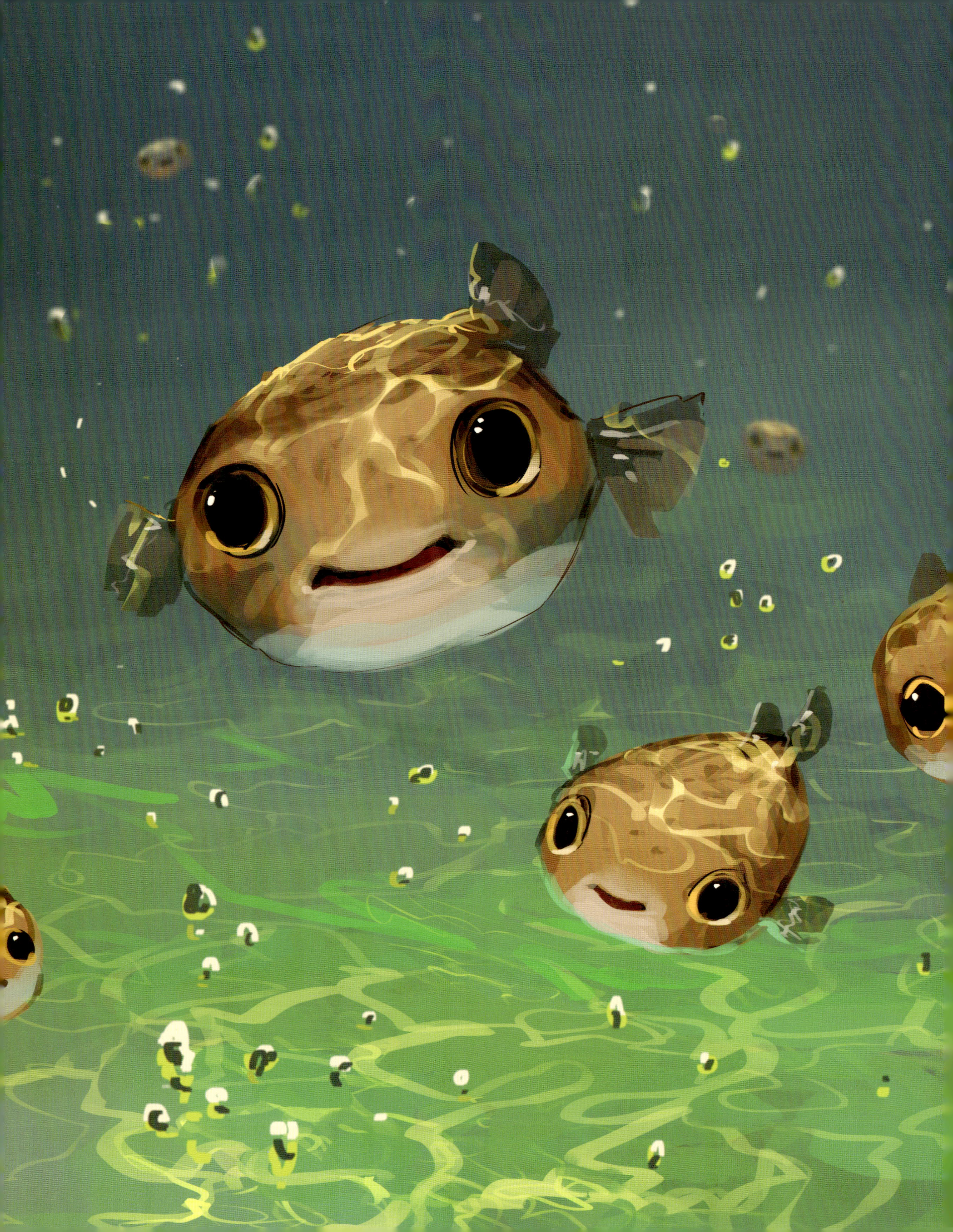

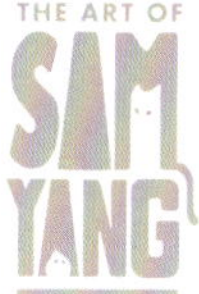

thank you

I want to take this opportunity to give my thanks to my parents for giving me all the opportunities in life and making it all possible for me. To my grandparents who raised me and looked after me. To my extended family back home, always the most warm, welcoming, and down-to-earth people with whom I feel like I belong. And finally, to my friends, to all of our adventures and the memories we share and cherish.

I would also like to thank those who inspired me along the way. Thank you to WLOP, Guweiz, Ramón, Aaron Blaise, Glen Keane, Atey Ghailan, and so many more artists. I can't list them all. You guys showed me what was possible in art and put me on the right path. I'd also like to thank Rossdraws, Ethan Becker, and Ergojosh; I admire your courage and drive to put yourselves out there and build up some of the most amazing communities on YouTube. I wouldn't have taken this step towards content creation if it weren't for you guys who did it all before me.

Finally, I'd like to extend my thanks to you, and to the global community of artists. You guys and your passion for drawing, creating worlds, and telling stories through your art inspires me each and every day. Thanks for hanging on to the little spark of creativity that so many people extinguish as they grow up. Keep nurturing that passion – it'll reward you in ways you could never have imagined.